AIR PIRACY, AIRPORT SECURITY, AND INTERNATIONAL TERRORISM

Winning the War against Hijackers

PETER ST. JOHN

Q

Quorum Books
New York
Westport, Connecticut
London

Library of Congress Cataloging-in-Publication Data

St. John, Peter
  Air piracy, airport security, and international terrorism :
winning the war against hijackers / Peter St. John.
    p. cm.
  Includes bibliographical references and index.
  ISBN 0-89930-413-3 (lib. bdg. : alk. paper)
    1. Hijacking of aircraft. 2. Hijacking of aircraft—Prevention.
  3. Airports—Security measures. 4. Terrorism. I. Title.
  II. Series.
  HE9779.S7   1991
  363.2'876—dc20   90-36031

British Library Cataloguing in Publication Data is available.

Library of Congress Catalog Card Number: 90-36031
ISBN: 0-89930-413-3

First published in 1991

Quorum Books, 88 Post Road West, Westport, CT 06881
An imprint of Greenwood Publishing Group, Inc.

Printed in the United States of America

The paper used in this book complies with the
Permanent Paper Standard issued by the National
Information Standards Organization (Z39.48-1984).

10 9 8 7 6 5 4 3 2 1

Copyright Acknowledgments

The author and publisher wish to thank the following for permission to use
material:

Extracts from *Winning Back the Sky* by D. E. Hubbard, copyright 1986 by
Saybrook Publishing Company, Dallas, TX.

Extracts from *Crusaders, Criminals, Crazies* by Frederick J. Hacker,
copyright © 1976 by Frederick J. Hacker, published by W. W. Norton &
Company, New York.

Extracts from *My People Shall Live: Autobiography of a Revolutionary* by
Leila Khaled and George Hajjar, by NC Press Ltd.

Diagrams—"the Secure Terminal" and "The Secure Airport"—by Cory
Phillips.

This book is dedicated to:
Rahul who inspired
Angus who encouraged and
Barbara who enabled

Contents

Preface

In late April 1985, my teaching assistant at the University of Manitoba, Rahul Aggarwal, a brilliant young Canadian of East Indian ancestry, presented himself for dinner at my home, as do all my teaching assistants every year. The dinner was a pleasant affair and included discussion of his forthcoming research trip to New Delhi where he intended to compare the Indian and Canadian experiences of middle-power foreign policy. It was the last time I ever saw him.

Two months later, Rahul boarded Air India 182 to fly from Toronto via London to New Delhi. The big jumbo jet never made it. Just off the Irish coast a terrorist bomb blasted the plane out of the sky and 329 people plunged to their deaths in the icy waters of the Atlantic Ocean.

The sabotage of Air India 182 had a profound effect on Canadians, much the same as the destruction of Pan Am 103 over Lockerbie, Scotland, in December 1988, had on Americans. Lax airport security, ignored warnings of terrorist attack, missed opportunities, ambiguous public information, and bungled investigations by security agencies—both during the incidents and in the years following—proclaimed the enormous problems facing airport and airplane security.

The death of Rahul was enough to ignite a growing sense of personal anger over cowardly bomb attacks on defenseless aircraft. The only useful therapy for that anger was to set to work to write a book on the problem of hijacking. Thus, a terrorist act of airplane sabotage was father to this study on how the United States, Canada, and other Western nations have and should confront attacks on commercial aircraft.

The purpose of this book is to give the reader a historical perspective as well as a contemporary analytical framework for achieving successful and effective airplane and airport security. The first two chapters describe the periods of historical development in this twentieth-century phenomenon—terrorist attacks on commercial aircraft—showing clearly how hijacks develop in repetitive patterns, accompanied by a marked copycat effect.

Chapter Three attempts to peer inside the mind of the terrorist and to determine his identity, his targets, and the psychology motivating his actions.

However, as the Federal Aviation Administration discovered, developing a psychological profile of a potential offender is all but impossible. Instead, I have chosen to classify eight types of hijacker and suggest how each might be handled.

Chapter Four looks at the whole vexed question of airport security. This is the key to controlling air piracy and at least 80 percent of the effort to prevent hijacking must be concentrated on that increasingly potent political symbol in Western states—the nearest national or international airport. In addition, I have articulated a holistic approach to airport security that takes into account the needs and threats of the 1990s.

Chapter Five deals with the dangerous theater of a hijack thousands of feet in the air. It examines the role of each actor in this drama and suggests how pilots, flight attendants, and passengers can prepare themselves for the emotional trauma during and after a hijack experience.

Chapter Six explores the ways various Western states have reacted to hijacks and evolved policies to combat their baneful existence. The initial government response to a first hijack experience seems to set the tone for nearly all subsequent policy behavior. When a move from soft-line to hard-line policies is attempted, the transition is usually painful and costly. Predictably perhaps, the reactions of Western European states to hijacking quite closely parallel the national stereotypes that have been largely dismissed in the late twentieth century.

The last chapter takes a global view of air piracy, for it is only at the international level that the whole problem can be controlled. Hijacking cannot be eradicated and even control depends on the political will for international cooperation, which has thus far been lacking. How many lives must be lost before nations make this common cause?

Many people contributed to the preparation of this book. Special thanks go to Professor Bill Thoms of the University of North Dakota Law School at Grand Forks, through whom the opportunity to write this book presented itself. Ray Salazar at the Federal Aviation Administration in Washington was very helpful in furnishing its all-important statistical record of hijacks; the American Air Line Pilots Association provided me with documentary material and an interview at short notice; Louis Haeck and Rodney Wallis at the International Air Transport Association in Montreal were of great assistance. Louis alone knows the debt I owe him and Rodney, who must be reckoned as one of the world's leading experts in air security, contributed accumulated wisdom and forward-thinking ideas which the international community would do well to heed. Larry Motiuk and Alan Poyner of the International Aviation Management Training Institute furnished documents and wise advice. Robert F. Selig, executive director of the Grand Forks Regional Airport Authority, answered my barrage of questions on several occasions as I sought to understand security from the airport manager's perspective.

Others who contributed substantially to my thinking were Captain E. V. (Ted)

Ryczko, Colonel Yoram Hamizrachi, Rehavia Ben-Shach, John T. Keenan, Norman Leach, Major Randy L. Perrett, Barbara Dunn, Professor Peter Hanappel, Professor William Thoms, David Kilgour, William Shea, John Bruneteau, Len Taylor, and the late Professor Larry Breen. Thanks are also due to Harvey Wasiuta who constructed the index at short notice.

But pride of place and warmest thanks must go to Captain Fred J. Deveaux, chairman of the Security Committee of the Canadian Air Line Pilots Association and longtime Air Canada pilot. Fred must be the doyen of all air security officers because of his tireless struggle to awaken government and the public to the need for air security. His many interviews and careful explanations of the problems of air security greatly helped in the writing of the book.

My wife, a seasoned journalist and editor, helped enormously in the redrafting process; the late Angus Murray, a longtime friend and owner of a Winnipeg bookstore, greatly aided me by his unswerving confidence and, perhaps most important, the emotional drive to write the book stemmed from the death of Rahul Aggarwal aboard Air India 182.

Abbreviations

AACC	Airport Associations Coordinating Council
ALPA	American Airline Pilots Association
AOCI	Airport Operator's Council International
ASALA	Armenian Secret Army for the Liberation of Armenia
AVSEC	Aviation Security Panel
BSO	Black September Organization
CALFAA	Canadian Air Line Flight Attendants Association
CIA	Central Intelligence Agency
CSIS	Canadian Security and Intelligence Service
DFA	Dangerous Foreign Airports
ECAC	European Civil Aviation Conference
EEC	European Economic Community
EPC	European Political Co-operation
FAA	Federal Aviation Administration
FATAH	Or al-Fatah (Victory)
FBI	Federal Bureau of Investigation
GSG9	Grenzshutzgruppe 9
IATA	International Air Transport Association
ICAO	International Civil Aviation Organization
IFALPA	International Federation of Airline Pilots Association
IFAPA	International Federation of Airline Passengers Association
INTERPOL	International Criminal Police Organization
IRA	Irish Republican Army
JCSS	Jaffee Centre for Strategic Studies
JRA	Japanese Red Army
NATO	North Atlantic Treaty Organization

NAYLP	National Arab Youth for the Liberation of Palestine
OPEC	Organization of Petroleum Exporting Countries
PFLP	Popular Front for the Liberation of Palestine
PFLP-GC	Popular Front for the Liberation of Palestine—General Command
PLF	Palestine Liberation Front
PLO	Palestine Liberation Organization
RCMP	Royal Canadian Mounted Police
SAS	Special Air Service
SERT	Special Emergency Response Team
SOAR	Special Operations and Research Unit
SWAT	Special Weapons and Tactics
TREVI	Terrorism, Radicalism, and Violence International

Chapter 1

The Evolution of Aerial Hijacking, 1931–1968

ELPIRATA COFRISI—1961

May 1, 1961, was a turning point in the evolution of air piracy, commonly known as hijacking or skyjacking.[1] On that day, just two weeks after the disastrous Bay of Pigs invasion, a National Airlines Convair 440, flying from Marathon, Florida, via Miami to Key West, was hijacked to Cuba by a man armed with a knife and pistol.

Before this first American airliner was diverted, the United States had appeared to condone the hijacking of planes. During the previous decade, refugees from Eastern Europe who used hijacked planes to facilitate their escapes were viewed as nothing more than freedom fighters fleeing evil Communist regimes. That policy held up at home as well. Since 1958, the U.S. government had granted political asylum to Cuban hijackers, never charging them in the courts or handing them back to Cuban authorities, even when they had killed or wounded people in achieving their escape. Nor were their aircraft returned to Cuba. Instead, American courts allowed hijacked Cuban aircraft to be sequestered by U.S. firms for debts allegedly owed by Cuba. By mid-1961 one firm, Harris Advertising of Miami, had seized nine planes hijacked from Cuba. So far, however, the flow had been all in one direction, from repression to freedom. Now an American plane had been hijacked and flown to a country with which the United States was almost in a state of war. It seemed a challenge to test American virility in foreign policy.

The hijacking began innocently at the National Airlines ticket counter in Miami. A slender, neatly dressed man with dark glasses bought a ticket and gave his name as Elpir Cofrisi. He then asked the clerk to add the letters "a-t-a" to his first name—Elpirata Cofrisi. The ticket clerk, completely unaware that Elpirata Cofrisi had been a pirate on the Spanish Main in the eighteenth century, missed the little joke. Who would have suspected, as author David Phillips later wrote, "that the man in the dark glasses was shortly to become the first of a new breed of buccaneer, the American sky pirate, a breed which, in a decade, would turn the Florida Straits into the Skyjack Main?"[2]

As the twin-engined Convair winged its way skyward at 3:30 P.M., the man who called himself Cofrisi emerged on the flight deck and shut the cabin door behind him. He stuck a knife to the throat of Captain Francis X. Riley, forced First Officer J. T. Richardson out of the cockpit at gunpoint, and ordered the plane to Havana. There was no question of resistance. The Convair, with its seven adult passengers and a baby, was making a historic flight into unknown and hostile territory—politically, psychologically, and legally, as well as geographically. Even should the plane survive the military shore batteries at Havana, there was a very real fear on board that the airliner would be impounded and the passengers imprisoned.

As they flew, in what would soon be recognized as typical behavior, Cofrisi began to tell Captain Riley about himself. He was an American citizen of Cuban origin who had served in the Korean War, he said. He had been offered $100,000 by General Rafael Trujillo Molina, president of the Dominican Republic, to assassinate Fidel Castro. But instead of going to Cuba to kill Castro, he was going to warn him.[3] There were a few tense moments when the Convair might have been fired upon before landing at Havana, but once on the ground, both pilots and passengers were treated in a friendly way, and within three hours the flight was on its way back to Key West. When last sighted, Cofrisi was being taken into custody and led away by Cuban soldiers. At a subsequent news conference in Key West, Captain Riley said he believed he had been skyjacked by a psychopath, marking the first time a mentally unbalanced passenger had seized an aircraft. Almost without exception, to this point, hijackers had been either political refugees or guerrillas.[4]

It was a significant turning point. A new kind of air piracy had evolved, and in the decade that followed, the skyjacker caused huge disruptions to civil aviation, not only in the United States but also around the world.[5] Aerial hijacks quickly escalated in the United States until, by 1973, two-thirds of all hijacks were occurring there. Between May 1, 1961, and December 31, 1972, 159 American planes were involved in skyjack incidents; of them, 85 were diverted to Cuba.

The attack on U.S. airlines was three-pronged: hijackers were political dissidents, common criminals, or people who were emotionally disturbed. All three types used the Havana route in an apparently endless wave of diverted flights that seemed impossible to contain and that greatly aggravated Cuban–American relations for almost 15 years.[6]

Elpirata Cofrisi was identified as Antulio Ramirez Ortiz by a federal grand jury in Miami on June 28, 1961, and soon came to symbolize a type of homesick Cuban returnee.[7] But his act of aerial piracy was to be emulated, in copycat fashion, not just in the United States but around the world, bringing death, injury, or psychological trauma to air travelers, flight crew, and pilots in almost every country. Even more serious, the Convair 440 had flown into a legal vacuum. There were no laws on the books for air hijacking, and the United States was forced to formulate new laws to face an unprecedented situation.

Later that year, President John F. Kennedy asked Congress for special antihijack legislation, making it "a federal offense to carry concealed or deadly weapons onto a plane. Also, to attempt to assault, intimidate or threaten crew members . . . so as to interfere with a flight."[8]

But Cofrisi's escapade was only one of a number of incidents that made 1961 the year of the hijack. In January there had been a severance of U.S.–Cuban diplomatic relations, and the subsequent two-way flow of skyjackings was a visible sign of the growing political gulf between the nations.

Then, on July 24, Wilfredo Roman Oquendo, an American born in Cuba, hijacked an Eastern Airlines Electra with 38 passengers and crew on board. Captain W. E. Buchanan, the pilot, radioed Key West, "I am proceeding to Havana at pistol point," a message that was to be heard all too frequently during the next decade. Oquendo didn't want to talk about himself, but Captain Buchanan noted that he acted professionally, like a trained agent, even to the point of giving the correct compass bearings for Cuba. The hijack differed from that of Cofrisi in another way. The Electra was worth $3,300,000, and Castro refused to return it, except in exchange for the 24 Cuban planes held by the United States. Secretary of State Dean Rusk explained publicly that 14 of the 24 planes had been returned to Cuba, and the other 10 had already been sold as a result of court orders. Negotiations continued, with the Americans using the Swiss Embassy in Cuba and the Cubans working through the Czech Embassy in Washington. In late July Castro threatened to put the whole matter in the hands of the U.N. Security Council. Castro suggested a hijacking treaty between the two countries, but the United States rejected the idea. Finally, on August 15 the Electra was released in exchange for a captured naval gunboat that Castro badly wanted back.

Before this, however, on August 9, the third successful hijacking of an American flag carrier took place. This time the target was a Pan American World Airways DC8 jumbo jetliner en route from Mexico City to Guatemala. It was hijacked by a French national, Albert Cadon, who was embittered by U.S. support for Algerian independence.[9] In the words of the pilot, Captain Carl V. Ballard, Cadon "looked insane," but the Cubans were delighted to receive the first jet to be hijacked successfully, with 72 passengers and 8 crew aboard. Plane, passengers, and crew were duly returned after the passengers had been feted and Castro had personally inspected the plane and asked many technical questions of the pilot. Columbia's foreign minister, Julio Cesar Turbay Ayala, and his wife were taken off and put up in a Havana hotel as Castro's guests.

It was as a result of these three major hijackings that President Kennedy initiated the special antihijack legislation, and security guards and sky marshals began to appear with some airlines. The Federal Aviation Administration (FAA), the Central Intelligence Agency (CIA), and the Federal Bureau of Investigation (FBI) were henceforth to be involved actively in the skyjack war.

But the most interesting hijack of the long, frustrating summer of 1961 took place on August 3. A gun-toting father and son, Leon and Cody Bearden, commandeered a Continental Airlines Boeing 707 jet in Phoenix, Arizona, and demanded to be flown to Cuba. The pilot, Captain Byron D. Richards, managed to convince the Beardens that a refueling stop at El Paso, Texas, would be necessary before proceeding to Cuba. By the time the plane landed, President Kennedy had been apprised of the situation and had given orders the plane should not be allowed to take off. He feared that a jumbo jet would give Castro too much leverage to blackmail the United States. It was assumed that the Beardens were in fact Cuban agents, so the FBI was told to keep the plane on the ground at all cost. For nearly nine hours the 70 passengers and crew awaited their fate as the Beardens threatened them. Finally, after a woman who was six months pregnant became hysterical, 63 passengers were released, while 4 passenger volunteers and the crew remained on board. Among the 4 was Leonard Gilman, a border patrolman in plain clothes. Gilman was later to break his fist while subduing Leon Bearden. At 6:50 P.M., the plane could be delayed no longer. With enough fuel to reach Cuba, it prepared for takeoff. But just as it was cleared, the Border Patrol surrounding the plane opened fire on the aircraft's ten huge tires. It was the first time a skyjacked airliner had been fired upon by law enforcement officers. The tires all went flat, gas began leaking from a bullet hole in the number two engine, and a pice of flying glass cut the cheek of one of the crew. Leon Bearden angrily ordered Captain Richards to take off anyway, but Richards, at great personal risk, refused. Bearden had a criminal record dating from 1941 and at the time was out on parole from a sentence for armed robbery. His was the first criminal hijack of an American airliner, the first in a long line of such attempts.

Finally, when FBI personnel came aboard to negotiate another plane, the Beardens were temporarily distracted and tricked into surrender. But the most interesting aspect of the El Paso hijack was that Captain Richards was the first airline pilot in the world to be hijacked twice. By a strange concidence, he had been the hero of the world's first, and also unsuccessful, hijack in Peru in 1930. It is to the beginning of hijack history that we must turn to gain some perspective on the whole.

By 1961 the contours of the problem as it applied to airplanes and airport security were rapidly becoming clear. From the four cases just cited, it can be seen that American planes were vulnerable targets, that the motives for hijacking would run the whole spectrum from emotional disturbance through criminal extortion to political motivation, and that the entire civil aviation industry was open and vulnerable to anyone who even threatened the use of a knife or a gun on board an aircraft. It became evident, too, that new laws would have to be enacted condemning and punishing aerial hijackers, and for them to be effective, many nations would have to cooperate by creating bilateral and multilateral agreements.

The handwriting was on the wall. In just four months between May and August of 1961, the warning of hijacking problems to come was made clear. But the United States failed to act on this warning, in part because the country was distracted by the larger Four Power crisis in Berlin, which would lead to the

Berlin Wall and the Cuban Missile Crisis in 1962. Partly, too, the United States was not prepared to come to grips with the political problem of a Communist-controlled Cuba just 90 miles off its southern coast; but mostly, the warning was ignored because after August 1961 there were no more hijacks of American planes. Moreover, for the next several years very few hijack incidents took place anywhere around the world. The Western nations were lulled into thinking the problem had gone away.

Viewed in historical perspective, it becomes clear that hijacking of aircraft has taken place in distinct phases or cycles that have repeated themselves with remarkable regularity. The year 1961 stands at midpoint in the evolution of aerial hijacking and, in restrospect, it is easy to see that more attention should have been paid to an evolving and dangerous phenomenon. There had already been 32 hijack attempts between 1930 and May 1961, and most had been successful. In the nearly 30 years since that time there have been 900 hijacks, and far too many of them have been successful to have brought an end to the problem.

Nevertheless, it is probably true that the hijack by Elpirata Cofrisi of May 1, 1961, brought the United States face to face with the problem in such a manner that the nation would ultimately be forced to become a pioneer in the field of prevention. The principal techniques of hijack prevention and measures for ensuring airport security used worldwide today owe much to the efforts, learned from sustained and painful domestic experience, of American lawmakers and security personnel.

THE EARLY YEARS OF HIJACKING

Captain B. D. Richards and the Peruvian Hijack

The first recorded hijacking was an isolated incident. In May 1930 Peruvian revolutionaries seized a mail plane belonging to Pan American and piloted by 22-year-old Captain Byron D. Richards. They wanted him to drop propaganda leaflets over the capital, Lima, but young Richards was intent on getting the mail through. He tricked the rebels into allowing him to deliver the mail first and then refused to fly on, at some risk to his life. Almost a year later, on April 3, 1931, he was awarded $100 for bravery. When the situation was repeated 30 years later, Captain Richards, who had been inspired to learn to fly by Lindbergh's solo flight across the Atlantic, distinguished himself again in Texas, preventing the Beardens from hijacking the Continental Airlines jumbo jet to Cuba.

Hijacks during the Second World War

During the Second World War there must have been a number of hijackings of military aircraft, but they were so much a part of a worldwide effort that they have never been sifted from the mass of other war events to stand alone as distinct episodes. The only one that did make an international splash was the sudden, strange flight of Rudolph Hess to Scotland in 1941. It has never been clear whether Hess thought he had a mission, as deputy fuhrer to Hitler, to negotiate with the British or whether he simply saw, long before his fellow Nazis, the writing in the sky.

HIJACKS SINCE 1945

Thus it is only since 1945 that any clear record of hijack attempts has been kept. But the evolving patterns of the postwar period have some real lessons for those maintaining the safety of the skies in the 1990s. The pattern of aerial hijacking or skyjacking has evolved since 1945 in the following way:

1947-1952	Eastern Europeans escaping communism hijack planes to gain political asylum.
1952-1958	Hiatus period as planes begin the move from propeller to jet age.
1958-1961	Raoul Castro initiates political hijacks in Oriente Province to gain power. Cubans of the Batista regime hijack to escape to political freedom in the United States.
1961/1968-1972	Reverse flow of homesick Cubans hijacking back to Cuba.
1962-1967	Hiatus period.
1968-1971	U.S. hijacks by the emotionally unbalanced, many to Cuba.
1968-1973	The Arab skyjack war. Political hijacks by FATAH, PFLP, PFLP-GC, BSO, NAYLP.
1971-1973	Criminal, extortion phase, initiated by D. B. Cooper.
1973-1978	The West fights back; airport security, bilateral agreements, international conventions, and counterterrorist teams at Entebbe (1976) and Mogadishu (1977).
1974-1978	Continuation of the Arab skyjack war against Western Airlines, though much more low key.
1979-1983	Hiatus period in Europe, but hijacking increases elsewhere in the world.
1983-1988	Moslem fundamentalist attacks on airplanes; continuation of the Arab skyjack war; Sikh hijack activity.

Eastern Europe: 1947-1952

Between 1947 and 1958 there were 23 hijack incidents, all but three of them inspired by the seeking of political asylum in Western Europe. In July 1947 a private plane on a domestic Romanian run was seized by three Romanian army officers who shot their way to freedom in Turkey. This was the world's first fatal hijack, since an uncooperative crew member was shot and killed. On June 17, 1948, a Romanian airliner was diverted to Austria with all but one of the 23 passengers aboard requesting political asylum. On December 16, 1949, a Polish airliner flying from Lodz to Gdansk was diverted to the Danish island of Bornholm where the hijacker and 13 other Poles requested asylum. There were hijacks from Czechoslovakia to the U.S. zone of West Germany, from Yugoslavia to Italy, and from Bulgaria to Turkey. Most of these incidents involved large numbers of refugees. On March 24, 1950, the first multiple hijack took place, anticipating a similar episode at Dawson's Field in Jordan in 1970. Eighty-five Czechs escaped in three airliners on the same day to U.S. Erding base near Munich. They were piloted by three Czech pilots who had flown in the Royal Air Force during the Second World War.

In each case out of Eastern Europe "the stolen plane went straight from point A to point B and everyone got off, claimed asylum, and disappeared into the new homeland."[10] The West regarded them as heroes and celebrated their actions without punishment. In these early years the only real crime was the theft of the airplane itself. As a result, planes were usually returned, but the killing of pilots or air crew went unpunished for political reasons. As James Arey pointed out, "There was a message in this if we had only read it: All hijackings, no matter what the motivation, infringe upon the basic human rights of other people and carry with them the seeds of injury or death."[11] The lack of punitive action by receiving governments against those committing crimes in the pursuit of political asylum set the stage for further hijacking.

The three other hijacks in this period were all in Asia, and one of them was important. On July 16, 1948, the flying boat *Miss Macau* was hijacked and crashed and sank in the ocean between Hong Kong and Macau. It was inevitable, perhaps, that Macau—a city renowned for its sea pirates—was bound to breed the first sky pirate. The plane carried close to $2 million in gold bullion on each flight to Macau, so when it was hijacked, the pilot and copilot instinctively tried to regain control of the aircraft. Eighteen bullets were fired, and the plane went down, drowning all but one man, who ironically was one of the hijackers. This attempted heist was the world's first criminal hijack and led to the first fatal crash of an aircraft hijacked in commercial use.

Between 1953 and 1958 there was a five-year lull in skyjacking, for no discernible reason. As David Phillips pointed out, "the dormant spell in skyjacking came during a period when there were good reasons for it to flourish."[12] The Berlin Airlift of 1948-1949 sustained the city of West Berlin with flights that came in every few minutes for a period of 11 months. Also, as David Hubbard pointed out, the Berlin Airlift "demonstrated that aircraft were almost invincible in their conquest of space, time, and political barriers."[13] Yet by the 1960s, anyone could fly on commercial aircraft. Suddenly, the exclusive and limited flying public of the 1950s became the large, amorphous, anonymous public of the 1960s. The bridging of this gap was accomplished technologically by the transition from the propeller years, up to 1958, to the jet age thereafter. By May 1952 the BOAC Comet was operating between Johannesburg and London, and in December 1957 the Boeing 707 made its maiden flight. Two months later a skyjack took place over South Korea, and eight months after that, Raoul Castro carried out the first political hijack of modern times.

Cuba, The Skyjackers' Haven: 1958-1961

Raoul Castro could certainly claim to be the father of the modern crime of sky-jacking. He was the man who initiated the Cuban malady and turned it into an international phenomenon. In the spring of 1958, as commander of Column Six of his brother Fidel's rebel forces, Raoul invaded northern Oriente Province. His intent was to harass transport and disrupt communications. Using his own public work corps and tractors, Raoul built a temporary air base in the jungle-covered mountains. It was to this base that guerrillas of Column Six hijacked two airliners owned by the Compania Cubana de Aviacion. Column Six seized the first Cuban plane on October 21, 1958, two weeks before the Cuban presidential elections, which the guerrillas were attempting to disrupt. Armed rebels, posing as passengers, forced the pilot to divert it to their camouflaged airstrip. Then, two weeks later, they repeated the performance with a second DC3. Between these two incidents, on November 1, 1958, four Cuban youths who aspired to join Column Six, seized a Cubana Viscount after it had left Miami for Havana. The plane crashed while the pilot was searching for a large enough airstrip on which to land in Oriente, and 17 of the 20 people aboard were killed, including the hijackers. Fidel Castro was embarrassed by the fatal crash. Nevertheless, this episode was indicative of future guerrilla tactics of illegal diversion and the use of appropriated landing strips—12 years before the PFLP's successful diversion at Dawson's Field, Jordan. There is no doubt that Raoul Castro's actions in Oriente Province provided the seed for the modern skyjacking era.

Ironically, skyjacking rebounded against Fidel Castro after he seized power in Cuba. On January 1, 1959, the day he won the Revolution, a Cubana Airlines was hijacked to New York by a group of ex-President Fulgencio Batista's supporters. During the next two and a half years a succession of planes were diverted from Cuba to the United States by those seeking to flee the socialist regime. Twelve of the 18 hijackings between January 1959 and July 1961 were by refugees escaping Castro's Cuba.[14] Even fishing boats were hijacked from Cuba to Miami and their occupants welcomed with open arms in the United States.

Responding to this exodus, Castro effectively, albeit temporarily, suspended aerial piracy by Cuban refugees with drastic security measures. He first tightened airport security, and then, when airliners began to be diverted by their crew, he placed sky marshals aboard flights to watch over both passengers and pilots. But as the flow was stemmed in one direction, it progressively increased in the other. The seesaw of planes diverted to one country or the other played a significant role in their worsening political relations. The United States thought that Cuban agents in the United States were deliberately waging war against its airliners. Yet until the first American airliner was diverted to Cuba, the United States appeared to condone skyjacking. Castro was, after all, a Communist, and if he had a skyjacking problem, it was just too bad, Americans reasoned. Those escaping his dictatorship were heroes.

It must be remembered, too, that the United States had no hostile borders until 1957. The Iron Curtain and the Cold War had all taken place in distant Western Europe. "When Fidel Castro commandeered the island of Cuba and figuratively hijacked it from our sphere of influence into that of the Russians, a new, exciting hostile border was brought into being, and skyjacking became a part of the American experience," stated David Hubbard.[15] The Cuban–American relationship was to bring out many unusual behavioral characteristics in Americans, most of which were to be mirrored in the ongoing saga of Cuban–American hijack acivities.

By the autumn of 1961, the full range of human, technological, and national problems involved in hijacking had emerged. The case of Elpirata Cofrisi made it clear that disaffected Americans would not hesitate to hijack American planes and take them abroad, if only to Cuba. It was a rude shock to American lawmakers and security personnel. In the case of the Electra in July, the difficulty of negotiating with a country that the United States did not recognize emerged. There was also the cost to airlines of having expensive machines sitting idle when they could be earning money. The El Paso hijack by the Bearden father and son heralded the beginning of criminal extortion aboard jetliners. The fact that they were Americans actually helped to spoil a growing conspiracy theory in the United States that the Cubans were behind all hijacking. Finally, the August hijack of the Pan Am DC8 by a French national indicated, very early, that the politics of Western Europe could have repercussions on United States air safety. However, the return of the Electra removed any incentive for a hijacking treaty with Cuba, and the ensuing lull in hijacks seemed to indicate an end to the phenomenon.

Hiatus: 1962-1967—"Reculer pour mieux sauter"

Between 1962 and 1967 there were only four hijacks per year at most, and only a few of the total number were significant. In October 1965 there occurred the first American hijack in more than four years. A Cuban exile, Luis Medina Perez, hijacked a National Airlines Electra en route from Miami to Key West. In the ensuing conversation with the pilot, Perez said he wanted his relatives out of Cuba. The hijack came to an end when the copilot clamped a fire axe over Perez's arms and body. But his wistful tale of freeing relatives in Cuba so tugged at the hearts of Americans that the lonely 21-year-old exile was allowed to go free by the jury that tried him. The public loved him. On November 17, 1965, a 16-year-old youth, Thomas Robinson, tried to hijack a National Airlines DC8 flying from New Orleans to Melbourne, Florida. Drawing two revolvers from his pockets, he went up and down the aisle lecturing the passengers on their need to "help the Cubans." Before he was wrestled into submission, the young man had fired nine shots into the cabin floor.[16]

During these years attempts were made to hijack Russian, Venezuelan, Portuguese, French, Dutch, and Argentinian planes.

But the year 1967 was to prove the fateful turning point in the evolution of aerial hijacking. This time, world political events half a world away would affect the safety of international air transport everywhere. Early in the year, a Russian-built Egyptian plane was hijacked to Jordan with 41 passengers aboard. It was the first Middle Eastern hijack. In the first few days of June the Six Day War took place between Israel and the Arab states, and the humiliating defeat of the latter set the stage for the Palestinian hijack war. Once the Palestinians realized there would be no further help from the Arab states for their cause, the need for a more radical strategy emerged. The idea for a hijacking war could logically have come from the Cubans, who were busy exporting their own revolution at this stage. Che Guevara was trying to start a revolution in Bolivia, and his death in 1968 reverberated across the anticolonial and idealistic Western student worlds.

Or perhaps it was an event that took place on June 30, 1967, that pushed the idea of politically motivated hijacking to the fore. On that day a private plane flying from Spain to Majorca was diverted to Algiers with the former president of the Congo, Moishe Tshombe, aboard.[17] It was the first plainly politically motivated kidnap on record, and as James Arey pointed out, "with it, a tiny little seed was sown; an ominous little seed that grew slowly, unobtrusively into an enormous, ugly, parasitic growth."[18] No one was sure why Tshombe was kidnapped or who hoped to gain from the act. When it was over, Tshombe, his hijacker, and the British pilots of the plane were all imprisoned. There then followed ten painful weeks of detention for the pilots, at the end of which the International Federation of Airline Pilots Association began to toy loudly with the idea of boycotting Algerian airports. The pilots were freed soon afterward. Tshombe died on July 1, 1968, of natural causes in his Algiers prison. A tremendous amount of press coverage surrounded the episode in both countries, and it was out of this hijacking that the idea of airline boycotts of countries harboring hijackers was born.

Between August 1967 and February 1968 a worldwide momentum began to build that was to lead to a virtual epidemic of hijacking. Indeed, the hijack statistics from 1968 to 1972 are the highest ever in the history of the phenomenon: There were 34 hijacks in 1968, 87 in 1969, 83 in 1970, 58 in 1971, and 62 in 1972, for a total of 364 hijacks.[19] See Appendix 1.

It was a worldwide explosion that was to catch the largely Western-run commercial air transport system by complete surprise, and it was not until 1973 that the West began to fight back with any effectiveness at all.

Chapter 2

Terrorism in the Skies
Goes International, 1968–1988

CRUSADERS, CRIMINALS, AND CRAZIES: 1968-1972

Suddenly, between 1968 and 1970, 121 hijacks of aircraft to Cuba took place, more than half of them from the United States.[1] Many of these incidents were engineered by criminals after ransom money, others who hijacked were simply mentally unbalanced, and still others claimed to be political refugees seeking asylum. Whatever the motive, Cuba became a magnet for misfits. In 1968 alone, 13 airliners were diverted to Cuba, along with 5 small private planes and 1 charter flight. Two Venezuelan, 2 Mexican, and 3 Columbian planes were also diverted there during the year.

What was to become a banner year in international air piracy began for the United States on February 21, 1968. Laurence Rhodes, Jr., wanted for a payroll robbery, forced a Delta Airlines DC8 to go to Cuba. Since this was the first successful seizure of an American commercial airliner since 1961, it was initially seen to be no cause for hysteria. But more hijacks quickly followed. Half of them were by Cuban refugees, from among the nearly half-million Cubans then living in the United States.[2] By 1968 they were facing visa difficulties, if they wanted to return to Cuba, as well as transportation problems since neither American ships nor airlines, unless they were hijacked, went to Cuba. Traveling via Mexico City was the one indirect way of getting there from the United States.

Since 1965 there had been Freedom Flights to the United States from Cuba on American planes, but there were no return flights. Thus hijacking basically meant direct transportation. From the North American perspective, flights diverted by unhappy returning Cubans were clearly the main problem, although there was no hard evidence that Castro encouraged them. Castro did, however, manage to make these frequent hijacks costly both for American airlines and American national pride. The Cuban authorities insisted that Haramas Jose Marti airport was too short to permit the takeoff of a fully loaded jet. Though American pilots disapproved, the Cubans wined and dined American passengers and then drove them 90 miles to Verdadero airport, reboarding them for their return to the United States after a complimentary tour of socialist Cuba.[3] As a result, every hijacked airliner to Cuba cost an additional $2,500 to $3,000 in hotel bills, fuel, and landing fees. In addition, the airlines lost $4,500 per day with the plane out of service. In an attempt to end these detours, on July 11, 1968, the State Department announced it would permit exiles to return to Cuba, but Castro turned down the idea.

From August 1968 onward hijacks escalated. The United States enlisted the support of the International Air Transport Association in opening a new avenue of communication, since both countries belonged to the organization. On January 18, 1969, the director, Nut Hammarskjold, went to Cuba and began talks that, much later, would lead to an American–Cuban hijack agreement. Meanwhile the Swiss represented American interests in Havana while the Czechs continued to represent Cuban interests in Washington.

In 1969 the rash of hijacks turned into an epidemic. In the first three months, 14 airliners were diverted to Cuba, more than the total number of hijacks to Cuba in all of 1968 and an average of 1 per week. By the end of 1969, there had been 40 hijack incidents, of which 33 were successful and all but 2 were diversions to Cuba.[4] Hijacking became a laughing matter as jokes like the following made the rounds:

A man enters the cockpit of a plane with a gun and orders the pilot to fly to Miami. The captain protests, "But this plane is going to Miami." The hijacker responds, "Don't kid me. I've taken this flight three times in the past month and all three times we ended up in Cuba. This time we're going to Miami."[5]

When they viewed it seriously, the American people felt the whole business was Castro's fault, and to a degree they were right, but the problem was much bigger than that.

Throughout this blitz there was discreet Cuban–American cooperation. Once a hijack was under way, Miami would phone Havana to announce the impending arrival of the plane. On February 10, the Verdadero expeditions were omitted, and gradually a new U.S.–Cuba understanding developed over the prompt return of hijacked passengers.

Clearly, Cuba was feeling the pressure of all of these hijacks. In September it announced it did not welcome pirates and would be willing to negotiate reciprocal treaties with other nations for the extradition of hijackers. This slowed the rate of aerial diversions by the end of 1969 and also brought about a change in the type of hijackers. The Cuban government began to realize that only a few hijackers were politically motivated, claims to the contrary notwithstanding. They soon began to conclude that the hijackers they were receiving were common delinquents, mentally deranged, socially alienated, or simply anxious to escape their country of origin for economic reasons.[6]

In 1969, too, there was a change in the pattern of hijacking as it took on an international dimension. In November a U.S. marine, Raffaele Minichiello, achieved the world's longest hijack, ending up in Italy after flying 6,868 miles across most of two continents and an ocean.[7]

The following year, the nature of hijacks became increasingly outlandish and bizarre. On January 8, a Frenchman, Christian Belon, seized a TWA B707 flying from Paris to Rome and diverted it to Beirut. It was the first direct threat to an American plane abroad. On March 15 John de Vivo, clearly deranged, boarded an Eastern Airlines DC9 shuttle flight between Newark and Boston and demanded that the crew "take me east."[8] Since only the Atlantic Ocean stretched east, the pilot and copilot were forced to attempt to overwhelm the hijacker physically. In the ensuing shootout, the copilot was killed and the pilot was wounded in both arms. Despite his injuries, he landed the plane, periodically subduing the hijacker each time he revived. It was the first shooting fatality aboard a hijacked American airliner.

On June 4 Arthur Barkley commandeered a TWA B727 flight from Washington to Phoenix with 58 passengers on board. Locked in a $100 million court case in which he was suing the United States over a $471.78 disagreement with the IRS over unpaid taxes, Barkley demanded the $100 million on the plane. TWA managed to collect $100,750, which was handed over at Dulles Airport, and the plane took off. Enraged at finding that he had been shortchanged, Barkley forced the plane to land again at Dulles, where the FBI shot out the aircraft's tires. In the final scuffle, in which the hijacker was subdued, Captain Dale Hupe was shot in the abdomen.

By the summer of 1970, therefore, hijacked American passengers could no longer joke with certainty, as they had in the past, that their destination would be Havana.

The problem was far from being solved, however. During the summer there was a growing fear that a B747 jumbo jet would be hijacked to Cuba, and on August 2 it happened. Rudolfo Rivera Rios of Puerto Rico made history when he hijacked a Pan American B747, with 360 passengers and 19 crew aboard, flying between New York and Puerto Rico. Captain Augustus Watkins explained later how Fidel Castro was at Jose Marti airport to meet the plane and was fascinated by the big jet.[9] After a conducted tour of the outside of the plane, Captain Watkins invited Castro to look inside, but Castro declined, saying, "I would probably scare the passengers." Within 52 minutes of landing, the jet was heading back to the United States.

For some reason, the Cuba run did not spur national action on security measures. However, the PFLP multiple hijack at Dawson's Field in Jordan in October certainly did. From this time forward the Nixon administration "became determined to win America's skyjack war, both at home and abroad."[10] But because Cuba was still such a diplomatic bone in America's throat, the administration failed to respond to the September offer of Cuba's foreign minister, Raul Roa, to enter into direct talks for a U.S.–Cuban agreement for the reciprocal return of both planes and hijackers. It was a treaty that the Nixon administration would be forced to sign less than two years later.

In September 1970 President Nixon appointed General Benjamin O. Davis to coordinate U.S. antihijacking efforts. He also ordered the creation of a sky marshal force of 2,000 men and urged allied support for a new international hijack convention.

Cuba remained the favored skyjack haven in 1971, but fewer managed to reach it. John Shaffer, chief administrator of the FAA, summarized the year this way:

This year's hijacking statistics remind me of those good news–bad news stories. The good news, of course, is that we have achieved a significant decline in the rate of successful hijackings. The bad news, on the other hand, is that we did not manage a meaningful decline in the total number of hijacking attempts.[11]

In 1968, 13 of 17 U.S. airliner hijacks had been successful; in 1969, 33 of 40 succeeded; in 1970, 17 of 26 were successful; and in 1971 it was 11 of 25, with 14 of them seeking refuge in Cuba;[12] only 9 of them made it.

Thus by 1971 Cuba had settled into being a troublesome sideshow. The real worry now was the introduction of the parajackers, men who skyjacked for ransom. The year was also one of other firsts in hijacking, all of which put additional pressure on the Nixon administration to take decisive action in the field of aerial piracy. On June 11 the first passenger fatality occurred, when Howard L. Franks was shot by a hijacker on board a TWA B727 between Chicago and New York. On July 2, a distance record was set in a hijack aboard a Braniff B707. During a period of 44 hours, the plane flew 7,500 miles, from Mexico City to Buenos Aires by way of Monterrey, Lima, Peru, and Rio de Janeiro.[13]

On July 23 an FBI marksman armed with a high-powered rifle shot the hijacker of a TWA jetliner on the tarmac at Kennedy Airport. The skyjacker had shielded himself with a flight attendant and was inside the plane, but he had made the mistake of standing beside a window. He was shot twice. It was the first time that an American hijacking an American aircraft had been slain on United States soil.

There was another first on October 25, when three sky marshals were aboard an American B747 that was seized between New York and San Juan by a Puerto Rican using a dummy gun. Finally, in October and November, two incidents took place that were to become significant in the light of similar events a year later. In the first, three blacks wanted in connection with the murder of a policeman rushed aboard a TWA B727 at Albuquerque, New Mexico, and ordered the pilot to fly to Cuba. In the other, Dale L. Thomas, a convicted killer on parole, seized a Wein-Consolidated B737 after it left Anchorage, Alaska, and then doubled back to allow the passengers to disembark. The latter hijacker was finally foiled concerning his destination and was arrested in Vancouver, Canada.

The events that provoked a crisis in American thinking on hijacking, however, were still a year away. In the meantime, the field was to be dominated by the mentally disturbed, criminal extortionists, and social misfits. It was not an easy combination for American aviation authorities to have to deal with.

EXTORTIONISTS AND PARAJACKERS: 1968-1971

No one knows for certain whether the first of the parajackers is dead or whether D. B. Cooper lived to spend the $200,000 ransom when he bailed out over the state of Washington on the night of November 24, 1971.[14] In the next seven months, five other Americans followed in his slipstream. Between them, they jumped with $1,555,000. Unlike Cooper, all of them were captured and all but $303,000 was recovered.[15]

It was actually a Canadian, Paul Cini of Calgary, who was the first to think of bailing out with the cash. But Cini had been overpowered by the crew while attempting to parachute from an Air Canada DC8 with $50,000 12 days before Cooper's leap, so Cooper became the focus for others with extortion on their minds.[16]

Ransom demands in 21 incidents in 1971 had exceeded $20 million and 15 pounds of gold, but Cooper's leap changed the course of hijacking. A surprising number of his countrymen admired and emulated his exploit, and a D. B. Cooper cult emerged, endowing the hijacker with heroic features. Eventually, a film was made of his life.

Parajacking's appeal was obvious. It appeared to let the skyjacker choose his escape route and keep his ransom. The hardest part of skyjacking had become the escape. Arrest on arrival seemed inevitable. Cooper used his own knowledge of parachuting to plan his getaway. He chose a B727 to skyjack because of its tail exit, enabling him to jump clear of the fuselage and the engines. His demands were for $200,000 in $20 bills to be put aboard at Seattle along with four parachutes. the money was the most ever turned over to an American hijacker at that point, and Cooper had obviously calculated its bulk. He also gave the pilot specific directions and instructions for his extremely risky nighttime drop. Most authorities believe D. B. Cooper never lived to spend his money, but extortion nevertheless became the fashion and ransoms and parachutes the vogue demand.[17]

Of the more than 14 subsequent attempts at parajacking, none was successful. Only five of Cooper's disciples even tried the leap from a moving plane, and most of those who landed successfully were apprehended through the use of bugged parachutes.[18]

Between November 1971 and November 1972 there were 21 skyjacks involving ransom demands of $20,512,000, and ransom of $9,155,000 was paid in 14 cases. Nearly $7,000,000 of that was recovered.[19]

Among the parajackers were some interesting cases, including that of Richard Floyd McCoy, Jr., who, on April 7, parachuted out of a TWA B727 during a flight from Denver to San Francisco. Ironically, it was a criminal in transit between two prisons who blew the whistle on McCoy, recognizing him despite a heavy disguise he used on board the plane. McCoy was also unwise enough to ask the teenagers who drove him home whether they had heard about the hijack. He was arrested two days after the incident and sentenced to 45 years in prison, a sad irony for someone who had been a police trainee before the escapade.

Probably, it was the stiff sentences, along with the efficiency of the FBI and the FAA, that finally killed the sport.

LOSERS, MISFITS, AND CRIMINALS: 1968-1972

In the United States, both the definition and the stereotype of the aircraft hijacker have changed over the years, from bold adventurer to ineffectual misfit. By 1971 the skyjacker was increasingly regarded as timid, cringing, weak, and sexually inadequate.[20] In the words of James Arey, "he is a dropout from everyday life, a malcontent, a political fanatic, a rebel with or without a cause, or an emotional disaster."[21] These hijackers did not fit neatly into any single, identifiable pattern, but they wreaked havoc in the skies of the United States between 1968 and 1973.

As Arey pointed out, the great majority of skyjacked flights originating in the United States have been basically apolitical.[22] The word had somehow gone around that hijacking was the thing to do, and sure enough, the ease with which hijackers took over planes seemed to corroborate this notion. Almost anything could be used to take over a plane—loaded guns and long-blade knives but also "toy pistols and such things as cans of mosquito spray, bottles of shaving lotion and candles concealed in newspapers . . . described by hijackers as grenades, bombs and sticks of dynamite."[23]

Most people would agree that under no circumstances can hijacking be considered the act of a well-balanced individual or group. In fact, one could go further and state that "all hijackers flirt, consciously or unconsciously, with the idea of death."[24] But the group that emerged after 1968 was particularly bizarre. In addition to those who decided to make their break for Cuba because of joblessness, marriage problems, or general disaffection with life in America, it included two categories of aberrant behavior. There were the emotionally disturbed, people who were psychiatrically ill or who seemed to have no objective other than death itself, and the criminally inclined, who were either transportation thieves and unreturned fugitives or forgers, burglars, robbers, two-bit smugglers, and narcotics peddlers.[25] The categories overlapped and intermixed.

On July 12, 1968, Oran David Richards hijacked a Delta Convair 880 flying from Baltimore to Houston. He met Senator J. O. Eastland at the lavatory door and shouted, "I am a sick man. Get back or I'll kill you." There was a gun to prove it. The 33-year-old forklift operator next told the pilot he was dying of cancer and had to get to Cuba. Suddenly, as he held the gun to the pilot's head, it occurred to him that he might be sinning, especially against the passengers in the plane. Ten minutes later he was sobbing on the floor and calling for his mother but still holding the gun steady. Finally, after an hour, he dropped the gun. The pilot picked it up and shortly after the flight, by now very low on fuel, made an emergency landing at Miami.

On November 1, 1969, which was his twentieth birthday, Raffaele Minichiello, a U.S. Marine, hijacked TWA Flight 85 out of Los Angeles and ordered it to Rome. He had a grudge against his Marine Corps paymaster who had told him there was only $600 in his personal account when he thought there should have been $800. This had occurred in January 1969 on his return from 28 combat missions in Vietnam. Brooding over the injustice in May, after drinking a considerable quantity of alcohol, he decided to break into the PX and collect $200 worth of goods in order to right the wrong. After the robbery, however, he passed out with the stolen goods still on his person. The resultant court martial was due to take place a day or so before he hijacked Flight 85.

Instead of facing his punishment, Minichiello took a much more drastic step. He committed the dangerous act of transatlantic piracy on a nontransatlantic aircraft. His hijack progressed from California to Rome by way of Denver; New York; Bangor, Maine; and Shannon, Ireland—nearly 6,900 miles in 17 grueling hours. During the odyssey, Captain Donald Cook was able to talk at considerable length to Minichiello and gain his confidence. It was no mean feat, since the young marine was armed with an M1 carbine and was not averse to using it. In fact, he fired one shot through the cockpit ceiling but fortunately did no serious damage. He was "deadly dangerous" and "ready to explode," as well as "extremely disturbed and obsessed with death," according to Captain Cook.[26] His wild mood swings kept the pilots and crew on edge during the whole flight. Finally, after commandeering a police car in Rome, Minichiello escaped into the Italian hills. He was captured a few days later in his shirt and underpants in a country church. Surprisingly, the Italians imprisoned him for only 16 months and fined him $580 but did not extradite him to the United States. Many young Italian girls wanted to marry him, and he became something of a hero in Italy.

Criminals were less admired. On November 4, 1968, Raymond Johnson hijacked a National Airlines B727 from Houston to Miami and ordered it to Cuba. A Black Panther, Johnson was one of the more vicious hijackers. He knocked off the copilot's glasses and ground them underfoot, and he reviled the passengers, calling them "economic devils." Then, demonstrating a streak of economic devilry himself, he forced one of the flight attendants to collect cash from 57 of the 63 passengers. It amounted to only $405, but the Cuban officials subsequently disapproved of his looting sufficiently to return all the money to the passengers.

Similarly, on March 5, 1969, Tony Bryant, commandeered a National Airlines B727 in New York. Released from prison in California after serving eight years for selling narcotics, Bryant robbed from rich passengers to give to poorer passengers and finally stepped off in Havana with $1,700 in cash filched from one wealthy traveler. The Cubans again returned the money.[27]

On May 28, 1971, ex-policeman James E. Bennett commandeered a New York to Miami Eastern Airlines flight. He ordered the plane to Nassau, where he demanded $500,000 ransom for the IRA. He was overpowered in Nassau.

On October 29, 1972, Charles Tuller, 48 years old, hijacked an Eastern Airlines B727 out of Houston. He had resigned from a $26,000 a year job with the United States Commerce Department because of diabetes, but he was also mentally ill. His illness stemmed from a hatred of his father who had held him responsible since childhood for the death of his brother in a road accident.[28]

Tuller's snapping point came three weeks after his resignation when he, his two sons, and their friend held up a bank. The raid failed, but he shot and killed the manager and a policeman. Shortly afterwards, in the Houston airport, the four men killed an Eastern Airlines ticket agent who tried to stop them, wounded a maintenance man in the arm, and hijacked the B727. On the flight from Houston to Havana, Tuller forced the 36 passengers to sit with their hands on their heads and cursed them. In a rage, he waved his gun about. Finally, he was arrested by Cuban soldiers.

This last category of hijacks in particular shocked the authorities into action. Certainly, by 1972, frequent repetition was removing some of the shock value of hijacking. Increased security at airports was also to help considerably, but even with a great deal of *target-hardening,* or building obstacles to hijacking, aerial hijacking continued steadily through the 1980s. This state of affairs is partly due to the fact that "it remains an unparalleled attention-getting device, and because . . . there is a type of personality almost irresistibly attracted to skyjacking as an activity," observed psychiatrist David G. Hubbard.[29]

THE YEAR OF RECKONING: 1972

In 1972 the FAA, the FBI, and the airlines realized they had to do something to stop the rampage of hijacks. At that time there were 531 airports in the United States that generated 15,000 flights and 500,000 passengers daily.[30] Although 95 percent of all Americans flew from 121 of those 531 airports, the security problem was still considerable, and it took a long time for the elements of an overall system of airport security to evolve in the United States. A number of different constituencies needed to be convinced singly and then collectively to cooperate with one another.

The stirrings and counteraction in 1961 under President Kennedy did not last; people quickly forgot about the startling events in the skies, and the FAA simply could not drum up enthusiasm for an antihijacking program.[31] Besides, no one was eager to pay for it.

The FAA did carry out a basic study of hijackers and tested a passenger screening system beginning in the late 1960s, nudged, by the epidemic of hijacking after 1968. The screening was effective, for in "a 16-month period ending in mid-February 1971, U.S. marshals, tipped off by airport detection devices, arrested 273 undesirables, confiscated 67 guns, one grenade, two rifles, and $1,500,000 worth of narcotics."[32]

For reasons completely unrelated to hijacking, however, the airline industry was faced with economic difficulties between 1969 and 1971, and the prospect of paying out more money when less was coming in did not exactly fill the airlines with elation.[33] Another factor in the lagging response to air piracy was the attitude of the airlines. American Airlines, for example, "sincerely believed that the reason they had so few hijacks was not that they flew on an East–West route but that their airline 'carries nice people—people of distinction, while others carry the great unwashed.' ''[34] Perhaps, too, the airlines were lulled into complacency by the number of unsuccessful hijacks. In 1969, 7 of 40 attempts failed; a year later, 9 of 26 were unsuccessful; and in 1972, 14 out of 25 failed.

For these and other reasons, from February 1968 to February 1969 there was a period of defeatism in the United States. With 150 million passengers or more traveling each year and an annual increase in passenger traffic of 17 to 20 percent, not to mention 57 cities with nonstop flights to Miami, how could the system respond?

The FAA task force began by concentrating on reducing the number of hijackings.[35] Beginning in February 1969, the concept of target-hardening began to emerge. Warning posters were used, and sifting of passengers continued by working on the behavioral characteristics of hijackers. The public also became aware that the airlines had a policy of nonresistance and gradually realized that what was happening was not a Cuban conspiracy but an epidemic of hijacks by amateurs.[36]

The problem began to expand worldwide. Between October 1969 and June 1970, there were hijacking incidents in 15 countries outside North and South America, and a shotgun approach to security began to evolve.[37] President Nixon's 2,000-strong sky marshal force was working as a deterrent in the air. At the same time, the FAA insisted on the importance of the application of psychological principles in law enforcement, and so work continued on psychological profiles. Simultaneously, the United States was pursuing international means of hijack control.[38]

The Tokyo Convention on hijacking had been signed in 1963, but it dealt only with the prompt return of passengers and planes, and it had not been ratified until 1969. On December 16, 1970, The Hague Convention for the suppression of illegal seizure of aircraft was passed by 74 votes to zero, with two abstentions (Cuba and Algeria).[39] The convention declared skyjacking to be both a criminal offense and an extraditable offense, but still the airlines lagged behind in security measures at airports, and this seemed to be the nexus of the problem.[40]

Finally, the FAA took the Big Stick approach. On March 6, 1972, it required that airlines develop a comprehensive antihijacking security program.[41] The next day, the shape of the future revealed itself when TWA was warned that four of its planes would be blown up at six-hour intervals unless $2 million in ransom was paid. One bomb did explode in a plane—on the ground—in Las Vegas, and another was sniffed out by a dog in John F. Kennedy airport. "Blackmail on the ground—piracy in the air" became the theme, and there was a huge spate of hijacks in 1972. Between 1961 and the end of 1972, 218 hijackers had been involved in 159 U.S. hijack incidents. Of the hijackers, 121 were still fugitives, 49 were convicted, 16 were placed in mental institutions, 9 were wounded or had committed suicide, and 15 had cases still pending.[42] It was not a cheerful picture. Then, on November 10, 1972, the hijack incident took place that was to galvanize the United States into imposing a complete system of airplane and airport security.

Three black escaped convicts, Henry Jackson, Lewis Moore, and Melvin Cale, hijacked a Southern Airways DC9 flying out of Birmingham, Alabama. Two of the three were out on bail, accused of rape, and the third was an escaped convict. The hijack was to last 29 hours, include nine forced stops, and involve two other countries. Fearing that the male passengers might be concealing weapons, the hijackers made them all strip down to their underwear. Jackson and Moore had a grievance against the mayor and police of Detroit, whom they had unsuccessfully sued for $4 million for brutality following their arrest 18 months before. After refueling at Jackson, Mississippi, the plane circled Detroit, and the hijackers demanded a ransom of $10 million and threatened to crash the plane into the atomic plant at Oak Ridge, Tennessee, if the ransom was not paid. The plane circled the nuclear plant until deteriorating weather conditions forced it to land at Cleveland with only eight minutes of fuel left. The plane sat on the tarmac while an FBI agent, stripped to his underwear in temperatures of 42° Fahrenheit, pumped 2,700 gallons of fuel into its tanks. The flight then took off for Toronto with the threat that unless the $10 million was handed over to them there, they would return to crash the plane into the Oak Ridge plant.

Another Southern Airways plane arrived in Toronto with $500,000, but this was not enough for the hijackers, and the plane took off again in the direction of Oak Ridge, where it circled for five hours. The hijackers threatened to "make this thing look worse than Munich," a reference to the massacre at the Munich Olympics.[43] The Atomic Energy Commission then evacuated more than 200 employees and shut down three nuclear reactors. Finally at 2:30 P.M., having again landed to be refueled by the underwear-clad FBI agent, the plane took off for Cuba. It arrived there after 19 hours of a nerve-wracking ordeal for the passengers and authorities. As two of the hijackers left the plane to negotiate with the Cubans, the pilot, Captain William R. Haas, considered jumping Melvin Cale, but Cale held a grenade in his hand.

The Cubans had no sympathy for the criminals but let them reboard the aircraft and take off again. This time a U.S. Navy DC6 chase plane tailed the DC9 with FBI agents at the ready, angering the hijackers, who announced they would fly to Switzerland. When they landed at Orlando, Florida, for more fuel and navigational aids, the FBI decided the hijacking would have to end and shot out the plane's tires. The hijackers responded by shooting the copilot in the shoulder and threatening to shoot all passengers, one by one, unless the aircraft took off, flat tires or not. It was "like driving a car with flat tires along a railroad," and pieces of tire entered the engines, causing serious overheating on takeoff.[44] The enraged hijackers then circled President Nixon's home in Key Biscayne before once again heading for Cuba and landing on a sea of foam at Havana. Finally, the Cubans arrested them.

A number of lessons were learned from this hijacking. The shooting of the tires nearly destroyed the plane with all of its passengers and turned the hijackers into raving maniacs. A serious threat to an American nuclear reactor had been made, but fortunately not carried out, and the vulnerability of the whole airport system had been mercilously exposed. As FAA director John Shaffer put it, "The Oak Ridge odyssey has cleared the air."[45] Suddenly, there was a real hope of a bilateral treaty, and indirect talks with Cuba began.[46]

On December 5, 1972, all U.S. airport operators were given 60 days to arrange for armed local law enforcement officers to be stationed at passenger checkpoints during boarding and reboarding.[47] On January 5, 1973, it became mandatory for all passengers at U.S. airports to be searched electronically and for their carry-on baggage to be searched.[48] Finally, 12 years after the first American hijack, the president of the United States swallowed his pride and signed a hijack treaty with Cuba.

On February 15, 1973, U.S. Secretary of State William Rogers announced in Washington that a five-year agreement had been reached covering not only planes but vessels.[49] Each government would henceforth prosecute hijackers severely in their own courts, and there would be no safe haven in the United States or Cuba. Canada, too, was included in this agreement.

But North America was not alone in the growing desire to secure planes and airports. Palestinian attacks on international airlines between 1968 and 1972 had a dramatic effect in Western Europe and the Middle East and a worldwide impact on security.

THE ARAB SKYJACK WAR, 1968-1972

The Palestinian hijackings began in 1968, following the defeat of the Arab states in the Arab–Israeli conflict of June 1967. The war had left the Palestinians without Arab support, on their own, and also deprived them of nearly all of their land bases for fedayeen raids across Israeli borders. Hijacking thus seems to have developed as one means of trying to achieve political objectives without recourse to direct military confrontation. It was the brainchild of George Habash, the leader of the radical Marxist wing of the Palestinian movement, the PFLP. Ten years after Raoul Castro had used skyjacking to disrupt communications within Cuba, Habash conceived the idea of shooting up El Al's B707s as a way of attacking Israel. The PFLP would "turn passengers into hostages, blow them out of the sky, attack them in terminals," said Habash.[50] He went much further than Raoul Castro; he used air piracy for the purpose of political blackmail as well as a tactic of terrorism. Habash's base was Beirut, but he was able to count on the support of many Arab regimes in the Mediterranean, especially the Algerians. Algeria became a sanctuary for hijacked planes and played a crucial role in the Arab skyjack war in Western Europe and the Middle East, which paralleled the Cuba–United States imbroglio from 1968 to 1972.

Between July 1968 and August 1978 the Palestinians and their allies carried out 35 hijacks or airport and airplane-related attacks on both Israeli and Western facilities. Twenty-three of them had occurred by December 1973 and were carried out by a bewildering number of groups. The PFLP started the process and was joined by the PFLP-GC, Japanese Red Army, Fatah, Black September Organization, Baader–Meinhof Gang, Black June, and, finally, the National Arab Youth for the Liberation of Palestine. In addition to these airplane and airport-related attacks there were many more different types of terrorist attacks launched simultaneously, which tended to inflate the impact of the attacks on the largely defenseless and certainly unsuspecting Western European air transportation system.

For the first year the Palestinian attacks were all against El Al, the Israeli National Airline, and were initiated at airports in Europe. The aim was to frighten passengers away from El Al and deter European authorities from accepting Israeli planes. In the case of the PFLP, maximum publicity for their cause and the use of blackmail for the release of captured or convicted terrorists were also major objectives.

In their first hijacking, on July 23, 1968, three PFLP guerrillas seized an El Al B707 on a flight from Rome to Tel Aviv. It was diverted to Algiers, where the Algerians released all non-Israeli passengers and later Israeli women and children, while holding the plane and 12 male Israelis and the crew hostage. The guerrillas demanded the release of 1,200 Arabs held in Israel.

On August 13 the International Federation of Airline Pilots Association (IFALPA) declared that it would boycott all flights to Algiers beginning on August 19 unless the plane and hostages were released. Thirty-nine days later, Israeli–Algerian negotiations, conducted through the Italian consul in Algiers, led to the release of both plane and hostages. They also led to Israel's release of 16 Arab infiltrators caught in the 1967 war. Although it was a year before the PFLP seized another plane, the group soon switched its focus to attacking El Al aircraft on the ground in European airports, first at Athens on December 26, 1968, and then at Zurich on February 18, 1969. In each case at least one Israeli was killed and others wounded. The result was that the Israelis improved their security measures on all El Al aircraft, including locked, bullet-proofed doors and armed sky marshals. This led the PFLP to turn to other nations' aircraft.

On August 29, 1969, a PFLP team led by Leila Khaled seized an American plane, a TWA B707 on a flight from Rome to Tel Aviv, and diverted it to Damascus. All passengers were allowed to disembark by the commandos, who then attempted to blow up the plane. The Syrians, however, held two of the Israeli passengers and exchanged them along with the repaired plane two months later for 13 Syrians held by Israel. Suddenly, the United States was fighting the hijack war on two fronts, at home and abroad.

Throughout 1969 more PFLP Hijack attempts were made, with many terrorists being apprehended in the process of boarding flights. In December 1969, for instance, three PFLP members were caught attempting to board in Athens with guns and explosives in their hand baggage. A suspicious airport clerk had noticed they all carried identical bags.

On February 10, 1970, the Action Group for the Liberation of Palestine tried to kidnap passengers in a transit lounge but failed. Exactly 11 days later, the PFLP-GC placed altitude bombs aboard two airliners. The first plane, a Swissair Coronado jetliner, crashed, killing all 47 passengers, including 13 Israelis. The second, an Austrian Airlnes Caravelle, managed to land at Frankfurt because the bomb had been surrounded by newspapers in the plane's baggage hold. Both planes were headed for Tel Aviv. There was worldwide revulsion to these acts.

On March 31, 1970, the Japanese Red Army carried out a dramatic hijack that was to be a teaching experience for the PFLP. It was the first skyjack to be televised as it developed, and there were two stages to the incident. The first lasted five hours at Fukuoka in Japan, and the second, nearly 80 hours in duration, was in Seoul, South Korea.[51] Each time, a television audience of millions watched nervously.

Nine Japanese men with Samurai swords seized a Japanese Airlines B727 flying from Tokyo to Fukuoka, 550 miles west, and announced that they wished to fly to North Korea. Since the flight was a domestic one, the hijackers had to agree to a stop at Fukuoka for fuel. In exchange for the fuel, 22 women and 1 old man were freed. The rest of the terrified passengers were tied to their seats and threatened with swords and explosive devices.

The Japanese government was totally unprepared for what it had always considered to be a Western malady and had not even ratified the Tokyo Convention (1963). When the plane took off again for North Korea, it was Captain Shinji Ishida's first flight over the South China Sea. He switched to VH121-5 megacycles in the hope of contacting Pyongyang as he flew near the Demilitarized Zone. To his surprise, a reply came for them to land, and two fighters escorted them to Kimpo Airport, Seoul. The South Koreans had already experienced two hijacks to the north and might have fooled the terrorists into thinking they were in North Korea but for the lack of posters of Kim il Sung around the airport. Then the hijackers saw a Northwest Airlines plane, which gave the game away.

Negotiations now commenced with the Japanese deputy minister of trade, Shinjiro Yamamura, taking personal charge. In the Samurai tradition, he offered himself as a hostage in place of the passengers. The swap took place 80 hours into the hijack, and finally the flight crew and minister flew into North Korea. The Samurai Nine, as they were dubbed, obtained political asylum, and the Japanese plane and occupants returned to a rapturous welcome in Tokyo.

But the PFLP learned some dramatic lessons from the incident. First, there was the protracted publicity of holding passengers in the eye of the television cameras. Then there was the act of keeping them caged up under the threat of extinction and playing on the emotions of public opinion. Holding them hostage to the indecisiveness of governments also had much propaganda value for the Japanese Red Army cause. "Another lesson was that a political group had detained an airliner full of passengers for four days at an airport while it negotiated with governments."[52] There is no doubt that this incident was a part of the inspiration for the dramatic multiple hijack in Jordan in September.

A transitional step took place July 22 in Athens, two days before the trial in that city of four imprisoned Arab terrorists. An Olympic Airways B727 was hijacked to Athens from Beirut with 47 passengers and a crew of 8. The hijackers used a threat that had been issued by the Red Army four months earlier in Japan. They demanded the immediate release of all seven terrorists held in Athens or said they would blow up the plane with the passengers. Aristotle Onassis was involved in the negotiations, and the Greek government was being tested. The government capitulated. After the trial of two of the hijackers, all were released within a month. As the Israeli foreign minister, Abba Ebban, observed, "If international hijacking is rewarded, the safety of the airways is very severely compromised."[53]

The stage was now set for the most dramatic multiple hijack in history, on September 6 at Dawson's Field in Jordan. The immediate prelude to this hijack was a severe Israeli reprisal to a PFLP attack on an El Al B707 at Athens airport, in which one Israeli was shot and killed and one engine was hit, nearly igniting the whole aircraft, which was full of passengers. So Israel launched a raid on the ground, which wiped out 13 aircraft of Middle Eastern Airlines at Beirut International Airport. There was severe criticism of the Israeli action worldwide, and the PFLP continued with grenade attacks on El Al offices in Brussels and Athens. Saboteurs and hijackers were becoming one.

On Sunday, September 6, there began a mass hijacking described as "the most remarkable event in the history of aerial piracy." First, a TWA B707 flying from Frankfurt to New York was diverted to Dawson's Field. Simultaneously, a Swissair DC8 flying from Zurich to New York was hijacked. The third plane commandeered was an El Al B707 flying from New York to Tel Aviv with a stop in Amsterdam. Leila Khaled and Patrick Arguello took on Israeli armed sky marshals in a battle that led to Arguello's death and Khaled's capture. The fourth airliner skyjacked that afternoon was a Pan American jumbo jet, which was taken by the two men who had failed to get on Khaled and Arguello's flight. They directed the huge jet to Cairo where the passengers were given eight minutes to vacate the plane before the $20 million aircraft was blown up. Finally, on Wednesday, September 8, the PFLP hijacked a British BOAC VC10 flying from London to Bahrain and Bombay in order to free Leila Khaled. It was the first British commercial airliner ever hijacked.

Five governments were now involved in negotiations over three aircraft at Dawson's Field. At the talks in Berne, the Americans, British, Swiss, Germans, and Israelis were all forced to negotiate with the PFLP. Typically, the Germans and Swiss wanted to negotiate immediately and independently. The Israelis adamantly refused to negotiate at all, and the British stood somewhere in the middle.

All five planes were major flag carriers on long-range international flights, and four of them were ultimately destroyed at a cost of $52 million. Four hundred and thirty passengers and crew were held hostage while a total of 769 men, women, and children were abused in the course of the five hijacks. The whole episode coincided with a civil war in Jordan, which greatly complicated the hostage situation and later led to the creation of another terrorist group called the Black September Organization. It took five weeks to unravel the whole hijack episode, but as George Habash stated, "We do not want peace! Peace would be the end of all our hopes."[54]

Both the United States and Western Europe were shaken by the severity of the multiple hijack at Dawson's Field. Suddenly, airport security became a priority for the Europeans.

There were other incidents that helped spur the move toward better security. On July 20, 1971, the first of a series of attacks was mounted by Fatah on Jordanian offices and aircraft in revenge for Black September in Jordan in 1970. For a year the attacks were carried out, without success, against the Jordanian airline Alia.

On July 28 and September 1, 1971, in two separate incidents, attempts were made by the PFLP-GC to blow up El Al planes by placing bombs in the suitcases of innocent Dutch and Peruvian girls on board.

On February 22, 1972, the PFLP returned to the attack when it hijacked to Aden a West German Lufthansa jet flying between New Delhi and Frankfurt. The 173 passengers aboard included the 19-year-old son of the late senator, Robert Kennedy, but the passengers were released since extortion was the purpose of the exercise. The PFLP demanded that the German government fly $5 million in ransom money for the release of passengers and 14 crew. Meanwhile, the terrorists wired the plane with explosives. The PFLP knew perfectly well which government would settle quickly, and their confidence in the efficacy of hijacking was quickly restored with such a large infusion of funds to be used for other heists. The South Yemen government also managed to extract $1 million from the West Germans for "landing rights."[55]

Basically, the weakness of the West German government had crowned a year of Arab terrorism with success. With 43 people dead and more than 80 wounded in three major hijacks, the German government had completely failed to buy off the Arabs or exempt themselves from terrorist attention. It was a bad mistake, even if the year was that of an Olympic Games and West Germany was trying to make them the "Happy Games." Sadly, "the wind sown at Aden was the whirlwind reaped at Munich."[56]

The growing confidence of the European hijackers was demonstrated by two hijacks, both of which occurred at Lod Airport in Israel in May 1972. In the first, on May 8, Black September hijacked a Belgian Sabena jet and forced it to land at Tel Aviv. The hijackers demanded that Israel release 317 Arab prisoners of war and threatened to blow up the airliner, themselves, 90 passengers, and 10 crew members.[57] On the first night, under cover of darkness, the plane was immobilized by the Israelis, who deflated the tires and drained the hydraulic fluid from the landing gear. As the minister in charge, Moshe Dayan, pointed out, with Israel committed to "no deals" with terrorists, there could be only three outcomes—destruction, capitulation, or capture.[58] In this instance it was the last of the three that came about at Lod. The International Red Cross joined the negotiations, both complicating and aiding the situation. As far as Dayan was concerned, the 50 Israelis inside the plane were going nowhere else. As he negotiated, the guerrillas put back their deadline. This breakthrough was followed by a second sleepless night for the two male and two female terrorists. At 10:00 A.M. the next morning their threat to blow up the plane may have been foiled by an abortive but dangerous attempt by Captain Reginald Levy to grab the leader's gun. The intervention and presence of the Red Cross enabled Dayan to learn that the two male hijackers were controlling the cockpit while the two female hijackers, who carried girdles with explosives around their waists and detonators in their bras, were to blow up the plane from the rear. At 3:45 P.M. on the second day of the hijack, 18 "mechanics" in overalls were sent to repair the damage to the plane, presumably preparatory to takeoff. The mechanics, when challenged by the Red Cross representatives, suddenly assaulted the plane, killing the two male hijackers and capturing the two women before they could act. The whole affair was over in precisely 34 seconds.[59] the one passenger shot and killed in the encounter was, unfortunately, one of those people so frightened that he stood up when told by the mechanics to duck down. This was the first effort made by the West to strike back at hijackers.

True to their word, the Israelis had established a policy of not negotiating with Arab skyjackers since July 1970, but this did not help them in the second hijack incident in late May. On May 31 three Japanese Red Army terrorists trained in Japan and North Korea and recruited by Wadi Haddad of the PFLP for further training in Lebanon, made their way toward Israel by plane. They flew to Paris, then Frankfurt, and then to Rome where they took an Air France plane to Tel Aviv. Their baggage was not searched. Once at Lod Airport, they opened their bags, snatched out assault rifles and grenades, and managed to kill 26 people. They also wounded 76 others, many of them Puerto Rican pilgrims visiting the Holy Land. Two of the three terrorists were killed, leaving the third, Kozo Okamoto, to languish in prison. He was the brother of Tekishi Okamoto who was one of the Samurai Nine mentioned earlier. This was the first of the Japanese "Arab" operations and the first of the transnational murder attacks. As General Richard Clutterbuck pointed out, "This incident shocked the world as no previous air piracy had done before."[60]

It was now becoming increasingly clear that the only way to counter such people was to stop them in the passenger-baggage pipeline, for the whole shocking episode dramatically revealed the extent of Palestinian international organization. Again, General Clutterbuck put it succinctly: "Japanese terrorists, trained in Japan, North Korea and Lebanon, had been provided with false papers in Germany, and Czech weapons in Rome, to board a French aircraft in order to attack international air travellers in Israel."[61] Ironically, all this coordination had come from a headquarters in the sanctuary of a refugee camp in Lebanon.

The year 1972 was only half over for hijackings. On September 5 the Munich Massacre took place at the Olympic Games. The killing of the 11 Israeli

Olympic athletes was not a hijack as such, but the West German government agreed to give the terrorists and their hostages safe passage to Egypt. Then, at Furstenfeldbruck Airport, West German sharpshooters opened fire. In the ensuing gunfight in and around the helicopter that was being used to transport them, all the hostages, five terrorists, and one policeman were killed. Millions of people all over the world saw the episode on television, and Black September was content to have made its point.

It was almost inevitable, given the attitude of the West German government, that Black September would at some time seize hostages to regain their hijackers in West German jails. Chancellor Willy Brandt's calling of an election was an ideal time to act, and so on October 29, a Lufthansa B727 from Beirut to Munich was hijacked to Damascus. The threat to blow up plane and passengers was enough to obtain the release of the three imprisoned terrorists. As one of the hijackers said to Captain Walter Clausen, "Your government has got wise."[62]

In February 1973 Italy released two Black September terrorists only six months after arresting them for putting a bomb on an El Al B707 at Rome Airport. Abba Eban, Israel's foreign minister, described the release as a "shocking surrender, a capitulation, and a weakening of the international stand against terrorism."[63]

Throughout the rest of 1973 a great deal of international terrorism took place, but by no means all in the area of hijacking. On July 20 a joint PFLP–JRA hijack took place between Amsterdam and Tokyo on a Japanese Airlines B747. One female hijacker killed herself when she dropped her grenade. The aircraft flew around the Middle East for four days until it arrived at Benghazi where passengers were released and the plane was blown up. The hijackers were arrested and jailed.

On August 5, 5 passengers were killed and 55 wounded in a machine-gun and grenade attack on passengers from a TWA plane that had just landed on a flight from Tel Aviv. The killers claimed to be from Black September but were later identified as the National Arab Youth for the Liberation of Palestine led by Abu Nidal.

On September 5 in Rome, Black September terrorists adopted electronic aerial warfare. Italian police arrested five Arabs armed with two Soviet Strela heat-seeking ground-to-air rockets (SAM 7s). The terrorists had rented an apartment in a house on the flight path to Rome airport and were planning to shoot down an El Al airliner. Finally, on December 17 in Rome, five terrorists set fire to a Pan American plane with thermite bombs, burning 32 passengers to death and injuring 40. They then hijacked a Lufthansa plane, murdered an airline worker, and flew to Damascus and Kuwait with hostages. Significantly, they were refused permission to land in any Arab country, including Libya, and the runways were physically blocked.[64] The terrorists belonged to Abu Nidal's NAYLP.

It was a bad year for European governments, with innovative and frightening means being developed to threaten airports, airplanes, and passengers. Also, the disarray of policy among the European governments was very obvious.

In summarizing the impact of the Arab skyjack war between 1968 and 1973, it can be seen that the multiple hijack at Dawson's Field really set in motion the process that led to the great reduction in hijacking in the United States by 1973. General Benjamin O. Davis realized the problem would have to be tackled on the ground and at the gates for boarding. The second Lod Airport episode with its passenger massacre had a big influence on the measures being discussed for counterhijacking. It virtually settled the argument about whether a mandatory search of all passengers should go ahead. The killing of 33 people at Rome airport was deeply shocking to the traveling public, and so on January 5, 1973, a mandatory search of both passengers and their luggage was ordered in the United States. The screening and search was made entirely by airline personnel in the presence of armed guards provided by the airport authorities. The cost was borne by the airlines and airports and thus indirectly by passengers in the cost of their tickets.[65]

By the close of 1973, 3,500 passengers had been prevented from boarding at gates in 531 airports in the United States. Three hundred declined to be searched and were turned away, 3,200 were arrested, 2,000 guns and 3,500 pounds of high explosive were seized, and 23,000 knives were confiscated. Such was the contour of the first skin of airport security, a system that was to last effectively for almost 15 years. There was also, by the end of 1973, a certain growing Arab disillusionment with hijacking.[66] As General Richard Clutterbuck stated,

The reason for the growing reluctance of the Arab governments to co-operate with the Palestinian terrorists is probably due to their double success in October 1973—first in wiping out the humiliation of the 1948, 1956 and 1967 Arab–Israeli Wars and second in proving that the oil weapon was far more effective than terrorism in exerting influence on the United States and Western European powers and in persuading them in turn to exert pressure on Israel.[67]

It is also interesting to note that whereas George Habash had set out in 1968 to drive El Al Airlines out of business, quite the reverse had in fact occurred. In 1967-1969 El Al did business amounting to $25 million, whereas in 1972-1973 it was $135 million, with a 69 percent load factor. More significantly, Israel's national carrier was forced to develop a system of airport and airplane security that was second to none in the world and even today might well be worth emulating by other Western powers.

THE WEST FIGHTS BACK, 1973-1978

Because of the Cuba run in 1961 and from 1968 onward, and because the United States had the largest share of international air traffic, it was inevitable that the first skin of airport security would originate in the United States. The system has several components and was developed at the insistence of President Nixon.

First was the passing of enabling legislation. Public Law 87-197 defined air piracy and its punishment in the United States. Second, a system of sky marshals was developed to guard planes while in the air. Third, security was implemented at all U.S. airports and was the responsibility of the airlines under the direction of the FAA. Fourth, a system of electronic surveillance and screening was developed for baggage and passengers. Fifth, the screening of passengers involved a profile that narrowed down the suspicious to less than 1 percent of all passengers. Sixth, air and cabin crews were instructed to develop policies of resistance to hijackers instead of inert nonresistance. Seventh, the FAA authorized crews to carry firearms if they were competent to use them and wanted to do so. Many pilots did not. Eighth, consultation of a transnational sort with foreign counterparts was encouraged with information sharing. Ninth, the deterrent effect was built up by the signing of multilateral conventions through the International Civil Aviation Organization dealing with hijacking. This included Tokyo (1963), The Hague (1970), and Montreal (1971). Finally, IFALPA, the international pilots association, was vocal in its determination to curtail aerial piracy, especially by refusing to fly into the airports of offending states. This could be quite a strong sanction. Basically, this is the technical system that has since comprised the first skin of airport security, and it was adequate until 1985.

In the case of the United States, the Canada–U.S.–Cuba hijack agreement of February 15, 1973, was very useful in regulating, if not controlling, the flow of hijacks between politically hostile countries. But the Western response to terrorism really began with the Israelis, who on May 8, 1972, used 18 ''mechanics'' to reverse the momentum in a hijack that had gone on for more than two days and nights. It was a blow for counterterrorism, in favor of the West.

On February 21, 1973, the Israelis shot down a Libyan plane over Sinai that they feared might take a bombing or suicide run at Tel Aviv. Then, on May 23, 1976, Dutch marines successfully assaulted a train that had been held for 20 days by South Moluccan terrorists. Two hostages and six terrorists died in the assault, and it demonstrated that elite teams could be used effectively against terrorists. If on trains, then why not on planes?

Not long afterward, on June 27, a joint Baader-Meinhof-PFLP hijack of Air France airbus ended up at Entebbe in Uganda. The Air France Airbus A300, with more than 250 passengers and crew on board, was hijacked shortly after its departure from Athens. It landed at Benghazi, Libya, to take on fuel and then proceeded to Entebbe. The hijacking was made possible by the collusion of the governments of Uganda, Somalia, and Libya. The hostages were taken to the airport buildings at Entebbe where the mixed gang of West German and Palestinian terrorists demanded the release of 53 pro-Palestinian prisoners in numerous countries in exchange for the hostages. During the negotiations, approximately 150 hostages were released, leaving behind those with Israeli passports and the Air France crew members.

On the evening of July 3, the hijack was brought to an end by a spectacular assault on Entebbe Airport by troops of Israel's elite Sagaret Matkal force. They killed two West German terrorists and five members of the PFLP. Three hostages were killed, but all of the others were rescued. It was the first great defeat of international terrorism, and it had an immense psychological effect worldwide. For one thing, the Israelis had sent a force hundreds of miles outside their own territory. For another, they had obtained not only Kenyan cooperation but also clear intelligence about where the hostages were and how to get them out. Finally, the raid was executed with perfect timing and minimum loss of life, and the hostages were airlifted safely back to Israel. It was quite a warning for the hijackers of the world.

One year later on October 13, 1976, a mixed band of PFLP–Baader–Meinhof terrorists hijacked a Lufthansa jet with 79 passengers aboard. The two male and two female terrorists, armed with pistols and plastic explosives, took control of the plane and ordered it to Rome for refueling. The hijackers demanded the release of 11 comrades imprisoned in Germany and 2 in Turkey and $18 million in ransom. The terrorists also threatened to kill the kidnapped German indus- trialist Hans Martin Schleyer. The plane made a wild flight around the Middle East, refueling at Rome, Cyprus, Bahrain, Dubai, the United Arab Emirates, Aden, South Yemen, and finally Mogadishu in Somalia. In South Yemen the pilot, Captain Jurgen Schumann, was murdered.

At Mogadishu the Somalian authorities not only gave permission for commandos to land and strike but also put their own troops at the disposal of the West Germans. The plane was stormed by West Germany's elite GSG9 Commando unit. At the same time, British Special Air Service (SAS) troops took part using stun grenades. As a result, three of the terrorists were killed and the fourth, a woman, was wounded. All passengers were rescued, though nine were wounded.

The main point here was that the West again seemed to be turning the tables on the hijack terrorists. Coming only months after the Entebbe raid, the Mogadishu rescue further shored up the morale of the West and served notice that Western countries would strike back at the terrorists. This strikeback capacity was demonstrated again in 1980 when the SAS went in and took out terrorists holed up in the Iranian Embassy in London.

Finally, at the Bonn Summit in July 1978, the government leaders of Canada, France, Italy, Japan, the United Kingdom, the United States, and West Germany agreed to impose sanctions against any state that aided and abetted in the hijacking of aircraft.[68] Even hard-line Arab terrorist supporters were reluctant to continue their support if the price was to have their airline communications with the outside world discontinued. Finally, after nearly ten years of free reign, the hijack terrorists were being shut down and deterred from their blackmail in the skies.

There was also a dramatic decrease in hijacks in 1973 because of the new U.S. airport security measures and the Cuban treaty. Hijacks worldwide plunged from 62 in 1972 to only 22 in 1973. Thereafter the number crept upward again, and between 1973 and 1987 the hijack average per annum was about 28. Indeed, the various Palestinian factions carried out at least 10 hijacks between 1974 and 1978, but some of them failed badly. The NAYLP of Abu Nidal, the PFLP,

Carlos, the Japanese Red Army, and the Baader–Meinhof Gang were the main culprits, but the increasing difficulty in mounting hijacks made them turn to other terrorist methods.

On October 8, 1974, a TWA airliner en route to Greece from Israel was blown up in flight over the Aegean Sea, killing all 88 aboard. The NAYLP was responsible. On January 13 and January 19, 1975, two attempts were made to destroy El Al planes with hand-held rocket missiles. Both attempts failed, indicating that airport security was improving. On September 10 TWA flight 355 from Chicago to New York was hijacked by five Croatian terrorists who were American citizens. The B727 was joined by a B707 in its 30-hour ordeal, which took them through Montreal and Gander, Canada; Reykjavik, Iceland; and London before finally terminating in Paris. The 86 passengers went through an emotional ordeal in which they fully expected to be blown up by bombs in cooking pots strapped to the male terrorists. The French government did not want Captain Richard Carey to land at Paris even though he was out of fuel, while the U.S. president would not allow negotiations. The whole hijack, which was watched on TV by millions, was undertaken with five one-way fares to New York costing a total of $400 and cooking pots and plastic putty. There were no bombs. Much publicity accrued to the Croatian cause, and another hole had been found in the airport security system.

On September 28, 1977, the Japanese Red Army hijacked a Japanese Air Lines plane, demanding and obtaining a $6 million ransom and the freeing of 11 Baader–Meinhof prisoners. The Japanese hijackers made their way to Baghdad. Japan had capitulated to the terrorists. On December 4 a hijacker commandeered a Malaysian Airlines System B737, and when the pilot tried to touch down at Kuala Lumpur instead of Singapore, the hijacker shot the crew and the plane crashed near Johore, killing 100 crew and passengers.

On February 18, 1978, two Palestinian gunmen from the PFLP murdered Egyptian editor Yasuf Sebai in Nicosia and then hijacked a Cyprus airliner, which later returned to Nicosia. The Egyptian commando mission sent to seize the terrorists tragically misfired, and 15 men died in a fight with the Cyprus National Guard. Finally, on August 20, members of Black June were reduced to attacking an El Al aircrew bus in London. They succeeded in killing a flight attendant.

There were only 27 hijacks in 1979, and none of them was noteworthy. Typically, this year marked a transition that ushered in a new and different phase of hijacking that crested in the mid-1980s.

FUNDAMENTALISTS, SIKHS, THIRD WORLD HIJACKING, 1980-1988

The most recent phase of aerial hijacking retains the dominant theme of Middle East-related attacks on airports, commercial offices, and jet planes. But it also is characterized by new actors on the hijacking stage, as well as the resurgence of some of the older ones. Hijacks remained at the level of almost 30 incidents per year; therefore, it is only accurate to talk about recurring cycles in hijacking and not about abatement. Hijacking has and will remain part of the overall international terrorist scene in the 1990s. The center of gravity in the 1980s moved, not surprisingly, to the Middle East, especially to Iran, Lebanon, Kuwait, and Libya. There was also significant growth in hijacking in Pakistan and India. Simultaneously, there were resurgences of hijacking from Eastern Europe and the United States to Cuba, and in the USSR and China.

Hijacks in the West, mostly in Western Europe, though fewer in number, were much more frightening and media intense. They reached a crescendo in 1985-1986 and coincided with a serious crisis in air safety accompanied in North America by the deregulation of airlines.

MIDDLE EASTERN AND ISLAMIC FUNDAMENTALIST HIJACKS

Between late 1979 and early 1982 seven hijacks took place, mostly of Middle Eastern Airlines planes out of Beirut. They were mounted on behalf of a Lebanese Shiite Moslem spiritual leader, Imam Moussa, who had visited Libya and had not been seen again. The last of these hijackers, in February 1982, demanded that there be a United Nations inquiry into the spiritual leader's disappearance. In 1983-1984 a new group called Islamic Jihad repeatedly struck at the airlines of Lebanon, Kuwait, Iran, and Libya and the West. Air France felt the bite first on August 27, 1983, when an Air France B727 was hijacked on its flight from Vienna to Paris. Four hijackers, armed with guns and grenades, seized the aircraft and hopped from Geneva to Sicily to Damascus and finally to Teheran. They demanded the release of Lebanese prisoners in French prisons and the withdrawal of French troops from Chad and Lebanon. After three days of negotiations the last of the 111 passengers and crew were released. On July 31, 1984, an Air France B737 flying between Frankfurt and Paris was diverted to Teheran. Islamic Jihad demanded the release of five Iranians jailed in France for the attempted assassination of a former Iranian prime minister. The French refused to give in to the demands, despite the terrorist threat to kill a French person each hour aboard the aircraft. Eventually, the hijackers blew up the flight deck, but it was clear that weapons and other support were coming from the Khomeini government.[69]

The next hijacking carried out by the Shiite International was in December 1984 and involved a Kuwaiti airliner flying from Dubai to Karachi that was directed to Teheran.[70] During six days of hostage terror the Shiite hijackers killed two Agency for International Development officials from the United States, wounded two Kuwaitis, and beat up and tortured others.[71] The Iranian government allowed some of the horrors being enacted in the plane to be broadcast. There was deep suspicion of Iranian complicity in the affair and the eventual "storming" of the plane by Iranian security men disguised as ground crew rang very hollow indeed. Islamic Jihad had deliberately revived the airplane hostage game just as airport security had seemed to be making hijacking more difficult and chancy to undertake. "By exploiting security weaknesses which always develop in long periods of calm before a storm, they had revived hijacking."[72] Moreover, they had learned the lessons from previous defeats and knew both what reactions to expect and the high value of propaganda. They also deliberately allowed the broadcasting of the screams and shouts of hostages and hijackers inside the plane for added impact on the media.

Islamic Jihad was planning a spectacular episode along the lines of Dawson's Field in 1970. The prelude to it was a bomb explosion in Frankfurt airport in early June 1985, which killed three and wounded many more. Probably, it was supposed to coincide with the TWA hijacking of June 14. On that day flight 847 was en route from Athens to Rome when it was hijacked by two of the three intended Islamic Jihad terrorists. The third was detained and arrested when weapons were found in his luggage at Athens. The 145 passengers included 120 Americans. The hijackers demanded the release of 700 Shiite prisoners of war in Israel, who had been captured in Southern Lebanon. They also kept the initiative throughout much of the hijacking by flying back and forth between Beirut and Algiers several times. With the Sixth Fleet and the American Delta force closing in, the hijackers would shift locale. Then they would release some passengers as a concession, before applying the pressure again. The pilot, Captain John Testrake, was distinguished throughout by his calm, professional behavior. But even he had to describe the hijackers as "homicidal maniacs." They singled out an American Navy diver, Robert Stethem, who was battered, tortured, and finally killed.[73] They then announced they would kill all Americans aboard, one by one. Later in the hijack they separated passengers with Jewish-sounding names from everyone else. The American television networks stumbled over each other in an unsightly and damaging, if unintended, collusion with the terrorists who managed to get unbelievable propaganda coverage of the episode—all two weeks of it.

It was a typical Middle Eastern scenario as the leader of the Amal in Lebanon, Nabih Berri, inserted himself between the Americans and the hijackers. All that his interaction accomplished was to remove 30 hostages to three safe houses and make a rescue operation impossible. Finally, when Berri could do nothing, President Assad of Syria intervened, and on June 30 all of the remaining 39 American hostages were driven across the Bekaa Valley to Damascus and from there flown to Frankfurt. The terrorists of Islamic Jihad proceeded to claim a great victory, and all terrorist groups were encouraged to strike again. It was a devastating defeat for the West, both in terms of airport security and in the inadequate way in which the crisis was handled. U.S. spokesman Lawrence Eagleburger summed it up fairly accurately when he said, "I don't think anybody has discovered an anti-terrorism policy that works. . . . we are all facing a new kind of warfare and we don't know how to deal with it."[74]

The hijacking of TWA 847 finally dismantled the effectiveness of the first skin of airport security, established in 1973, and encouraged all sorts of terrorist groups to return to airplane hijacking. It was very bad news for Western airport security and the safety of the Western traveling public.

Until December 1985, Abu Nidal, alias Sabri al-Banna, who heads a break-away group of the Palestine Liberation Organization (PLO), had never been involved in air piracy. But as Christopher Dobson and Ronald Payne pointed out, "of all the bands of hit men travelling the world in search of prey, none were more persistent, revengeful and outrageous than those controlled by the Abu Nidal organization."[75] TWA 847 tempted Abu Nidal irresistibly, especially since terrorism thrives on imitation. On November 23, 1985, Abu Nidal terrorists hijacked an Egyptair B737 on a flight from Athens to Cairo. The security guard shot one of the terrorists but then was himself killed. The plane landed at Luqa Airport in Malta, where the hijackers proceeded to murder Jewish and Western passengers one by one. The hijackers were not sane enough to negotiate rationally, and after 22 hours of negotiation and five deaths, the plane was stormed by Egypt's elite counterterrorist force, Thunderbolt. The rescue operation turned into a tragedy as the plane caught fire. It is still not established whether the terrorists' grenades or the commandos' explosives, used to blow open the cargo doors, caused the conflagration. The point was that 57 of 98 passengers died in the inferno. It turned into the bloodiest hijack to date. For Abu Nidal, the terrorists were expendable. In fact, a month later on December 27, Abu Nidal's organization coordinated attacks on El Al check-in counters at Rome and Vienna airports that killed 19 people and wounded more than 100. Three terrorists were killed at Leonardo da Vinci Airport, with one wounded and captured. Austrian police managed to ambush the terrorists in Vienna, killing one and capturing two others. A document found on the sole survivor at Rome threatened a "river of blood."

It was still not the end of Abu Nidal's efforts, for on April 2, 1986, a TWA B727 flying from the United States via Rome to Athens and Cairo suddenly experienced an explosion at 11,000 feet. It was discovered that a six-foot hole had been blown in the side of the jet from a bomb planted under Seat 10F. Four Americans, including a baby, were sucked out of the hole and died. Abu Nidal's Arab revolutionary cells claimed the credit for bombing Flight 840. Again on October 5, 1986, four Abu Nidal terrorists hijacked a Pan Am B747 at Karachi with 390 passengers and 13 crew. The pilots of Flight 073 managed to escape, thus immobilizing the plane. But when the generator ran out of fuel at night and the lights went out in the plane, the terrorists, thinking counterattack, fired on the passengers, killing 22 of them and injuring 125. There was considerable criticism of the Pakistani handling of the incident and of the poor security at Karachi airport.

Another similar secret terrorist group operated out of Baghdad and was called the "15th May Organization." Its leader, Abu Ibrahim, was a graduate of the PFLP and had extraordinary expertise as a maker of almost-undetectable suitcase bombs. Thinly rolled explosive was molded into the fabric of the suitcase and a miniature detonating device was hidden in the metal studs. After some years of experimentation, Abu Ibrahim manufactured six identical brown suitcases as deadly weapons calculated to explode in American or Israeli airliners in order to destroy them in midflight and create panic among passengers flying to Israel.

The particular evil genius of these suitcases was a refinement of the technique of linking the barometric detonator to a timing device.[76] This meant, for example, that a suitcase bomb put on a flight to Athens could arrive there safely, be transferred to another plane heading for Israel, and still not explode until the airliner flew in over Tel Aviv. The explosion low over the city would then cause a double catastrophe.

This technique almost moved from the realm of theory to actual practice on April 17, 1986, when El Al security at Heathrow Airport in London found a cleverly concealed bomb in the luggage of a pregnant Irish girl, Ann-Marie Murphy. She was being used as an innocent dupe by her Palestinian lover, Nezar Narnas Mansur Hindawi. Interestingly, it was her nervousness at flying for the first time that triggered a further security search of her belongings. The ten pounds of high explosives found in the bottom of her suitcase would have destroyed the plane, killing 400 passengers.

Nothing better illustrates the growing crescendo of activity that accompanies a surge of hijackings than the pattern in the Middle East between 1983 and 1986. In 1983 there were 5 Middle East-related hijacks. There were 11 in 1984, 12 in 1985, and 4, of a total of 13 for the year, in 1986.

The extremist Sikhs in the Punjab who are trying to create an independent Sikh state started hijacking Air India planes in 1981 and 1982. Two more hijacks occurred in 1984. The first of them on May 7 was an Indian Airlines A300 with 264 passengers and crew flying between New Delhi and Srinagar in the Punjab. They demanded $25 million for damage done to their sacred temple and the return of treasures looted by the Indian government. They were forced to surrender. Then on August 24, seven Sikh terrorists hijacked an Indian Airlines B737 on the same run, diverting it this time to Karachi and Dubai, on the Persian Gulf. Using their ceremonial daggers to hijack the aircraft, the Sikhs then demanded the release of fellow Sikhs in Indian jails as well as safe passes to the United States. They, too, were forced to surrender.

The next Sikh terrorist attack took place in North America and left an indelible mark on the minds of Canadians. On June 23, 1985, an Air India Boeing 747 flying out of Toronto and bound for London and New Delhi disintegrated in midflight over the Irish Coast with a loss of 329 lives. The evidence gathered by Canadian and Indian authorities points almost conclusively to a Sikh terrorist bomb that had actually been detected in the luggage scan in Toronto but was wrongly identified as a machine disfunction. The bomb probably exploded in the forward luggage hold, which was situated right next to the jumbo jet's nine computers, which would explain why the plane went so abruptly off the radar screen at London airport.

On the same day there was an explosion in the luggage of CP Air Flight 073 at Narita Airport, Tokyo, which killed two baggage handlers. The bomb had exploded prematurely, and it appears that it was intended to detonate after transfer to an Air India flight in Tokyo. Had the CP Air flight not arrived 15 minutes early due to favorable head winds, approximately 700 passengers would have died in one day of Sikh terrorism. The case against the Sikhs is still being actively pursued.

Once again, on May 30, 1986, an attempt was made by the Sikh terrorist organization Babbar Khalsa to blow up an Air India plane from JFK Airport in New York. In this case the two terrorists were apprehended, the bomb intercepted, and the guilty convicted on December 23, 1986, and sentenced to life imprisonment. More terrorism can be expected from the Sikhs since a virtual civil war is raging between Indians and Sikhs in India. Unfortunately, Canada and the United States are being used as safe havens for Sikh extremists to raise money, encourage Sikhs in India, and blow up Indian planes flying to India whether or not they contain North American citizens.

The first half of the decade of the 1980s also witnessed a resurgence of escapees from Eastern Europe, as in the period between 1947 and 1952. In 1981 there were seven hijacks from Poland to the West, sometimes successful and frequently landing at Templehof Airport in West Berlin. In 1982 there were four more hijacks from Poland and one each of Balkan Airlines (Bulgaria) and Aeroflot (USSR). So the Communist world is not exempt from the Western disease of hijacking.

Another striking trend in the 1980s was the resumption of hijacks to Cuba. In spite of the U.S.–Cuba hijack agreement of 1963, nearly all of them were successful. There were only three Cuban hijacks in 1984, which strongly suggests the copycat effect coming in to play.

Another trend that was becoming evident in the 1980s was the length of certain hijacks for political or propaganda purposes. On March 2, 1981, a Pakistan International Airlines plane was hijacked by followers of the former executed president, Ali Bhutto, of Pakistan. The hijack lasted for 12 days with President Zia finally capitulating and freeing 54 political prisoners. The hijacking of TWA 847 in Beirut lasted from June 14 to June 30, 1985, 16 days, the longest hijack to date. It was deliberately planned to become an international incident that would put maximum pressure on the U.S. and Israeli governments. But on April 5, 1988, the longest uninterrupted skyjacking ever took place with Kuwait Airlines Flight 422. The airliner was seized between Bangkok and Kuwait just as it neared the Strait of Hormuz. It then began a 3,200 mile journey from Mashad in Northeastern Iran to Larnaca, Cyprus, and finally to Algiers. The hijackers, Lebanese Shiites, were intent on freeing 17 terrorists jailed in Kuwait in 1983 for lethal bomb attacks on the U.S. and French embassies. Three of the 17 terrorists were under sentence of death. These same hijackers had been involved in at least two other hijack attempts for the same cause, including TWA 847 in 1985. It was believed that one of them was Imad Mughniyen, a Lebanese who was both cousin and brother-in-law to one of the 17 jailed terrorists.

At a basic level the long, agonized hijack was part of the continuing struggle with Iran and sought to destabilize Kuwait for participating in the Iran–Iraq war on the side of the latter. But the more general impact was to remind air travelers dramatically all around the world, for 15 days, that continued air travel would be a calculated risk and that an innocent traveler could all too easily become a political pawn.

Yet another theme of hijacking in the 1980s was the increasing loss of life connected to hijacking. It has already been mentioned that 60 people were killed and 35 injured in the bloody Valletta, Malta, hijacking of November 23, 1985. Earlier in the summer 329 passengers died aboard the Air India B747 over the coast of Ireland. On September 5, 1986, when the generators failed aboard Pan Am Flight 073 at Karachi, 23 people were killed and 125 wounded. Just five days later a bomb exploded in Kimpo Airport in Seoul, killing five and injuring 29 others.[77] On November 25, 1986, a shootout occurred on Iraq Air Flight 163, a B737 with 107 passengers on board between Baghdad and Amman. The shootout, which included grenades, caused the plane to make a crash landing that killed 65 and wounded 42 on board. On November 29, 1987, a Korean airliner B707 vanished near Burma with 115 people aboard. It is suspected that the North Koreans were involved. Whichever way one looks at it therefore, there is an increasing death rate of innocent passengers aboard planes because of shootouts, hostage dramas, or lethal bombs planted aboard aircraft.

CONCLUSION

After 30 years of serious hijacking since 1958, it can now be assumed that the phenomenon is here to stay. It is not suddenly going to cease or disappear. Hijackers are not going to stop commandeering planes. Therefore, the need to maintain airport security and guard against terrorist attacks is likely to remain all over the world. But at the same time hijacking is only one of the means by which international terrorism expresses itself. Kidnapping, explosive bombing, armed attacks, sabotage, and assassination are also means of terrorism, and they need not depend on the presence of a commercial airplane. The result of the perseverance of hijacking is, therefore, that it tends to develop in distinct phases. This has held true since the subject began to be studied seriously after the Second World War. It is a striking fact that hijacks seem to have progressed in five-to-seven-year periods, growing more intense toward the end of the period and then being followed by a distinct hiatus. The hiatus may be as long as the hijack period preceding it but is characterized by a severe diminution of terrorist hijacks. It seems that a hiatus is a furlough or rest period similar to the in-between period of a volcanic eruption. The hiatus phenomenon can clearly be seen from 1947 to 1987, a 40-year period worthy of assessment:

1947-1952   Eastern European hijacks

1953-1958   Hiatus: Propeller to jet age

1958-1961   Cuban hijacks by Raul Castro and Batista followers to the United States

1962-1968   Hiatus: "Reculer pour mieux sauter"[78]

1968-1974   The Arab skyjack war; PFLP

1968-1973   U.S. hijacks on the Cuba run; extortionists, criminals and the mentally unbalanced

1974-1979   Relative hiatus, certainly in the United States

1980-1986   New hijack phase in Middle East and Western Europe by fundamentalists; growing Third World hijacks

1987-1988   Hiatus in terms of number of hijacks (13 yearly)

If there are regular, predictable hiatuses between intense periods of hijacking, the forecasting of the nature and location of the next set of attacks on airports and airlines becomes feasible. Defenses can be strengthened and target-hardening can take place in anticipation of terrorist violence. Intelligence can be gathered from the right sources.

Another striking fact about hijacking has been its political nature right from the beginning. The first hijack of May 1931 was in the midst of a Peruvian domestic power struggle. The flight of Rudolph Hess to Scotland in 1941 was laden with political overtones.[79] The political escapes from both Eastern Europe and Cuba were basically part of the East–West Cold War. Because these early hijacks were part of the political struggle between the Communist world and the West, not much attention was paid to the illegal activities of the escapees. In both Eastern Europe and Cuba, pilots and flight crew were killed in the course of hijack escapes, and the criminal law of the receiving countries was not invoked against them for political reasons. The result was that the ability to invoke international law against hijackers later when hijacking escalated was severely inhibited and was often subject to political agreement. When the Western nations, who owned most of the world's airlines, came under worldwide terrorist hijack attack, it was discovered with surprise that their laws were completely inadequate.

For centuries piracy on the high seas was recognized as a heinous crime detrimental to the interests of all nations. Perpetrators of the crime found themselves subjected to the jurisdiction of any state that apprehended them. The latter could take immediate and effective action to prosecute the pirates under the customary international law principle of universal jurisdiction. When seizure of aircraft began in earnest in the 1940s, it was natural to refer to such incidents as "air piracy." It was also assumed that the pirates involved could be seized and prosecuted by the state where the aircraft landed, as with incidents on the high seas.

As the number of attempts to divert aircraft illegally increased, the use of the term *air piracy* declined and was replaced with a variety of descriptive terms, such as aerial hijacking, unlawful seizure of aircraft, or *skyjacking.*[80] Moreover, along with the decline of the concept of air piracy came the recognition of universal jurisdiction over the persons who had seized the aircraft. Thus the failure to prosecute alleged "pirates of the sky" on the part of many nations in whose territory the illegally seized aircraft landed demonstrated that no law pertaining to piracy in the "high skies" in fact, existed.

Only when the act of piracy had been committed in a place not within the territorial jurisdiction of any state did it violate customary international law, which considers the high seas to be the common heritage of all humankind. Consequently, piracy per se cannot be considered a crime against the law of nations. Rather, the crime must be defined according to the municipal law of the prosecuting state.

Evidently, common elements exist between these two concepts of piracy: They are both threats to international transportation; both possess universal jurisdiction as a sanctioning force; both use municipal legal systems to enforce prosecution of offenders; both require private vessels for the commission of the crimes; and both call for legal definitional distinctions in municipal and international law. Yet the crimes are not the same.

By definition, an act of sea piracy must be committed on the high seas, external to any state's territorial jurisdiction. Unlawful aircraft seizure, on the other hand, usually occurs entirely or partially within the territorial airspace, or territory, of some state. Even if it is committed outside national airspace, the plane must land in some nation's territory. Second, sea piracy requires one private vessel randomly plundering a flagship of any nation. Unlawful aircraft seizure occurs only aboard one aircraft and is usually committed by a passenger. Third, traditional piracy, as defined, was undertaken for "private ends." Aircraft hijacking involves other motives, often with political overtones. Thus it has taken almost 30 years to establish a legal system of rules that will apply to hijacking. Many states have not signed the Hague, Tokyo, and Montreal conventions, which deal with the legal status of hijackers and hijacked aircraft. Many states will still receive hijacked planes as an act of political sympathy with the hijackers. Therefore the system will probably never became foolproof simply because different parts of the world see the phenomenon of hijacking either as politically defensible or as a political necessity.[81]

After 1968 new actors entered the hijacking scene, mostly in the United States. These actors included the mentally unbalanced, who hijacked planes for personal and idiosyncratic reasons; the extortionists, who hijacked to obtain financial gain by holding hostage passengers who were the responsibility of the air carriers while in transit; and the criminals, who hijacked to escape to Cuba or elsewhere and sometimes practiced extortion on the side when faced with all of those wealthy passengers. In all three categories there was a marked copycat effect. One hijack would cause other hijacks to take place, because the idea was reported in the newspapers or on television. Indeed, throughout the period under study and in every category of hijacking, the copycat effect has taken place. It has always been this way in the evolution of political violence.

The most spectacular recent example was in the Islamic Jihad's hijack of TWA 847 between Algiers and Beirut in June 1985. Not only did Islamic Jihad look back to September 1970 and Dawson's Field to plan its hijack, but three other Middle Eastern groups immediately reentered the hijack field as a result of the TWA hijack. These three groups were Iraq's April 13 group, the Palestine Liberation Front (PLF), and Abu Nidal's Revolutionary Council. Without doubt, the media reports of a particularly agonizing hijack tend to precipitate other groups into similar operations, clearly hoping to capitalize on the available publicity and propaganda for their cause.

Modern terrorism has been called a "theater of fear," the "weapon of the weak," and the "propaganda of the deed." It is a phenomenon that feeds, ironically, on the best that modern civilization has to offer through mass communications and advanced technology. Were it not for the gleaming jet airplanes that became a favorite target and the television cameras that riveted world attention on such exploits, many terrorists would probably have remained at home. Many terrorist incidents that were routinely covered on the back pages of the newspapers got prominent exposure in television newscasts because of their visual drama and excitement. David G. Hubbard called such practice "social pornography," because it caters to the sick, unmet needs of the public. In his words, "its effect is sedition, whether deliberate or not."[82] Not only do skyjackers, deranged or otherwise, learn new techniques from the media, but constant attention paid to skyjacking undoubtedly has turned certain individuals' minds in the direction of hijacking. In one case, a skyjacking was built entirely around a television film. Although it was a bluff, the real-life skyjacker got away with it because he had given enough essential facts to the authorities to persuade them that a bomb actually was aboard a plane. As Christopher Dobson and Ronald Payne put it:

Of the available forms of theatre, few are as captivating as a skyjacking. The very fact that 200-300 potential hostages are packed into the metal shell of a jet airliner hundreds of times a day and sent hurtling through the skies provides terrorists not only with a target whose cosmopolitan innocence imbues it with a "there but for the grace of God" emotionalism, but one that is packaged with a supermarket flair, ideal for selling through millions of television sets.[83]

As early as 1970 an analysis of world airline traffic showed that the United States and Western Europe dominated air carrier services. In that year the United States was flying 180 million passengers annually while the rest of the world was flying only 36 million passengers, including 18 million from Western Europe. Therefore as the Western air carrier services catered more and more to business people and tourists, so the terrorists found an increasingly lucrative vein to mine in their pursuit of hostage blackmail. The realization of just how vulnerable this system was came in 1972. There were far too many successful hijacks in the United States, and the traveling public was no longer prepared to put up with the onslaught. The new system of security concentrated initially on the 531 commercial airports of the United States, thus bestowing airports with political significance for the first time. By the late 1980s there was a gradual realization of the political symbolism of airports because of the political statements being made there by terrorists. The attack on passengers near the ticket counters at Rome and Vienna in December 1987 showed that the entire airport was a community to be alerted and guarded from terrorist attack.

The guarding of airports and the upgrading of their security was followed by the use of sky marshals in the air, but it was a political agreement of the bilateral kind that did the most to stop the Cuba run.

By 1976-1977 special counterterrorist teams like the West German Grenzshutzgruppe 9 (GSG9) and the British SAS were developed for the final stages of a hijack confrontation when negotiations had failed. The increased sharing of intelligence information demonstrably curtailed the terrorist networks in Western Europe, while the Tokyo, Hague, and Montreal conventions began to put international sanctions in place against hijacking.

By 1980-1981 a new wave of assassinations of leaders of states was under way, and it seemed to security forces that hijacking would probably die down. But this turned out to be inaccurate. The new force of Shiite Islamic fundamentalism, which was born of the 1982 Israeli invasion of Lebanon and the Iranian Revolution, returned to hijacking with a violence hitherto unknown. It gathered momentum in the Middle East in the early 1980s but was unleashed on an unsuspecting Europe in June 1985. Because Islamic Jihad was ready to blow up planes and because its members were willing to die with their hostages, the Western system of airport security was suddenly outmoded. The first skin of airport security was exposed as insufficient, and a second, more costly skin of security was called for. The real lesson being learned was that there is no clear-cut, decisive way of preventing the determined hijacker from striking at airports and airplanes. This is the real vulnerability of the West, that it can only react to the maliciously inspired, hostile initiatives of others.

By the mid-1980s the hijackers were not hijacking as many planes, but they were making much better use of the ones they did commandeer. The media became deeply involved in a process that created heavy propaganda for the terrorist cause. When bombs were planted on planes, they exploded with a lethal violence that caused many deaths. By the late 1980s hijacking was spreading steadily to the growing Third World air carrier systems. There was a conspicuous growth in the number of Asian airlines affected by hijackings. It was also significant that by the end of the 1980s Western tourists were flying in greater numbers than ever before to the warmer, southern Third World countries where political violence was most frequently manifest. Many experts believe that political terrorism, including hijacking, is seen as a logical Third World response to the opulence and economic exploitation exercised by the Western countries. If this theory is true, increasing numbers of Western planes will be taken hostage as they fly tourists into the Southern Hemisphere. At this point not security but political negotiations will be necessary, and the true political dimension of terrorism will come into its own.

It is significant that between 1968 and 1988 it was one unresolved political issue in the Middle East that dominated the field of hijacking. That issue is the question of Palestine. The most fearsome innovators in air hijacking have all come from the ranks of the Palestinian National movement. Between 1968 and 1974 it was George Habash and Wadi Haddad. Between 1974 and 1983 it was Carlos and the PFLP and its allies in the Japanese Red Army and the

Baader–Meinhof. After 1983 Abu Nidal and the Islamic fundamentalists domi-nated. It is tempting to suggest that if a negotiated settlement of the Palestinian problem were to come about that the cause of much international hijacking might be removed.

But the final issue concerning hijacking may be that of sustained terrorist hijack attacks on the airports of North America in the 1990s. The U.S. airports are by far the most vulnerable in the world because of the heavy traffic that pours through them daily. It could be argued that attacks on North American airports are just a question of time. Middle Eastern and Islamic fundamentalists have moved westward into Europe in their attacks on Western and American airlines. The growth of political terrorism in Central America is already spilling north-ward as the Cuban problem did in the 1960s. North America has not yet experienced the airport and airplane problems faced by Western Europe, but if it does, the system will be incredibly difficult to defend.

Chapter 3

A Practical Profile of the Hijacker

After 20 years of continuous air piracy, a certain amount of information exists about the hijacker, his outlook, and his habits. Psychiatrists David Hubbard and Frederick J. Hacker not only have interviewed a number of hijackers but also have written books about them. In *Crusaders, Criminals, and Crazies,* written in 1976, Hacker outlined three basic types of terrorist, though he was clearly more interested in the psychotic than the political terrorist. Hubbard was also primarily interested in skyjackers of the psychotic variety. In his first book, *The Skyjacker and His Flights of Fantasy,* he explored the role that gravity, sex, and the American moonshots of the 1960s played in the creation of the psychotic hijacker. This is anything but a mainstream book on hijacking, but during the next 17 years, he and the staff of his Aberrant Behaviour Centre and its successor, the Behavioral Research Centre in Dallas, traveled nearly 2 million miles, further researching the subject. The results led Hubbard to write his second book, *Winning Back the Sky: A Tactical Analysis of Terrorism* (1986). This book is extremely valuable because it adds analysis on the behavior of the political hijacker, and has a section on the human dynamics in an airplane hijacked in flight.

Only one terrorist has actually written about the experience of hijacking a plane. In her autobiography, *My People Shall Live: Autobiography of a Revolutionary* (1973), Leila Khaled of the PFLP has written gripping accounts of what went on in her mind during two hijacks in 1969 and 1970. The accounts are sensitively written and tell a good deal about the terrorist's perspective during a hijack.

The other two sources that deal in part with the hijacker are the two main accounts of the historical evolution of hijacking, David Phillips's *Skyjack: The Story of Air Piracy* (1973) and James A. Arey's *The Sky Pirates* (1972). It is interesting that no major work on hijacking and air piracy has been written since 1973.

By extension, therefore, very little has been written in the past 15 years about the mind-set and predisposition of terrorists who hijack planes. In fact, very little is known about terrorists and particularly about those of the political variety. Since terrorism virtually amounts to a new form of international warfare, it is surprising that so little is known about its main characters.

Professor Jerrold Post has written that most comparative studies find there is no uniquely terrorist "mind" or "personality." Most terrorists, he contends, are psychologically normal; they arise from all strata of society and derive from a wide range of cultures, nationalities, and ideological causes.[1] Researchers have begun to understand, however, that certain kinds of personalities are drawn disproportionately to terrorism. There are, for example, a high percentage of angry paranoids, many of whom share the tendency to externalize, to seek outside sources to blame for what has gone wrong with their lives. Post referred to studies done in Germany that found that many of those who enter terrorist groups have experienced failure at school or at work. They tend to come from broken or troubled families and to have been socially isolated. Developing as isolated loners, these young people come to adulthood with a deficient sense of self-esteem.

As a result, joining a terrorist cell may represent the first real sense of belonging, after a lifetime of rejection. The cell gradually becomes the family the youth never had. "Underlying this strong need to belong—generally shared by terrorists around the world—is a fragmented identity: often the only way a member feels reasonably complete is in relationship to the group."[2]

Furthermore, membership in a terrorist group seems to result in a common rhetoric that is strongly believed. The language is absolutist, black and white, with no shades of grey. "The world is polarized into an idealization of 'us' (the group) and a projection onto an undifferentiated 'them' (the establishment) of all that is wrong."[3] Such psychological schema permit terrorists to rationalize and carry out the most violent of actions.

Finally, no one becomes a terrorist overnight. The road to terrorism is gradual, step by step, but occasionally a critical event may occur that will precipitate the leap into terrorism. The Germans call this "der Sprung," or the leap. Ex-Red Army Faction member Michael Baumann wrote in his auto-biography that when West Berlin police shot and killed a friend of his during a 1967 demonstration, he had a tremendous "flash" that eventually convinced him to fight without mercy. In a similar fashion, Leila Khaled was obviously traumitized as a little girl when she and a friend crouched under the stairs of her home in Palestine as the Israelis invaded her town. The friend ran out to retrieve her doll, and her body was riddled with bullets right in front of Khaled. From reading Khaled's autobiography it is clear that the delayed impact of the shock of this childhood event led directly to her finding release in joining the PFLP, hijacking airplanes, and even undergoing painful facial plastic surgery.

Identifying commonalities is further complicated by the fact that the terrorist group itself is not uniform in its behavior patterns. At least three basic types can be found worldwide among terrorist groups: the anarchic ideologues, the nationalist–separatists, and the religious fundamentalists. Anarchic ideologues such as West Germany's Red Army Faction and Italy's Red Brigades are disloyal to parents and families who are loyal to the existing system. They tend to live in a charged atmosphere since they are antiauthoritarian; yet they themselves allow no dissent and call for unquestioning compliance. They usually embrace Marxist or anarchist philosophies wholesale. Nationalist–separatists, such as the PLO and the Irish Republican Army (IRA), are loyal to families but disloyal to their regime. With the support of family and the ethnic community, the members of this group are usually better adjusted and may operate relatively openly. As psychiatrist and educator Franco Ferracuti pointed out, "the Palestinians, for example, have achievable, non-utopian goals, and that makes it easy to recruit members."[4] But if the nationalist–separatists tend to be lionized as heroes in their villages, the anarchic ideologues, by contrast, make a total break from society and lead a hermitic, underground existence. The third group, the religious fundamentalists, are a recent and growing threat to the West. They never question the moral authority of their group since the intended audience of their terrorism is the deity. Again, in the words of Jerrold Post, "These messianic true believers think they must participate in a struggle to 'force the end.' One way of doing this is by expelling or eliminating those who interfere with propagation of the truth."[5] In the case of hijacking, one thinks immediately of Shiite terrorism, encouraged and sanctified by the theocracy in Iran and by Hizbollah and Amal in Lebanon. All three groups have hijacked planes. All three groups are considered deranged or fanatical. But Raymond Kendall, chief of the Interpol police network, has stated: "They prepare their operations very carefully. If I were a professional criminal going to rob a bank, I would behave in the same way. It is a criminal approach."[6]

This raises an important issue about the terrorist: Can he be both deranged and fanatical on the one hand and yet professional and well trained on the other hand? In other words, are terrorists psychotic or psychopathic, unable to control their behavior and needing psychiatric care, or are they sane, deliberate, and highly politically motivated? The experts seem to disagree on this matter, and it is therefore extremely difficult to develop a psychological profile that would be a reliable guide for flight and cabin crew aboard aircraft.

The late Larry Breen was a forensic psychologist at the University of Manitoba in Canada who has specialized in hostage situations. He pointed out that the psychopath has no conscience or sense of guilt, a sign of a completely under-aroused autonomic nervous system. He could "quite easily cut someone's throat and then go and eat a Big Mac immediately afterwards."[7] He knows precisely what he is up to but has no sense whatsoever that it is wrong or socially unacceptable. He has no affective feeling of right or wrong. The psychopath does have a keen sense of self-preservation, however, and does not wish to get hurt. He is therefore a classic manipulator of others. The psychotic, on the other hand, is completely out of touch with reality. If God or the Devil told him to do something, he would go off and do it, even if it was a suicide run. "Most hijackers are psychopaths," said Breen, and he included in that group religious fundamentalists, criminals, and political terrorists.[8] The combination of a political motive and psychopathic behavior, however, is extremely dangerous and even deadly. As Breen pointed out, both types were evident in the TWA 847 hijack. The leader, "Saïd," was psychopathic—calm, in control, deadly. But his partner, "Castro," was psychotic, ranting and raving, taking karate kicks at passengers, and ready to crash the plane on Tel Aviv.

It seems clear, therefore, that at this point it is not possible to develop a clear and helpful psychological profile of hijackers that would be of use in a hijack situation. Even if flight crew were to learn all about psychosis and the behavior of psychopaths, there would still be the question of how to cope with a harrowing and frightening situation that was complicated by political or religious fanaticism. Perhaps the best way to develop a clear image of the hijacker is to examine closely the events of the past 30 years. During the period under study, at least eight kinds of hijackers can be distinguished. Once these categories have been established, it becomes possible to instruct pilots and flight crew in how to approach differently motivated hijackers and simultaneously provide protection for the passengers and a happy issue from the hijacked flight.

"The anatomy of skyjacking," as Peter Clyne called it, has evolved as follows during the last 30 years:

1. Escaping refugees, 1947-1952, 1958-1972, 1980s
2. For purposes of transportation, 1961-1988
3. The mentally unbalanced, 1961-1988
4. Political terrorists, 1968-1988
5. Escaping criminals, 1971-1973
6. Extortionists, 1971-1973, 1975-1977
7. Religious fundamentalists, 1983-1988
8. Bomb saboteurs, 1984-1988

ESCAPING REFUGEES

The category of escaping refugees includes those persons who illegally seize aircraft to flee from an oppressive political regime. In international law certain immunities or exemptions for foreign aircraft and their occupants entering in distress were recognized, by analogy with the immunity of foreign ships in distress. In a large majority of cases, a degree of immunity has been granted to aircraft in distress, including those arriving under control of hijackers, and political asylum has been given to those hijackers trying to escape from countries whose governments deny or disregard human rights and do not usually permit their citizens to leave the country lawfully. Countries most frequently relevant to this category are the Soviet Union, Poland, East Germany, Czechoslovakia, Yugoslavia, Romania, and Cuba. The first wave of escaping political refugees occurred from Eastern Europe or the Soviet Union to Western Europe. In all of these cases, restrictive exit regulations prevented people from freely leaving the Soviet sphere and so bred a desperate and ruthless type of hijacker.

PURPOSES OF TRANSPORTATION

Unlike political refugees, some persons use hijacking simply as a convenient means of traveling, without the costs and legal formalities of departure and entry between countries. The majority of cases involved Castro supporters in Colombia, Venezuela, and the United States. Since no regularly scheduled commercial air service operated between these countries and Cuba, one of the easiest means of transportation was to divert an aircraft unlawfully. Cuba's scheduled air services were limited to Mexico, Spain, and various Soviet Bloc nations during most of the 1960s and 1970s. In other cases, the hijackers had been refused permission for a visa to Cuba. This category also included people on both domestic and international runs who simply could not afford the airfare and so hijacked the plane. This type of hijacker flew mostly between 1961 and 1972 but is still a possibility on domestic runs, even in the age of lower cost fares and airline deregulation.

THE MENTALLY UNBALANCED PERSON

The mentally unbalanced category includes mentally disturbed individuals and "attention seekers," a product of what the chief surgeon of the FAA, has hypothesized as the "hijacker syndrome." This offender believes he can prove himself an effective human being by commandeering an airplane. Hubbard's comprehensive studies of this "hijacker mentality" outline "individuals who are seriously sick in a psychiatric sense and are using this action either as a direct expression of their illness or as acted-out behavior to escape some less personally acceptable intent."[9] There is also the idea in the hijacker's mind that he can start life anew elsewhere, gaining fame and glory and recognition in the process. Another variant of this category is that some offenders use the hijacking experience as a rationalization for suicide. In short, this category describes the person who is plagued by mental, emotional, and social problems and seeks wide publicity to compensate for personal failures in life.

POLITICAL TERRORISTS

Radical political groups use aerial piracy for protest and propaganda purposes as well as for political blackmail. Perhaps the best known of them is the Palestianian Front for the Liberation of Palestine, but others have grown to emulate them, including the Black Panthers, the Japanese Red Army, the Baader–Meinhof Gang, the Eritrean Liberation Front, the Croatians, the Armenians, and the Sikhs. Not only have these groups hijacked planes or sabotaged them in the air, but they also have attacked airports and used any form of disruption or hostage taking that would enable them to put pressure on governments. This form of political blackmail is aimed at achieving their own political ends, whether those ends be the destruction of a hostile regime or the establishment of their own regime. Hijacks for protest, propaganda, blackmail, and the release of jailed terrorists began in the Middle East in 1968 and have been a continuing threat and challenge to Western civil aviation in the intervening two decades.

ESCAPING CRIMINALS

Unlike the fleeing political refugee, escaping criminals include those persons with criminal backgrounds who have used illegal aircraft diversion to escape trial or prosecution. Most hijacks of this type took place from the United States to Cuba, the inference being that such fugitives thought that they would be safe from prosecution if they reached Cuba.[10] Also counted in this category are criminals who, in the process of being transported from one confinement location to another, manage to escape current sentences by diverting the aircraft to another nation. With at least two-thirds of world air traffic in the 1970s, the United States has inevitably had the largest share of this type of hijacking.

EXTORTIONISTS

In recent years hijacking attempts for profit have become a common occurrence. On numerous occasions they have included the robbery of individual passengers, as well as ransom demands of large sums of money to ensure the safety of the airplane, the passengers, and the crew. It was primarily the lack of punitive action that set the stage for a whole spate of hijacks in this category. Peter Clyne called this type of hijacking "old-fashioned larceny committed in a jet setting, or Jesse James skyjacks."[11] In this category the initiating criminal was D. B. Cooper, and his exploit was widely lionized and emulated. His new twist on an old cops-and-robbers game so appealed to Americans that in one 17-week period in 1972 there was a hijacking every single Friday, and the last day of the work week became known as "Skyjack Friday." It took a great deal of effort and very severe prison sentences to bring this category of hijack under control. While airplanes continue to fly, extortion will continue to be a problem.

ISLAMIC FUNDAMENTALISTS

Hijacking by Islamic fundamentalists began, tentatively, in 1980. During the next two years, seven hijacks were engineered by Shiite Moslems in Lebanon who were trying to obtain the restoration of their spiritual leader who had disappeared in Libya. There were also numerous hijacks to and from Iran as the civil war between the religious and secular forces worked itself out in that country. The Israeli invasion of Lebanon in the spring of 1982 displaced more than 400,000 Lebanese Shiites, who then began to strike back at their oppressors. First the Israelis, and later the American peacekeeping forces in Beirut, were hit with suicide bomb attacks. Then, in 1984, Islamic Jihad began to hijack regularly scheduled Western airliners. The culminating act was against TWA 847 in 1985; it proclaimed to the world that Islamic fundamentalists were ready to die for their cause and that the death of innocent Western passengers was of no particular concern to them. Certainly, the fundamentalists had political aims as had the PFLP earlier, but their fanatical religious behavior and apparent willingness to die in a suicidal manner made Western air carriers realize they were in the presence of a new type of airplane hijacker.

BOMB SABOTEURS

Bomb saboteurs are a new and deadly addition to the realm of air piracy. The saboteur is a clever and ingenious technologist, who plays the role of the hidden brain behind some of the most devastating hijacking schemes and is never found at the scene of the crime. From his concealed headquarters, the saboteur sends lethal weapons of destruction on to doomed planes full of passengers. Sometimes these deadly instruments are carried by his own people, but more often, they are placed in the luggage of an unwitting passenger, who boards the plane unaware that his computer modem or radio tuner has been doctored. The advent of plastic explosive and its use against airplanes has caught airport security by surprise, giving the bomb saboteur an enormous advantage. He is an evil genius who is fundamentally challenging air security as never before.

It remains to be seen whether these eight categories will stand the test of time, but an examination of the almost 900 hijack incidents that have occurred since 1931 validates the continuing nature of each category. At present, the only complete assessment of all hijacks in the world to date comes from a massive FAA study.[12] As can be seen from figure 1, the category of escaping political refugees is still by far the largest, and it is striking that there have been 78 hijacks of this type between 1981 and 1986. The great majority of these escapes have been by disturbed Cubans, unable to speak English and threatening to

Figure 1
Categories of Hijacker

	1947-67	1968-72	1973-80	1981-86	Total
Escaping pol. refugees	59	53	60	78	250
Psychotics	3	29	27	19	78
Political terrorists	4	28	30	40	102
Escaping criminals	4	8	11	12	35
Extortion attempts	1	30	30	1	62
Fundamentalists			7	14	21
Bomber-Saboteurs				12	12
Palestinian attacks			44		44
					560

wreck the plane unless it was immediately headed for Cuba. The continuing number of these hijacks has been hidden from public view because of a lack of media coverage and because of the effectiveness of the U.S.–Cuba hijack agreement of February 1973. But pilots, flight attendants, and passengers still have to deal with the sometimes traumatic rerouting of what was expected to be a routine flight.

It is difficult to distinguish between escaping refugees and hijacks for the purpose of transportation. The two categories tend to merge, and the FAA study does not make such a subtle motivational distinction, but the eight categories of hijacker account for only 560 of a total 830 hijacks detailed (until 1987) by the FAA; therefore it must be assumed that many foiled hijacks, in which the hijacker was frequently killed, were in these two categories.

The second largest category of hijacker consists of political terrorists, whose objectives are complex and multifaceted. It is clear from figure 1 that their numbers have remained both high and consistent since 1968, and their continuance is a basic statement about the condition of international politics. Psychotic, or mentally unbalanced, hijackers constitute the third largest category, and it is interesting to note their continuing attraction to airplanes. It was thought that the psychotics would be weeded out after 1972 with the first skin of airport security, but this clearly has not been the case. Extortionists make up the fourth largest category. They flourished between 1971 and 1973 and between 1976 and 1977 mainly in the United States and Latin America, clear evidence of the impact of the copycat effect. The fifth largest category has been that of escaping criminals. Because prison inmates are moved around by plane it is almost inevitable that they should attempt escape through a hijack. This becomes easier when an airline pilot, who is, after all, responsible for the lives of his passengers, refuses to allow anyone to carry a gun on his aircraft. If anything, the number of escaping criminals has increased over time. The final two categories—Islamic fundamentalists and bomb saboteurs—are growing quickly, markedly increasing the threat to airlines and their passengers. So the depressing news from the statistical study is that all eight types of hijacker are still very much present in the skies and that it will be necessary for pilots, flight attendants, and the authorities on the ground to continue to deal with hijackers and to learn to distinguish among them. In the section that follows, therefore, an attempt is made to describe the behavior patterns of the eight types of hijackers and to present suggestions on how an air crew might practically deal with them.

ESCAPING REFUGEES AND HIJACKING FOR PURPOSES OF TRANSPORTATION

It is difficult to distinguish between escaping refugees and those who are seeking transportation because these two categories account for such a consistently high percentage of all hijacks. The hijackers are nearly always desperate, and conventional deterrents are of little use. When an individual, or even a group of people, decides to forsake home and job and nationality and take the desperate risk of hijacking an airplane, violent behavior can be expected. In the period between 1947 and 1952, 50,000 people per month were escaping the Communist tyranny in Eastern Europe. These were people with a tradition of democracy who were suddenly submitted to the Leninist–Stalinist tyranny. They knew that hijacking a plane was illegal, but the cost of remaining in place was a slow, progressive spiritual and emotional death. The first hijack, in July 1947, involved three Romanian army officers who were so intent on escaping to Turkey that they killed the copilot to force the crew to divert the plane.

The atmosphere surrounding the lowering of the Iron Curtain across Europe was extremely tense, and the Berlin airlift of 1948-1949 played an important role in raising that tension to a fever pitch. For 11 months allied airplanes took off and landed every few minutes with supplies for the beleaguered garrison of West Berlin. As a result, airplanes became a powerful symbol of freedom for subjugated peoples. If it was necessary for escaping refugees to wound or kill pilots and air crew, it was felt that this was the cost of freedom. Western courts seem to confirm this impression with fairly lenient jail sentences, allowing the refugees quickly to get on with a new life. Unfortunately, Communist pilots and air personnel did not always realize that the line of least resistance was the most sensible approach to take.

In the case of Cuba in 1958, the situation was handled differently. Between 1958 and 1967 a total of 17 planes were hijacked from Cuba to the United States. On some occasions there were shootouts, and a few of the hijacks failed in a blaze of gunfire. But beginning in May 1961, the hijacks were all in the other direction, engineered by people wishing to reach Cuba for a multiplicity of reasons. The hijackers were nearly all disillusioned Cubans who wished to return to their homeland and for whom there was no means of legal transportation. Half a million Cubans were in the United States, many of them living in the Florida Peninsula. Clearly, many, if not most, expected to return to Cuba with a victorious military force at the time of the Bay of Pigs in 1961. When that failed, the doors to Cuba closed to them. Visa problems and a lack of air and sea transport stymied their return. The only way to go home was to hijack a plane, and that is still the case. The passage of the U.S.–Canada–Cuba hijack agreement has made absolutely no difference in the number of hijacks, but it has regularized and routinized the process of transportation from the United States to Cuba. It was often lamented that the 1965 Freedom Flights from Cuba to the United States had no return capacity. But even in 1988 Castro was simply not interested in receiving Cubans back from the United States. Between 1968 and 1972 there were 21 hijacks to Cuba; between 1972 and 1980 there were 23; but between 1981 and 1986 there were 30 planes diverted there, and a dangerous new tendency emerged. Frequently, the hijackers stood up and shouted instructions in Cuban, necessitating translation by Spanish-speaking people on the flight. Worse, they produced not only knives but containers of gasoline, which they poured over the seats of the aircraft, down the aisles, and sometimes over themselves and even flight attendants, threatening to light the gasoline if the plane was not flown immediately to Cuba. In some cases the hijackers were so emotionally overwrought that they actually tried to light cigarettes after spilling the gasoline. Not much has been said publicly about these episodes, but they are a growing danger to aircraft, and if the United States is unable to negotiate a better political arrangement with Cuba, perhaps Spanish-speaking flight crew and formalized procedures should be implemented to ensure passenger safety in all flights to or from the Florida Peninsula.

Escaping refugees are not confined to the United States. Between 1947 and 1986 refugees hijacked planes from 60 countries. Throughout the period there have been numerous hijacks between Latin American countries, and it is not always clear whether they are freedom oriented or politically motivated. In the Middle East, 16 countries have been involved in hijacks by escaping refugees, and again, there was confusion as to whether a political or religious message was being sent or whether the hijackers were simply seeking asylum. They frequently claimed asylum after a long and harrowing hijack episode. Another facet of these Middle Eastern hijacks was the use of violence, which led, on a number of occasions, to the midair destruction of entire aircraft. The onset of Islamic fundamentalism in the area has resulted in a number of desperate escapes between Iran and Iraq and between these and other neighboring Persian Gulf states.

In the 1980s it was not simply a question of stealing a plane to transport oneself from point A to point B. Refugees from civil war and persecution, real or imagined, were beating a path to the wealthy, prosperous states of the Western world. They did so on Western airliners, and they remain desperate and often dangerous people. It is much better to deal with them on the ground than in the air. Therefore, the role of the flight crew is straightforward in the case of escaping refugees: facilitate and ameliorate their passage to the desired country and let the people on the ground deal with the result of the hijack.

ESCAPING CRIMINALS

"Criminal terrorists," stated F. J. Hacker, "want nothing different from what most other people want, but they are willing to resort to socially disapproved methods in order to achieve their goals."[13] Many criminals are severely disturbed people to begin with, and once they decide to exploit an aircraft for personal gain, they can be very dangerous indeed. Convicts often feel themselves to be victims of racial persecution and sometimes believe the evil forces in society are responsible for their plight.

There is a predictable side to the criminal hijacker, however. He is perfectly rational in his commission of a crime for financial purposes. For one thing, the criminal is not going to take unnecessary risks. Also, conventional deterrents are often effective against him, since he knows there is a high risk of being caught and punished.[14] The rational hijacker is one of the most likely to negotiate and compromise; after all, what could be more rational than instant financial gain.

There was little rational about the criminally inspired November 10, 1972, hijack of Southern Airways Flight 49 out of Birmingham, Alabama, however. The $2 million ransom money demanded during a 29-hour hijack with nine forced stops in the United States and two other countries has already been described. This was a case in which the three hijackers were undoubtedly mentally disturbed and therefore doubly dangerous. Their anger at not being given the full $2 million increased when the aircraft's tires were shot out on the runway and illustrates the extreme care that needs to be taken when criminals are thwarted during a hijack. From "docile maniacs" they turned into "raving maniacs," one passenger observed, and it is worth observing that escaped convicts who have already killed or raped are likely to have no compunction about doing it again.

Not only did this hijacking provoke the familiar first skin of airport security, but it was an object lesson in how not to handle a criminal hijack. Untested responses by law enforcement officials exacerbated a dangerous encounter and could very easily have resulted in a widespread loss of life. This hijack was particularly interesting because one of the hijackers, Henry Jackson, carried on a revealing dialogue with an older female passenger.[15] Through this dialogue many of the vulnerabilities and doubts of the hijackers were revealed but too late to be of any use during the hijack. In retrospect, however, there is another lesson here for the flight crew: If some form of emotional bond is created between a passenger and a hijacker, it might be used to defuse the hijack.

EXTORTIONISTS

On November 24, 1971, D. B. Cooper bailed out of a B727 over Washington State with parachutes and $200,000 ransom. He was never seen again, but the really surprising result of the publicity that followed this extortion was the number of people who admired his exploit. Suddenly, a D. B. Cooper cult began to grow, and extortion became the new twist to hijacking. Extortion was popular at the time anyway. A close scrutiny of the FAA statistics shows that between May 18, 1971, and January 4, 1973, there were 29 extortion attempts. There were 18 more hijacks by extortionists between 1973 and 1980, before they suddenly seem to have disappeared. Some of the above earlier incidents had violent endings, confirming earlier evidence with escaping criminals that it is probably wisest to follow the hijacker's directions closely and ensure the safety of the passengers.

Not all extortionists were violent. Richard Floyd McCoy, Jr., was a 29-year-old student majoring in law enforcement at Brigham Young University in Utah when he hijacked a plane and successfully parachuted out of it with $500,000. He was arrested two days later through carelessness, circumstantial evidence, and his own vanity.

But Frederick William Hahnemann, who jumped over Honduras with $303,000 ransom, was not pleasant at all. The pilot, Captain W. I. Hendershot, said of him later, "that hijacker is the most ruthless individual I've ever come across. He had a gun on one of the two stewardesses throughout. I believe we're all lucky he didn't blow one of our heads off."[16]

Extortion could easily be revived in Third World countries, and the Western tourist trade would be an obvious target. Even a planeload of wealthy holiday travelers might do.

There is one final and irritating variant on the extortionist–criminal type of hijacker—the bluff artist. According to Peter Clyne, "He is simply after money—or escape. What distinguishes him from others is that he really has no weapon at all, but relies on the airline's unwillingness to take chances."[17] The primitive bluff simply takes the form of threatening the pilot or crew with a toy gun, a harmless package, or a liquid claimed to be high explosive. A much more deadly form of this game was staged in Sydney, Australia, where a "Mr. Brown" rang Quantas airways and told them to look in a particular airport locker. There they found a letter that had enough scientific detail to convince the airline that a bomb placed on the 8 A.M. service to Hong Kong might indeed explode as it came down from cruising level to 10,000 feet. While there was even the smallest chance the threat might be real, it was decided to hand over the $25,000 that the extortionist had phoned and asked for and then had come and picked up in person.

He might have gotten away with the game had he not begun to spend his money too quickly. He was arrested and the money recovered. As Clyne pointed out, one of the interesting aspects of this affair was that a TV film shown in Sydney exactly four weeks before the crime obviously provided the blueprint: A bomb was set to go off as the plane descended to an altitude of 5,000 feet; the skyjacker, who (in the film) had set a real bomb, phoned in for the money but unfortunately suffered a heart attack before he could be paid—and the plane was saved only because it landed at Denver airport, altitude 5,200.[18]

THE MENTALLY UNBALANCED HIJACKER

As can be seen in figure 1, the mentally unbalanced hijacker is a category of hijacking that refuses to disappear. After 30 years, it is still the third largest category. Also, as mentioned earlier, many of the escaping political refugees to Cuba display genuine signs of mental disturbance, and therefore the actual numbers may in fact be much larger than are indicated here.

Whatever their numbers, dealing with a mentally unbalanced hijacker is fraught with particular difficulties. As Hacker pointed out, "the emotionally disturbed are driven by reasons of their own that often do not make sense to anybody else."[19] Dealing with them is simplified somewhat by the fact that they usually work alone and do not have accomplices, as political terrorists do, but this is small consolation when one considers the problems even one unbalanced sky pirate can cause. The problems caused by hijackers who are mentally unbalanced touch on both unpredictability and illogicality. The mentally ill wish to attract public attention and generally tend not to count the cost, leading them to take unnecessary and often dangerous risks. As a result, conventional deterrents frequently will not work against them. The unbalanced hijacker often reacts violently to what he reads in books or newspapers, and the media have paid a lot of attention to hijacking. Furthermore, it is very difficult to judge, from outward appearances, whether or not a passenger is mentally ill. There is no guarantee that an unbalanced hijacker will give himself away by foaming at the mouth, and frequently his demands are the same as those of a rational hijacker.[20]

There is nothing rational about his motivation, however. In his research with Hubbard in Texas, Hacker found that

fantasies about finding ultimate asylum, rest and possibly death in the airplane were curiously mixed with expectations of achieving omnipotence by replacing the pilot and with notions of unrestricted release of aggression. Exhibitionistic publicity expectations regularly provided crucial motivations, and the satisfaction of having brought about an exciting, possibly even a world-shaking event pervaded the thought processes of the sky-jackers, attracted by the mystique of sovereignty, in which the airplane represented the home or territory of an independent, tightly knit community under the command of an all-powerful leader.[21]

Negotiating with a person who is mentally ill is a psychiatric problem that may depend on several factors. According to Clyne,

An approach which might be quite suitable for use on a manic-depressive, bent simply on suicide, would be eminently unsuitable if used on a man who suffers from the paranoid delusion that there is some vast conspiracy to imprison and study him for life because he holds the secret of eternal youth; and even an approach suitable for that paranoid would be quite unsuitable if used on a paranoid who is obsessed by some totally different kind of delusion, and would be still less suitable for a schizophrenic in whose crazy universe red ties mean imminent and deadly danger.[22]

This makes successful intervention on the part of flight crew much more difficult. Yet there are situations in which an observant and well-prepared cabin crew may be able to take the upper hand and bring an end to a hijacking of this type. Flight attendant Elizabeth Rich told the story of a hijacker called "Sam" who "requested a drink, asked the flight engineer to hold his gun for him and relaxed. When he finished his whisky, the flight engineer politely handed his gun back to him."[23] Unbalanced hijackers have frequently been known to disarm themselves in the course of a hijacking, and crew management of such incidents would involve anticipating and reacting to such self-defeating behavior.

The Cuba run has been a particularly popular one for mentally ill hijackers. As early as 1973, Rich pointed out, "The U.S. began to suspect something the Cubans must have known for 10 years—that severely-disturbed United States citizens were travelling to Cuba in stolen airplanes at great risk to many lives to seek mental rather than political asylum.''[24] Since it is clear there is no simple solution to the political problem of Cuba, and since it is equally evident that the psychological profiles developed by the FAA have not made it any easier to spot would-be hijackers of the unbalanced variety before boarding, it is not surprising this problem refuses to go away. It might be argued that severe legal deterrents with the threat of long imprisonment or death would effectively halt the psychotic hijacker, but as Hacker wrote, "Expectations of punishment, particularly the death penalty, serve as attractions rather than deterrents because of extremely strong aggressive tendencies that are directed against the self, culminating in suicide fantasies.''[25] (See Appendix 2)

So it remains with the flight personnel in the hijacked plane to deal, without much assistance, with an unbalanced hijacker. The important thing is to see him as a sad spectacle who is really crying out for help. Wrote Elizabeth Rich, ''From my first days of interest in skyjackers it occurred to me that they might be frustrated, desperate people who saw airplanes as glamorous yet vulnerable symbols of power—also symbolizing a spectacular means of escape from their problems and a public forum for saying to society 'look what you have driven me to do.' ''[26]

Nevertheless, the subject is remarkably complex, as Hacker's psychological profile of the unbalanced hijacker shows. Citing Hubbard's work, he wrote,

Most of the 52 skyjackers he examined were disturbed, inadequate, often physically weak, frustrated, egotistical daydreamers, frequently with deep-seated, overly manifested sexual problems. They were depressed, with suicidal fantasies and strong tendencies toward dissociation. Practically all were paranoid to a degree, and many of them suffered from paranoid schizophrenia.[27]

In a second paragraph Hacker outlined the parameters of the psychotic hijacker's behavior:

Almost without exception, the men were self-punishing, passively oriented and ineptly striving to placate their wives, who reviled and cuckolded them. In their youth, the skyjackers typically had many flight and fall dreams; and throughout their development, most of them displayed infantile fantasies of omnipotence and meglomanic ideas that often reached the intensity of delusions. The skyjacking usually followed a frustrating professional or personal experience and was motivated by revenge for injustice or by rage over failure. Hubbard also suggests that a subtle disturbance of the inner ear, affecting the skyjacker's body image and sense of gravity, is a distinguishing factor. My own experiences and investigations, some of them made in collaboration with the Abberrant Behavior Centre in Dallas, confirmed many of Hubbard's findings.[28]

The FAA and the psychiatrists differed over this analysis of hijackers, and the gap grew wider over a court case concerning Mexican immigrant Ricardo Chavez-Ortiz, who hijacked a plane in 1972. The penalty was a 30-year prison sentence, and the issues were clear-cut. ''The prosecution wanted Chavez-Ortiz to be classified as a criminal terrorist so that he could be punished and serve as a deterring example. The defense seemed to place the interests of the cause over those of an anonymous, confused, and resourceless defendant.''[29] In short, the prosecution wanted a long prison sentence due Chavez-Ortiz as a criminal, whereas the defense wanted a sentence that would make him a martyr, a symbol of injustice and persecution perpetrated on all Mexicans. Hacker, taking a third perspective, believed Chavez-Ortiz to be mentally ill, a crazy terrorist with crusading overtones. But, as he concluded sorrowfully, ''The medical experts only explain, advise, and suggest; they do not decide.''[30]

It would be a great mistake for the FAA to continue to ignore Hubbard's work, for not only has he interviewed more than 250 imprisoned terrorists, but in his book *Winning Back the Skies* (1986), he displayed a crucial evolution in his thinking. His encounters with Islamic fundamentalists in the Middle East have given him an important insight into both political hijacking and the Islamic mind.

POLITICALLY MOTIVATED TERRORISTS

According to Hacker, ''Crusading terrorists are idealistically inspired. They seek, not personal gain, but prestige and power for a collective goal: they believe that they act in the service of a higher cause.''[31] Furthermore, the typical political or crusading terrorist, whether he is a volunteer or carefully selected, appears to be psychiatrically normal no matter how crazy his cause or how criminal his behavior. Hacker has found that the political terrorist

gains his strength not only from his comparatively intact ego but from his enthusiastic membership in a group onto which he has projected and externalized his conscience. He is neither a dummy nor a fool, neither a coward nor a weakling, but a professional, well-trained, well-prepared and well-disciplined in the habit of blind obedience.[32]

In their study *Terrorism: Threat and Response,* Eric Morris and Alan Hoe wrote that ''the terrorist mind operates within the bounds of moral psychology rather than displaying signs of mental illness which can be diagnosed by orthodox psychiatric methods. Terrorists are intelligent, fit, usually well-trained and highly motivated individuals when it comes to working for the cause.''[33] Although some unbalanced people are attracted to political causes, as Hacker pointed out, ''Within limits, the differentiation between crazy, criminal and crusading terrorists remains useful and valid, sometimes even vital, because the distinction determines the widely ranging courses of action for meeting or treating the terrorist challenge.''[34]

The political terrorist knows exactly what he wants or what his instructions require him to do, and as Peter Clyne pointed out, ''He is totally regardless of consequences, either to himself or to others, and this is what makes him so dangerous. On the other hand, he lives in the same universe as we do, not (like a schizophrenic) in some strange universe where two and two make five.''[35] We must try to understand what goes on in the mind of the political terrorist, for if we don't there will be no negotiations, and if there are no negotiations airline passengers will perish. Fundamental to dealing with a political terrorist is the understanding that he must not be startled or panicked; nor is it a good idea to break faith with him. The West has been a long time in understanding these basic principles.

Since 1968, the Palestinians have dominated political hijacking. Their activity has been persistent and their aims unchanging—the release of prisoners, the coercion of Western governments, ransom money to fund their movement, and, above all, dramatic, striking publicity for their cause. Compared to their record, other groups are inconsequential, and many of them have aped the Palestinian style and methods. As can be seen in Figure 1, the number of political hijackings is second only to those engineered by escaping refugees, and, perhaps more significantly, the numbers of the former have increased in spite of target-hardening in airports around the world. Of the 102 political hijacks mentioned above, more than 60 have been perpetrated by the Palestinians.

George Habash and Wadi Haddad, both Palestinian medical doctors, initiated the full-scale onslaught of political hijackings of commercial aircraft between 1968 and 1972. Habash was the "progressive" philosopher and founder of the Marxist PFLP, whereas Haddad was the revolutionary man of action, and it is probably he who created the international alliance that carried out the first campaign of terrorist hijackings in Western Europe and the Middle East.[36] By 1972 the PFLP had carried out 19 hijacks or attacks on commercial aircraft, driven by a philosophy deliberately bent on traumatizing Western nations. Said Habash, "the murder of one Jew where it will provoke shock and outrage is better than killing 10 Israeli soldiers in a border incident."[37]

Between the first hijack in 1968 and the Munich Olympic attack of 1972, Habash "decided to force the entire world to pay attention by bringing the (Palestinian) conflict onto the television screen in everyone's living room."[38] It was stunningly successful. Millions viewed the resulting hijacks on TV, and the West had no idea how to respond. The shock value did not last, however. The PFLP ceased airplane hijacking in 1972, likely because Habash had developed a severe heart condition.[39] But perhaps it also stopped because one of the main drawbacks of these hijack spectaculars was that frequent repetition reduced their publicity value.[40] Both Fatah and the PFLP decided to desist. Besides, by 1973 the PLO had decided to opt for the diplomatic route, and terrorist hijackings were incompatible with PLO speeches at the United Nations General Assembly in New York.

Wadi Haddad disagreed, and after a row with Habash, he stormed out in 1972 to form a splinter group, the Special Operations Group, with the help of the Iraqi and South Yemen secret services.[41] Haddad continued to specialize in plane hijacking, and between 1974 and 1979 "more than any other Palestinian leader he made terrorism international."[42] He recruited Carlos into the Palestinian cause and involved him in a number of prominent hijackings, including those involving the Organization of Petroleum Exporting Countries (OPEC) oil ministers, Entebbe in Uganda, and Mogadishu in Somalia. Carlos the Jackal, alias Ramirez Sanchez, the son of an Argentinian millionaire Communist, typified the attention-getting nature of the hijack terrorist when, in December 1975 during a hijack involving the OPEC oil ministers, he stated, "I am Carlos. You have heard me. Tell the world."[43] Haddad also drew the Japanese Red Army and the Baader- Meinhof Gang into his operations, which became increasingly outrageous, until they were even condemned by both the Soviet Union and China.[44] But still he planned other attacks with the assistance of Eastern European terrorists.[45] These attacks were never carried out however, for Haddad died of leukemia on March 28, 1978, in an East German hospital, and that ended the second phase of Palestinian hijacks.[46]

There was a hiatus in hijacking between 1978 and 1981. The focus of international terrorism seemed to be on assassination of heads of state, military leaders, and government officials. It was quite a shock, therefore, when a third Palestinian leader, far more vicious than the others, returned suddenly to the practice of aircraft hijacking. Abu Nidal is the *nom de guerre* for Sabri al Banna, the son of one of Palestine's wealthiest landowners. Trained as a teacher, he heads the Fatah Revolutinary Council, often known as Black June.

Israeli intelligence has credited Abu Nidal with 100 terror attacks and 200 deaths during a period of 13 years. According to James Adams of the *Sunday Times,* London, Nidal has carried out 56 acts of terrorism that are responsible for the deaths of more than 240 people since 1983. Choosing the avenue of radicalism in 1974, he was expelled from the PLO, but that did not prevent him from trying to assassinate PLO leader Yasir Arafat. He has been sentenced to death, in absentia, by the PLO. Since 1974 he has carried out at least six hijacks under the name of the National Arab Youth for the Liberation of Palestine and Black June. Since 1985 he has carried out six more attacks on aircraft that have cost many lives.

According to Adams, "Nidal is the nearest thing to a total psychopath around in terrorism today." He is completely ruthless and his anonymity has made it extremely difficult to counter his actions. "He is so terrified of an attempt on his life," added Adams,

that he refuses to eat or drink anything prepared by others and he sleeps in a different place each night. He never talks on the telephone or radio because he fears he may fall victim to an electronically detonated bomb such as the ones planted by Israeli intelligence, which killed a number of his followers in the early 1970s.[47]

It is not surprising that Abu Nidal had heart surgery in 1977, 1984, and 1986. There is obviously considerable stress involved in continually killing one's enemies, one's allies, even one's own family, as well as the innocent traveling public. Between 1982 and 1986 Abu Nidal operated out of Baghdad, Damascus, and Tripoli, as well as both Western and Eastern Europe. The difficulty from a Western point of view is how to deal with such a killer when he chooses to target Western airlines.

If earlier Palestinian hijackers were ready to negotiate a peaceful end to hijacks, this has rarely been true of Abu Nidal's group, which numbered between 150 and 200 active members. His three- to seven-member cells have worked with savage intensity to carry out several appalling massacres. In February 1978, his men seized a Cypriot airliner, which, when Egyptian commandos later stormed it, resulted in 15 deaths. In November 1985, Nidal cells held an EgyptAir B737 at Luqa Airport in Malta. The hijack ended with a rescue attempt that resulted in nearly 60 deaths. The next month Abu Nidal cells attacked El Al check-in counters at Rome and Vienna airports killing 19 people and wounding more than 100. It is also likely that Abu Nidal was connected to the bomb blast in TWA 840, which killed 4 passengers as the flight approached Athens Airport in April 1986. In September 1986, at Karachi Airport, four Abu Nidal terrorists panicked when the generators failed at night aboard a hijacked Pan Am B747. Opening fire on the passengers, the terrorists managed to kill at least 20 people. In short, 20 years after the first Palestinian hijacks, the situation for Western air carriers is as deadly as ever.

Indeed, it appears that the terrorist leaders of the increasingly numerous Palestinian splinter groups are getting more destructive as the years pass, which adds weight to Brian Jenkin's assertion that the later generations of terrorist groups are less intellectual, more criminal, and more destructive than were their predecessors.[48] Therefore, the logical way to safeguard the lives of innocent airline passengers would seem to be political negotiations aimed at finding a solution to the problem of the Palestinians.

Other unsolved political situations have also led to hijacking. There were Croatian hijacks in 1974 and 1976, with the latter crossing the Atlantic and entering five countries over 30 hours with millions of television viewers. In 1983 the Secret Army for the Liberation of Armenia (ASALA) prematurely exploded a bomb in Orly Airport, which resulted in the deaths of 7 people and injuries to 60. In 1984, 1985, and 1986 Sikh separatists attempted to create an independent Punjab state hijacked and placed bombs on Air India planes with a considerable loss of life.

But as Yossi Melman has stated, "individual terror has never achieved its aims. It has killed rulers, liquidated symbols of power, executed innocents, disturbed peace and tranquility, but has never succeeded in realizing its aims."[49] Melman believes that terror has become an end in itself for Abu Nidal and that he and his successors will continue to torment the West in the years to come. He therefore concluded, "Now that the terrorist groups have internationalized their struggle, the West must realize that its response requires internationalizing the battle against terrorism."[50]

ISLAMIC FUNDAMENTALISTS

It is not always realized that the anger and violence of the Shiite revival in the Middle East is two-pronged. The initial thrust came from the Khomeini regime, which began to spread its theocratic, Islamic revolutionary message as soon as the Ayatollah assumed power in Iran in 1979. Naturally, the United States, "the Big Satan," was the chief enemy, and not far behind was "Zionist" Israel. But as the war with Iraq dragged on in the 1980s, Iran spread its revolution and sought ways to weaken states aiding the Iraqis, including Kuwait, Bahrain, and Saudi Arabia, all of which, like Iraq itself, have sizeable Shiite minorities. But the other prong of Khomeini's influence was the defiant and angry Shiite community in Lebanon, caught in the middle of the fighting between Israel and the PLO during Israel's 1982 invasion of Lebanon. Nearly 400,000 Shiites were rendered homeless by the Israeli invasion, and they ended up as a resentful, angry, and explosive ghetto on the outskirts of Beirut.

Eric Morris and Alan Hoe described

the suicidal commitment of the Shia, whose religious traditions of martyrdom and protest are so much more amenable to terrorism; they present a formidable threat. They are children of Lebanon's civil war generation. . . . They are men and women with a readiness to die which is always the deadly strength of the fanatic. The world is against them and all they seek is release into paradise in bloody spectaculars.[51]

The result of these twin tragedies in the Middle East in the early 1980s created, by 1984, a Shiite International that has been called Islamic Jihad. The coalition is made up of four groups: Amal (Hope), led by Nabhi Berri; Al Dawa (Call of Islam), led by Sheik Fadlallah with Libyan connections; Hizbollah (Party of God), led by Abbas Mussarsi, and the Iman Hussein Suicide Brigade in West Beirut.

In 1983 these groups carried out six suicide bombings that resulted in 45 deaths in the U.S. Embassy and 300 killed at the U.S. Marine barracks, both in Beirut. But on December 12, 1983, the key event turned out to be suicide bomb attacks on the U.S. and French embassies in Kuwait. Five people were killed and 87 wounded. However, one hand of the suicide bomber was found, and he had already been fingerprinted. This led to the arrest of 18 accomplices, who were imprisoned, some of them under sentence of death. One of the imprisoned happened to be the brother-in-law of the head of security for Amal in Lebanon, a man called Imad Mughniyah. The latter is a Lebanese Shiite who is a key figure in the pro-Iranian Islamic Jihad movement. According to Oliver B. Revell, the FBI's assistant director for investigations, "Mughniyah is the single most dangerous terrorist alive today."[52]

Mughniyah has been tied to the abductions of six American, one British, and five French hostages, as well as to three hijackings and two mass bombings that killed more than 250 Americans.[53] In 1988 it was considered that this man had masterminded more terrorist attacks than the legendary Carlos and had more impact than Abu Nidal. It was also agreed that the incoming Bush administration would find him a tough adversary as it grappled with the issue of the remaining nine American hostages in Lebanon. Perhaps Mughniyah's menace lay in his elusiveness. The leader of a small cell of Lebanese Shia extremists, which is part of Islamic Jihad, he was trained by the Iranians but has moved into an independent stance that reflects his own personal agenda. That personal agenda has been shaped by the violence of the Arab–Israeli struggle, the passion of Islamic fundamentalism, and almost fanatical loyalties to family and clan.

It took two years for American intelligence to trace his name, though they were partly helped by former hostage David P. Jacobsen, who met him and described him as a "man not crazed, but obsessed."[54] All sources agree that the motive of his obsession is to free the 17 hostages in jail in Kuwait because his brother-in-law and cousin, Mustafa Badreddin, is among them. The cousins have been lifelong friends, had lived near each other in southern Beirut's slums, and had fought in the same militias. They were a lethal combination since Mughniyah was the planner and Badreddin the explosives specialist. They were both linked to the Marine Barracks bombing in Beirut, which killed 241 U.S. servicemen, and the U.S. Embassy bombing in 1983, which killed 17 Americans. Their teamwork was terminated with Badreddin's capture in Kuwait, and Mughniyah has been trying to free his former accomplice ever since.

There have been three attempts so far to free Badreddin, all of them hijacks. The first took place in December 1984 and involved a Kuwait Airways jet. The second was TWA 847 in Beirut in June 1985, and the third was another hijacked Kuwaiti jet in April 1988. Mughniyah is a particularly menacing figure for the international airline industry because he combines political and religious extremism with a deadly personal fanaticism.

The hijack of TWA Flight 847 was of particular interest because of the light it shed on the new type of hijacker, the Islamic fundamentalist. The two terrorists who took over the plane, Ali Younis and Ahmed Ghorbieh, were described by the passengers and Captain John Testrake as "homicidal maniacs." In the early stages of what became a two-week ordeal, they shouted and screamed at the passengers. One of them moved from verbal to physical violence, and demands throughout the nearly two-week ordeal were made partly in devout religious and partly in obscene language.[55] At the same time, however, the hijackers knew their drill very well. For much of the hijack they kept the initiative in at least two ways: First, they shunted back and forth between Beirut and Algiers just in time to avoid assault by either the U.S. Sixth Fleet or the Delta force from Fort Bragg, Texas. Second, they would make a gesture by releasing some passengers and then increase the pressure on the Western negotiators by threatening to murder passengers or blow up the plane. To show they were serious, they tortured and finally shot U.S. Navy diver Robert Stethem and dumped his body on the tarmac. Later, their numbers augmented by reinforcements, they separated the U.S. and Jewish passengers from the rest of the hostages, a grim reminder of both Entebbe and the Holocaust practices of Nazi Germany. Finally, the hijackers lost the initiative, and instead of killing the hostages or committing suicide, they dissolved into the environs of Beirut.

A film, *The Uli Derickson Story,* was subsequently made, detailing the role played by the senior flight attendant on TWA 847. Because she spoke German, as did one of the terrorists, and had spent two years in Saudi Arabia, she was able to play a crucial part in the hijack and is credited with saving many lives. Later, Thomas M. Ashwood, chairman of the Security Committee of IFALPA, conducted a tape-recorded interview with Derickson that forms a chapter in his book *Terror in the Skies* (1988). This chapter is perhaps the best available account of Islamic fundamentalist behavior during a hijack.

Derickson was thrown violently against a door and kicked in the chest in order to intimidate her. Violent, nonlethal blows and loud verbal assaults were used to gain control and subdue resistance. The hijackers moved people about the aircraft like pawns in a chess game and also beat women and children, as well as the male passengers, in a brutal show of maintaining control. They were not on drugs and were very clear-headed; yet they kept shouting, "We have come to die."[56] One thing that was painfully evident to Derickson was the ritualistic aspect of the killing of the navy diver. Stethem was beaten half senseless and then left to die with his hands still bound together. Afterwards, the hijackers scrawled slogans on the aircraft doors in his blood.[57]

At times the younger of the two terrorists, who has since been labeled psychotic, was almost completely out of control and might have killed many other passengers or crashed the plane had he not been restrained by his partner. At the same time, however, the terrorists seemed to be in complete ignorance of the technical aspects of aviation; they were frightened by some light turbulence in flight, and because of language barriers, they were unable to communicate verbally with their victims.

THE BOMB SABOTEUR

"The bomb is the meanest of weapons. It kills indiscriminately and without risk to the terrorist—once he has assembled and placed it," wrote British author General Richard Clutterbuck.[58] But a bomb placed on a commercial aircraft, risking hundreds of lives, is a particularly savage terrorist weapon. If the hijacker has decided on sabotage and murder, only the airline and airport security systems stand between him and success. The sabotage of aircraft by bombs also makes detection of the cause of a crash difficult in some cases, which may be why the more than 80 known attempts to explode bombs in planes since 1968 are probably only about half the number actually attempted. (See Appendix 3.)

Attempted sabotage of aircraft dates from at least the 1940s, when members of the Second World War German conspiracy to remove Hitler, the Black Orchestra, placed a bomb in Hitler's plane on one of his trips to the Russian front. It was calculated to go off at a certain height, but the weather was very cold and the firing mechanism froze, with the result that the bomb was rendered harmless, and the saboteurs quickly had to remove the bomb from the plane when the flight landed safely.[59] So if the "good guys" initiated aerial bomb sabotage, it was inevitable that the "bad guys" of international terrorism would follow suit.

Very little is known about bomb saboteurs. The people who are caught are usually couriers, who simply deliver the bombs and are either unwilling or unable to lead police to the hidden brain behind the operation. At present, therefore, more is known about sabotage operations than about saboteurs' personalities or their thinking.

Early attempts at airline sabotage mainly involved furnishing innocent passengers with tape recorders containing hidden bombs geared to go off in flight. On July 23, 1974, an airliner carrying 92 passengers and crew from Belfast to London made an emergency landing in Manchester after an IRA telephone call, ten minutes into the flight, warned of a bomb on board. Sure enough, a bomb was discovered in a bag under one of the seats. The firing pin had gone off but had failed to detonate the charge. Had it done so, all 92 people aboard would have perished.[60] The aircraft was chosen because it was carrying two policeman to London to receive gallantry awards from the queen, and the chief constable of Northern Ireland, a Roman Catholic, was accompanying them.

Then, on September 7, 1974, the bombers suddenly got lucky. They chose a TWA flight from Tel Aviv via Athens to the United States. It blew up in flight over the Ionian Sea, killing all 88 people on board. The NAYLP, linked to Abu Nidal, was responsible for the destruction, but only four days after the disaster, Ahmed al Ghafour, the leader of the NAYLP, was shot dead by a Fatah execution squad of the PLO. When no bombs exploded on board planes for several years following al Ghafour's death, it was wrongly assumed he was the bomber.

Gradually, Western intelligence became aware of a new Iraqi-based terrorist group, both sinister and secretive, called the "15th May Organization." The date was that of Israeli independence, and the leader of the group was Mohammed Omari who goes by the pseudonym of Abu Ibrahim. According to Christopher Dobson and Ronald Payne, "he is one of the most technically dangerous and cunning terrorists in the world."[61] He was a graduate of the old PFLP Special Operations Group and originally came from Tripoli in Lebanon, though he is Palestinian. Apparently, "Abu Ibrahim's power to cause fear stems from his extraordinary expertise as a maker of clever bombs, and his callous lack of discrimination in using them against innocent people."[62] His particular craft has been to manufacture suitcase bombs that are almost undetectable. As described earlier, he was known to have refined the technique of using a barometric detonator in combination with a timing device. Apparently, Ibu Ibrahim was experimenting with the device as long ago as 1972. Four years later he experimented in San Francisco by trying to place a device aboard a Pan Am flight to Tokyo. That attempt was discovered by American security, but now he was perfecting a new weapon in the form of six identical, brown, soft-sided suitcases sold under the trademark "Lastric." "The plan," said Dobson and Payne, "was to place them in American and Israeli airliners in order to destroy them in mid-flight and create panic among airline passengers, especially those flying to and from Israel.''[63]

The first of these suitcase bombs was planted by his agents in Athens on a gullible English businesswoman who did some work in both Greece and Israel. She actually flew to Israel with the suitcase, but it failed to explode, so she returned to Athens, still with the suitcase. Somehow, Western intelligence became involved, and there was a first-class row between the Greek and American governments, which ended in a CIA station chief being expelled. Five of the other brown suitcases, however, were recovered with thinly rolled explosive molded into the fabric of the suitcase and detonators fixed into the metal studs to avoid X-ray detection. In 1983 one young Arab was blown to pieces by his own bomb in the Mount Royal Hotel in London, and the 15th May Organization declared him a martyr.[64]

On April 17, 1986, El Al security found a bomb with ten pounds of explosive in the luggage of Ann-Marie Murphy at London airport. Her Palestinian lover, Nezar Narnas Mansur Hindawi, not only had got her pregnant but also was sending her to certain death en route to Israel along with 400 other passengers. The sophisticated bomb had already cleared the normal screening process and was subjected to El Al's stringent hand search procedure only because Murphy was so frightened and nervous about flying. Two months later, at Madrid's Barajas Airport, a small-time crook was conned into carrying a suitcase into an El Al security lounge. When opened, it burst into flames and injured 14 people. In both cases a form of Czechoslovak-made plastic explosive called Semtex was used. The Eastern Europeans have exported this dangerous product to the Palestinians, and traditional airport X-ray techniques cannot detect these explosives. But behind the traffic in plastic explosives lies the fact that one skillful and immoral terrorist wishes to put maximum pressure on the U.S. and Israeli governments to abandon Israel. Western security will always be one step behind as the attacker of innocent airline passengers takes the initiative.

Airplane bombings have not been the sole prerogative of the Palestinians. In copycat fashion, other groups have adopted the practice, making the 1980s the worst time for airplane sabotage to date. Among the most lethal are the Sikh separatists, whose rationale for attempting to destroy 700 people with two airplane bombs in one day is very difficult to understand. The Air India bombing has angered Canadians and set them against the cause of an independent Punjab state.

Other separatist groups that have tried aircraft sabotage include the Armenians and the North Koreans. On July 1, 1983, the Armenian ASALA group exploded a bomb at Orly Airport, Paris, which killed seven and injured 60 others. On May 8, 1986, a bomb exploded aboard an Air Lanka jet on the ground but nevertheless killed 16 and wounded 41 others. On September 14, 1986, the North Koreans exploded a bomb in a garbage receptical at the entrance to Kimpo Airport, Seoul, South Korea, just before the Asian games scheduled to be held there in October.[65] A year later, in December 1987, Korean Air Lines Flight 858, a B707 with 115 passengers (mostly Koreans from the Middle East), vanished from the radar screens. Two North Korean agents who deplaned in

Abu Dhabi were suspected of placing a bomb aboard the aircraft. One of them bit a cynide capsule and died; the other, a woman, confessed to the sabotage.

The subsequent trial of this young woman appeared to confirm that the government of North Korea had deliberately trained its agents at great length and expense for the sole purpose of disrupting the Seoul Olympics and thus destabilizing the South Korean regime. In other words, this was state terrorism.

On August 24, 1988, a bomb exploded in an American-made C130 transport plane belonging to Pakistan, which was transporting President Zia ul-Haq and 29 others, including 10 senior Pakistani army officers, and Arnold Raphael, the U.S. ambassador to Pakistan. The plane was taking off for a flight to Rawalpindi, 500 miles north, when it was suddenly engulfed in flames and crashed. No one survived; indeed, only a copy of the Koran survived the charred wreckage. It was clearly a bomb sabotage and most likely planted by the Soviet KGB, which had been threatening Pakistan over its support of the Afghan rebels.[66] Zia ul-Haq was the first head of state to be assassinated by airplane bombing sabotage. It might also be deemed a second example of state terrorism in this field.

In November 1988 the West German police discovered the constituent elements of an airline bomb of the type to be placed inside a radio tuner in the possession of the PFLP—GC of Ahmed Jibril. This ought to have been a warning to Western intelligence, because even after several telephoned hints in November, a bomb was somehow placed aboard Pan Am 103 either in Frankfurt or London on December 21. It exploded over Lockerbie, Scotland, en route to the United States, killing 259 persons on board, including 189 Americans. By mid-1989 nothing had been proven, except that it was bomb sabotage, and the evidence seemed to be pointing toward a collusion between Jibril's PFLP-GC and the Iranians. This would mean that the flight was destroyed by the PFLP-GC, probably for a price in order that Iranian fundamentalists could be avenged for the shooting down, by the USS *Vincennes,* of one of their planes over the Persian Gulf in 1987.

The shock value of the destruction of Flight 103 was incredible. It galvanized the whole system of airport security worldwide and created great anger and revulsion at the Islamic fundamentalists.

The real difficulty is to know how to deal with this vengeful variation on the theme of aerial hijacking. It may be that the tough response to air hijacking around the world has pushed the terrorists to plant bombs on planes. It may even be that the lack of political solutions is making terrorists more vengeful and destructive, but one fact is unchallengeable. Only really good airport security stands between these terrorists and the deaths of hundreds of innocent passengers. Since a high standard of airport security is highly dependent on good intelligence, as Jossi Melman has stated, the West will have to internationalize its response by very close cooperative efforts if it wants to defeat this costly and destructive new form of international warfare.

Chapter 4

Airport Security: Ground Rules for a New Game

For the past two decades the Western civil aviation industry has been subjected to a calculated campaign of terror from terrorist groups around the world. Western planes have been attacked and bombed. Ground-to-air missiles have been fired at commercial aircraft. Airports and ticket counters have been attacked, and even airline offices have not been spared in terrorist attempts to intimidate governments and prevent the Western public from flying. Although terrorism directed at the civil aviation industry comprises only a small percentage of terrorist incidents worldwide, a successful attack produces the results most desired by a terrorist organization—mass publicity and chaos within the system. It is primarily for this reason that Western governments ought to make airport security a key element in their battle against terrorism.

In the past 20 years the airport has become a highly symbolic and politically significant place. Terrorists, criminals, and even the emotionally unstable have undertaken acts of violence at airports to make statements of one kind or another. Airports are vulnerable, difficult to defend against attacks, and visited by millions of people daily. Any kind of attack is sure to attract immediate attention from governments and the media. Terrorists simply cannot leave airports alone; nor does it make sense to do so, since they are the weak point in Western defenses.

Since the airport is a symbolic stage for both domestic protest and international grievance, terrorists have created a seemingly endless number of ways to attack it. As we enter the 1990s, a number of questions cry to be answered: Why is this state of affairs allowed to drag on? Is it impossible to create foolproof airport security? Is there such a thing as a secure airport, and how do we go about creating one?

PROBLEMS OF AIRPORT SECURITY

There are several basic problems that have so far inhibited effective airport security. First, both Western democracies and the civil aviation industries have continuously upgraded their security capabilities only sufficiently to match the known methods of terrorist attacks. This practice has given rise to a reliance on security standards that do not improve with advances in related technological fields. This creates the following merry-go-round: A terrorist operation carried out successfully reveals the inadequacies of an outdated security system; new updated measures are then adopted that will in turn remain in place, regardless of technological advancement, until they are circumvented by yet another terrorist action.[1] As Paul Robinson, former associate director of national security at Los Alamos National Laboratory, pointed out, "The number of things that a terrorist can do is far greater than can ever be defended against. We'll always be in the position where deterrence presupposes a rational adversary."[2]

The second problem standing squarely in the way of improved airport security is that the implementation of more stringent security procedures is based on the perceived terrorist threat within individual countries. A country that has just experienced a terrorist attack tends to invoke increased security measures, whereas a neighboring country that has been spared the same terrorist hostilities sees no need to upgrade its own security measures. This syndrome has been particularly true for Euroterrorism in France, Germany, Austria, and Italy. The resultant patchwork system of "security according to threat experienced" has left international air travel with many exploitable gaps. Even the United States has been guilty of this particular practice. After 1973, when the number of air hijacks had dropped to a worldwide low of 22, the United States thought it had the problem licked. The result was a relaxation of security and a failure to plan for the future. Canada is in a far worse situation because both the government and the populace feel somehow protected by Canada's international reputation of basic decency. Canadians think they are simply far too nice for any terrorist to attack their civil aviation system. Even after 331 people died on one June day in 1985 as a result of air terrorism in Canada, the government scarcely changed its policy of studied neglect of the airports of Canada.

A third basic problem in developing effective airport security concerns the international means of enforcement that have evolved. At least three conventions and one declaration were developed between 1963 and 1978. The Tokyo Convention of 1963, the Hague Convention in 1969, the Montreal Convention of 1971, and the Bonn Declaration in 1978 together, in theory, effectively outlawed air terrorism and put enforcement sanctions in place. Even with the International Air Transport Association (IATA) and the International Civil Aviation Organization (ICAO) presiding over these international sanctions, however, individual countries have chosen, always for political reasons, to ignore their provisions. The result is a complete lack of concerted international enforcement of antihijack measures. Even though 54 of 120 aviation-related terrorist attacks were foiled between 1983 and 1987, "once terrorists set out to attack civil aviation, their chances of achieving at least partial success are better than 75 per cent."[3]

A fourth problem inhibiting the development of effective airport security has been the attitude of the airlines themselves. For the world's airlines, transportation of people and goods by air is a profit-making concern, and the development of air terrorism has been a regrettable but almost unavoidable hazard of the profit-making process. There is now cutthroat competition between the world's airlines to obtain ever-larger shares of the burgeoning air carrier business. In 1970 there were 216 million passengers flying, of which total the United States accounted for 180 million. By 1977 the number of passengers worldwide rose to 610 million, by 1981 it was 752 million, and by 1986 it reached 938 million passengers.[4] The story of international air travel has been about the rest of the world catching up on the very large American head start. In 1979 the United States deregulated air travel, fully expecting Western Europe and Japan to follow suit. Neither of them had done so ten years later; rather, national governments have chosen to nurture and encourage their national airlines. By 1981 there were 110 airlines worldwide, and it was estimated that one year earlier was a turning point, when for the first time the number of non-U.S. citizens flying to the United States may have equaled, if not exceeded, the number of Americans flying abroad.[5]

By 1984, of 846 million air passengers worldwide, the American share was 363 million, which meant that the United States had lost its monopoly on international air travel. Throughout the 1980s both the rejectionist Palestinians and the Islamic fundamentalists began to attack American airliners with sabotage and hijacking. In 1986, reacting to the terrorism of the year before, between 50 and 70 percent of Americans declined to travel to Western Europe, which gave Western European airlines a further advantage. Since the U.S. government is not now supporting its air transportation industry, competition for a declining share of world markets is fierce among the airlines, which leaves scant resources for dealing with expensive counterterrorist systems at airports.

A fifth and final problem blocking effective airport security is that the whole system of airports worldwide is only as strong as the weakest link in that chain. In 1985 the series of attacks on both airports and airplanes seemed to be nullifying the work of years in building up to a safe worldwide system. Airport security was found wanting in Toronto and Montreal in June 1985, as the Air India flight crashed off Ireland. In the same month TWA 847 was ferried almost at will by the terrorists back and forth between Beirut and Algiers. This latter episode caused an angry listing of the ten weak-link airports by *Newsweek.*[6] The list included Athens, Beirut, Karachi, New Delhi, Manila, Teheran, Tripoli, Conakry, Lagos, and Yaounde. It might also have included Algiers, which along with most of the above-mentioned airports is a place that hijacking terrorists know they can flee to, since they are likely to encounter at least a neutral, if not friendly, reception there. The continuous use of these airports by terrorists and the collusion of the respective governments involved make a complete mockery of any effective worldwide system of airport security.

In December 1985 Palestinian terrorists mounted the ramps overlooking the El Al ticket counters at Rome and Vienna airports and opened fire on innocent people with automatic weapons. The overall result was 22 people dead and 121 wounded in two airports that were considered to be reasonably secure against terrorists. On September 5, 1986, the Palestinians attacked more passengers on board a Pan Am B747, bypassing the security system at Karachi Airport and commandeering the aircraft. Again, in April 1988 Algiers was used by the Islamic fundamentalists, and they received enormous support, plus an escape to freedom, courtesy of the Algerian government, after killing Kuwaiti hostages. Finally, the explosion of Pan Am 103 over Lockerbie, Scotland, on December 22, 1988, which killed 270 people, convinced Western nations that even Frankfurt and London are now "unsafe airports" when it comes to bomb sabotage. It was enormously discouraging to have to face the fact that both Third World airports and Western ones were vulnerable to and likely to receive additional terrorist attacks in future. Therefore it is important to know what has been achieved so far in the process of building airport security, as well as how to cope with the security threat that lies ahead.

THE ISRAELI SYSTEM OF SECURITY

Airport security is a feasible goal. Proper airport security is not only possible but is being practiced successfully by one state in the world: Israel. Israel exists in a state of war with the Arabs, and the price of survival has had to include the political will, the acceptance, and the expense involved in mounting a successful system of airport security. Western airport security therefore has a standard by which it can continually measure itself. No attempted hijacking of an El Al airliner has been recorded since September 6, 1970, and that one failed because of the presence of sky marshals.[7] Israeli airport security was implemented immediately after the hijack of an El Al plane by the Palestinians in 1968. The plane ended up in Algiers, but the incident resulted in no loss of life. Nevertheless, the Israelis instituted a series of boarding checks of all passengers on the aircraft. All passengers were thoroughly searched physically for weapons and then psychologically for inconsistencies. Every passenger underwent an extensive character check to ensure that each was really who he or she claimed to be.

To facilitate this character search, the ticketing process changed. Complete identification is required upon purchasing an El Al ticket to allow security officials to compile a reference file on the individual. "The security staffs of El Al also conduct passenger interrogations of a depth not characteristic of any other airline."[8] Passengers are usually asked to arrive at least two-and-a-half hours before flight time to allow sufficient time for baggage security procedures and questioning.[9] They are asked whether they did their own packing, whether they packed any electronic devices and where they bought them, and whether they are carrying anything, even a present, given to them by someone else. They are asked whether anyone has had access to their luggage after it was packed. If security has any suspicions they cross-check by telephone with friends or family of the passengers.[10] It is this kind of human security that has made El Al safe from hijacking for two decades.

The other element in Israel's security system consists of an extensive technological process of baggage screening. Baggage destined for the plane's cargo compartment is first individually X-rayed and then placed together in a sealed container where the air is depressurized to simulate in-flight conditions. It is expected that if an explosive device is concealed within the bags the X-rays would discover it visually or the drop in air pressure would detonate it prematurely.[11] As we have learned at great cost, bombs activated by pressure changes have been a favorite tactic of terrorists recently. In the event that a bomb does escape detection, there is still the further protection of the plane. The cargo holds of all El Al airliners are reinforced with armor plating, to limit the destructiveness of an explosion.[12]

The third element in the Israeli security system actually takes place aboard the aircraft. Passengers boarding the flight and in possession of carry-on luggage are not allowed to take such articles to their seats.[13] All carry-on luggage is stored in a compartment at the front of the plane, thus eliminating any chance a would-be hijacker would have of using a weapon that had earlier escaped detection. Along with the cargo compartment, the cockpit of the aircraft has been reinforced so as to separate and protect the pilots from any activities occurring within the passenger section. In combination with this practice, the crews of El Al aircraft are given extensive intructions and training as to the proper responses to make in a hijack situation.

In-flight security on El Al aircraft is further strengthened by the presence of well-armed and well-trained sky marshals. Sky marshals have been a controversial option in the United States and elsewhere, but for El Al they have proved their worth again and again. Israeli sky marshals, or the "007 Squad" as they are known, work most often in pairs, with one situated near the front of the aircraft and the other at the rear.[14] In this way the entire passenger section is under surveillance. Sky marshals are recruited from the Sayaret Matkal.[15] This is an elite force that is highly trained in the areas of hand-to-hand combat, marksmanship, and, perhaps most importantly, the terrorist psyche.[16] In the moments immediately preceding her second hijack in 1970, Leila Khaled was very much aware of the two sky marshals watching her with suspicion. Such is the impact of body language on a trained observer.[17] (See Appendix 4.)

The fifth element of El Al security is something of which most passengers would be unaware. There are protective devices under the wings of El Al planes that can alter the flight of most surface-to-air missiles that a terrorist might launch along the incoming or outgoing flight path of the plane. The result of this intense concentration on security in the fight against terrorism is that El Al is considered the world's safest airline.

It might well be asked, in view of Israeli success, why have other airlines neglected to implement these measures fully? The answer is that different conditions exist in Israel. The first and most apparent characteristic of the situation in Israel is the logistical one. El Al is a small, highly centralized airline company handling a relatively small volume of passengers. Compare El Al to other foreign air carriers such as Air France, KLM, Lufthansa, TWA, and Pan Am, all of which have massive operations, and the problem of instituting security of this kind becomes apparent. For these airlines to adopt El Al's security measures and initiate its meticulous passenger and baggage checks would prove to be too time-consuming based on the large volume of passengers needing to be examined.[18] Under closer scrutiny, however, it can be seen that Western aviation security efforts have been plagued by a different problem. The adage, where there is a will, there is a way, can be applied to their efforts but in reverse. The Western governments and their aviation industries have had the knowledge and the technology but not the will to enforce El Al-like security procedures.[19] The question is whether a really effective system can be developed that does not jeopardize the efficient running and all-important profit margins of the large airlines. The answer to this question was still not apparent in the late 1980s as terrorists sharply escalated the nature and destructiveness of their attacks on Western civil aviation targets. In the meantime, each airport manager must assess the security threat to his own airport and make sure an adequate level of security is maintained within his own jurisdiction.

THE EVOLUTION OF AIRPORT SECURITY SINCE 1974

From the beginning, the United States has had the most comprehensive aviation network in the world and has therefore had the largest stake in maintaining the security of this mode of travel. As Robert G. Bell pointed out in 1976, "more than 40 per cent of hijackings around the world since 1960 have involved American aircraft."[20] In the United States in 1973, the FAA specified three areas that should be designated for increased security measures: the ticket counter, the boarding gate, and the inside of the aircraft itself. At the first of these areas, increased security was accomplished with ticket agents being instructed to be aware of persons fitting what has become known as the terrorist profile. In 1969 an FAA task force under the leadership of Evan W. Pickerel identified 35 behavioral characteristics common to past hijackings. It was decided that a 100 percent search was not necessary since a great number of air travelers were businessmen or regular fliers. Various forms of profile were attempted, not so much to detect suspicious persons as to eliminate unsuspicious ones. "One of these profiles was to eliminate all except those between 16 and 65 who had bought a single ticket for cash. Surprisingly, this left only two per cent to be searched. Other profiles—which were kept confidential—further narrowed this to half of one per cent."[21]

At the boarding area major steps were taken to screen all passengers to prevent concealed weapons from being brought on board. At all major airports in the United States and, later, Western Europe, walk-through metal archways were installed as well as X-ray machines to examine carry-on luggage. The insertion of these devices into aviation security was seen as a very successful step toward safer air travel. The two machines would do in a span of two or three minutes what the Israelis do in 10 or 15 minutes or even more, that is, the thorough inspection of all passengers boarding an aircraft. Security was also intensified on the flight itself, with the issuing of a set of FAA guidelines. Armed sky marshals were to be present on the aircraft and operate in much the same manner as their Israeli counterparts. This, however, was a short-lived security measure as so many airlines protested it. They argued, legitimately, that these marshals were not adequately trained to deal successfully with a hijack situation within the confines of an airplane. The airlines also pointed out that an ill-trained, armed sky marshal attempting to disrupt a terrorist operation could lead to a worst disaster. Except for the sky marshal program, the introduction of the new security standards appeared to be a success. In the United States alone, the first year of X-ray and metal detection machines yielded more than 2,000 guns and 3,500 pounds of explosives with the number of hijackings reduced from 29 in 1972 to 2 in 1973.[22] In attaining these results, 165 million U.S. travelers were screened by the new security procedures. This is where the security system stopped developing, however, since it was assumed that the enemy was static, rational, and unable to adapt. Unfortunately, the U.S. security measures at airports did not seem so impressive when some important conditions were taken into account.

First, the brand of air terrorism the United States was facing was different from that which prevailed in the Middle East or even Western Europe. The vast majority of hijackings in the United States were carried out by individuals who needed a means of escape or transportation to another country, generally to Cuba. Otherwise, U.S. hijacks were carried out by the mentally unstable, criminals, and extortionists. These attempts were not staged to gain publicity for a political cause and carried out by individuals willing to sacrifice both passengers and plane to achieve their aims. Because of this, U.S. aviation security has never been exposed to the relentless efforts of terrorists to circumvent its workings and gain political advantage as have the countries of Western Europe. Second, the flaws of U.S. security measures have best been exposed when they were put into practice in Western European airports. The initial element of the system, the use of the terrorist profile, has been found to be extremely ineffective in identifying would-be terrorists. Apart from suspecting every Arab on the flight, there are no longer any tell-tale ways of pinpointing suspect individuals. Modern terrorists are well aware that their appearance comes under careful scrutiny and accordingly disguise themselves in well-tailored suits and travel as businessmen or fly together as husband and wife teams.

The next designated area of security checks, the electronic screening of passengers and their hand luggage, also fared poorly in Europe. Both the metal detector and the X-ray machine were found to be only as effective as the individuals operating them. It was discovered that the large volume of passengers going through the screening process produced the "assembly line" syndrome, causing security personnel to become much less vigilant. This, coupled with terrorists' success in disguising weapons by dismantling them and distributing them among themselves, made it all too easy to circumvent this security measure.

There were also some areas of security that the United States neglected altogether, one being the failure to examine checked baggage. In the United States, the lack of political terrorists in hijacking made such a measure unnecessary. In Europe it was quickly realized that the failure to check baggage traveling in the aircraft's hold constituted an exploitable gap in security procedures. To remedy this lack, European airlines formulated the method of matching the baggage within the cargo hold to the passenger on board.[23] Any unclaimed luggage was removed. With this method in place, if an in-flight bombing were to occur it would have to be, in most cases, a suicide attempt, which was a rarity in the 1970s. Even this system was penetrated, however, when one terrorist organization planted a bomb in an unsuspecting accomplice's luggage.[24]

These inadequate security measures persisted throughout the 1970s, and as a result, the civil aviation industry, principally in Western Europe, suffered through an abundance of horrific terrorist operations. For some strange reason, during this period Western governments concentrated their energy and resources not on improving their security standards but on upgrading their rescue capabilities. This state of affairs was exemplified with the Entebbe and Mogadishu raids in 1976 and 1977, in which elite commando units from Israel and West Germany and Great Britain successfully rescued all passengers off the hijacked planes with a minimum loss of life. Immediately after these incidents all Western nations developed specialized or paramilitary forces, as if this was the panacea for hijack prevention. In so doing they neglected the vital deterrent effect of target-hardening in the form of progressively improving airport security. It was as if the West was surrendering to the fact that it could not prevent a terrorist assault from occurring but that it could affect the event's outcome.

The United States, meanwhile, consistently pursued largely international solutions to air terrorism that touched only tangentially on airport security. On February 15, 1973, the Memorandum of Understanding on Hijacking of Aircraft and Vessels and Other Offenses was signed by the United States and Cuba. The result of years of painstaking negotiations, the agreement would at least take some of the stress off airports. Later, in 1973, "The diplomatic offensive waged by the American delegation at the 1973 ICAO Conference in Rome denoted the high-water mark in U.S. leadership of the response to terrorism against international civil aviation."[25] The strategy used by the United States was aimed at eliminating all terrorist "safe havens" by establishing the ICAO sanctioning authority. Unfortunately, the Europeans felt that sanctions would not reach non-U.N. states, but before a confrontation could develop, on August 10 (two weeks before the conference), "The Israelis, with an appallingly poor sense of timing, forced down a Lebanese commercial airliner in order to search for Palestinian guerrilla leaders suspected of being on board."[26]

After the subsequent collapse of the Rome conference, the United States considered the multilateral approach as being closed. Congress now went on to create Public Law 92-366, which was entitled The Anti-Hijacking Act of August 5, 1974. The provisions of the act promised 20 years or more or death for hijackers, suspension of landing rights to secondary boycotts for offending countries, FAA control of law enforcement for aircraft in flight, and legal status for airport security and passenger screening.[27]

One problem concerning jurisdiction at airports was clearly delineated, much to the relief of the airline pilots. The act changed the definition of an aircraft in flight. It placed an aircraft in flight "from the moment when all [its] external doors are closed following embarkation until the moment when one such door is open for disembarkation, or in the case of a forced landing, until the competent authorities take over the responsibility for the aircraft and for the persons and property aboard."[28] This provision resolved a painful issue for pilots, best demonstrated in the case of Captain W. R. Haas in November 1973, when the FBI shot out the aircraft's tires and the hijackers forced him to take off at enormous risk to plane and passengers.[29] The legislation enabled the secretary of transportation to revoke or impose conditions on airlines from outside the United States that did not maintain adequate security. The FAA had already found eight major foreign airports with "grossly inadequate" security measures: Beirut, New Delhi, Bangkok, Brussels, Rome, Buenos Aires, Copenhagen, and London.[30] A final provision of the act, which the American Airline Pilots Association (ALPA) lobbied to obtain, was a federally controlled and funded law enforcement organization to oversee security at airports. The Senate went along with the suggestion, but the House of Representatives balked at the idea, and so "qualified state, local and private security people were given the security maintenance task."[31]

The United States also pursued the support of Foreign Technical Prevention programs abroad. A large number of countries participated, at their own expense.

As of 1975, 11 governments had requested inspection of their aviation security systems by FAA experts, representatives of 17 nations had attended the Department of Transportation Aviation Security training course in Oklahoma City, and more than 50 countries had received audio-visual programs on such subjects as explosives, security and in-flight hijacking defense tactics.[32]

Concern about air security increased in 1977, when hijack attempts within the United States began to mount again. Worldwide, the figure rose to 32. John O'Donnell, representing IFALPA's 50,000 pilots from 64 nations, addressed the Senate Foreign Relations Committee: "If terrorists cannot hijack, they will destroy. . . . our society does not lend itself to the concept of turning our airports . . . into armed camps."[33] In 1978 the number of hijack attempts in the United States more than doubled, while globally, the total was 31. On January 30, O'Donnell made a statement to the Governmental Affairs Committee of the U.S. Senate that strongly indicated the direction being taken by the IFALPA and

ALPA. He began by paraphrasing Mark Twain on the weather, "Everyone talks about terrorism but nobody does anything about it."[34] He went on to state,

We are totally convinced that the United Nations has neither the will nor the means to effect any meaningful solution. We have consequently arrived at the inescapable conclusion that strong, unilateral and bilateral action by a few powerful nations is the only practical path to follow.[35]

O'Donnell then commended the provision that required the president to compile a list of Dangerous Foreign Airports (DFAs). The use of this provision would, he felt, establish a standard or criterion for worldwide airport security. "Experience has shown," he continued, "that the state of security at given airports can range from non-existent to very good within a matter of hours. The change occurs with local political situations, possibilities of attack or being a host airport for a hijacked aircraft."[36]

The number of attempted U.S. hijacks remained steady at 13 in 1979, but in 1980 it jumped to 22 with 41 hijacks worldwide. It was clear that hijacking was on an upsurge again after the usual hiatus period, and since international attempts to obtain aircraft security from governments had failed, the civil aviation community would have to start looking within for better airport security.

It is hard to put a finger on the precise turning point, though the new secretary of the pilots association, Captain Thomas Ashwood, did not pull any punches. Addressing the U.S. Senate on May 7, 1979, he pointed to an ominous trend in terrorism—the use of small surface-to-air missiles to shoot down unarmed civilian airliners. Incidents of this type had happened twice in Rhodesia. Only three weeks later, four baggage handlers were injured in a bomb blast at JFK Airport in New York. Ashwood expressed his alarm "that this country has no specially-trained force comparable to those of Britain, Germany or Israel."[37] In May 1979 he criticized the State Department for opposing automatic sanctions on the grounds that they would "hinder our tactical flexibility."[38] He then went directly to the point: "Effective screening of passengers at the airport before boarding is the single most important action foreign governments could take to cut down on hijackings."[39]

Almost prophetically, Ashwood closed his speech to the U.S. Senate Committee on Governmental Affairs by stating, "We do strongly support the use of taggants because we believe they will act as a significant deterrent to acts of sabotage."[40]

The age of aircraft sabotage had finally arrived, and airport security would have to be reevaluated in the light of this new and menacing development. Between 1980 and 1984 the number of hijacks worldwide never fell below 28, and in 1983, 19 of 34 hijacks around the world were linked to U.S. civil aircraft.[41]

In the 1980s, it was clear to anyone examining the statistics that the American philosophy of airport and aircraft security would have to change. The revolution in Iran had spawned not only a new source but also a new location for the practice of terrorism. This has gradually become known as Islamic fundamentalism and it called for the destruction of all "Western decadent democracies." Preoccupation with the U.S. Embassy hostages in Iran, wonderment at the savagery of the Iran–Iraq war, and blithe innocence and naivete in placing American marines in Lebanon all distracted the U.S. government from realizing it was becoming the prime target of Islamic fundamentalist terrorism.

In March 1983 the United States could congratulate itself that "over the last decade 4-5 billion passengers and 5.5 billion pieces of carry-on luggage were screened. In the process, 25,000 firearms were detected and confiscated and more than 10,000 related arrests were made."[42] But in the summer of 1985 both the Islamic fundamentalists and the rejectionist Palestinians made such a mockery of airport security around the world that it became clear that radical changes and a far different quality of airport security would be called for to deal with the new hijack menace. When it became apparent through the ruthless murdering of U.S. citizens that the United States was the specific target, the government and airline industry were forced to go into action. Writing in 1986, James Ott pointed out that "the U.S. aviation industry initiated efforts to upgrade its security systems that have been unparalleled to date."[43] But how could he know that in December 1988, a new and deadly game of sabotage of aircraft was being undertaken by the enemies of the West. As 1989 dawned it was very clear that a whole new approach to airport security would be called for to deal with the destruction of Pan Am 103.

What is so very striking in all of these developments is that by 1989 there was still no concerted attack on the many and vulnerable airports of North America. A concerted attack against U.S. and Canadian airports by terrorists would likely cause complete confusion and chaos in a system of airport security that had not had to change in a basic way since 1973. In anticipation of the inevitable escalation of attacks against civil aviation all around the world, now would be an ideal time to develop a completely new skin of airport security and maybe a new philosophy to animate that system.

A NEW SKIN OF AIRPORT SECURITY FOR THE 1990S

It would be perfectly acceptable to some people to state that "a new system" of airport security is needed for the 1990s. But that would imply that we should discard the old system and replace it. The whole process of airport security, in place since February 1973, is excellent as far as it goes, and most of it should be retained. The hijack of TWA 847 in 1985, however, and subsequent major attacks on U.S. aircraft have begun to make us think in a different way about implementing airport security. It is no longer acceptable to speak of "beefing up security," which Canadians love to do. It is not a question of throwing more expensive technology at the problem of terrorism in the hopes it will disappear. When describing a "new skin" of security, one is talking about a living, changing organism that covers a body. When skin is absent, there is infection and bleeding. In other words the whole "system" is mutually interdependent. One area of vulnerability affects the whole; thus the analogy of a stretched skin covering the body and masking it from infection and invasion from without is an apt description of airport security. What is needed in the 1990s is a comprehensive, yet flexible, system of aviation security that, while continually in place and working, is nevertheless able to adapt to fluctuations in the terrorist threat worldwide on different levels at different locations and at different times. Good airport security involves planning and anticipation. It involves a delicate balance of human and technological expertise in which the human element takes the lead. Good airport security involves outthinking the terrorist. It also involves close cooperation between all agencies that can, together, block all security loopholes that exist in a process that begins with an individual's decision to buy an airline ticket and ends as the plane leaves the ramp and taxies out for takeoff.[44]

A complete and integrated system of airport security must embrace at least seven facets of the total life of an airport. These seven facets need to work together as one for good security to result. They are:

1. The physical layout and design
2. X-ray and sniffer technology
3. Security personnel
4. The airport's human communities
5. Emergency response teams and policing
6. Shared jurisdictions—airlines, airports, and government
7. The role of the airport manager[45]

Note that diagrams of terror-proof airports can be found in Appendices 5 and 6.

Physical Layout and Design

In describing the relationship of design and layout to security at an airport, it is possible to follow the passenger step by step through his journey. For the passenger, it's a journey, but for airport security personnel it's a process of security in which the chief objective is to keep the terrorist or his bombs off commercial airplanes. As Thomas Ashwood, security chief for the American Air Line Pilots' Association, has said, "If we turn airports into armed camps, the terrorists have won."[46] Therefore the idea behind good airport security must be to keep a balance between freedom of travel and effective, informal security.

Some cities have used downtown terminals in which both tickets and baggage are checked before the bus or quick transit railway even approaches the airport. The airport of the future should seriously consider reviving this habit as much for economic as for security reasons. There is a need to redesign the approach areas in front of terminals, which at present place parking or a drop-off area a short distance from the terminal building. Here, instead, there would be prelimi-nary destination and flight identification for both passengers and their baggage.[47] Passengers would then be whisked to the terminal on moving sidewalks or shuttles by train or bus. Unfortunately, the practice of letting passengers' relatives and friends accompany them to both the airport and the boarding gate would have to end. This process is called sterilization, and it would be very useful in reducing the chronic crowding and confusion at many airports, which creates a nightmare for security and a perfect cover for the terrorist to evade detection. As early as July 1985, Rodney Wallis, director of facilitation and security for the IATA, was arguing that "it may eventually be necessary to keep everyone except passengers with tickets out of terminal buildings."[48] The trade-off here is that air travel has become routine for most citizens, and therefore the social function of airports must bow to the security aspect when airlines world-wide are under terrorist attack. Even the approach to the airport might need to be guarded by a perimeter fence that is intruder sensitive or even patroled by armed guards. Amman Airport in Jordan is equipped with watchtowers and patroled by military police. The same is true for Narita Airport in Tokyo. With the creation of a sterile area beyond the first security checkpoint, as Thomas Ashwood pointed out, "the passenger can be jostled, cajoled, herded and bothered into going in the right direction until he or she reaches a choke point in the path."[49] At present only an hour's lead time is required for passengers on numerous flights originating from the same airport to go through a process of ticketing, check-in, seat assignment, and security. Some of them may want to eat some-thing in a restaurant on the way through or even visit a bar. The passengers also run a gauntlet of specialty shops that often cater to the most bizarre whims and that further impede forward progress.[50]

This is where airport design and layout become all-important. Most North American airports were not built with security in mind, and they are characterized by large crowds of people milling in huge open areas. They were built to accommodate the maximum flow of passengers in and out with a minimum of delay and "choke points."[51] Even Rome and Vienna airports suffer from the large, open concourse system that made it only too easy for the terrorists to create a terrible carnage there in December 1985. The security principle demands that crowds of people be dispersed into small bits of narrow, easily managed space. The smaller the perimeter, the smaller the problem, and the more the situation can be contained.

According to Ashwood, London's Heathrow Airport, Terminal 4, is probably the only security-designed building currently in use. In building it, security experts and architects blended the need for crowd control, direction, and con-tainment with streamlined security checkpoints equipped with the most modern technology of search and detection.[52] Both covert screening and surveillance ability were built into the structure with esthetically pleasing decor so that small areas could be controlled and isolated by few security personnel. Terminal 4 services British Airways and sensitive airlines like El Al.

Continuing on the journey to their flight, the passengers check in at the airline counter, where the next line of security defense is located. It consists of both overt and covert security checks. The famous but still-elusive profile is applied at this point, and the elimination of nonsuspicious people begins. Since the passengers part with their baggage here, a system of passenger and baggage reconciliation must be initiated. In the meantime, the passengers are assigned a boarding gate and a time when they may start the boarding process. Usually, they then go through the formal security clearance with X-ray machines and the arched magnetometer, manned by watchful security personnel. Both overt and covert security can be carried out here as passengers are forced to stop and submit to a search of their person and carry-on luggage. Once this point of search and surveillance has been reached, the passengers are considered to be sanitized. Fingers or concourses radiate outward in most airports, and this hub and spoke design now carries the passengers through a "sterile concourse."

As British security expert Major General Richard Clutterbuck said of the sanitized areas, "Once you are in, you cannot get out. There should be no backwards or sideways, but only straight into an aircraft."[53] The passengers arrive at the boarding gate where they surrender the all-important boarding pass. This is a further opportunity for passenger profiling, before a traveler steps onto the jetway or out onto the ramp.[54] On a high-risk flight a further hand-luggage search, body pat-down, or checkover with a hand-held portable metal detector can be made. At the same time surveillance will continue to monitor all boarding passengers.

Finally, the passengers board the plane, usually by seat numbers, which further breaks up the crowding process. This enables the flight crew to make a fairly close scrutiny of those boarding. Flight crew members are usually properly trained security observers, and since they spend so much of their lives aloft in planes, they have inner sensors that quickly indicate when something or someone is out of place.[55] By breaking up and elongating the whole process of boarding an aircraft, considerable behavioral study of the passengers can take place. For the ordinary, innocent passenger, such a process both calms and builds confidence for a safe journey. But for the terrorist, whose adrenaline is already dangerously high, often with drug-induced stimulants, the whole process of security surveillance is nerve wracking and sometimes fatal. This is just the way that good security would want things to happen.

X-ray and Sniffer Technology

In November 1985 Steven Ashley wrote an article in *Popular Science* entitled "Can Technology Stop Terror in the Air?"[56] In many ways, it's a misleading question since technology is only as good as the human personnel who deploy it. Yet there is a widespread belief that new technology is the answer to sniff out the increasingly deadly bombs being placed aboard commercial airliners.

Such sophisticated technology is needed at the security checkpoints to detect weapons or bombs on the persons or in the carry-on baggage of passengers. It is needed to check the baggage that goes into the cargo hold of the plane.

Technology is needed to detect the presence of weapons on board before the aircraft reaches the point of takeoff. In the form of video cameras and other surveillance paraphernalia, it is also relied upon within the airport. British expert Paul Wilkinson believes that "security *can* be improved without sacrificing passenger convenience by using new technologies for detecting explosives and by designing efficient security systems for checking passengers' identities."[57] He said that more than 90 percent of aviation terrorism now involves the use of false passports. Therefore the introduction of a high technology identity document, a computerized air travel permit the size of a credit card that could be checked against the bearer, would detect many terrorists. The widespread use of stolen passports would be neutralized, and the whole process would not take longer than four seconds.[58] The scheme would be widely emulated once the advantages of better screening and quicker passenger throughput became apparent. Then more time could be spent by security in checking the passengers from countries like North Korea, Libya, and Iran who would undoubtedly refuse to join the scheme. Wilkinson also raised the issue of the obvious gap in security that was exposed by the blowing up of Pan Am 103 over Lockerbie. Clearly, vapor-sniffing machines should be used to augment inadequate X-ray machines.[59] This would call for "a top priority research and development program to develop better explosive detection using neutron bombardment, dielectric measurement and thermal imagery."[60]

There is one advantage on the side of those waging war against air terrorists at the airport terminal and that is that the potential hijacker or saboteur has a relatively limited choice of weapons. Finding these weapons eliminates much of the terrorist threat. He can use guns and knives, but these weapons usually contain enough metal to be caught by baggage X-ray systems or the magnetometer. But the most serious problem arises when the terrorist smuggles or sends explosives aboard an outward-bound airliner. Fortunately, there is one common denominator among almost the entire range of explosives, and that is that they contain nitrogen compounds.[61] That one feature is now the basis of most approaches to bomb detection presently under investigation. According to Stephen Ashley, "the most promising high-technology bomb-detection device . . . is based on a technique called thermal neutron activation."[62] In this system, thermal, or low-energy, neutrons would be directed at luggage passing by on the conveyor belt. If the luggage contained an explosive, a gamma-ray detector would instantly detect the presence of photons and set off an alarm.

Another process under consideration is called chemiluminescence, and it takes advantage of the fact that certain compounds—for instance, explosives—can be made to glow in easily detectable ways under the right conditions.[63] Yet another system would involve a supersensitive chemical detector, now used to analyze air pollution samples and to find cancer-causing additives in preserved meats, adapted into an accurate bomb sniffer.[64] Finally, chemical and electronic tracers can be used as taggants in the electric blasting caps employed in many bombs, making them detectable by using special devices.[65]

By 1989 only one machine, the thermal neutron analyzer, had met the new

FAA standards that require that explosives be detected and diverted without human intervention. These machines can spot a wide range of explosives, including plastic explosives, and by the beginning of 1990, the first six were being installed at a cost of $1 million each. Their reliance on computers gives a quick and usually accurate reading of most baggage. The process has been 95 percent accurate on tests carried out in California. On August 30, 1989, the FAA ordered 40 airports around the world that handled outgoing or incoming planes from the United States to meet the new FAA standards.

According to Carl H. Lavin, in an article entitled "New Machines Can Detect Terrorists' bombs, usually," in the Science Section of the *New York Times,* September 12, 1989, FAA consultant Lee Grodzins of the Massachusetts Institute of Technology said that given enough money, two types of nuclear probes could be ready for airports within three years, which would make it almost impossible to bring an explosive in luggage onto a plane. Apparently, a third technology that detects molecules of explosive material in vapors given off by bags or passengers is already in use at a few airports abroad.

The thermal neutron analyzer passes suitcases through a cloud of subatomic particles and analyzes the radiation produced for signs of nitrogen, which is in all known types of explosives. There is some radioactivity in the baggage as a result, but the shielding material means that the machine weighs almost ten tons. Also the californium type of isotope used might raise objections in nuclear-sensitive countries. But the principal problem, as the public now knows, is that a plastic explosive can be rolled out as thin as two record albums, which would enable it to mimic the density of wool or silk, which also contains nitrogen. The thermal neutron analyzer usually diverts about 4 percent of bags in normal operations, but to detect a one-pound bomb, which was believed to have destroyed Pan Am 103 in December 1988, the false alarm rate would have to go up to about 10 to 15 percent. This would cause an unacceptable time delay for a plane the size of a 747. Thus to improve the process, the FAA has ordered $150,000 X-ray machines that, coupled with the thermal neutron analyzer, would give an even clearer picture of what is inside baggage. The X-ray device would then cut the false alarm rate to about 2 percent. At present the FAA is spending at least $6 million a year on explosives detection, but as Grodzins has pointed out, the development of the two promising new technologies will cost about $10 million each.

Israeli scientists are developing the resonance-absorption method, which calls for an accelerator to shoot protons at a carbon sample that reacts by emitting gamma rays on a particular frequency. The machine would pass a bag through a beam three times at different angles, almost guaranteeing an edge-on view of any sheet explosive. The big advantage of this technique is that fast neutrons produce clear, unique gamma rays from at least three of the important elements that constitute bombs—carbon, nitrogen, and oxygen.

The third device that is being experimented with sweeps up vapor in a collector the size of a hand-held vacuum and chemically analyzes it for molecules of explosive substances. This device cannot find an explosive in a bag, but it can detect explosives carried by people, which is important, since many bombs have been left on aircraft by passengers. In spite of these new and expensive prospective technological solutions to bombs aboard commercial aircraft, however, the need for increased human vigilance will be every bit as important.

In a special report in *Discover* in June 1986, the question of plastic explosives was raised. The report indicated that plastics such as C-4 and Semtex are about one-third again as powerful as TNT, which in turn is about twice as powerful as common dynamite.[66] Plastic explosives were developed during World War II and were useful for their environmental stability. They can be set off only by a detonator. They also can be made to look like bricks, shoe leather, clothesline, or Silly Putty.[67] The detonation velocity of C-4 is 26,400 feet per second, which creates enormous pressure waves that in turn produce a shattering effect called brissance on nearby objects. It would take very few pounds of such a material to make even a jumbo jet such as Air India Flight 182 or Pan Am Flight 103 completely disintegrate without warning. Semtex plastic has more impurities than C-4, and it can ooze vegetable oil when warm. This very feature may have been one of the things that led El Al security men at Heathrow airport to detain Anne-Marie Murphy whose luggage contained enough plastic to have blown up 400 passengers on an El Al jumbo jet on April 17, 1986. Now that plastic explosives have been used on a number of commercial aircraft, there is a race to develop technology that will detect them and at an acceptable price.

Any practical system of security must be able to process at least ten bags per minute. It must be affordable, but above all, it must not cause many delays. Airline executives have stated that each hour a passenger plane is on the ground costs them $20,000.[68] With from two to five bombs coming through in 400 million to 500 million bags each year, a detection system must have a false alarm rate of less than 1 in 200 million bags in order to avoid unnecessary delays.[69]

In Saudi Arabia, Philips Electronic Instruments, Inc., has provided a check-in baggage X-ray screening device that is built right into the ticket counter. In this system, a trained security technician analyzes the X-ray image of checked baggage from a remote location and presses a green for "go" or red for "stop" button, depending on whether he sees weapons. If the baggage looks suspicious, a guard is alerted to do a hand search, and in this way the passenger and baggage are kept together until both have been checked. One remote station can process seven or eight check-in counters simultaneously.

Generally, checked baggage presents a different problem, and sometimes dogs have been used to sniff out explosives, but even dogs become tired of sniffing and after a short period become confused by competing scents. Dogs are also costly to train, have a limited accurate smell effectiveness period, and work better when a specific bomb is being searched for, in an airplane for example.

On May 2, 1986, an explosion aboard a Sri Lankan airliner killed about 20 passengers. The bomb, which may have been planted by Tamil separatists, was hidden among vegetables in the cargo hold of the plane. This incident led to a system whereby air freight is now kept for a period of 24 hours so that any bomb will explode before it reaches the cargo hold of a plane. This is one alternative for poorer countries that cannot afford the very expensive bomb sniffing technology, but there are nevertheless problems and vulnerabilities in a system in which a terrorist can send weapons from an undefended airport system into a highly defended one in the Western world. The West also has to recognize that the level of terrorist technology may be driven up by the level of counterterrorism practiced at major airports. The terrorists' reluctance to use new and unproven technology may ultimately be overcome by their sense of outrage and political desperation. Terrorists usually have fairly limited technical competence, and their prescribed political objectives have drawn many analysts to conclude that terrorism will remain a relatively primitive endeavor. The main problem, then, is not with the technology developed to counter the terrorists' weapons. It rather has to do with the chinks in the armor, the loopholes that are still far too plentiful in a Western commercial aviation system more finely tuned to profitability than to security. In short, where there is a will there is a way.

Colonel William T. Corbett is vice-president and European general manager of International Security Management and has long worked in the field of counter-terrorism. Writing an article in October 1989, in *Security Management,* "Air Terrorism: Flight or Fright," he insisted that the future emphasis in air security must be on people. He believes that properly trained and motivated and well-supervised personnel with standard equipment can mount a successful security program. When conducting surveys, he first looks at the ratio of dollars spent on equipment to dollars spent for initial training, subsequent training, and supervision of personnel. The latter is usually far outspent by the former. He then looks at whether all of the elements of the approved security program are being implemented. There is usually a large discrepancy between promise and performance. In the words of Wilkinson, "With the exception of Israel, no democratic country has been able to sustain the will and sense of urgency to combat aviation terrorism."[70] One wonders how many hijacks and sabotaged planes and deaths it will take to give international aviation the will to mount foolproof airport security.

Security Personnel in Airports

In the wake of the Pan Am 103 disaster in December 1988, the airline commissioned a report from a private security consultant, Isaac Yeffet. Yeffet was director of security for El Al airlines from 1978 to 1984.[71] His 200-page report, based on a survey of 25 Pan Am branches around the world, concluded that "under its security system which is virtually unchanged even now, Pan Am was highly vulnerable to terrorist attack."[72] Running through the whole report are a number of themes that Americans and Canadians will not want to hear at this time, but they are nevertheless both true and very likely prophetic. The seven themes that follow are clearly a warning to American airports to start taking seriously the whole human dimension in airport security.

Yeffet stated, "As international security tightens, the United States, with its lack of safeguards at airports, becomes more inviting to terrorists."[73] It is already well known that American carriers are at particular risk, since 20 percent of all terrorist attacks are carried out against U.S. citizens or property. But America's chief enemies at the moment are the rejectionist Palestinians and the Islamic fundamentalists, both of whom have promised to strike at and in the United States. One secret service official from the State Department has stated that "it's going to come here also, it's just a matter of time."[74] Indeed, North America has been extremely lucky so far in avoiding the kind of attacks that are commonplace in Latin America, Western Europe, the Middle East, and West Asia.

Second, Isaac Yeffet maintained that "there is no airline security in the United States. What little is being done to protect passengers is not done well."[75] It quickly becomes clear that he is criticizing not the considerable expenditure on surveillance and X-ray machines but rather the enormous gaps in the human security that must monitor and interpret these machines. Human security broke down badly at every one of the six major U.S. airports he visited.

Third, Yeffet pointed out that "airline executives have made security a low priority. There is no reason to believe this will change until there is a major disaster at an American airport."[76] By placing expensive machinery (the technological solution) at most major U.S. airports the air carriers feel they are following FAA regulations. In fact, they are hiding behind FAA regulations to avoid blame for both air crashes and the sabotage of planes. They would do better to recognize that security pays for itself in decreased insurance fees and increased ridership.

Fourth, in Yeffet's opinion, "In America there does not seem to be an awareness among security people that seemingly abandoned luggage could pose a threat."[77] Luggage left in European airports has exploded with considerable loss of life, but North American security personnel have little awareness of this fairly simple form of terrorist attack.

The fifth theme mentioned by Yeffet amounts to another major weakness in U.S. security. "The airlines put their trust in gadgets—metal detectors and X-ray machines—spending millions on equipment and little on the people who operate it."[78] Humans alone can make judgment calls. Yet Americans place the decision as to whether or not a plane is secure in the hands of a poorly trained, underpaid, unmotivated, and overworked contract employee. The remarkable success of El Al security is due to the fact that it focuses on the passenger rather than the luggage. In Canada and the United States it's the other way round.

The sixth problem with U.S. airport security lies in the relationship between the FAA and the airlines. The latter rely on FAA regulations to determine security levels; yet the regulations are inadequate. Yeffet said, "Just changing FAA rules won't help. The FAA has to rethink the concept of airport security and reevaluate security systems twice a year. . . . Routine is the enemy of security. As it stands now, American carriers use FAA regulations as a bastion against lawsuits after they fail to prevent disasters."[79]

The central problem in both U.S. and Canadian airports is that the security personnel are completely inadequate for the job. In both countries the government has left the task of maintaining security to the air carriers. The air carriers are in the business of transportation to make money, so it stands to reason that they will hire the security firms who mount the lowest bid for the task of maintaining airport security. The personnel that result from this process are poorly trained, are scarcely motivated, are paid subsistence wages, and are given little incentive to feel good about themselves or their jobs. It is now well known that guards operating the X-ray scanners lose effectiveness after only 20 minutes because of boredom and fatigue. A sensitive supervisor might rotate workers around the different tasks at the magnetometer and the X-ray machine, but the prospect of maintaining this for eight hours completely dooms any possibility of effective security. At Stapleton Airport in Denver, Yeffet spoke to a guard who was responsible for X-raying all baggage for international departures on a 5:30 A.M. to 1:30 P.M. shift. During that time he got time off for lunch and a coffee break. He was paid $3.60 an hour and would be paid $25.00 for each gun he found. The man told Yeffet that his training consisted of one eight-hour session on how to operate an X-ray machine, and he remembered vaguely that the color green was metal; dark spots were usually books but could be bombs, and if he saw something suspicious he was to ask the passenger what it was. If the passenger told him, he was told to trust the answer and let the person go through.[80]

At Pearson International Airport in Toronto, Canada, the top rate of pay for security firm employees in 1988 was $6.25 (CDN) per hour. Each received three days of training, including a lecture from an examiner, a video, a manual, and two-and-a-half days of on-the-job training followed by an examination by a Transport Canada inspector.[81] At least this was the official line, but on March 22, 1988, CBC Television aired a program entitled "On Guard for You: Canada's Shaky Airport System." Transport Canada's director for transportation security and emergency planning, John Rodocanachi, was interviewed first and stated that Canadian airport security was "among the world's best." The interviewer then spoke to individual security employees who said they had no idea what a bomb would look like on the X-ray machine. David Bruce, age 24, working for Metropole Security Services, said he had received a two-and-a-half hour lecture, no practice on the X-ray machine, and no exam and was at work three days later. He had to watch other employees to know how the X-ray machine worked, and after three hours on the job he was detailed to train a new guard. He knew there was a silent alarm to call the Royal Canadian Mounted Police in case of trouble, but he didn't know where it was. Security guards interviewed all stated that working conditions were bad, morale was poor, and there was a 15 to 17 percent turnover in personnel each month. More than half of the guards quit in their first year of work.

At Winnipeg International Airport, a security guard recounted the following points:[82] He found a lack of standardization in the airport among different airlines that left serious security gaps. He stated that the security guards had a demoralizing lack of authority that put them at the mercy of rude or overbearing passengers, that the training system was completely inadequate, and that the attention paid to terrorism was very little. He called the airport a very stressful location to work, since constant delays caused people to miss connecting flights and made them irate and impatient. Stress builds, he said, when long lines of people begin to accumulate at the X-ray choke point. Security breaks down, for airline representatives frequently instruct security people to lower security standards in order to break up the logjam. "No wonder," he said, "the turnover in the job is 100 percent every year; and no wonder I was a supervisor within two months." He added that he became so mesmerized by the process that he failed to realize he was checking the persons of the leader of the national Liberal party and his wife, people he knew well by sight.

Routinely, security personnel are tested by undercover police and journalists, as well as by intelligence operatives, and in a majority of cases they fail to detect weapons. In San Francisco International Airport, Yeffet and a *Life* magazine photographer managed to get a gun and a disarmed grenade past boarding-gate guards by staging a diversion. At the same airport, the two men walked up to a security gate: The photographer set off the metal detectors and rather than empty his pockets, he proceeded to place his coat on top of the X-ray machine. He walked through the magnetometer without setting it off and was promptly handed his coat, which had not been checked.[83]

In April 1988 I was boarding a plane at Reno Airport bound for Canada. When I asked if the film in my camera would be affected by the X-ray machine, the lone security attendant became so irate that he totally forgot to examine either my ticket or my wife's ticket. The tickets were not checked at the boarding gate either, but we felt that more than security was at fault when the plane ran out of fuel in the two-hour flight to Winnipeg and we were forced to land at a military base in North Dakota to refuel.

In his book *The War Against the Terrorists,* counterterrorist expert Gayle Rivers stated, "Security measures taken at airports, I am sorry to report, are largely insufficient."[84] He went on to relate how the frisking process is so poorly done—with guards checking both sides of the torso and both sides of each arm and leg—at some American airports that a knife in the small of his back or an ankle holster would never be detected. Furthermore, Rivers pointed out, airline employees are not kept up to date on changes in terrorist habits and activities. Today many terrorists are indistinguishable from thousands of well-dressed businesspeople.

In 1988 a civil servant of the Manitoba government boarded a plane at Winnipeg International Airport, having flown numerous times on government business. He was carrying a revolver in the modem of his computer. He had successfully convinced countless security personnel in the past that a modem carries data that must not be opened or disturbed. Later on the same day in Halifax Airport, on the east coast of Canada, a security official must have known that hard or floppy disks, and not modems, store information, and the gun was duly discovered. It was one more embarrassment for the Canadian airport security establishment. Even worse was the incident in late 1987, when a security guard "accidentally" passed an Indian baby, wrapped up papoose-style, through an X-ray machine. There was an uproar across the country that should have led to basic changes in the security system. But Canadians, like Americans, refuse to change their way of doing things unless a disaster occurs. Canada did suffer a disaster on June 22, 1985, when 329 died aboard Air India 182, but somehow this still didn't change the system. Perhaps the Canadians were looking to follow an American lead.

Airport security in Western Europe and in most parts of the world now requires that passengers on certain flights and in certain circumstances be questioned. As stated earlier, El Al security agents ask the following questions at the check-in counter: To whom does the luggage belong? Who packed the bags? What presents or gifts are you carrying? Who gave them to you? Where has the luggage been since you packed it? What are you carrying that does not belong to you—or that you do not know the contents of?[85] The questions asked all demand more than a yes or no answer and give security agents a chance to scrutinize people for telltale signs of lying. Frequently, a passenger's eyes or body language will indicate the need for further investigation. In 1980 El Al thus intercepted a German ex-convict who was innocently going to his death, thinking the packet he was carrying, and for which he received a $5,000 fee, was diamonds. It was, instead, four kilos of explosives.[86]

In the United States the FAA requires the airlines to elicit certain information from passengers on international flights, but this job usually falls to the ticket agent, who is probably facing a long line and is certainly too preoccupied to start asking leading questions. Besides, a ticket agent in the United States or Canada lacks the authority to ask serious questions of a suspected terrorist. At San Francisco International Airport, just four weeks after the Lockerbie disaster, Isaac Yeffet watched the loading of a Pan Am flight to Guatemala and El Salvador. Agents boarding passengers asked no security questions.[87] This kind of lax security and the vulnerable airports that result from it are almost certain eventually to attract terrorists.

An absolutely crucial gap in airport security in both the United States and Canada is the lax attitude toward luggage and boxes that are routinely left unattended, around airports. "In America there doesn't seem to be an awareness among security people that seemingly abandoned luggage could pose a threat," said Yeffet. For the most part, he is right, because we have had very few bombings in North American airports. On December 29, 1975, a bomb exploded in the baggage area of La Guardia in New York, resulting in 62 dead or injured, but the memory faded quickly. By contrast, in Western Europe many bombs have gone off in airports. On July 15, 1983, at Orly Airport in Paris, an Armenian bomb exploded, killing 7 and wounding 60 people. In June 1985, at Frankfurt Airport, a bomb exploded inside the terminal just a couple of days before I met my wife arriving off a flight from Canada. On September 14, 1986,

I arrived in Kimpo Airport in Seoul, South Korea, after a 23-hour flight from North America. Just two hours after I left the airport, a bomb exploded in a garbage container, killing 5 and injuring 29 people.[88]

It is because of incidents of this type that unattended luggage is targeted by security within seconds in Israel and Western Europe. The planted suitcase bomb is one of the easiest and deadliest types of terrorist attack. It nearly always kills and wounds, and it creates great fear and insecurity. At Heathrow Airport speakers on the public address system warn passengers in public areas at ten-minute intervals not to leave baggage unattended. The point is, good security must be able to monitor absolutely everything that happens in an airport. But in North America at present, more attention is paid to illegal parking of cars in the airport entrance than to security.

Finally, there is the question of showing airline tickets before boarding planes. Perhaps the worse breach of security in the United States takes place with the curbside check-in system. This allows luggage to go directly to the cargo hold of the plane without being X-rayed and without the bag being opened. For that matter, there is no real check whether passengers owning the suitcases being loaded on the flight will actually board. In the case of Air India 182 in 1985, passengers checking in for other flights remember the anxious behavior of the Sikh who loaded his suitcase at the ticket counter and then left the plane to fly to its doom. In the United States, you frequently do not have to show a ticket to board, and in cold weather, the skycaps huddle inside terminal doors, leaving hundreds of destination tags unguarded.[89] Most Canadian airlines check and recheck passengers' tickets, but the volume of traffic is much less than in the United States.

The very serious and alarming major hijacks since June 1985 have caused some concern in Canada about airport security, but that concern has been voiced mainly by the public, the media, and certain concerned academics who specialize in counterterrorism. The resultant pressure on government has caused a slight upgrading in airport security. Long-planned renovations and additions to Canadian airports were made to look like the creation of a new security system, but within a year of the Air India disaster the Canadian system had lapsed into the same old lethargy, with government ministers and civil servants stating either that security was satisfactory or that improvements would cost too much money. Nevertheless, a parliamentary committee decided in December 1988, after a three-week study of European airports, that the preboarding screening in Canada was inadequate. As a result, the 11 members of parliament involved strongly urged the government, in a report tabled on December 14, to take over full responsibility for security checks of passengers and carry-on luggage. That responsibility is now shared with the airlines. The members of Parliament and members of the House of Commons' Standing Committee on Transport recommended that either Transport Canada or airport operators take over the hiring of screening personnel and train them to work with regional police and the Royal Canadian Mounted Police (RCMP).

In 1989 there was intense airline competition because of deregulation in

Canada, and by February one major airline, Wardair, had been forced out of the marketplace. In such a competitive environment, the airlines will obviously continue to select the cheapest security services available. Steve Vody, a spokesman for Local 2413 of the International Association of Machinists and Aerospace Workers, a union that represents nearly 400 security guards at Toronto's Pearson Airport, stated that airlines should now begin to screen baggage electronically on domestic flights, a procedure that has so far been in place only for international flights. The director of Transport Canada's security replied that domestic baggage screening was both unnecessary and irritating to passengers. Vody replied, "They [Transport Canada] are acting as though we are located on another planet—the Middle East isn't that far away."[90] He added that planes are frequently allowed to take off on international flights with unmatched bags in their cargo holds. Liberal member of Parliament Fernand Robichaud confirmed that the transport committee had learned of 12 such alleged incidents in the past six months. Vody also called for the upgrading of security for carry-on baggage since, "If you let someone through and a bomb does go off, that's a pretty heavy responsibility to ask someone to take for $6 an hour."[91]

The answer to all this attribution of blame and denial of responsibility is, for Canada, that the Department of Transport should be fully responsible for all airport security. Furthermore, the RCMP should take over sole responsibility for airport security, liaising with local police forces. In this way someone would take responsibility for what happened to airports and airplanes, and properly trained law enforcement personnel would bring a new attitude toward airport safety.

In the United States, precisely the same kind of evasion of responsibility takes place. The FAA issues its directives but leaves so much responsibility for security with the airlines that it amounts to a shared jurisdiction. When all goes well, both sides claim the credit, but when disaster strikes, each blames the other for the breakdown. In both Canada and the United States, airport security cannot effectively be carried out either by the air carriers or by airport managers. Airport security is a national responsibility because the airport is now a politically symbolic place.

In rebuttal to Isaac Yeffet's stinging assessment of U.S. airports, the FAA's director of security, Ray Salazar, argued that if threats were to materialize, changes would be made overnight.[92] These arguments really belong to the period before 1985, however, and now, after the Lockerbie disaster, it must be realized that even American airplane security abroad is faulty.

Yeffet and other specialists in security have been consistent in their calls for better airport security. The following changes ought to be considered seriously by both American and Canadian governments:

1. Eliminate curbside check-in and match all bags to passengers.

2. Station security people—not just ticket agents at check-in counters—to ask questions and divert suspicious passengers. The ticket agents' job is to get people on the flight, not keep them off.

3. Mark each bag after it has gone through security and make sure only those bags are loaded.

4. Have special seats on board for suspicious passengers, located where flight crews can monitor them.

5. Keep nonpassengers out of domestic and international concourses.

6. Isolate passengers on connecting flights coming from airports where security is weak and send them through security again.

7. Have one security system for the entire airport. At present, as many as four or five different agencies work the same terminal with little or no coordination.

8. Raise the caliber of security people. Choose bright, educated people; train them well; test them frequently; and pay them a decent wage. At $3.60 an hour, you get what you pay for.

9. Perform preboard security X-rays on all domestic as well as international luggage, but never rely on them exclusively.

10. Take responsibility for security out of the hands of anyone involved in day-to-day flight operations. The security director should have the power to postpone or cancel any flight.[93]

THE AIRPORT'S HUMAN COMMUNITIES

Winnipeg International Airport in Canada was 60 years old in 1988. By that time the airport was generating approximately $250 million worth of economic activity for the city of Winnipeg. According to airport manager George Elliott, "The city has an airport that can support bigger conventions, summer games, you name it. We're the front door to the city and the spinoff benefits can be tremendous in terms of functions the business community can host without fear."[94] What began in 1928 as a small but hopeful enterprise now employs more than 7,000 people, who together facilitate the boarding process for 2.3 million passengers and the arrivals and departures of 150,000 flights each year. As Elliot observed,

an airport is like a city within a city, we maintain our own roads, sewage fire, police and RCMP services. It is costly to run and if we are to continue to maintain our high level of service and meet the demands of a growing flying population we have to develop more ways to generate revenue.[95]

In a forward-looking article in *American Airport Management,* William F. Shea wrote: "U.S. airports are a precious commodity, a true national asset." They are also, he continued, "the gateways to their areas, the real economic generators that create jobs and provide economic progress as well as transportation."[96] He pointed out that JFK International Airport is the largest employer on Long Island. The failure to keep up standards and grapple with increasing traffic can actually cause one city to be bypassed in favor of another in today's deregulated culture. In short, airports are clearly big business.

This is particularly true in the United States, where there are 531 commercial airports and where, by 1992, there will be a total of 3,668 landing facilities. Canada, by comparison, has a total of 139 commercial airports, 10 of which are international facilities. It is little wonder that security in the United States has such a low priority.

It is little wonder, too, that it's difficult to achieve. Each one of the more than 500 American commercial airports is a hive of activity, as any passenger can tell with just a cursory glance outside his window after boarding. On the tarmac are trucks, tugs, carts, all manner of strange vehicles, people in overalls, people in uniform, and people in street clothes all milling around with apparent purpose. To prepare a flight for departure there must be mechanics, baggage loaders, commissary workers or caterers, fuelers, cleaners, lavatory tank trucks and their operatives, and food kiosk workers who work airside of the airport X-ray line. There are people ensuring the safe loading of U.S. or Canadian mail and occasionally armed guards who are supervising the safe loading of bullion or other valuable cargo. Most of the jobs done by these people are paid near the subsistence wage level. Almost inevitably such people are from minority groups, many of them recent immigrants and frequently from countries prone to terrorism. Throughout Europe, for example, guest workers from the Middle East operate food concessions that serve passengers in departure lounges. So, for the most part, the relatively wealthy travel, and their needs aloft are met by workers from the poorer sectors of society, workers who might be forgiven for envying them and who might have cause, as a result of their background or heritage, to wish Western air travelers harm.

It is perhaps because international airport terminals are the crossroads of the world that so many attacks were mounted on them in the 1980s. In an article entitled "International Terrorism and Civil Aviation," Israeli terrorist authority Ariel Merari traced attacks on international civil aviation between January 1, 1983, and December 31, 1987. He found a total of 229 actual or attempted terrorist attacks against civil aviation worldwide. They were carried out against three types of targets: Airlines accounted for 100 incidents or 44 percent of the total; airline offices were attacked in 78 cases or 34 percent of the total, and airports were attacked 51 times or 22 percent of the total.[97] The most frequent mode of attack was bombing, which accounted for 132 incidents or 58 percent.[98] A further breakdown of the distribution reveals that bombings constituted only 20 percent of the attacks on airlines. Nevertheless, this last statistic is nothing from which to take comfort. To circumvent security precautions, terrorists have used a whole range of special methods and means. According to Merari they include such techniques as the recruitment of naive couriers who are unknowingly supposed to die with the other passengers; special explosives and sophisticated concealment methods that would pass ordinary luggage checks; smart detonating methods, such as barometric pressure-operated detonators that activate the bomb when the airplane reaches a predetermined altitude; and sophisticated electronic pressure-activated devices, designed to be concealed under a passenger's seat.

As airport security has tightened up in Western Europe, the terrorists have typically chosen easier targets for their bombs. In the cases of the Armenians at Orly in Paris in July 1983, the Islamic fundamentalists at Frankfurt in June 1985, and the Abu Nidal faction at Rome and Vienna airports in December 1985, the perpetrators were able to walk into a heavily peopled airport area and place bombs or shoot innocent victims with no one even suspecting what was about to happen. In the case of Pan Am 73 at Karachi in 1986 there was proven collusion between airport personnel and the terrorists, who were able to bypass the security process completely and enter the plane from the airport apron. In the case of the Air Lanka explosion of May 1986, the bomb is reported to have gone off in a container of vegetables. In still other hijacks, including TWA 847, the cleaning staff must have placed grenades and guns in the washrooms of planes that the terrorists could easily pick up during the flight. The clear message from all of these developments is that the various human communities of the airport can just as easily be used by terrorists in attempting to bypass increasingly effective security.

The only way to counter the terrorist exploitation of the human communities is through better intelligence. To begin with, it is necessary to check the background of each employee thoroughly and to insist that all ground crew wear ID tags whenever they go airside of the airport security zone. But that is only the beginning, since airport ID has proven no harder to come by for a determined terrorist than fake passports. What is more, pressure can be so easily exerted on a previously reliable employee to carry out terrorist instruction by the simple expedient of advising him of the danger to his family that a refusal might entail. It is not ony in poorer countries that people can be tempted by money to place a little plastic bag in a lavatory of an aircraft. Local dissident nationals have helped to effect the death of passengers on hijacked planes. Then, as Gayle Rivers pointed out,

Can you blame airline X that it didn't know of all of the affiliations of that attractive reservations clerk, whose current boyfriend happened to be a member of Abu Nidal's hit squad, and asked her to do a small favour by putting his heavy suitcase on the conveyor belt to save him overweight charges on a flight that he, as it happened, didn't take?[99]

With the right sort of bribe any number of people in the communities serving a plane could be talked into placing a small plastic bag inside an airplane. After all, much of the drug traffic is well known to be traveling via airport baggage handlers. If one of these people were to see that a plane subsequently blew up in midair, he would be far too frightened to come forward and admit to placing a bomb. Indeed, this may be the answer as to how the bomb got aboard Pan Am 103.

The Canadian approach to tightening security among the airport's human communities may be a sad and cautionary tale for American authorities. In the wake of the worst terrorist attack on an airliner in aviation history, that of Air India 182 in June 1985, Canadian authorities came to the conclusion that a contributing factor was a lapse in security procedures when a CP Air check-in agent was persuaded to allow an unaccompanied suitcase aboard the Air India B747. There was likely another slipup when the Condor sniffer was applied to the suitcase containing the bomb. Apparently, it made a smaller noise than it had when it was earlier demonstrated to the employee using it, and so the suitcase was passed through because of assumed malfunction of the Condor. These were just two of several instances when better training could have saved the lives of 329 people.

Following the Air India tragedy, the Canadian government ordered a $60 million program to upgrade airport security. This applied, in particular, to Canada's 50,000 to 60,000 airport workers, who were now to be screened before being issued restricted-access ID passes for working airside of airport security. The situation was typically worse at Toronto's Pearson Airport, which handles 46 percent of Canada's international passenger traffic.[100] There, more than 10 percent of the 29,500 employees had not been screened for security risks. They included baggage handlers, check-in attendants, and security guards. It was also found that across the country more than 7,000 airport workers did not have permanent Transport Canada passes, which are issued only after they have passed a security check.[101] The turnover was so high among security guards that often a guard had moved on before the Canadian Security and Intelligence Service (CSIS) could get around to checking the individual's background. Therefore, Transport Canada had to bend its own rules and issue thousands of temporary passes to airport employees.

At Toronto Airport, 17,000 airside security passes had been issued to personnel by May 1986, but the governing and issuing body for these security passes, Transport Canada, either ignored or chose not to have the mandate to check an applicant's immigration, criminal, or subversive status before issuance of a pass. Such passes allow access to almost anywhere in Pearson International. It was then found that a number of airport employees, legally in possession of security passes, were illegally resident in Canada. Until May 1986, Canadian immigration investigators had arrested six such illegals working at Pearson Airport. The ultimate black humor of this situation was that although Transport Canada had issued security passes to illegals, they refused immigration investigators the same passes to assist in the investigation of the illegals. In eary 1986, a cleaning company supervisor at the airport was charged with knowingly employing illegal immigrants after investigators found two cleaners with forged social insurance cards.[102]

As one police investigator said in frustration: "It's ludicrous, the airport here in Toronto has no employee security whatsoever. They hand out passes without any checking of any kind. It's made to order for terrorism."[103] Unfortunately, this was not the end of the matter, for on September 30, Transport Minister John Crosbie announced that along with screening procedures the federal government would start fingerprinting all airport workers. This provoked sharp criticism by the union, which represents 8,500 maintenance and ramp workers across the country.[104] The union leader said he was not opposed to better security at Canadian airports, "but what is the point of fingerprinting our members when there is only a cheap, eight-foot chain-link fence around the perimeter of Toronto International Airport? There are no surveillance cameras. Anyone who wants to get in can do it.''[105]

After this distressing litany of inefficiencies one might be tempted to throw up one's hands and simply say that airport security is impossible because of the large human communities and the huge economic interests at stake. But this need not necessarily be so. Rather, governments in both Canada and the United States have steadily refused to take full and direct responsibility for airports in the same way they have done for other politically significant symbols of power.

In the United States a computerized card access security control system will soon be required at 269 airports as a result of amendments to the FAA's Federal Aviation Regulation 107, which deals with airport security. This ruling, which was passed in the spring of 1988, came in the wake of the Pacific Southwest Airlines crash of a British Aerospace 146, believed to have been caused by a former US Air employee who opened fire with a gun while the plane was in flight. Under the proposal, computerized control systems must be capable of granting access to secured airfield areas to authorized personnel only and denying access to unauthorized personnel. As Karl Bremer, managing editor of *Airport Services,* wrote,

Most systems allow for additional means of identification to be used in conjunction with the cards to prevent the use of lost or stolen cards before their access authorization can be revoked. The most common method is a personal identification number assigned to each card holder that must be entered on a key pad at the access point and verified by the card holder. Other backup techniques used to positively identify card holders include eye retina scanners, digitized images or finger prints, and voice prints.[106]

Unfortunately, a controversy has developed about the cost to the industry over a ten-year period. According to the FAA, the cost of these systems would be $149.5 million in 1987 dollars.[107] But the Airport Operator's Council International (AOCI) has pegged the total cost to the industry at nearly $878 million in 1988 dollars, excluding maintenance. The FAA apparently estimated that an average of 128 doors per airport would require control systems. But the industry found that closer to 260-280 doors would need security controls.[108] A preliminary survey at Miami International found that almost 900 doors would require security controls.[109] Apart from the cost, computerized card access control is a new concept for most airport managers, and some may well feel overwhelmed by the array of systems and techniques available to choose from. For now, a coalition of aviation groups have proposed a lead airport program in 4 selected airports to be used as a guide to designing systems for the other 266 airports. In French airports new identification cards with magnetic information strips and visual code bars will eventually be issued to all employees, from airline workers to cleaning crew personnel. The estimated cost is about 100 million francs, or $17 million.[110] For the larger airports of the world the computerized system will be a necessity for security in the near future. But for smaller airports, like the one in Grand Forks, North Dakota, Director Robert Selig said, "We watch for foreigners on the ramp, and you can always tell when someone is there who ought not to be, because he doesn't know how to behave there. He sticks out like a sore thumb."[111] Selig also confirmed that FAR 107 requires verification of an employee's background for the past five years. The turnover in personnel at Grand Forks is very small, and so the security community develops a quick sense of an intruder. In a larger international airport, like the one in Winnipeg, only 150 miles north across the border, the sense of community is much weaker. At Toronto's Pearson Airport or Chicago's O'Hare, there is not even a faint hope of community operating among thousands of employees. There, computerized security systems, with their own attendant bureaucracy, need to be put in place.

POLICING AND EMERGENCY RESPONSE TEAMS

Under the constitution and laws of the United States, the protection of life and property and the maintenance of public order are primarily the responsibilities of state and local governments, which have necessary authority to enforce the laws.[112] The federal government may assume this responsibility and this authority only in certain limited circumstances.[113] Since most major acts of terrorism are violations of both state and federal law, concurrent criminal jurisdiction is usually the rule. Thus the federal government can either act or defer to state jurisdiction, depending on the incident. Those terrorist incidents that involve some sort of crisis interaction between perpetrators and government require careful management and are termed "incidents of duration."[114] Crisis management for a specific terrorist incident is exercised by that agency which has the primary responsibility by virtue of constitutional or statutory authority or executive branch directive or understanding.[115] As stated earlier, the U.S. Senate wanted a federal force in place at airports as early as 1974, but the House of Representatives balked at the idea, and so a local program was decided upon. The 1974 act states that operators of airports "regularly serving CAB certified air carriers are required to establish security programs that provide a law-enforcement presence. The operators may use the services of qualified state, local and private security people."[116] In the case of Grand Forks Regional Airport, the local Grand Forks police are contracted to arrive within 15 minutes of an emergency call from the airport. As Robert Selig pointed out, "If the incident at an airport remains within the airport, it comes under state law and therefore, the criminal jurisdiction of the local police."[117] In the case of larger airports, there is authority for the airport operator to have its own police force on hand at all times. In 1979 the American Air Line Pilots Association strongly protested an FAA ruling that removed the armed policeman at each screening location and freed him to roam, alone or in groups with his colleagues, throughout the airport. The pilots' reasoning was that a visible law enforcement officer was a deterrent to would-be hijackers. But modern thinking, and that of the FAA, is that a group of law enforcement officers approaching a hostage or hijack situation would have a better chance of taking the initiative to terminate the incident.

But the moment a plane is hijacked, the incident falls under the jurisdiction of the FAA and the FBI. The FBI has regional offices all over the United States. These offices have contingency plans for acts of terrorism; they have hostage negotiators and psychologists. Their Special Operations and Research Unit (SOAR) is made up of FBI special agents who are trained in psychology and criminology and are available during a terrorist incident. In addition, the FBI has Special Weapons and Tactics (SWAT) teams, trained for use in a situation such as a siege or hostage taking. The SWAT approach is the last resort when negotiations fail.[118] If a domestic terrorist incident cannot be resolved by civil police forces, the military force option would be used. This might involve the Delta forces of the U.S. military which are usually employed for overseas use.

It is probably relevant to mention Canada's very different policy at airports, since there is so much traffic between the two countries and since a number of hijacks have operated back and forth between the United States and Canada. The Canadian Airport Security Program is based on federal government ownership of all 139 airports in Canada. Security is primarily the responsibility of Transport Canada.[119] In Canada the screening of passengers and their carry-on baggage is the responsibility of the air carriers, and Transport Canada provides screening equipment, sets standards, and supplies training programs to the air carriers.[120] The solicitor general is the lead minister for managing hostage-taking situations that require federal government involvement. He is responsible for the RCMP, which, by virtue of a Memorandum of Agreement with Transport Canada and a mandate from the federal cabinet, has responsibility for the provision of police and security services at 10 international airports and 8 of the largest major domestic airports. The RCMP Airport Policing Program is currently being enhanced; however, it does not affect the responsibilities of the local police with criminal jurisdiction at these 18 airports. The police continue to be responsible for enforcement of the Criminal Code and provincial statutes. In 1986 the Special Emergency Response Team (SERT) was created in Canada to deal with terrorists and hostage situations. It was attached to the RCMP, rather than the Department of National Defence, which was a surprise. The SERT is Canada's principal antiterrorist assault force, though logistical support would have to come from the Department of National Defence, and there is no legal provision for it to act overseas.[121] Apparently, the location of the SERT within the national police force was not without precedent. A review of the practice of 24 Western and other governments in the location of their national terrorist emergency response teams showed that in 14 countries the armed forces were responsible, in 6 countries the national police were responsible, and in 3 countries a hybrid system existed.[122]

In the United States, the federal air marshal program—not to be confused with the sky marshal program of the early 1970s—began in 1980. The air marshal program has created

an elite group of highly-trained aviation security professionals who work in teams and in very close co-ordination with airlines and flight crews. Their primary responsibilities include checking airport and aircraft security while on assignment—monitoring passenger screening operations, inspecting cargo and baggage-handling activities and ensuring that airport operations areas, roads and perimeters are secure.[123]

Assigned only to high-risk or known-risk flights, they are "highly trained aviation security specialists with major responsibility for establishing and checking pre-boarding and ground security at airports used by U.S. carriers and by carriers flying into the United States."[124] An important aspect of the program is the requirement that flight crews not only are informed when air marshals are to be aboard but also participate in a preflight security coordination briefing.[125] This FAA program, enhanced through the revision of FAR 108 in the wake of the TWA 847 hijack in 1985, could become a crucial and effective force in the struggle against terrorism, especially if an assault on the American domestic civil aviation system ever develops.

SHARED JURISDICTIONS: AIRPORTS, AIRLINES, GOVERNMENTS

Governments, airlines, and airports share jurisdiction when it comes to security. Their interests do not always coincide though, and when conflict arises, security suffers. Usually, airport and airline management get along, since they share the same facilities and have the same interests. "Unfortunately, this level of cooperation is lacking on the part of some governments," said Rodney Wallis, director of security for IATA, "and a lot of work remains to be done between airports, airlines and governments. All too often, governments have made decisions in isolation which have actually led to a decrease rather than an increase in the effectiveness of security measures."[126] But even airport managers and airline executives can disagree. In May 1986 the forty-eighth annual conference of the American Association of Airport Executives was held in Seattle. According to a report on the conference, "Airport Security issues rising from the increasing threat of international terrorism are among top concerns of U.S. airport owners and operators, while U.S. airlines regard the level of concern as unjustified."[127] Richard Lally, Air Transport Association assistant vice-president for security, characterized concern in the news media and on Capitol Hill for the security of air travel as being unfounded. "The facts do not support that high level of concern, and if people are really worried about the state of their travel they probably ought to worry more about getting into their automobile to go to the airport than about the second leg of their trip on the aircraft."[128] Obviously, Lally had no idea what casualties would soon be affecting U.S. airlines. In June 1987 the FAA responded to criticism of U.S. airport security from Congress with the following statistics:

The FAA monitors airline security procedures closely and from 1982 to 1986 issued 197 enforcement actions resulting in $275,661 in fines to the airlines. During that time, more than seven billion passengers and nine billion pieces of luggage were inspected, with 36,000 firearms detected and more than 15,000 related arrests. By our count, 117 hijackings or related crimes against aviation were prevented.[129]

The FAA further pointed out that research and development funding for security equipment had increased from $1 million-$2 million before 1985 to $11 million-$12 million per year in the last two fiscal years.[130] From September to December 1986 screening personnel detected 79 percent of the test weapons for X-ray tests, 82 percent for metal-detector tests, and 81 percent for physical search tests.[131] Other congressional criticism was directed at U.S. airlines, which were accused of a penny-pinching attitude toward security. The Air Transport Association "disagreed that airlines are cutting corners on security, saying the industry accepts it as a cost of doing business."[132] Also, U.S. airlines spent about $200 million annually in passenger screening alone within the United States. Lally estimated that the real overall cost was closer to $500 million a year.

But the destruction of Pan Am 103 suddenly transformed a situation of domestic bickering into one of urgent need to cooperate in the struggle against the new form of terrorism called airplane sabotage. One of the first moves by the FAA, responding to widespread criticism of security on the Pan Am flight, was to order the computerized card access security control systems mentioned earlier. Immediately, both airlines and airports replied that the FAA order was too abrupt and not thought through carefully enough from a cost perspective. In January 1989 one U.S. official said,

the FAA has made the U.S. airlines responsible for working out the new security arrangements, even when this requires dealing with foreign governments, police and military authorities and airport operators. The FAA puts the responsibility of implementing the security squarely on the shoulders of U.S. airlines, while in Europe it is generally governments that handle it.[133]

As a result, U.S. airlines asked the federal government to take a more active role in securing airports and aircraft. They wanted FAA inspectors to be stationed at high-threat locations overseas and asked the government to "oversee, co-ordinate, assist and monitor and deal with the host governments."[134] The airlines also expressed the desire to have the ICAO create an international police force under its auspices in Montreal.

In Britain, immediately after the Pan Am 103 bombing, the Department of Transport said primary responsibility for security at airports lay with the airport operator and secondary responsibility with the airline. But the British Airport

Authority, which operates Heathrow and other major British airports, referred all security questions to the Department of Transport, stating that security operations at the airport were the responsibility of the British government.[135] Not to put too fine a point on the matter, both government and the airports and airlines were trying to distance themselves from being saddled with responsibility for the bombing.

In Britain three levels of airline security have been established. The highest is for El Al, the second level is for U.S. flag carriers, and the third is for European and Asian carriers. Transport Secretary Paul Channon, under attack in Parliament for inadequate airport security, ordered a postcrash review of airport security arrangements. But this kind of intense pressure situation served only to complicate, not to integrate and solidify, cooperative relations among airlines, airports, and governments.

The destruction of Pan Am 103 has had a traumatic effect on the security planners in Western countries, although diplomatic delays, bureaucratic inertia, and the inevitable practical difficulties of changing airport and airplane routines have stood in the way of reforms. John H. Cushman, writing for the *New York Times* news service in May 1989 stated "that a few airports had found it impossible so far to implement a demanding new rule calling on all U.S. airlines to inspect with x-rays or by hand every piece of luggage leaving Europe or the Middle East."[136] To help foreign airlines comply with their new role, which called on them to obtain the agency's approval for security on flights to and from the United States, the FAA drafted a model security plan. The French government balked over the new rules and launched a diplomatic protest, but the commercial need to continue flights to the United States will quickly bring it into line. Raymond Salazar, associate administrator for aviation security at the FAA said, "if we are going to fight a common enemy, terrorism, it isn't sufficient that one state have very good security and another mediocre and another none at all. We all must basically strengthen together."[137] Despite disagreements, officials in Europe achieved substantial cooperation over security, and Aurello Cozzani, the Italian Interior Ministry's police director said, "the problem of terrorism has done a lot to break down bureaucratic barriers. We security people are in very direct, personal communication with our colleagues from other European countries and from the U.S."[138] In West Germany, France, Italy, and Greece, airlines and government agencies are not waiting for the ICAO to act. They are investing in new security equipment, adding to their security staffs, and imposing new procedures that inevitably slow passenger traffic.[139] The conclusion to be reached then is that the Lockerbie disaster seems to have pushed governments, airlines, and airports together in necessary cooperation because of possible future threats of the same nature.

THE ROLE OF THE AIRPORT MANAGER

Airport managers seem to be shy, unseen people with little desire for life in the limelight. They are administrators responsible for a small village situated within a city, though admittedly, the village is a high-tech endeavor with a disproportionate volume of human traffic. But increasingly, terrorism is forcing airport managers out into the open and directing their concerns more and more toward security. At The Hague Conference on Aviation Security in January 1987, Jan Willem Wegstapel, president of Schiphol Airport in The Netherlands, said,

I think that airports are playing a key role in preventing aviation terrorism. Also because according to AACC, the Airport Associations Coordinating Council, which represents the two international airport associations, AOCI and ICAA and their 400 member-airports in over 100 countries throughout the world, aviation security must be regarded as the most serious challenge civil aviation is facing today.[140]

In the two years after the TWA 847 incident, Wegstapel pointed out, far more security personnel had been deployed in airports; security measures at check-in and boarding positions had been stepped up and tightened; and airports and airlines had greatly tightened security procedures and had taken steps to reduce the number of staff with access to airside operation or restricted areas. All of these measures had been time-consuming, expensive, and a cause of upheaval and had certainly detracted from the traditional economic role the airport had come to play in modern society. Security had to react to the increased attacks on airports, and as Wegstapel pointed out: "Airports have realized that they are actually the last line of defence against acts of violence."[141] This meant that the Airport Associations Coordinating Council (AACC), IATA, ICAO, and FAA are just some of the organizations putting increased pressure and demands on the airport manager. It is interesting that in his speech to the delegates, Wegstapel stated categorically that existing security should be greatly improved before any contemplation is given to banning well-wishers from the terminal building:

If we should do so, for instance, at Amsterdam's Schiphol Airport, it would, among other things, mean that we would have to close down all public restaurants and shopping facilities outside the customs area, simply because there would not be enough customers to make such facilities profitable. I wonder whether we do not submit too easily to fear when we forbid non-passengers to enter the airport compound.[142]

Wegstapel said that airports must not be turned into armed camps, for they are by definition places of an open character; that airport designs had not taken security into consideration at all; and that airports should refrain from competing with each other while striving for a uniformly high standard of effective security. He repeatedly insisted "that governments have the ultimate responsibility to fight terrorism" but that airlines and airports should assist them in cooperation with the ICAO.[143] In his closing remarks, he hinted that the Dutch government was threatening to erode its longtime management role in the field of security and make its airports shoulder both the responsibility and the cost for airport security. Traditionally, European governments have taken responsibility for security measures, but an erosion of that responsibility, presumably in the interests of cost cutting, could unload enormous burdens on airport managers, burdens they cannot and should not be asked to carry.

An airport manager can positively and cost-effectively affect security by controlling the nature of information that is divulged to the public through the media. When security is poor and muddled and disorganized at a major international airport, like Toronto's Pearson, members of the media delight in writing about the airport's shortcomings. They seek to prove its vulnerability by attempting to test the airport's security themselves. Although this may prod governments into upgrading security, what it is more likely to do is present an invitation to terrorists. Here is an airport worth attacking, such reporting says. Design problems, hopeless overcrowding, extreme inefficiency, and a lot of media attention have made Pearson International absolutely ripe for a major terrorist incident. Many major U.S. airports are also in a similar situation, and only time will test whether or not they are ready for a determined terrorist attack.

Robert Selig manages the Grand Forks, North Dakota, international airport, which, he estimated, generates just over $100 million a year in direct and indirect economic activities. He likened an airport to a hospital, "in that you use it only when you need it, always count on it being there, are annoyed if it is not working properly and certainly don't expect it to impede your quick progress about your own business."[144] Selig believes that terrorists will tend to hit the major airports of the world because they are interested in the widest possible publicity. He said one has to decide on a certain level of security and then get on with the job of getting people through in the quickest possible time. "You have to find a balance," he said, "between treating 99 per cent of people as normal honest human beings and yet keeping the guns and knives out of the planes."[145] Selig believes that the main weakness of the U.S. airport system is the problem of reverse screening. Passengers coming from a small airport to a larger hub airport mingle with other screened passengers in a large concourse area, and this is when a terrorist could easily strike because he has not been adequately screened for the continuation of his journey.

A determined continuation of international terrorist attacks against civil aviation or even a series of attacks against North American airports could make the careers of airport managers short, stress filled, and unpopular.

A LOOK AT MAJOR INTERNATIONAL AIRPORTS

The system of airports in the United States is the largest and most complex in the world. At the end of 1984, there were 16,075 airports on record with the FAA. Of them, 4,806 were publicly owned, and the rest, 11,269, were privately owned. See figure 2. These figures for airports account for almost half of the world's total. Yet even this statistic inadequately conveys the extent and volume of aviation activity in the United States. The United States has half of the world's airports, but it also claims two-thirds of the world's 400 busiest airports in terms of passenger enplanements. Collectively, U.S. airports handled more than 343

Figure 2

U.S. Civil and Joint-Use Airports, Heliports, STOLports, and Seaplane Bases on Record by Type of Ownership as of December 31, 1984

TOTAL and STATE	Total Facilities	By Ownership Public	Private	Paved Airports[1] Lighted	Not Lighted	Unpaved Airports[1] Lighted	Not Lighted
Total	16,075	4,806	11,269	3,446	367	506	1,257
United States Total[2]	16,009	4,761	6.905	3,426	362	506	1,244
1. Texas	1,556	329	1,237	308	28	11	63
2. Illinois	901	99	802	89	1	20	8
3. California	881	302	579	206	51	1	14
4. Pennsylvania	708	78	630	92	6	27	38
5. Ohio	689	132	557	122	2	28	43
6. Alaska	609	405	204	35	5	50	236
7. Florida	542	132	410	94	11	10	19
8. Indiana	495	80	415	79	4	9	27
9. Minnesota	480	147	333	93	1	36	21
10. New York	480	83	397	84	12	25	51
11. North Dakota	457	94	363	62	4	16	24
12. Michigan	427	132	295	116	9	35	64
13. Missouri	423	122	301	109	6	11	24
14. Wisconsin	413	104	309	97	5	16	29
15. Washington	385	121	264	79	12	13	29
16. Kansas	384	131	253	101	5	25	27
17. Nebraska	341	95	246	73	3	12	23
18. Oregon	336	96	240	53	17	9	27
19. Oklahoma	335	137	198	113	10	7	40
20. Louisiana	317	77	240	61	6	1	15

[1]Among public use airports only.
[2]Excludes Puerto Rico, Virgin Islands, N. Mariana Islands, and South Pacific.

Source: FAA

million passenger enplanements, both domestic and international, in 1984, more than three-quarters of the world's total outside the Soviet Bloc. Since 1982, the FAA has classified airports in four major categories: *Primary airports,* which are public-use commercial airports enplaning at least 0.01 percent of all passengers annually enplaned in the United States; *commercial service,* which are public-use airports receiving scheduled passenger service and enplaning at least 2,500 passengers annually; *general aviation airports*, which are strictly for private and business aircraft and have fewer than 2,500 annual enplanements; and *reliever airports* for relieving congestion.[146]

The 281 primary airports, or less than 2 percent of the total in the United States, handle virtually all airline passengers. Roughly half of the primary airports handle very little traffic, just 5 percent of the total annual enplanements. The top 20 airports account for almost two-thirds of all enplanements and the top 10 account for 40 percent. "In fact," said Alexander T. Wells, "close to one-quarter of all airplane passengers board their flights at one of just five airports—Chicago O'Hare, Atlanta Hartsfield, Los Angeles, Dallas–Fort Worth, and New York Kennedy.''[147] Metropolitan areas are designated ''hubs'' by the FAA and are divided into four classes according to percentage of the total passenger enplanements: large, medium, small, and nonhub.[148] Twenty-six large hubs handle 72-80 percent of all traffic.

According to Wells in his book *Airport Planning and Management,* published in 1984, the airports with the largest volume of traffic in the United States were Chicago's O'Hare with 19.1 million enplanements annually, Atlanta–Hartsfield (18.9), Dallas–Fort Worth (15.3), Los Angeles (14.5), Denver (12.8), Newark (11.7), New York–JFK and San Francisco (both 10.5), and New York–La-Guardia (9.4).[149] An updated rating of the ten busiest airports in the United States four years later in the January 1988 issue of *Condé Nast Traveler* shows O'Hare with 54.7 million enplanements annually, Atlanta–Hartsfield (45.1), Dallas–Fort Worth (39.9), Denver–Stapleton (34.6), Newark (29.4), St. Louis–Lambert (20.3), Detroit–Wayne County (17.6), Minneapolis–St. Paul (17.0), Greater Pittsburgh (15.9), and Charlotte–Douglas (11.9).[150]

The following study of terrorist attacks on airports was based on two sources. The first is the FAA study, which is hemispherically oriented. The result can be seen in figure 3. The emanating airports of the FAA list of hijacks from 1931 to 1988 was analyzed, and topping the list were Miami (with 29 hijacks); New York (26); Beirut (22); Los Angeles (15); Chicago (13); San Juan, Havana, Prague, and Frankfurt (all with 10 hijacks); and Barranquilla, Colombia (9). The second source of attacks on airports is less complete statistically and deals predominantly with the European and Middle Eastern traffic between 1968 and 1988. It comes form Christopher Dobson and Ronald Payne's *Never-Ending War.* The result is Paris and Rome (10 incidents); London (8); Athens and New Delhi (7 each); Vienna, Frankfurt, and Tel Aviv (all with 6); Karachi and Tokyo (both with 5); and Amsterdam (4).[151] These statistics do not prove a great deal, though they do provide a network of the most hijack-prone airports. There is, in fact, not a great deal of evidence to back up *Newsweek*'s 1985 summary of the most unsafe airports being Athens, Beirut, Karachi, New Delhi, Manila, Teheran, Tripoli, Conakry, Lagos, and Yaounde. It is true that the first six have experienced a lot of political instability, but the list is typically uncritical of the American condition, especially when the FAA listing shows that four of the five most hijacked airports in the world are in the United States. Toronto could also be added to the list as one of the most unsafe and potentially terrorist-prone airports in the world. In his *Life* magazine article of January 1989, Isaac Yeffet made serious criticisms of the terrorist vulnerabilities of La Guardia Airport in New York, O'Hare in Chicago, Stapleton in Denver, Miami International, Los Angeles International, and John F. Kennedy Airport in New York. It will be interesting to see what changes come about, as a result of this widely read article.

In early 1989 John H. Cushman examined European airports for the *New York Times* news service and found a mixed picture. He dealt with Heathrow and

Figure 3
Emanating Airports of FAA List of Hijacks, 1931-1988

Miami	29
New York	26
Beirut	22
Los Angeles	15
Chicago	13
San Juan	10
Havana	10
Prague	10
Frankfurt	10
Barranquilla	9
Paris	8
Caracas	8
Newark	8
Tokyo	7
Mexico City	7
Rome	7
Atlanta	7
San Francisco	7
Bogota	7
Istanbul	7
Teheran	7
New Delhi	7
Athens	6
Gdansk	6
Buenos Aires	6
London	6
Amman	5

Gatwick in London and with Paris, Frankfurt, Rome, and Athens. Heathrow is perhaps the busiest airport in the world with approximately 35 million passengers a year. New government rules have demanded a much closer inspection of items taken on board, including radios and computers. High-risk flights, including American carriers, have all checked baggage screened. Both government and the aviation sector have recently been embarrassed by incidents of deliberate unauthorized entry. In one case, reporters disguised as cleaners gained access to airliners. Worse, three youths climbed aboard an empty British

Airways jumbo jet and filmed themselves in the cockpit. In an in-house report more than 100 security flaws were found at Heathrow. Gatwick is installing a machine using thermal neutron analysis to detect plastic explosives. It is being installed by the United States for its flights through London, but its capacity is restricted to only one jumbo jet each hour.[152]

In Paris the security at both Orly and Roissy-Charles de Gaulle airports is directly controlled by the government through three of its police agencies. The United States and Israel hire their own security people in Paris; otherwise, as the security director for the French civil-aviation agency, Jean-François Bouisset, said, "we are not going to privatize security. We want the state and only the state, to be in control."[153] Bouisset also complained that small independent security services at Paris airports were complicating the task of the French police forces in charge. In 1989 Pan Am increased its security force by 50 percent adding 74 people, and under instruction by the FAA it sought to install new X-ray machines, but French authorities complained that they were obstructing movement at the airport. Bouisset insisted that the growing congestion around U.S. ticket counters "may actually attract terrorists."[154] For flights of El Al and Air India and U.S.- and Israel-bound flights, all considered "sensitive," the French have guarded enclosures where all checked or transferred baggage is X-rayed and hand luggage is searched.

Unlike the French procedures, the West German procedures at Frankfurt diverge from those recommended by the Americans. For instance, many but not all bags are X-rayed. The airport also has a special low-pressure chamber in which some luggage, but not all, is tested under decompression. Another difference is that the Germans believe the thermal neutron analysis is "theoretically functional, but not yet practically applicable."[155] Lufthansa, however, is not resisting the FAA's rule calling for the filing of security plans for its flights to the United States as have the French.

At Rome's airports, security is often cited as being among the best even though flights are delayed, armed guards are everywhere, and confusion appears to reign. Extra-tight security is imposed whenever the pope goes on one of his worldwide trips. Rome's security begins well before arrival at the airport as police monitor traffic. Selected people are searched by armed police at the airport entrances. Check-in counter employees interrogate passengers, referring some of them to police for further searches. Passengers then go through metal detectors, their luggage is X-rayed, and their carry-on luggage is limited to one piece, which is carefully examined. A final check is carried out at the boarding gate where some passengers may be searched again. Police cars escort buses across the runway for boarding, and police monitor the boarding of planes parked near the terminal. Armed cars escort the planes when they taxi, and police guard parked planes. Police regularly inspect the documents and bags of cleaners, caterers, and technicians. In an unusual procedure, the Italians even use a helicopter to escort high-risk planes when they take off.[156] The Italians are sanguine about the new American regulations and have tried to meet all the FAA demands, but as Aurelio Cozzani, police director of the Italian Ministry of the Interior, said, "There is such a thing as national sovereignty and they cannot expect to dictate the same regulations for the entire world as if it were all the United States territory."[157]

Athens airport is the only one ever publicly identified by the United States as unsafe from a security stand point. Although Athenian authorities insist this has changed, many travelers, journalists, and security people have noticed considerable discrepancies in Athens' security system. There is concern that as the European Community moves toward eliminating most border controls by 1992, that Greece will be a soft spot in the overall security system.

In the final analysis, there remain some fundamental differences between U.S. and Western European airport security. The latter airports have experienced sustained attack by politically motivated terrorists, many of them members of expatriate communities living within the European capitals. The European approach has been to increase the quality of human security in its airports and at the same time insist on maintaining normal relations with other Mediterranean and Middle Eastern countries. Such a strategy has refused to acknowledge terrorism as anything more than a temporary and manageable nuisance. On the other hand, the American approach has been to rely heavily on technology, and because its many airports and heavy air traffic have been virtually untouched by the political terrorists, it has not concentrated on the human side of security. Under President Reagan, terrorism was designated the foremost enemy of the democracies; therefore it was much easier to insist that European airports elevate their standards to protect American travelers than it was to insist on similar action at home in the United States.

Continental North America has been incredibly lucky so far, but the dream cannot last forever. It has been virtually untouched by political terrorists. In trying to safeguard its nationals in Europe, the United States is really dictating security to the Europeans through the FAA. But if politically motivated attacks begin in the United States and Canada, Europeans may make uncomfortable demands on North America that we will have great difficulty in meeting. The world may be very close to the point of being forced into adopting universal standards of airport security, and that should be the business of the ICAO. But this organization has given poor and unimaginative leadership in recent years, whereas the AACC, IATA, and IFALPA, all with much less political clout, have given vigorous support to airport security schemes.

Still, airports are the key to controlling hijacking, and major efforts must be made to help weak links in the chain with both security training and financial aid.

Chapter 5

Countering Terrorism in the Air: Dealing with the Hijacked Plane

Skyjacking seems to be a subject that unravels the lunatic fringe decorating some part of all our psyches.[1]

Elizabeth Rich, flight attendant

I shouldn't tell you this, but the unwritten directive is to shoot the hostess if the skyjacker is using her as a shield and that's the only way to get him.[2]

Sky marshal to flight attendant

In one almost absurd incident, two different crewmen actually held the weapon for the skyjacker without taking him prisoner . . . because of the image they had in their heads.[3]

David G. Hubbard, psychiatrist

Of the available forms of theater, few are so captivating figuratively, as well as literally, as skyjacking. The boldness of the action, the obviousness of the danger, the numbers of people involved as hostages and therefore potential victims, the ease with which national boundaries can be traversed and international incidents created, the instantaneous radio and television linkages, all these combine to make this crime one of the most immediately attractive forms of terrorist action.[4]

Thus does Jan Schreiber summarize the most spectacular aspect of international terrorism and at the same time one of the most risky ventures for the terrorist himself. Hijacking is, in at least one respect, unique in the catalogue of criminal activities in that "no other crime in the world can pick itself up, its perpetrators and its victims, and move them from point to point at just under the speed of sound."[5]

The hijacking of airplanes is a special form of theater in which the notions of spectacle, fear, and excitement and a message are all concentrated inside the hull of a modern commercial jet. It is a form of theater in which airport property, or even the plane itself, may be blown up. Human lives may be threatened or taken. The threats—backed by periodic torture or even killings—may be used to extort money or to obtain the release of prisoners, the publication of manifestos, or safe conduct to another country far from the scene of the crime. Not only is the terrorist act theater, but it is "theater by surprise and in the interests of a political program."[6] As Jan Schreiber pointed out, "It is possible to diagram the process of terrorist communication by means of a triangle in which the terrorist is the subject, the opposing government is the object and the victim is the medium."[7] (See figure 4.)

The messages sent by the terrorist are varied: release our prisoners, pay our ransom, put pressure on the government, don't fly your planes into enemy territory. Underlying these threats is one single message that demands notice, if not respect—the promise of menace if the situation and the terrorists' anger are not taken seriously. These are not requests, pleas, or supplications to the recipient government; they are the demands of one belligerent to another and are backed up by the threat of violence, which, as terrorists have frequently demonstrated, are likely to be carried out.

The choice of victim, the third point in the triangle, is often random or incidental. He dies not because the group has anything against him personally but because his death (or the threat of it) will alarm many people and thereby demonstrate to society at large that his killers or kidnappers are deadly forces, however small their numbers. The resulting terror in the population at large compels the unwary government to overreact.[8]

There is also a fourth element that should be included in figure 4 and that is the opinion of the public, whether in a particular country or in the world at large. That opinion is swayed negatively or positively by the electronic and print

Figure 4
The Process of Terrorist Communication

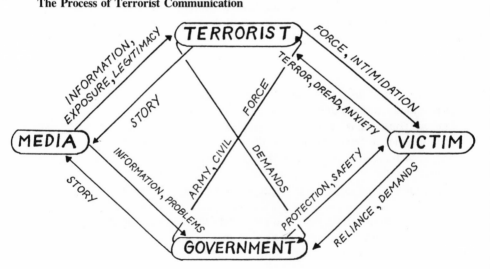

media. Hijacking is so very effective because of the special characteristics, both psychological and political, that make it an ideal media event. As David Hubbard pointed out,

The high visibility of skyjacking derives from the ongoing human drama and international conflict which it creates, and which the media in turn exploits. The human and political factors which are specific to skyjacking net great amounts of public interest, but get very little in the way of hard-headed analysis. This is unfortunate because, ironically, the same characteristics which make skyjacking so effective for terrorists could be turned to our own use against them if we would only learn the game.[9]

It is clearer today than ever that we must learn the game; hijacking is still flourishing as strongly and perhaps more dangerously than ever.

In her book *Flying Scared,* written in 1973, Elizabeth Rich pointed out that people who feel beaten down and defeated by the world and who are repeated failures in everything might conceive of hijacking as a means of reversing the process and rising above all the hassle. This thought led her to conclude,

When a plane leaves the ground, it becomes an autonomous microcountry or political unit. While it is in the air, the captain is king of the country, the crew his lieutenants and the passengers his subjects, whose lives depend on his skill and their obedience to his orders. Simply by using a threat, the skyjacker brings about a coup d'état, putting himself in the position of authority and controlling the outside forces he feels have put him down all his life. He in fact becomes king, the passengers and his crew his fearful subjects.[10]

This notion of the jet airplane as kingdom is not a bad place to start in analyzing how to go about controlling hijacking activity. In fact it is possible to go even farther and break down the constituent actors or involved parties in this kingdom.

David Hubbard prefers to use the image of an improvised play in which all the actors are amateurs, though none are volunteers except the star.

The cast includes the skyjacker himself (often the producer of the piece as well as the starring player), a crew of co-starring pilots and flight attendants, and a collection of walk-on bit players who are called "the passengers." The play itself has a scenario but no script, and is improvised in response to all sorts of unpredictable factors, including the weather. Audience response, the impulses of the actors, and the competence of the technical crew (that is, the aviation industry) can all affect the outcome of the play. The run of the show depends, of course, on how much public interest can be generated.[11]

There are a variety of actors in hijack theater. Not only is there the captive cast in the play—the pilots, flight attendants, and passengers, along with the ever-present chroniclers, the media—but also there are the crews behind the scene—the airline owners, maintenance crews, police, government authorities, and special antiterrorist SWAT teams. As Hubbard indicated:

The "plot" can be prolonged through an almost unlimited series of maneuvers, threats, demands and relocations. And the audience can be manipulated into putting pressure on various governments either to give the skyjackers what they want or to make martyrs of them. But on the other side of the coin, the cast and the technicians may have other options than going along with the skyjacker. Insofar as they are necessary to make the crime a real production number and not just a monologue, they have some power over the skyjacker.[12]

A hostage-taking episode on an aircraft in flight with a terrorist in charge takes on the character of a dynamic psychosocial process. First, a hijack usually lasts for a considerable time, long enough for the terrorist to experience challenges to his initial resolve and his carefully prepared state of mind. Second, during this same period the victim continuously confronts the terrorist and is the latter's total responsibility. At the same time the hijacker is confronted from time to time by the pilot and the negotiators on the ground. These factors both genuinely affect the terrorists' feelings and actions. Third, the victim or hostage is affected by the whole experience in ways that are impossible to predict, a factor that tends to complicate the hijack situation further. Finally, the complex pressure-process of response and counterresponse between hostage taker and captive suggests that the negotiators may be able to pursue a strategy that will both avoid a violent outcome and maybe even persuade the hijacker to surrender. Such an outcome has happened on a number of occasions during hijacks in the past 20 years.

Public opinion tends to identify with the victims for the very good reason that reporters concentrate on the victim's point of view, and if the public sympathizes with the victim, the terrorist will be seen as the villain of the piece, representing an evil cause. Such media identification is inevitable, since through no fault of their own the passengers' lives hang in the balance. Such random victimization is painful to experience, but it sells papers. At the same time a hijack is also a harrowing experience for the hijacker since the outcome for him, too, may well be death. Options are severely limited in an act of air piracy. If challenged by the crew while in flight, the suicidal destruction of the plane may be the terrorist's only option. Once the plane has landed and is surrounded by hostile authorities, there is an even greater chance that he may die.

As Jan Schreiber pointed out,

Every hijack attempt is therefore a serious flirtation with death. And in spite of his almost religious dedication to his cause, his willingness to die for it if necessary, the hijacker is uneasily staring death in the face for hours and even days on end. In the course of an exploit he is in the state of heightened emotional responsiveness, sometimes edging perilously close to hysteria.[13]

When two groups of people are both facing an unknown outcome to an intractable situation, they are naturally susceptible to emotional involvement. Captive and hijacker may develop strong bonds because they are both in a small, enclosed space facing a hostile world outside. Among psychologists, this bonding is called the "survival identification syndrome." The results of such a mutual attraction can work both for and against the terrorist. They work for him when the captives support him against police and authorities on the ground but against him when his concern for his captives betrays him into a potentially fatal error of judgment.

This interesting process of mutual bonding by a hijacker and his innocent victim in the course of a life-threatening hostage situation is known by several other names—"the just world hypothesis" and, the most frequently used description, "the Stockholm Syndrome." This last term emerged during a bank robbery in Sweden in 1973 in which the unique psychological relationship between captive and captor began to be widely recognized for the first time. On the morning of August 23, 1973, a professional thief, recently escaped from prison in Stockholm, entered and held up the Sveriges Kreditbank. Jan-Erik Olsson produced a submachine gun and demanded money but was foiled in his attempt to escape by the quick arrival of the police. Eventually, isolated on the first floor of the bank, he took four hostages, three of whom were female. To this group was added a second convict from prison, and the six retreated into the bank's vault. For six days they stayed there, connected by telephone to the police outside.

During the six days, a female hostage tried, unsuccessfully, to talk Prime Minister Olof Palme into letting Olsson carry out his plan to escape with his captives. This development rather surprised the police. Another female hostage shunned contact with the police and indicated she was emotionally allied to the group inside the vault. Furthermore, during the standoff one of the female hostages allowed Olsson to fondle her, although she drew the line at sexual relations, and Sven Safstrom, the sole male hostage, remembered with confused credulity how grateful he felt when Olsson said that he would only shoot him in the leg to show the police that he really meant business. Eventually, when the police teargassed the vault and Olsson and his partner surrendered their weapons, the hostages refused to leave without their captors and their obvious loyalty and affection was mutually reciprocated. It was, in short, a classic study of the unique emotional impact of hostage situations on both captive and captor. The insights provided were not, however, sufficiently developed in the mid-1970s to allow any public understanding as to why heiress Patty Hearst should suddenly start behaving like Che Guevara.

The survival identification process does not always set in during a hijack situation. If the terrorists are very angry and fanatical, it may not occur at all, but under normal circumstances this psychological bonding between captive and captor can set in anywhere between 15 and 75 minutes into a hostage situation. This initial period is the most dangerous and volatile, and it is here, as Eric Morris and Alan Hoe pointed out, that "in psychological terms, the hostage takers could be said to be in a state of emotional erection. They are frightened; though the adrenalin is pumping and excitement is high, they are akin to cornered animals, ready to fight to the death, and to kill anyone who challenges their authority or their purpose."[14]

Once the hostage has survived this period, survival identification can begin, given the right conditions. The hostages survive initially by keeping calm, though some may suffer injuries that will add to the effects of shock. Usually, escape is impossible, and so victims feel numb and no longer in control of their own situation. Much of the initial stage of denial or disbelief is due to a natural suppression by the brain so that the individual will not suffer excessive stress reaction. As Morris and Hoe put it, "without the numbness of the denial state, the situation would become unbearable."[15]

After a time, things begin to settle down; the hostages realize that they will not be executed as long as they explicitly obey their captors. This phase is often called the "disengagement of reality phase," which will then be followed by a realistic comprehension of the real predicament being faced. The hostage then either goes into a state of depression or else begins to identify with his captor. As the period of captivity progresses, the hostages regress to an almost childlike state, known as "traumatic psychological infantalism."[16] They begin to display childlike, submissive behavior toward the captor. In these circumstances sexual attractions can be aroused, and later, hostages may even impede rescue operations because of this stress-bonding effect. Hostages who have been subjected to maltreatment do not generally develop the Stockholm Syndrome. It is clearly in the interest of the hijacker, the flight crew, the passengers, and the authorities for the Stockholm Syndrome to set in, for there is then less likelihood of the plane being blown up and the passengers being killed. Also, as mentioned above, the survival identification process may be the very way in which the hijacker will ultimately defeat himself.

The first task in a hijack is to get the plane on to the ground, as flight crew well know. Failing this, the next task is to try to induce the hijacker to surrender peacefully. The ultimate horror is when negotiation has ceased, and captives are being shot one by one in anticipation of a commando raid. Just such a scenario occurred at Luqa Airport, Malta, in 1985 when an Abu Nidal group began systematically shooting hostages. At this point, it is each person for himself with the attendant danger of death from the terrorists, death from the invading commandos, or injury in attempting to escape from the plane.

By the late 1980s there had been hijacks that lasted just a few hours, hijacks that lasted 15 days, and in one case a hijack that lasted on and off for 40 days. Naturally, during a hijacking, there are critical moments when the configuration of relationships may ultimately be seen in retrospect to have affected the outcome of the whole episode. These moments unite to form a pattern that, if clearly understood, could greatly aid flight crew in the management, and maybe even the foiling, of hijacks.

Lufthansa, the German airline, commissioned a Munich psychologist, Wolfgang Salewski, to interview passengers and crew who had been involved in a number of incidents. His report, "Luftpiraterie," was the basis for a training film used to help crew cope with hijacks. As Jan Schreiber pointed out,

What is most interesting in Salewski's conclusions for our purposes is his depiction of the curve of emotion that is perceptible on a hijacked plane over the course of the episode. It is an oscillating curve, rising and falling between the extremes of desperation and euphoria and tending, with the protraction of the episode, to retreat from both extremes.[17]

In Salewski's script, and indeed throughout almost any hijacking, it is possible to gauge the feelings that develop from certain events and hear the self-assessment of the various actors involved at critical moments. The denouement of a hijack is a highly theatrical process. It begins when the terrorist stands up in a state of heightened excitement and anxiety, ready to take control of the aircraft. To wrest control from the pilot and flight crew, he is often violent and cruel, which causes acute fear in the helpless passengers. This fear and tension begins to subside as the flight attendants are allowed to resume their normal activities in the plane and a certain emotional collusion occurs between the flight crew and their new captain.

Even one unexpected incident, however, can set the terrorist off into a fresh paroxysm of anger, which can appear even more dangerous than the original state of terror. Lives are again threatened, and the passengers once more experience the fear that the plane might be blown up in midflight.

When the plane does finally land and negotiations begin, there is again a chance of passenger hysteria should conflict develop between the hijacker and the authorities. The whole process is frequently complicated by extreme heat on an open airport tarmac, the loss of air conditioning, restricted access to washrooms, hunger, or unsuccessful negotiations.

The sole purpose of a simulated hijack training film would be to instruct flight crew to be aware of the response phases in a hijack situation so that they will be better able to cope with the real thing. Such a training film helps them to intellectualize the experience and so aids in the development of a measure of control.[18]

At some time all flight crew of commercial aircraft should be required to confront the possibility of their involvement in a hijack so that they can begin to anticipate the emotional journey such an experience would involve.

David Hubbard has rightly distinguished the three groups most directly involved in a hijack as pilots, flight attendants, and passengers, but there are in fact other important actors who participate. They include "ground controllers," the airport controllers who direct planes from one airport to another, and the government, which implements policy over hijacks and other crises in the sky. In the case of the United States, the FAA has the last word on how a hijack is to be handled because it develops policy; therefore "ground control" and "ground authorities" may well be two different agencies in the denouement of an airplane hijacking. The final actor in hijacking theater is the terrorist himself. In the section that follows, an attempt is made to deal with these five groups of actors that are always involved in hijacks.

In characterizing pilots "a strange and interesting bunch," David Hubbard is probably referring to an older cross-section of pilots.[19] The younger ones do not necessarily have the military connections or the war experience of the older generation. Like their more senior colleagues, however, they are self-confident individuals who must be methodical, careful, and disciplined; after all, they are responsible for many lives. They wear their uniforms with pride and play a role that is calculated to project an aura of competence and command, deliberately distanced from the flying public. With the extraordinary automation of modern aircraft, it is conceivable that the pilot and copilot have less work to do than their earlier counterparts had in the days of propellers; yet in today's world of deregulated competition, the attributes of an experienced commercial pilot are perhaps more important than they ever were. Certainly, the pressure to deliver passengers safely and speedily to their destination is greater than it ever was. This, in part, is why a hijack is so effective; it not only jeopardizes the safe arrival of the flight, but it also challenges the position and prestige of the captain of the aircraft, and each pilot may react very differently to such an unaccustomed afront. Unlike faulty instruments or bad weather, a hijack attacks the emotional and personal side of a pilot. This is an event that does not normally happen in the course of a year or even a career, and the limited training presently available does not adequately prepare pilots for the trauma of a hijack.

Flight attendants, on the other hand, have been hired to deal with people, to ease the passage of angry, troubled, or confused passengers through the sometimes frightening experience of jet flight. Hubbard contends "that feminity takes the edge off the flight" and allows passengers to "to regress to an infantile mode of existence, to a point where an attractive young woman tends our needs, tucks us in and brings us a bottle."[20] This sexist approach to flying is now changing as North American airlines increasingly hire both men and women as flight attendants and treat them as career employees, rather than sweet and single young things interested in travel or mating or both. This increased professionalism together with their proximity to the passengers give flight attendants the best opportunity to influence the course of a hijacking. They also tend to have the least chance of being injured.

Because they are younger, often female, and certainly less threatening than the pilot, flight attendants take the edge off the violence of a confrontation with a terrorist. This enables them to act as a shield of protection for passengers and other crew members and to intervene to defuse a hijacking. At times, they have been asked to go even farther, to "mother" the infantile behavior of an adrenalin-pumped terrorist, a tactic that has proven to work far better than treating him as a rebellious adolescent as male crew members might do. Unfortunately, however, flight attendants get even less training in hostage situations than pilots.[21] Looking after the physical, emotional, and food needs of a planeload of passengers, even for a few hours, is exhausting. Just ask a flight attendant how she feels at the end of a flight. But to have to handle the extreme stress of a life-and-death hijack situation is more than most people can handle unless they are exceedingly resourceful or extraordinarily well trained or both.

The final member of this triumvirate is the passenger. With no authority and no knowledge of how a jet operates, passengers are of use to the terrorist only as a bargaining chip. What is worse, they have no active role in a hijack. Since passengers are anonymous and expendable, they become the logical target of threat and intimidation and are used to manipulate or influence both crew and ground authorities. Because of their essentially passive role, passengers experience far greater fear and frustration than crew and flight attendants who at least are able to remain busy doing things for safety, direction, and comfort. Passengers are an "anonymous, unpredictable collection of human beings to be controlled by the skyjacker if he is to succeed."[22] They are usually bunched together or physically humiliated and then left to brood in their own complete helplessness in a hijack. In most cases the hijacker is not acting out his rage or rebellion against the passengers (in fact, he usually has no desire to kill them), but there are hijack situations in which, to regain the initiative, the hijacker may be convinced that he has to kill one or more passengers.

In the opinion of David Hubbard, there is usually psychological but not physical damage to the passenger as a result of a hijack. He considers the mental stress in a hijack to be no more than in an ordinary car accident. Even keeping in mind that people react differently to car accidents depending on whether they are psychologically vulnerable to sudden shock, often including injury, or whether they have the physical and emotional resilience to jump quickly back into normal life and driving, Hubbard's opinion is not widely shared. Psychologists and psychiatrists differ as to the long-term impact of hijacks, especially traumatic ones. They know hostages often regress to a childlike state, referred to as "traumatic psychological infantalism."[23] In this condition they will impede rescue attempts, hide their captors from intervening troops, or even refuse to testify at trials against the terrorist. In addition, psychologists are aware that long after the hijack incident the passenger may suffer flashbacks, frightening dreams, feelings of being followed, and general insecurity bordering on paranoia. Undoubtedly, many passengers need but do not get posthostage therapy to help them get over the trauma. However, very little study has been undertaken on the need for passenger aftercare in airplane hijackings simply because, until now, nobody thought it was important. A few well-chosen court cases against airlines resulting from hijack stress coupled with airline neglect could quickly change this perception.

It is very clear that the passenger, too, is in need of training and education about his attitudes and behavior in a hijacking. It is ironic that we go through a long process of driver training or defensive driving with road vehicles. Similarly, people aboard ships and boats have to go through drills for emergency situations and hypothermia and its effects. Yet millions of passengers of all social strata board one flight after another without the slightest idea of how to behave should their plane be hijacked by terrorists.

It is time that all three groups mentioned above should start to receive specific instruction as to what to do and how to cope with the trauma of a hijack. Better training of all three constitutencies aboard commercial aircraft could dramatically shorten or even terminate a number of hijacks. Since hijacking shows no serious signs of abating after 30 years of continuous activity, it seems safe to suggest that the participants should be taught to handle the experience with as little stress as possible.

It is certainly worth asking what goes on in the mind of a terrorist as he hijacks a plane. Unfortunately, very few have committed their thoughts to paper, though there has been one interesting exception. The only female hijacker to live through two hijackings, PFLP member Leila Khaled, wrote two detailed accounts of what went through her mind in both hijacks, and there is no reason to doubt the veracity of her story. The full text of both hijacks appears in Appendix 4.[24] But it is worth mentioning a few points that are relevant to this discussion on how to handle a hijack in the air. She stated, "I had trained for every conceivable contingency; I had mastered most operational details of the great Boeing 707."[25] In fact, she had mastered the details so well that she caught the flight engineer lying about how much fuel they had left. This certainly demoralized him and put the flight crew on the defensive. But Leila Khaled was unprepared for the human encounters before and during the flights. In her own words, "there was something, however, I did not train for: the human situation. How to deal with idle or curious conversationalists. How not to arouse their suspicions or be rude to a seat-mate. I had to improvise and felt very uncomfortable. I imagined that all the Westerners aboard knew about my mission."[26]

The direct questioning of fellow passengers rattled her, and the direct approach of small children almost made her abort both hijack attempts. Children have always been Leila Khaled's weak point; she worked with them in refugee camps after her hijacks. Another revealing aspect of her account is how the attentions of the crew brought out her nervousness. She wrote: "But they (the flight attendants) made us nervous, as they kept returning and asking us if we wanted anything else. I pretended that I had a stomachache and asked for a blanket. Innocently I placed it over my lap, so I could take my hand grenade out of my purse."[27]

The final point to be made here is about motivation. Concerning her first hijack, of a TWA flight in 1969, she wrote: "We diverted Flight 840 because TWA is one of the largest American airlines that services the Israeli air routes and more importantly because it is an American plane."[28] Also, "It was a momentous second in my life when I put my fingers on the trigger and ordered the enemy to obey my command. All my life I dreamt of carrying arms to aim at the enemy—that vengeful enemy who raped our land and has expropriated our homes without compensation."[29] The evidence from contemporary hijacks in the late 1980s seems to be that the emotional and human factor is one of the terrorist's weaknesses, and to a certain extent it can be exploited by a watchful crew.

The various actors involved in the hijack theater aboard a plane have now been identified, but a hijack is a dynamic process, ongoing, with ebb and flow, and it is really the interaction between these actors that makes a hijack situation so stressful. Perhaps, then, it would be useful to examine how each actor in the relationship behaves toward the others during a hijack situation.

THE ROLE OF THE PILOT

The pilot is the prime player in the hijack situation becaue he controls the aircraft and the crew. Once the hijacker has convinced the pilot that he is serious and that the crew must do as requested, he becomes the man in charge. He supplants the authority of the captain. Fortunately, so far, because of his inability to fly the aircraft, the hijacker must place a certain amount of trust in the pilot while he directs the aircraft and the actions of the crew. It is in this necessary trust that the pilot has an opportunity to thwart the hijacker and bring about an early end to the hijack.

The first concern the pilot has, after ensuring the safety of his passengers, crew, and aircraft, is to advise the ground authorities that he has been hijacked. Often the hijacker prefers to do this at a time of his own choosing, in which case the pilot must resort to covert methods to ensure that a warning is issued. The pilot has various means whereby he can secretly advise ground controllers that he has been hijacked. Since all flights are radar controlled, most commercial aircraft have a transponder that receives a ground-based signal and replies automatically. The controllers advise the pilot to select a given frequency that identifies the flight and its altitude, course, speed, and position. Should the pilot reset his transponder to a special code, alarm bells will advise the ground controllers that a problem exists. The controllers would immediately call the plane and should the pilot confirm that his transponder is correctly set, the controllers will acknowledge that fact and ask if the pilot can provide further details. Should the pilot respond that he cannot, the controllers will continue to monitor the flight and pass the fact of the hijack along to control agencies farther along the jet's route. As is well known within the industry, pilots can select special codes for emergency situations on board (code 7700), for communications' failure (code 7600), or for skyjacking in progress (code 7500). Should the pilot be unable to activate his transponder, he could still advise ground authorities by the use of code words. The code word *trip* used in combination with the aircraft call sign will identify the flight as one that has been hijacked.

Once the ground system is advised of the hijacking, any necessary clearances for the aircraft to penetrate unfriendly airspace or to land at a given airport can be negotiated. This information will be relayed to the pilot; however, it is normally kept from the hijacker to try to convince him that it is necessary to go to a site more favorable to the crew. In keeping with this concept, the crew will normally try to be as negative as possible to all of the hijacker's demands. Since many hijackers are unfamiliar with flight operations, it is possible that the crew can convince the hijacker that an immediate landing is necessary because of engine problems, a lack of fuel, or inclement weather. It will be to the crew's advantage to be as slow and methodical as possible in their actions since this will serve to confuse and tire the hijacker. Some people reach their acceptance threshold of negative responses and delaying actions before others, and so the crew will have to be attentive to the attitude of a hijacker.

After the ground system is alerted to the hijack, the crew should endeavor to use the ground authorities to terminate the hijack. Potential destinations can be identified by simple techniques such as the pilot explaining to the terrorist that he must have weather data for a particular airport so he can prepare the landing calculations. Once given permission to get weather conditions for a particular airport, the ground controllers can advise the police or military, as well as calculate the estimated time of arrival.

Hubbard mentioned a case in which a hijacker left Los Angeles and intended to stop at Miami before attempting to cross the Atlantic.[30] Since the plane would not have made it across the Atlantic, El Paso ground control sent a spurious weather warning that caused the terrorist to divert the plane. At New Orleans, the same tactic was repeated, and the crew responded in the same way. "When the Miami controller told him firmly that the plane could not go on, the skyjacker acceded, and the skyjacking ended."[31] This raises the issue of problem-solving pilots who ignore leads like the one cited above and insist on overcoming engine and weather problems when they could be used to get the aircraft onto the ground. Apparently, this problem-solving behavior has raised the success rate of hijackers a good deal more than necessary. The desirable objective here would be for crew deliberately not to use backup systems when problems arise but, rather, to use the latter to good effect against the hijacker.

As mentioned in Chapter 2, when the Samurai Nine hijacked the B727 from Tokyo to North Korea in 1970, the plane actually landed in Seoul, South Korea, without the hijackers being any the wiser.[32] The hijack might have ended then had there been photos of the North Korean leader Kim il-Sung around the airport and had the terrorists not spotted a Northwest airlines plane on the tarmac. Similarly, on December 11, 1988, a Cuban from Miami who tried to hijack TWA 469 en route from San Juan to Miami and take it to Havana was foiled when the flight was diverted to Grand Turk in the Bahamas instead. Bahamian police arrested him as he stepped out of the plane, a tribute to ground–pilot cooperation.

Finally, the pilot must use all of his calm and reason to control the situation. Risky acts such as overhandling the aircraft to disorient the hijacker or aircraft depressurization to render the hijacker unconscious, are both methods that may result in injury or death to passengers or crew members. Depressurizing the aircraft has often been suggested as a technique that will eventually render the hijacker, as well as all those not on oxygen, unconscious in a matter of minutes. This is not advised because the actions of people vary as they deal with altitude sickness or hypoxia. Normal, rational people can become angry and uncontrollable and could inflict a considerable damage before passing out. Aside from these physical problems, it may be difficult to explain to the hijacker why the crew is on oxygen and why it is not necessary for him to be on oxygen as well.[33]

THE ROLE OF THE FLIGHT ATTENDANTS

Although the pilot is most often the focus of a hijacking, flight attendants nearly always play a major role as the liaison between pilots, passengers, and hijackers. They are the pilots' eyes and ears in the back of the airplane and may, on occasion, coordinate the actions of passengers in situations such as evacuating the airplane or rushing the hijacker. Their friendly, helpful manner can be a major factor in preventing confrontations, aiding passengers in coming to terms with a hijack, and creating an atmosphere to both calm and obtain the trust of the hijacker. The last objective, obtaining the trust of a hijacker, sometimes requires treating him in a manner that might be termed infantile.

David Hubbard told a story that illustrates the vital importance of the female buffer role. On a flight from Anchorage to the Aleutians,

one of the flight attendants, the 20-year-old daughter of a veteran pilot, was making her first flight as a newly trained stewardess. The other was an older, more experienced woman. About an hour out of Anchorage, an enraged, drugged male shoved a gun at the younger woman's head and made the usual change of course, cash and head-for-Mexico routine. The older attendant tried to discipline the hijacker in a bossy way and his violent behaviour escalated. The younger women then took over consoling and calming the man for several hours at the end of which she talked him into surrender.[34]

As early as 1973, flight attendant Elizabeth Rich wrote: "Information now available could help crew members play their roles during a skyjacking in such a way as to make a high percentage of hijackings unsuccessful."[35] Those roles include being alert to self-defeating moves by hijackers. In the aforementioned case of "Sam," who requested a drink and handed his gun to the flight engineer, the hijack should have ended then and there. In the case of Rafaele Minichiello, the hijacking should have ended when he took his gun apart to clean it.[36] Such crew management of hijackings requires more training for both pilots and flight attendants, focusing on ways they can cooperate to end a hostile takeover.

On November 12, 1971, there was a hijack aboard an Air Canada flight between Calgary and Toronto. The hijacker, Paul Cini, was clearly mentally disturbed, as well as being the first parajacker. The incident began when Cini left a note in the washroom of the DC8, announcing that this was the Doomsday Flight and nobody was going to survive. To back his threat, Cini carried a bag full of dynamite to which he was wired (this was in the period before airport security), as well as a gun and a sawed-off shotgun. He had been jilted by his girlfriend and was determined to get even. He also demanded money and passage to Ireland. As one witness observed, "The man was completely off the wall."[37]

The hijack lasted eight hours, while the plane floated back and forth across the U.S. border. Cini first wanted to go to Cuba, then wanted to go to Ireland, and finally, allowed the plane to land at Great Falls, Montana. Thanks to a flight attendant called "Mary," who had been able to get through to the disturbed man and create a bond of sorts, the women and children on the flight were allowed to disembark. The random money Cini demanded was picked up, and the flight continued, with the hijacker deciding to jump out, through a window over the wing. As he got ready to jump, he had his hands full of communications equipment from the flight deck. To get his parachute out, he put his gun down. The pilot, who happened to be close by, seized the weapon and threw it several seats away. The scuffle that ensued ended abruptly when the assistant purser felled the hijacker with a fire axe.

The Uli Derickson story, as related to Captain Tom Ashwood (see Chapter 3), also has some lessons for flight attendants. Derickson not only was a senior member of the flight crew but also was psychologically prepared for this hijack. She had received training on hijacking and had mentally reviewed what she might do in such a situation. So when it happened, she made decisions instinctively.[38] The training carried her through the initial period of surprise and shock and comforted her when one of the hijackers attacked her, trying to intimidate her with karate kicks. Recovering quickly, she was able to take the initiative against her tormentors. The things she had been taught echoed through her mind: *"Delay, delay, delay. I must delay and try to talk to them."*[39] As the beatings and shouting continued, she realized the diatribe was being directed against the Americans on the flight. She stopped the two Palestinian hijackers by telling them, in Arabic, that she was German and perhaps she could help them.[40] They stopped their assault in astonishment.

Having thus established communications with one of them in German, Derickson began to work at building rapport. The opportunity came during a quiet period in the first class section when, in a lengthy exchange, she learned the hijackers felt they had been treated like animals by the Americans. She was able to empathize, saying she, too, had been a refugee, twice escaping communism. She also sang to them, so moving the elder hijacker, who had lived with a German girl and fathered a child by her, that he made a promise to let Derickson go free. Later in the hijack, when things looked bleak, she reminded him, "You promised me over the lips of Allah," and he immediately stopped, at least temporarily, his brutal attacks on the passengers. Building rapport involved displaying some sympathy for the terrorists, which also calmed them. Derickson said, "In my opinion, it is necessary to convince them that you are understanding and cooperative. That does not mean, however, that you should do everything they tell you to."[41]

How did Derickson keep the situation from escalating into total destruction once rapport was established? She recalled, "It was simply a case of never telling them 'yes' or 'no.' If I was to say 'yes,' I would commit myself totally to something and if you say 'no,' you get them angry. I tried to equivocate in a reasonable manner."[42]

Another important factor in her success was that in two years in Saudi Arabia she had learned enough to be able to tap into the hijackers' religious convictions. They said their prayers on mats in the aisle of the plane and insisted on putting blankets over the legs of women in shorts. Allah the Merciful is one of the precepts of Islam, and she was able to use this with the hijackers when they beat passengers mercilessly.

Derickson was also able to see the hijackers' vulnerabilities, which gave her the courage she needed to act in time of crisis. They failed to convince her there were five terrorists on board, they clearly had no idea about flying and were upset by turbulence, and they were emotionally insecure. Derickson saw all of these things and stored the knowledge for a time of confrontation. That time came when the terrorists demanded the passports of all passengers, a scene that was vividly portrayed in the television movie made of her role. She managed to dispose of dangerous passports, to conceal the identity of Jewish Americans, and, finally, to dissuade the terrorists from persisting with the passport charade. This is full-blown crisis management, and Derickson did very well indeed. Twice more she intervened at risk to her own life, once when it seemed the younger hijacker would beat another passenger to death and later when she reboarded the plane for a further eight hours after having been freed and managed to negotiate the freedom of a number of female passengers and her flight crew. She played her heroic role to the hilt, even to the point of putting a $12,500 gasoline charge on her Shell credit card in Algiers. Throughout, the big lesson we can learn is that prior experience and training of the right sort undoubtedly enabled Uli Derickson to save many lives.

Barbara Dunn, a flight attendant of many years experience and also an executive member of the Canadian Air Line Flight Attendants Association, said, "Flight crews all go out together as a group and their relationship is unique, almost like a family."[43] You spend so much time away from home living out of a suitcase "that you only have one another as social contacts," said Dunn.[44] But the contact can be as sporadic as it is personal. Someone you might have dinner with on a layover somewhere might not come into your life again for six years.

Barbara Dunn has not experienced a hijack but prepares for it mentally and psychologically all the same. She is very insistent on building on two results of her experience in the air. The first is teamwork. Cooperating in a crisis, whether terrorist or otherwise, means that flight attendants and pilots must listen carefully to one another and get past the quirks of personality. The second lesson she has learned from experience is that "over the years, the more you fly, the more intuitive you become. We can spot the drinkers and those who will be impolite and rude."[45] Spotting the terrorist is more difficult, she believes and contends that no one could have spotted the terrorists aboard TWA 847.

THE ROLE OF THE PASSENGERS

The passengers are usually of little use to crew members in combatting hijackers. Their primary role is that of an unspoken threat, since hijackers must be on guard for any kind of rush by one or more passengers. On a remarkable number of occasions passengers have overpowered hijackers or have simply got up and walked off a hijacked plane. Also, one never knows how a group of people who have never met before will react to the trauma of a hijack. In some cases a group may be very docile and do absolutely nothing for themselves. In other cases, determined leadership may emerge. In El Paso, in August 1961, a border patrolman in civilian dress who volunteered to stay on in the plane as a hostage finally knocked Leon Bearden out and terminated a lengthy hijack. On several occasions in the 1970s all of the passengers simply got out of their seats and deplaned on their own. In the case of the June 1970 hijacking by Arthur

Barkley, the passengers simply started deplaning and ignored the shouts of an armed psychotic.[46] Captain Dale Hupe was shot in the abdomen as he struggled with the hijacker, but it did not stop the spontaneous deplaning process. Clearly, in the 1990s one cannot expect a jumbo jet full of people to start crowding the plane's exits for an escape. As James Arey pointed out, "panic among passengers carries almost as much danger as a gunman in the cockpit."[47] Also, most hijacks take place in the air, and passengers therefore cannot exit the plane, but they must learn somehow to handle a mostly passive role during a very frightening experience. As we have seen, both pilots and flight crew are kept very busy during a hijacking, but for the passengers there is usually only waiting and fear.

In a number of recent hijacks between 1985 and 1988, however, the role of the passenger has suddenly come to the fore because of some dramatic events. One was the hijack of TWA 847, which, though it occasioned a great deal of less-than-sensitive press coverage by the American media, at least served to illustrate the dilemma faced by the victimized passenger. First, the passengers were subjected to the sight of Robert Stethem, an American navy diver, being tortured and shot in cold blood. Next, the hijackers demanded the passports of passengers so that they could ascertain who were Jewish and who were American—the chosen enemies of the Islamic fundamentalists. In this case heroic flight crew flushed incriminating passports down the lavatory, probably saving the lives of the owners, but this is a role flight crew and passengers can play together: to conceal the personal details of nationality and ethnic background from hijackers who are ready to murder Jews, Americans, or anyone else for that matter, because they happen to be enemies of their cause. Another significant factor in the TWA 847 hijack was that, at least initially, two very frightened and short-handed hijackers faced 155 passengers, and it seems in retrospect that the whole episode might have been terminated early on with a little passenger initiative. At one stage, three male passengers developed a plan to jump the terrorists, but they were separated by three rows and seated near the windows, and Uli Derickson warned them that one of the terrorists held a hand grenade from which he had pulled the pin. Barbara Dunn quoted Tom Strentz of the Hostage-taking School in Quantico, Virginia: "If passengers take on the terrorists, they had better make sure it works, because they won't get a second chance."[48]

Even if it is argued that passenger heroics should not be encouraged in hijacked aircraft, the Malta episode of November 1985 raises serious issues for passengers as victims. An Egyptair 737 was hijacked on a flight from Athens to Cairo by members of the Abu Nidal faction. The plane was forced to land at Luqa, Malta, where the hijackers, who had already shot a security guard in flight, started to murder Jewish and Western passengers one by one. There was no Stockholm Syndrome operating here, since the hijackers behaved like crazed fanatics from the start. Passengers of the offending nationalities would be summoned, stood in the open hatch of the aircraft, shot in the back of the head, and then pushed out onto the tarmac. One Australian businessman realized as his turn came that it would be better to break a leg or arm jumping out of the open door down onto the tarmac than to be shot in the back of the head. He did, and it saved his life.[49] Finally, Egypt's elite antiterrorist Thunderbolt force stormed the plane. Whether from the hijackers' grenades or explosives used by the commandos, the plane caught fire, and 57 people perished, all of them innocent passengers.[50] Twenty people died and 125 were wounded in the hijack of Pan Am 73. In November 1986, 65 passengers died and 42 were wounded in the firefight crash of Iraq Air 163.

The year 1986 should have been called The Year of the Passenger and ought to have been dedicated to the pain and grieving of crash victims' relatives. But before passengers can even begin to think of an active role in hijacks, it is vitally necessary for them to learn to handle the emotional experience of psychological transference as encountered in the Stockholm Syndrome. Assuming that transference has set in, what should a passenger do to clear his mind and create an atmosphere that is as positive as possible?[51]

The Counter-Terror Study Centre in Winnipeg, Canada, has developed a list of 15 things passengers can do in a hijacking.

1. Don't be a hero. Accept your situation and be prepared to wait. Most hijackings are over within 72 hours, and there is nothing you can do to speed that process.

2. The first hour is the most dangerous, since the hostage takers are in a highly volatile, intensely emotional state. This is the time when they are most likely to strike out at any interference or hesitation. Follow directions precisely.

3. Never speak unless spoken to. Try to appear neither hostile nor overly friendly.

4. Try to rest. A hijacking is extremely stressful and rest is essential.

5. Don't make suggestions. If your captor takes your suggestion and it goes badly, he will blame you.

6. Don't try to escape unless you are absolutely sure your attempt will succeed. Escape attempts are not recommended.

7. Let the hostage taker know, calmly and quietly, if you have a serious health problem or need special attention, but don't pester him.

8. Be observant. You may be released or escape, and your observations could help the authorities.

9. Be prepared to speak to negotiators once a radio or phone link is established, but don't attempt to send signals.

10. Don't be argumentative. Reactions of this type only serve to agitate the hostage taker and other passengers.

11. Treat your captors like royalty. Don't ever turn your back on them unless ordered to. A hijacker is much less likely to harm someone with whom he has eye contact.

12. Be patient. It may seem that nothing is happening, but in reality negotiators are very busy developing a course of action to bring the situation to an end. Remember that hostage situations take time to resolve.

13. When rescue comes, follow orders exactly and be prepared to be frisked and identified by police.

14. Women need not be concerned about rape. There are no cases in which it has occurred.

15. And finally, if food is admitted, eat it. It will not be drugged or contaminated in any way.[52]

It is important to realize that each hijacking situation must be judged on its own merits from the counterterrorist point of view. It is easy to point out specific actions that should or should not have been taken after an event, and it is probably wrong to second-guess flight crew actions. Nevertheless, questions about the role of ground control and security forces on the ground and pilots and flight attendants in the air are being raised, particularly in relation to some recent hijacks.

The important issue to keep in mind is that not all terrorists are fanatics, preferring to die rather than negotiate. In fact, most of them wish to live and would greatly like to know the impact of their hijack action on their overall cause. That's human nature. Furthermore, many of them would rather be heroes than martyrs, and this is their weak point. Flight crew must be aware of any opportunity to disrupt the hijacker's plans and confuse him. Once the aircraft is on the ground, every effort should be made to ensure that it does not return to the air. The hijacker's fundamental requirement is to maintain his mobility long enough to reach a hospitable country, and he will issue effective threats until someone who has the authority to grant his demands caves in.

It is usually through the patient and cooperative actions of crew and ground control that the terrorist's pattern of activity can be interrupted to terminate a hijacking. Obviously, the best way to defeat an enemy is to know his strategies and defenses. This is now much more feasible because in recent years the terrorists, in seeking protracted propaganda victories, have inadvertently revealed a great deal about themselves and their methods. Such is the cost of high-publicity exercises.

The 1985 hijack of TWA 847 and the 1986 hijack of Pan Am 73 are two recent events that received much media coverage. Because of this, enough is known about them to teach us some valuable lessons in crew-management and ground-crew coordination.[53]

TWA 847, JUNE 1985

Flight 847 was on a scheduled run from Athens to Rome and turned out to be the most reported hijacking of the 1985 season. For some 17 days the Western world was forced to absorb the details of the saga of this B727 jetliner as it flew about the Mediterranean looking for a haven from which the terrorists could begin negotiations.

An Iranian-backed terrorist group—part of the Hizbollah, or Party of God—sponsored the hijack of TWA 847 by three members of the Lebanese Shiite militia. Since the flight was heavily booked out of Athens, only two of the three hijackers made it onto the plane. The group's leader was kept on the ground. Once airborne, however, the two who did get on the flight improvised and rushed the cockpit. Apparently, they expected to be welcomed in Beirut, but they were not. The Beirut runways were blocked with trucks and heavy vehicles, and it was only after the crew was threatened that the runways were cleared. The Beirut authorities listened to the terrorist demands, allowed them to refuel, but then ordered them to depart. An otherwise textbook hijack was beginning to develop problems as the hijackers chose to go to Algeria, since that country was deemed neutral and perhaps sympathetic to the terrorists' needs. After a short stay in Algiers to refuel, the hijackers ordered the plane to return to Beirut, probably because of a rumor that an American Delta force team might attack the plane in Algiers. These teams can be sent anywhere in the world in 8 to 12 hours, and the hijackers must have felt the pressure. Again, Beirut was closed to the aircraft, but Captain John Testrake, who knew the plane was very short on fuel, decided to land anyway, at night, and the runway lights were put on just before the plane touched down. At this point the hijackers stood to lose their initiative completely, and they concluded that killing a passenger would be the only way to tap the source of support that they knew they had somewhere in Beirut. Robert Stethem, an American navy diver, was killed in a slow, inhumane fashion, which greatly angered the Americans.[54] The result was that the Amal militia of Nabbi Beri sent a representative aboard the aircraft. During the night several other terrorists went aboard to provide assistance, but an unfounded rumor of an Israeli attack forced the terrorists to fly back to Algiers. After only a day there they returned once more to Beirut, took the remaining 30 or so passengers, and escaped into the city.

There are two very different and contradictory pictures that emerge from this hijack. On the one hand, the terrorists appeared to have both mobility and a specific purpose; on the other hand, they could be seen as desperately improvising during a number of setbacks and barely escaping as Western counterterrorist forces closed in on them. Even from the terrorist perspective, it could hardly be called a success.

The initial demand for Israel to free Lebanese prisoners was foolish because they were scheduled to be freed soon anyway. The demand for the United States to stop oil and arms trade with the Arabs would obviously not be met. The Americans stated throughout the event that they would do everything possible to gain the release of the hostages, but they would not negotiate over other issues. The frantic, moment-by-moment coverage of the hijack by the American media appeared to underline the inabilty of the U.S. government to stop, prevent, or control terrorism against innocent Americans. Perhaps this was the strongest message that the terrorists could send to the American people, with a desire to instill fear in the average American citizen; maybe it was also the true rationale behind the hijack. Otherwise, the terrorist goals "were obviously to attract international attention, to cause dissension among Israel's allies, and to provide a rallying point for other militant fundamentalists."[55]

But the really striking feature of the TWA 847 hijack, on closer inspection, is the confusion, fear, and improvisation that characterized the terrorists' actions. This, too, is where the opportunities to terminate the hijack lay unexploited. First, only two terrorists made it aboard, and they were panicky and afraid from the start. In spite of these obvious signals, which were noticed by the crew and passengers, everybody cooperated fully with the terrorists and helped to tip the situation in their favor. These terrorists were clearly not maniacs ready to die: They were two vulnerable and frightened thugs threatening more than 150 people.

Second, the hijackers expected to be welcomed in Beirut but were not. This probably meant that Druze and other Moslem factions hostile to the Hizbollah were in charge of the airport, and here was an opportunity for Western intervention.

Third, once the hijackers were out of Beirut, they were in considerable trouble and desperately needed a secure place to rest and then conduct their propaganda campaign. Although it is true that Algiers was neutral, the pilots may have had an opportunity to use a different location. Should one of the pilots have become ill, or had engine or weather problems developed, the aircraft could have been diverted to a country favorable for the crew. Italy, Greece, Spain, and the island of Crete all have large American military populations, and even a forced military diversion to one of these places might have led to an early termination of the hijack.

Fourth, it was obvious that neither terrorist had any real concept of the functioning of the aircraft, and the pilots could have used this ignorance. The concept of being as negative to hijackers as possible is standard airline training. Once the air crew determines that hijackers are ignorant of flight procedures, it is in their best interest to search for a spot where they would rather be, other than where the hijackers want them to go. Knowledge of the local geography will then help the pilot in outwitting the terrorist and landing in friendly territory. Military interceptors, or a "sudden problem," could have diverted the aircraft to Europe and would have then forced the terrorists to negotiate from a weaker position or perhaps even surrender. In this incident, hindsight has shown that had the hijackers lost the mobility of the airplane, they would probably have been more likely to surrender than to kill hostages.

Fifth, it is time that terrorists, like everyone else, should learn that 727s require regular, specific maintenance procedures. The pilots twice had an opportunity to "find" some problem with the aircraft that could make it unable to fly. Even a delaying tactic due to a simulated malfunction might have given the U.S. authorities time to organize a rescue attempt or plan a forced diversion.

Sixth, the hijackers gambled that if they killed a passenger they would be helped rather than assaulted in Beirut. In restrospect, however, the impact of that death has been deeply injurious to the Hizbollah cause, not only because of the savage way in which it was carried out but as a result of the court proceedings in the United States that condemned and exposed the movement's essential lawlessness.

Seventh, when the terrorists took their remaining hostages and dispersed into the civilian population in Beirut, an abrupt end to the media search for sensation-alism would have brought the whole hijack to an effective close. It soon became apparent that the hijackers had no realistic plan for completing their crime. In the words of David Hubbard, "these men needed time to find support and to build strength, and they got that time, partly from the capricious goodwill of nature, partly from the automatic problem-solving of the crew and partly from the passivity of the passengers."[56]

This is not a criticism of the way in which everyone behaved on board TWA 847; it was a harrowing experience, but again, in the words of Hubbard,

it is impossible to say that any particular action would not have made the situation worse rather than better. But what I *can* say with certainty is that these skyjackers were not unbeatable, just very lucky. This skyjacking succeeded almost in spite of itself. There was every possibility of it failing and yet none of these possibilities was exploited. The plot of a skyjacking is not written ahead of time by the perpetrators and played out smoothly in the air. It is invented as it goes along, and we should keep that carefully in mind if we want to get the skyjacking problem in a sensible perspective.[57]

In the case of TWA 847 there were opportunities to intervene and change the hijackers' plans, both inside the aircraft between Beirut and Algiers and in Beirut itself. In other words, it was a "soft" hijack that had potential for manip-ulation. In the case of Pan Am 73 in Karachi a different kind of terrorist enemy was in control.

PAN AM 73, SEPTEMBER 1986

It has been frequently said that terrorist attacks come in groups of three. The hijack of TWA 847 was the third by Islamic Jihad in 1984-1985. Similarly, Pan Am 73 was the third hijacking attributed to the Abu Nidal group in the period of 1985-1986. It took place on September 5, 1986. Four terrorists drove a replica of a Karachi Airport security van to the boarding steps of Pan Am 73, which was about to continue its 21-hour flight from Bombay and Karachi to Frankfurt and New York. There were 374 passengers and 15 crew aboard the jumbo jet, which was just minutes from takeoff time. In an act of calculated brutality, the terrorists randomly picked a U.S. citizen and shot him dead.[58] Perhaps it was this act that enabled the crew to lock the cockpit door and escape through the cockpit emergency exit. The terrorists demanded to be flown to Larnaca, Cyprus, but airport authorities stalled for time by stating that a crew would have to be flown out from Europe. The hijack had taken place at 6:05 A.M. and the first deadline set by the terrorists was 7:00 P.M. That was later superseded with hijacker approval and set for 11:00 P.M. Unfortunately, toward evening the oil pressure began dropping in the auxiliary generator that powered the plane's lights, air-conditioning, and instruments. It was calculated that by 10:00 P.M. both the generator and the emergency battery would be nonfunctional and the plane would be plunged into darkness. But because of language difficulties, it proved impossible to make the hijackers understand what was about to happen. Accordingly, at 9:55 P.M., the lights went out, and fearing a commando attack, the hijackers opened fire with guns and grenades on the passengers who were crowded into the aisles. The result was 17 dead and 125 wounded, 50 of them seriously.

After the massacre, one of the terrorists tried to melt into the crowd but was angrily seized by escaping passengers.[59] The rest were captured and thrown in jail, though one was gravely wounded and died. The Pan Am 73 hijack came only four months after the American raid on Libya and was followed a few hours later by an attack by the Abu Nidal group on Jewish worshippers in a synogogue in Istanbul. Apart from the savagery of the attack on the passengers, there were some significant lessons to be learned from the Pan Am hijack by Western authorities.

First, the hijackers attacked in the airport itself, which probably meant that security measures by airlines around the world were making it harder for terrorists to slip their weapons past security. This was the third time that an Abu Nidal attack had not moved beyond the airport. The hijackers made it clear that they wanted to fly to Larnaca, Cyprus, where they meant to bargain for the release of fellow Palestinians in jail there, imprisoned for an attack on Israelis in a yacht some months before. Since Larnaca had already announced its refusal to let the plane land, it is likely that the plane, had it taken off, would have ended up in Beirut or Algiers in a potentially much more exploitable situation.

Second, the hijack took place in Karachi, far away from the usual Abu Nidal locale. Perhaps the climate for a hijack in Europe or the Middle East was considered to be "too hot," and a new venue was needed. There had been no intelligence reports indicating the possibility of a hijack in Karachi, so the terrorists certainly achieved the element of surprise, but at the same time, the choice of Karachi seemed to indicate that the terrorists were being pushed to the outer geographical limits of their effectiveness.

Third, the decisive factor in the hijack was the failure of the terrorists to gain control of the cockpit. The instant the flight crew heard of the hijack (by way of a telephone call from an alert flight attendant), they locked the cockpit door and escaped through an overhead hatch, lowering themselves to the ground on a cable. By so doing, they rendered the aircraft immobile and so fulfilled new FAA instructions to keep a hijacked plane on the ground if at all possible. Because of the deaths later in the hijack, critics suggested that the pilots should not have deserted their passengers. They also maintained that because Karachi was inaccessible, U.S. "planners" would have preferred to see Pan Am 73 land in Cyprus. Presumably, this would have given the Delta force some opportunity to move in.

The strong argument against that is that Larnaca had refused to allow Pan Am 73 to land anyway. This might have caused the hijackers to land in Beirut, where there would have been the potential for another TWA 847 situation. Apart from these arguments, the primary principle is always to prevent terrorist mobility and ground the aircraft. This means that the options will be shootout, surrender, or compromise escape, any or all of which are preferable to a midair catastrophe. Finally, the failing generator that precipitated the hijackers' panic would not have been affected by the presence of the pilots, since there was both a linguistic and a communication problem that heightened the terrorists' panic toward the end of the hijack.

Fourth, the effective grounding of the aircraft now opened the way to stalling-for-time tactics by airport authorities. The issue was the flying in from Frankfurt of another flight crew. By nightfall, already two of the terrorists' deadlines had passed without incident. The terrorists had even relaxed sufficiently to play with some of the children aboard the plane. Up to the final failure of the plane's emergency batteries, the security forces on the ground had had 17 hours in which to prepare for an assault on the aircraft. The important principle was to buy time, and this was successfully achieved—but unfortunately, it was not properly exploited.

Fifth, according to one informed student of this hijack, "the greatest crime of this operation was the execution of the raid by the Pakistani military forces."[60] Once the terrorists started shooting at 9:55 P.M., the passengers and crew began to open doors and escape from the aircraft. In spite of this action, the ground forces did not attempt to enter the aircraft until some 20 minutes after the shooting had begun. It seems incredible that, given 15 or more hours in which to establish a plan and knowing that a power failure, which would probably upset the terrorists, would occur near 10 P.M., these forces were nonetheless unprepared to assault the jet. The ground forces did not even have ready access to a ladder to climb up to one of the numerous hatches, or on to the wings, should they find it necessary. Once the shooting started, it was reported that some 15 to 20 mintues elapsed before a ladder could be found to access the plane's hatches.

Subsequent evaluations of the incident revealed that the Pakistani commandos realized that a firefight was likely but were unprepared for it. In addition, the commandos were placed too far from the aircraft, they waited too long to storm the plane, and they did not have a plan in which to gain control of the situation. Pakistani authorities at first hinted that they had been anticipating the failure of the power unit and hoped to exploit it by staging a commando raid. Later, they changed their story, maintaining that the lights failed earlier than expected and that the panicky hijackers began shooting wildly. Piecing together a clear picture of what really happened has been complicated by "the inconsistency of Pakistani authorities in explaining what they had done."[61] But several authoritative observers suspected the Pakistanis were trying to cover up a bungled commando operation. After a detailed study of the Pan Am 73 attack, a Canadian air force pilot stated, "It must be concluded that the Pakistani forces and their ineptitude contributed to the deaths of 17 people and the injury of many more."[62] The Pakistanis would not allow the American Delta force teams to intervene, even with 80 American lives at stake, which clearly demonstrates the kind of bureaucratic, logistical, and diplomatic obstacles that remain in the way of keeping international airways clear.

Sixth, there was the question of security at Karachi International Airport. In the summer of 1985, Karachi, Beirut, and Athens were listed among the ten airports in the world with the poorest security by a *Newsweek* study.[63] The terrorists at Karachi chose their method carefully. The airport had recently passed the U.S. government security inspections with high marks and was supposed to be on an FAA alert, but the hijackers bypassed the Pan Am security system when they entered the tarmac from the airport perimeter, which is the responsibility of the airport authority and the local government. They also attacked on the Moslem holy day, Friday, when security is weakest. The crucial question was whether local security or airport personnel aided the terrorists in getting to the plane. The hijackers were not known by sight to the airport employees.[64] As a Pakistani official stated, "It's really hard to see how they could have expected to get past [the airport gate] without speaking the language and without proper identification."[65]

Apparently, investigators established that the first terrorist arrived in Karachi just 19 days before the hijacking, giving him little time to gather weapons, familiarize himself with airport procedures, and arrange a disguise. Also, one of the hijackers arrived from Bahrain, where many Pakistanis work at the local airport; therefore it is clear that the hijack was made possible only with substantial inside help at the airport and with logistical support in Karachi. Although the government of General Zia ul Haq maintained good relations with Washington, it is nevertheless true that there was both strong left-wing opposition to his regime in Pakistan and widespread anti-Americanism among the Pakistani people.[66] According to a U.S. State Department official, "the terrorists may have been abetted by security guards of Pakistan International Airlines who are said to be politically left-wing and opposed to the police and the government."[67] If terrorists can enlist the support of left-wing airport employees to enable the mass killing of American citizens on regular international flights, the future of the American tourist industry around the world could well be in jeopardy. Many international travelers have pointed out the fact that in nearly all large airports of the world, low-paid and mostly foreign workers perform most of the menial but security-sensitive jobs. It is to be hoped that the State Department and the government of Pakistan have worked out jurisdictional problems, but they may well spring up elsewhere for American air carriers in future hijacks.

Seventh, there are some lessons to be learned about pilot–flight attendant–passenger relations in the Pan Am 73 hijack. It was an alert cabin attendant who, seeing a hijack was in progress, quickly telephoned the cockpit from the passenger section to warn the crew. This caused a critical setback to the terrorists from which they never recovered. That cabin attendant surely saved many lives. Sadly, she lost her own when she fell upon some children to protect them from gunfire. One thing that Pan Am 73 lacked was an Arabic-speaking member among its crew. When a particular flight is regularly crossing the entire Arabic-speaking world, it might well be worth having at least one member out of 15 aboard conversant in Arabic, if only as a courtesy to the countries being served. In this case an Arabic-speaking person might have prevented the concluding firefight in the plane. Also, when the pilots have left a hijacked plane on the ground, there needs to be a flight attendant designated to take command. In the case of Pan Am 73 the flight attendants opened exit doors under fire, had their hair grabbed by the terrorists, persistently calmed panicking and fearful passengers, and somehow managed to hide crucial American passports from the terrorists who were collecting them.

Still, the flight attendants were unprepared when, as the battery-fed lights were fading, the terrorists ordered the passengers to gather in the aisles between the rows of seats. If there remained any doubt at this point, the terrorists' prayer session, followed by a concerted countdown, should have triggered the flight attendant in charge to signal some passenger reaction to the terrorists. With the encroaching darkness in the aircraft, an assault on the terrorists by all the hostages might well have ended the hijacking. Even hitting the floor would have saved lives. Aran Athavale, of El Toro, California, saw a family of four sprayed by bullets but escaped injury himself by falling to the floor. As he stated later, "Most of the people who got killed didn't duck."[68] It is a life-saving reaction in any shootout anywhere to duck and stay down. The terrorists who took over Pan Am 73 were neither imaginative nor innovative. They bungled their hijack badly without achieving any of their aims, stated or unstated. Even if the killing of Americans or martyrdom was being aimed at, they failed. A bomb placed on the plane would have been more effective than their anaemic performance. Also, the killing of Pakistani nationals aboard the plane could only deal a blow to the terrorists' cause.

In conclusion, the civil aviation industry is, to a large extent, a closed shop. Its members are reluctant to speak about problems of safety, jurisdiction, or terrorism. Each sector has its own perspective and its own union management, and as a result, there is no feeling of community among the constituent parts of the industry. Indirectly, this greatly aids the terrorist.

Speaking about the relationship between pilots and flight attendants, CALFAA's Barbara Dunn suggested that "a coordinated training program is needed and we are not where we should be in this respect."[69] An industry task force was appointed in Canada after the Air India explosion in 1985, and the CALFAA developed such a training program, but after the furor over the tragedy had died down, it was put on the back burner. In the United States, the FAA's response has been to put flight attendants in the classroom for eight hours. "This is no answer," said Dunn, reiterating her strongly held view that joint training for pilots and flight attendants is needed. Such joint sessions have been attempted on a trial basis in Canada, with some unexpected results. The pilots were surprised, said Dunn, at how knowledgeable and capable flight attendants can be in an emergency situation. "In a hijack you need to know one another's role and we have not come to that point yet. After all, we are not dealing with emotionally disturbed hijackers anymore, but with a highly trained group of people who know exactly what they are doing.''[70]

Just as flight attendants had to be nurses in case of a crash in the early days of civil aviation, so today perhaps they should become much more conversant with the technical and electrical systems of an aircraft. In the same vein, perhaps pilots should learn a good deal more about the emotional and psychological trauma that is being played out on the other side of the bulkhead. As Barbara Dunn said, ''We need to learn how to be hostages and there is already a good deal of expertise to draw on to help us in that regard.''[71] Larry Breen of the University of Manitoba recommended the Rogerian nondirective approach for flight attendants.[72] ''Don't criticize, don't agonize,'' he urged, ''and the terrorists won't become outrageous. If possible, talk them down off their adrenalin-pumped-up high.''[73] When a terrorist is all revved up, it is the time to be calm, counseled Breen, and even if he pulls the pin in his hand grenade, don't panic; keep talking; he is not there to die, even if he says so; otherwise he would not have hijacked the aircraft in the first place. Help the passengers to cope with their terror, urged Breen. ''Most people never see a gun and even the sight of one freaks them out. Having one pointing at you is traumatizing.''[74]

Flight attendants have to act as role models in a hijacking, so the more relevant video training films they see, the better their psychological preparation. Often stress management is conditioned by the absence or presence of a crucial piece of knowledge. Stress can come from unforeseen circumstances. The 1971 Air Canada hijack, mentioned earlier, ended when the assistant purser hit the hijacker over the head with a fire axe, but the psychological trauma was just beginning. The problems stemmed from the assistant purser's conviction that he could easily have murdered the hijacker. He kept this trauma to himself and continued to fly, but it became worse as the years passed. Finally, in 1981, a group of survivors of the hijack created a video titled *The Invisible Injury* and, for the first time, openly discussed the trauma of the accident. In the words of one participant, ''It was a mission of love and a tremendous help for all those involved.''[75]

There is now considerable posttraumatic stress help available for the flight crew, but unfortunately such services can not be made available to passengers because they are so terribly litigious when incidents happen. In the background, a lawyer is frequently urging passengers not to accept anything. If the psychological trauma of a hijack is not dealt with suitably, no amount of money from litigation will do the victims the slightest good.

In the meantime, there is a lot of ground to be covered in coordinating the various groups that manage airport and aircraft security. Somehow, pilots, flight attendants, passengers, air controllers, airports, airlines, governments, and intelligence agencies must all integrate their efforts to create a finely tuned net of security that will hold the terrorists at bay. ''For the moment,'' said Barbara Dunn, ''we are simply resting on our luck.''[76]

Chapter 6

International Responses to Hijacking: The Good, the Bad, and the Ugly

One would think the response of nation states to terrorist attacks on their own citizens and civil aviation would be immediate and decisive. But this is not the case. The exercise in state sovereignty, even against the terrorist, is as much a political as a legal process. Punishment of the wrongdoer is by no means the chosen path of the Western democracies. It is worth pursuing some of the reasons why states fail to punish terrorists, because it goes a long way toward explaining why exploitable gaps exist in Western defenses, even today after 30 years of serious hijacking.

First, governments rarely implement preventive measures that anticipate future terrorist attacks. Instead, the implementation of more stringent security measures and procedures are usually taken either as a result of a direct attack or attacks or at least on the basis of perceived terrorist threats to an individual country. Thus after experiencing an attack, one country will undertake increased security measures, while a neighboring country, which has been spared terrorist hostilities, will see no need to upgrade security. This tendency has created a patchwork system of security for international air travel both within Western Europe and within the Western Alliance, especially between North America and Western Europe. Terrorists have been quick to exploit these gaps.

Second, as Paul Wilkinson pointed out, "traditionally governments have taken the view that they must retain sovereign control."[1] The jealous control of state sovereignty has meant that the global response to terrorism has been greatly weakened. At a conference on aviation security in The Hague in January 1987, Robin E. Hill stated,

There must develop, as part of a general anti-terrorist scheme, a distinct and coherent response to airborne crime in governments, in alliances, in ICAO and within the industry itself, with increasing collaborative efforts between these tiers of authority. . . . Traditionally, governments have been reluctant to cede jurisdictional and other legal powers to international bodies.[2]

Third, most democracies at certain times have little direct experience with terrorism and so do not perceive the problem in perspective. As a result, their enthusiasm for action often dissipates rapidly once public shock over a specific outrage has dissipated. The fear of revenge attacks or of the loss of commercial markets induces a kind of double standard in a state's policy that quickly amounts to decision-making paralysis over terrorism. Good contemporary examples of this syndrome are the French attitude to the Armenians and Syrians, the Greek attitude to the Palestinians, and the Italian attitude toward the Libyans and Palestinians. These attitudes alone seriously compromised the development of a concerted policy toward terrorism in Western Europe during the late 1980s. Another important factor is the growth of ideologies and subcultures supportive of terrorism in some Western countries. This includes not only the homegrown variety of terrorism that goes under the heading of Euroterrorism but also the large Middle Eastern Arab worker populations established in many Western European cities. At the same Hague conference on aviation security mentioned above, Geoffrey H. Lipman, director general of the Geneva-based International Foundation of Airline Passengers Association, presented a paper entitled "A Passenger Perspective," in which he stated:

It's hard to avoid cynicism when exposed to the daily farce of governments condemning terrorism and dealing covertly with terrorists, or the speedily released hijackers to protect national interests abroad, or the head-of-state calling for the death sentence for hijackers one day and re-positioning himself the next after a discussion with "friendly foreign interests."[3]

Fourth, democratic governments have somehow managed to convince themselves, from time to time, that it is not their responsibility to respond to acts of transnational terrorism, even when that terrorism is directly aimed at their own national airlines. An interesting example of this outlook took place at the Hague conference. In the opening address of the conference, The Netherlands' minister of transport and public works stated:

The (terrorist) offender must be punished, but, of course, there may be extenuating circumstances or even moral or human justification for the act. The offender may be a true terrorist, or he may be a freedom fighter or simply a freedom lover. The problem is that he may be a freedom fighter as far as one state is concerned while he is a true terrorist in the eyes of another state.[4]

This statement was a perfect example of the liberal state attempting to slide out from under its clear-cut commitment to security, and many speakers reacted to the minister's remarks. The first to do so was Jan Willem Wegstapel, the manager of Schiphol airport in Amsterdam. He closed his own address in the following way:

The Dutch government is planning to pass on to the Dutch airports not only the responsibility but also the cost of security measures at these airports. This is something the airports and airlines vigorously oppose. I find it basically unfair that airports and, through them, airlines and passengers should foot the bill for costs incurred by the government to protect them against terrorist attacks. The safety of persons and goods is the concern and responsibility of the government—a state duty—that can not and should not be shifted on to the third parties.[5]

Earlier Wegstapel had pointed out that the final responsibility for the safety of civil aviation lay with the states "because they are in fact the very ones terrorists are trying to hit in their attacks. (The terrorists) see airlines, airports and passengers simply as extensions of these states."[6] It is in fact the collusion of offending governments and the passivity of others that are the crucial assumptions on which international terrorism operates. "International terrorism," Wegstapel continued, "would simply not be possible if all states denied sanctuary to terrorists and stopped promoting their activities. Governments have the ultimate responsibility to fight terrorism, but airports and airlines must assist them in safeguarding civil aviation."[7] There is no increasing evidence of international terrorist cooperation on a bilateral and regional basis; therefore the only way to beat transnational terrorism is through a flexible, carefully coordinated program of national and international measures. Only national governments are capable of such action.

Typically, perhaps, the Federal Republic of Germany's ambassador to The Netherlands, Otto von der Gablentz, took the opposite side of the argument to his Dutch colleague when he stated: "My basic suggestions would be that the case of governments trying to secure the safety of air traffic is largely a case of political responsibility, political leadership, and only partly legal responsibility." He acknowledged that government decisions were influenced by all sorts of considerations. He also pointed out that governments do not like to be led by other governments. But in the end, he came to the conclusion that a process of slow concensus building, accompanied by a certain amount of political pressure and political leadership from time to time, was the answer. Speaking on behalf of airline travelers everywhere, Lipman concluded: "Terrorist attacks are not aimed at airline passengers. They're aimed at states. The objective is not to disrupt aviation—that's only a means—the objective is to destabilize governments."[8]

In attempting to assess the reaction of different states to aircraft hijacking, it is necessary to study their behavior over a period of time. The following analysis therefore covers the period from 1968 to 1988, when between 800 and 900 hijackings took place. After careful analysis, it was estimated that about 100 of these hijacks, or just under 10 percent, were internationally significant. The number of hijacks that accrued to each state's national air carriers was then noted, but of particular significance was the way in which each state handled the incidents. Clear-cut national responses emerge from this study, though some countries seem to have faced the problem in very different ways at different times during the 20-year period.

There were two countries that were under constant terrorist attack throughout the full 20 years, and they were Israel and the United States. Israel played a major role in the emergence of modern hijacking by its overwhelming victory in the Six Day War of 1967. The Arab and Palestinian attacks on its aircraft, offices, and nationals are thus attributable to the latent state of war between the two parties. In the case of the United States, Palestinian attacks on its civil aviation started in 1973 and intensified in the mid-1980s. The reasons for attacks on American aircraft probably have to do with its close association and unwavering support for Israel and the fact that the United States, as a superpower, could take action to ameliorate Palestinian grievances if it chose to do so.

The full list of hijacks appears in Appendix 7 so that readers can draw their own conclusions. The list of states attacked and on what occasions appears in Appendix 8. This reveals the time patterns of terrorist activity. Finally, the victims of hijacks are recorded by nationality in Appendix 9. It is interesting to note that attacks on Israel, the United States, West Germany, Holland, Japan, the United Kingdom, Austria, France, Italy, India, Kuwait, Canada, Greece, Belgium, Switzerland, and Malta account for 91 of the 100 most significant hijacks. It can be assumed therefore, that "the West" is the target in the overwhelming number of aircraft hijackings that are both internationally and politically significant.

The main objective of this chapter is to trace the evolution of national policies toward terrorist hijacking and to indicate where gaps exist in trying to reach a Western concensus on the control and prevention of hijacking generally. From Appendix 8 it is clear that West Germany, the Netherlands, Japan, Austria, and the United Kingdom faced the problem in the 1970s and that France, Italy, India, Kuwait, Canada, and Greece came under fire in the 1980s. Before looking closely at the evolution of national policies, however, there are a number of regional variations and behavioral characteristics that need to be addressed in order that an overall evaluation of national policies can take place. There are four major issues that are addressed: First, the division between the United States and Western Europe over how to handle international terrorism; second, the division within Western Europe about how to deal with the regional onslaught against civil aviation; third, the varied and contradictory policies carried out by Western governments in the 1970s in contrast to the 1980s; and fourth, the spectrum of governmental response that has evolved in reaction to terrorist attacks, undulating between soft-line and hard-line policies, with intermediate stages in between.

Christopher Hill has written in a British publication a chapter on terrorism dealing with the political dilemmas for Western governments. As he pointed out, it is only since the beginning of the 1980s that terrorism has begun to create major problems for West-West relations. His thesis is "that Western governments now recognize the need for a concerted policy on terrorism reflects changes both in Western attitudes and in terrorist practises, and to some extent is a mark of the ability of international terrorists to force a change in states' priorities."[9] This state of affairs is a recent phenomenon.

In the 1970s the United States was not in the front line of terrorist attacks. The Weathermen, the Symbionese Liberation Army, the Black Panthers, and even the Hanafi Moslems did not affect civil aviation except on rare occasions. Also, the process of Arab embitterment at the United States was mostly quiescent in the 1970s. There were attacks on U.S. citizens and on U.S. civil aviation abroad, but they were seen as specific events and not generally as a threat to U.S. superpower leadership in the international system. To state that the United States was largely free of major international threats from terrorism, however, does not mean that it was free of hijackings. On the contrary, domestic aviation was in acute crisis between 1969 and 1972, but this consisted of hijacks by the mentally disturbed, extortionists, and escaping refugees, mainly homesick Cubans wishing to return to their native country. Stopping this rash of hijackings was essentially a national problem for the United States, with some bilateral action with Cuba and other Latin American countries.

It was the Europeans who were the principal victims of politically motivated terrorist attacks during the 1970s. After 1969, Palestinian attacks were directed principally at certain Western European powers, which also became the playground for international terrorists like Carlos and the target of international terrorist attacks. The kidnapping of the OPEC ministers in 1975 falls into this category. As can be seen in Appendix 7, the Arab terrorist attacks were aimed selectively at certain Western European states; therefore there was no perceived need for either an European or an alliance response to terrorism as such.

Another factor that prevented terrorism from becoming a major problem was what Christopher Hill called "the very success of Western governments in prophylaxis—or rather, 'containment,' for terrorism survived in one form or another whatever its opponents did."[10] At first, European governments were horrified by the terrorist attacks at Dawson's Field, Lod Airport, the Munich Olympics, and other places and seemed frozen into immobility. But the Western counterattack in civil aviation came with the implementation of American airport security measures and national special forces that performed so effectively at Entebbe and Mogadishu. Throughout the period from 1969 to 1979 Western governments, and particularly those of Western Europe, opposed terrorism firmly but also played down its potential as a strategic threat. As Christopher Hill remarked: "To raise the temperature to the level of crisis would have been, it seemed, to play into the hands of the terrorists, whose very intention was to put target societies into a state of siege, to polarize public opinion within them and to focus attention on themselves."[11] Western European states preferred to make terrorist activities seem bizarre and marginal, not a major challenge to the status quo. Above all, they were determined not to react like the Israelis, who were in a state of war.

During 1972 and 1973 the new airport security measures in the United States ended a torrent of 159 hijacks. In 1974, 165 million people passed through the new security with only 3 hijacks occurring. But the United States was facing a different game from that in Western Europe. The security of U.S. civil aviation was not exposed to the relentless efforts of political terrorists to circumvent its system. Also, since the U.S. system was inadequate for Western European conditions, other countermeasures had to be developed to contain the terrorists. Governments during the late 1970s concentrated their energy and resources not on improving their security standards but on upgrading their rescue capabilities. All Western nations developed specialized military or paramilitary forces to deal with terrorist crises. It seemed as if the West was surrendering to the fact that its members could not prevent a terrorist assault from occurring, and they were instead content to affect the outcome of events.[12] Between 1979 and 1981 there was a relative hiatus in hijacking and it is possible that Western governments concluded the problem would go away. How wrong this assumption was.

As a result of President Carter's Camp David initiative in 1978 the United States became directly involved in the fate of the Palestinian–Israeli issue. The rejectionist front of states and groups redoubled their efforts to attack Israel and its principal ally, the United States. Direct attacks against the United States and Israel were now in the planning stage, and it was clear, well before President Reagan took office, that U.S. civil aviation would soon become a direct target of Palestinian rejectionist anger. The Iranian Revolution was an unanticipated accelerator of this process after 1979. It also created significant links between Islamic fundamentalists based in Lebanon and Khomeini's regime in Iran. "What followed," wrote Christopher Hill, "is the now-familiar chronicle of outrages against targets which more and more tended to have an American component or denomination."[13]

The very fact that the United States had now become the main target for Middle Eastern terrorist attacks thrust terrorism to the forefront of policy debate in all Western States. There were two key events in the Americanization of international terrorism. The first was the attempted assassination of President Reagan in 1981, which led the administration to designate terrorism as the main enemy for the rest of the decade. Conveniently, Claire Sterling's *Terror Network* designated but completely failed to prove that terrorism was entirely a Communist plot to destabilize the West. But it was all the Reagan cabinet needed to become active against terrorism. The second event, which led directly to the present adversarial involvement of the United States in world terrorism, was the Israeli invasion of Lebanon in 1982. This invasion must now be seen as a strategic mistake that was to unleash terrorism on and against Israel, the United States, and Western Europe in an unprecedented fashion. Although the Israeli invasion was aimed at dislodging the PLO from Beirut and dealing a death blow at the movement generally, what it really did was strengthen the rejectionist groups and dispossess the Shiites of Southern Lebanon. The seizing of American hostages in Lebanon and the strategic retreat of the United States from peacekeeping duties there with the multinational force, when more than 240 American marines were killed in a suicide bombing, was merely a prelude to

American problems still to come. Between 1983 and 1985 the pattern of hijackings between Iran, Iraq, Kuwait, Lebanon, and Libya grew in intensity to the point at which American civil aviation was sure to be attacked. That the main attack was delayed as long as the summer of 1985 was in itself remarkable. But the central combination of Islamic fundamentalism and rejectionist Palestinians created, after 1985, a crisis in Western civil aviation from which both Western Europe and the United States are still reeling. With 36 to 53 percent of all terrorist attacks occurring in Western Europe—of which 25 percent were of Middle Eastern origin—after 1985, it was difficult enough to develop a Western European response. But when the United States and Western Europe were divided over how to respond to terrorism, suddenly minor differences over the North Atlantic Treaty Organization (NATO) strategy looked insignificant beside the furor that followed. The story of this furor and its consequence belongs later in this chapter, engaging as it does, not only West-West relations but relations within the Western European community itself.

According to Paul Wilkinson there are two main poles in the reactions of states to terrorism—the soft-line approach and the hard-line approach. The soft-line approach consists of "a readiness to make a deal with terrorists, to gain the release of hostages and a rapid end to each terrorist attack."[14] Wilkinson cited a Rand Corporation study stating that statistically, terrorists have a 79 percent chance of success, that is, of evading death or imprisonment. In the soft-line approach terrorists are allowed to react with bolder and more demanding attacks. They will cause other terrorist groups to emulate their methods, and the price of this democratic reaction is further humiliating defeats. The hard-line approach, on the other hand, "means combining harsh and effective temporary measures to isolate and eliminate terrorist cells . . . but still maintain democracy."[15] The key to a hard-line policy is not to panic and become repressive but to mount "a consistent policy of maximizing the risk of punishment run by the terrorists and minimizing their potential rewards."[16] So, according to Wilkinson,

to counter terrorism effectively the tough-line approach involves waging two kinds of war: a military-security war to contain and reduce terrorist violence, and a political and psychological war to secure the popular consent and support which must be the basis of any effective modern democratic government.[17]

There are many options that fill the graduated spectrum between soft- and hard-line policies. There is "retaliation," or the use of force, a tit for tat philosophy. There is "no compromise," the basis of which is the assumption that concessions simply lead to further demands. There is "flexibility," in which a latent sympathy for the terrorists may be mixed with concessions and emergency measures from time to time. Finally, there is the policy of "concession and accommodation." These four policy postures range from hard line to soft line and will be accompanied by a mixture of diplomatic and economic action, preventive measures, deterrents, the application of legislation already in place, international cooperation, and police and intelligence assistance. There are just about enough different options available for the democracies not to have any two nations reacting in exactly the same way to the threat of terrorism.

J. Bowyer-Bell of Columbia University is responsible for the above typology in a trail-breaking work called *A Time of Terror*, published in 1978. Under the heading of "retaliation" he cited the 1976 Entebbe raid by Israel, in which the latter agreed to negotiation policy.[18] But then they struck with lightning speed and great success by using a military force to free the hostages. This incident had a temporary salutary effect on terrorist hijacking worldwide, but it did not demonstrate that retaliation was the panacea for governments. Under the heading of "no compromise," Boyer-Bell stated that "the base of the policy . . . is that concessions simply lead to further demands; to save a few lives now would put more lives in jeopardy in the future,"[19] He cited the French position of "no compromise" in the Croatian hijack of September 1976, which almost, and quite unnecessarily, resulted in the deaths of a planeload of American passengers that the French government would not allow to land even as it ran out of fuel circling over Paris. Both the British and Dutch learned some vital lessons in the 1970s about policies of "no compromise" laced with judicious negotiation to their own advantage.[20]

The policy of "flexibility" has been consistently followed by Sweden but at considerable cost to that state both in financial terms and in terms of prestige. The West Germans and the United States learned sharp lessons from this soft-line approach. The West Germans were hard line with their own domestic terrorists but softer with the Palestinians. In the case of the United States, hijack policy remained "no negotiation and no concession" until the Croatian hijack of September 1975. After that chilling experience of inflexibility the Carter administration adopted a more balanced approach, which then paid off handsomely in the Hanafi Moslem siege in downtown Washington on March 9, 1977.[21] Under the heading of "concession and accommodation," Bowyer-Bell included Cyprus, Spain, Haiti, and Austria, among which the Austrians have remained stubbornly soft line, consistent with their policy of neutrality, to the dismay of certain other Western European states. Throughout the 1970s governments acted without serious, prior planning. Largely spontaneous and reactive, their response was determined by the posture and politics of the moment. Throughout the decade, as Bowyer-Bell pointed out, it can be seen that "each Western democratic state evolves a response as a result of a mix of factors, habit, history, personalities of the moment, traditional prejudice, intuition and usually an eye on the public's desires."[22]

The section that follows traces the specific evolution of policy in Western nations toward the hijacking of civil aviation. Some states changed their policies as a results of their experiences. Other states remained at the extremes of soft-line or hard-line policies. By the end of the 1980s the problems of national-international coordination among the Western powers were more severe than they had been ten years earlier. It is hoped that this short historical section will illustrate some of the breakthroughs and pitfalls in what has been a largely experimental period of dealing with the terrorist threat to civil aviation.

ISRAEL

The state of Israel was the lightning rod that attracted the Arab skyjack war. Between 1968 and 1976 Israeli counterterror policy was worked out by trial and error. After 1976 very few hijacks directly affected Israeli planes, and so policy could remain constant.

On July 22, 1968, an El Al B707 from Rome to Tel Aviv was hijacked to Algiers by the PFLP. Negotiations dragged on for almost two months, and the incident was terminated only when the pilots of the IFALPA threatened to boycott Algiers. At an early stage Israel made clear its intention to use "retaliation," and on December 28, in a raid on Beirut airport, 13 Middle East Airlines planes were surgically destroyed. On August 29, 1969, Leila Khaled of the PFLP hijacked TWA 840, a B707 out of Rome en route between Los Angeles and Tel Aviv. The flight swooped low over Lod Airport, was almost shot down by accompanying Israeli fighters, and finally landed in Damascus. The Syrian government bartered with the Israelis for the lives of some Jewish passengers. Following the incident, Israel announced its intention of never again giving in to hijackers' demands.[23] In December 1969 three PFLP terrorists with carryall bags full of weapons were arrested at Athens airport. By July 1970 there were seven Palestinian terrorists in Greek jails. Only two days before the trial of these seven, an Olympic Airways B727 was hijacked, and the Greeks quickly released the Athens seven in exchange for the plane and its passengers. Abba Ebban, the Israeli foreign minister, was furious and warned that if international hijacking was rewarded, the safety of the airways would be very severely compromised. Taking a tough stance themselves, the Israelis announced they would not, in the future, release imprisoned Arabs in exchange for Israeli passengers.

In February 1970 Ahmed Jabril of the PFLP-GC announced his intention to stop airlines from flying to Israel. His method was to place bombs aboard Swiss Air and Austrian airline planes on February 21. Both bombs exploded; the Austrian plane survived, but the Swiss plane disintegrated with a loss of 47 lives, 15 of them Jewish. In October 1970 an Israeli plane was involved in the mass hijacking to Dawson's Field, Jordan. An El Al B707 flying from New York to Tel Aviv was boarded in Amsterdam by Leila Khaled and her partner. Armed sky marshals killed her partner, Patrick Arguello, and captured Khaled, ending her second hijack attempt. But in the ensuing international negotiations, the Israelis adamantly refused to take part. Throughout 1971 and until early 1972 the Palestinian hijackers aimed their attacks at Jordanian planes, but with very little success.

On May 8, 1972, members of Black September struck at a Belgian Sabena aircraft headed for Israel. They hijacked the plane, landed at Lod Airport, and demanded the release of 100 Arab prisoners in Israel, threatening to blow up the airliner if their demands were not met. Moshe Dayan, the minister of defense, personally directed the incident, stating that only three outcomes were possible: "Destruction, capitulation or capture."[24] The hijack ended with capture as Israel made good on its July 1970 policy decision of nonnegotiation with Arab skyjackers.[25] On September 5, 1972, Black September struck again, this time at the Munich Olympics. In the shootout that followed at Furstenfeldbruck Airport, all 11 Israeli athletes were killed. Three terrorists survived and were imprisoned. The Israelis were as stunned as the West Germans, but their relatiatory instinct was only sharpened by the event. Israeli Prime Minister Golda Meir declared war on the Arab terrorists involved: "We have no alternative solution," she said, "but to strike at the terrorist organizations wherever we can locate them."[26] Later, in April 1973, Israel created the Mirtah Elohim or Wrath of God. Based on the retaliatory principle of "an eye for an eye and a tooth for a tooth," the Israeli counterterror squad set out to assassinate the perpetrators of the Munich killings. Although such a response by the Israeli government was understandable, the counterterror policy would prove to be politically costly. As David Wilkinson pointed out, it was "counter-productive in terms of foreign and diplomatic support."[27] It was also politically and morally questionable. When an innocent Palestinian waiter was assassinated in Norway by the Wrath of God, there was an international outcry.

In 1973 there was a partial hiatus in Palestinian hijacking because of divisions within the PLO and because of the Arab success in the 1973 war. But on September 7, 1974, a TWA flight from Israel, which had landed en route to Athens, was blown up by a bomb in midflight over the Ionian Sea, killing 88 people. This cowardly act simply fanned the embers of the Israeli desire for revenge and retaliation. Then, on June 27, 1976, a French A300 airbus with 250 passengers was hijacked by a joint Palestinian–Baader-Meinhof Gang team and ended up in Entebbe, Uganda. The Israelis pretended to take part in the negotiations for more than 100 Jewish passengers while organizing a military raid to free all of the hostages. It was an enormously risky strategy but a successful one, for the rescue team freed all of the hostages but one and lost only one soldier in the raid. The impact of Entebbe was to turn the psychological tide of defeat being felt in the West over hijacking and to confirm to the Israeli government its belief that only a hard-line, retaliatory policy would work against hijack terrorists.

WEST GERMANY

By the late 1980s, both Lufthansa and German airport security were among the best in the world, but they were not so in the beginning. According to the Bowyer-Bell typology, the West Germans between 1973 and 1977 shared a place with the Swedes and the Americans in subscribing to the "flexibility" approach, or the third category of hijack response. The West German response really began at Dawson's Field in September 1970.

It is worth recalling that the aircraft of five nations were attacked simultaneously in this mass hijack, called by one author "the most remarkable event in the history of aerial piracy."[28] In it, a TWA B707 was diverted between Frankfurt and New York; a Swiss Air DC8 was diverted between Zurich and New York; an El Al B707 was unsuccessfully attacked between Amsterdam and New York, and a Pan Am jumbo jet was diverted to Cairo from its Amsterdam-New York flight.

All of these hijacks took place on September 6, and then on September 8 a British VC10 flying between London and Bahrain was hijacked to free Leila Khaled who was languishing in a British jail after her capture aboard the El Al B707. The result was that now five governments were involved in the negotiations to free hostages and save $50 million worth of aircraft that had been taken to Dawson's Field in Jordan. The aircraft, a jumbo jet, which landed in Cairo; was blown up on arrival. Thus the American, British, Swiss, German, and Israeli governments were involved in the remaining negotiations. It was deliberately, on the part of the PFLP, a drawn-out process. The Palestinians wanted to savor the moment. They wanted both messages—of the Palestinian plight and of Western vulnerability—to sink in. They also wanted to explore the possibilities for divide and rule between the weaker and stronger Western governments. They were not disappointed in the least. The positions of the governments involved in the negotiations looked like this:

| German and Swiss negotiate immediately and independently. | British and Americans are in the middle. | Israelis are adamant in refusing to negotiate. |

George Habash and the PFLP saw that they could squeeze the weaker-responding governments for greater concessions, creating temptations to attack them again at a later date. For the West Germans, that later date came on February 22, 1972. In a 48-hour drama, the PFLP hijacked a West German airliner flying between New Delhi and Frankfurt and diverted it to Aden. All of the passengers were released because the purpose of the hijack was extortion. The PFLP demanded and got from the West German government $5 million in cash, which was handed over at Beirut airport. The PFLP already knew from experience which government would settle quickly. This "Aden coup," as it was called, restored the Arab guerrillas' self-confidence and made hijacking attractive once again. As David Phillips pointed out: "Their confidence was restored by the speed with which the West German government agreed to settle, thus giving a huge infusion of guerrilla funds."[29]

The Aden coup was a costly hijack for the West, and it unleashed a series of events that, by 1977, taught the West Germans a severe lesson. It is highly likely that the weak attitude of the West German government led to a rejuvenation of

Arab terrorism at this time. What the West Germans hoped would be exemption from further attention resulted instead in a high cost in dead and wounded passengers. It was, after all, the year of the Munich Olympics and West Germany was spending DM 1,972 million to make them the "Happy Games." But "the wind sown at Aden was the whirlwind reaped at Munich."[30] The lessons learned by the West Germans in this period were available also to the other Western states observing the drama.

On September 5-6 eight members of Black September shot their way into the Israeli quarters in the Olympic Village. As indicated earlier, 11 hostages were taken to be exchanged for Arabs imprisoned in Israel, but in the ensuing shootout all died save three Arab terrorists who were put in jail. They didn't have long to wait there, however, it was inevitable that the terrorists would soon seize hostages to free the hijackers in German jails. On October 29, 1972, the West German government stumbled into yet another trap in the wake of an election call by Chancellor Willy Brandt. Lufthansa Flight 615, a B727, was hijacked between Beirut and Munich and flown to Damascus, where it was announced that the plane would be blown up unless the Munich trio was handed over. An HS125 executive jet with no less a luminary than Lufthansa's chairman arrived with the Arab prisoners aboard. In the words of an unidentified Arab who was involved: "Your government has got wise." Abba Eban, Israel's foreign minister, described the release as a "shocking surrender, a capitulation, and a weakening of the international stand against terrorism."[31] Simultaneously, the West German ambassador to Israel, Otto von Puttkamer, explained that although he was extremely sympathetic to the reaction of the Israeli government, his own government was in an awkward predicament. He insisted that West Germany was not at war and that therefore his country would have to make every effort to stay within the law and make the saving of German lives the top priority.[32] But as Bowyer-Bell pointed out: "The German government agreed with such alacrity that many suspected the hijacking of Flight 615 had been previously arranged."[33] Like other European states, the West Germans did not want to hold on to poison pawns, meaning Arab terrorists, who would then engender fresh rounds of hostage taking. Unofficial estimates are that in the five years following, 150 Arab terrorists were arrested in Western Europe and released without trial.[34]

Between 1973 and 1976 the trials of the Baader-Meinhof Gang were taking place, and the German government was preoccupied with internal terrorist problems. The terrorists who had abducted Peter Lorenz in 1975 were given an airplane and safe passage to South Yemen. All five subsequently returned to West Germany to resume their terrorist activities. They actually took part in the abduction of Hans Martin Schleyer in 1977, but by then things were changing, and they were astonished at the tough line taken by the government when they were captured. As one diplomat remarked: "This was proof that giving in is self-defeating."[35] The Schleyer episode took place in September 1977, and the turning point for West Germany in hijacking occurred in the days following

October 13. On that day a Lufthansa B737 flying between Palma and Frankfurt was taken over by four hijackers belonging to the joint PFLP-Baader-Meinhof. They demanded the release of 11 prisoners in Germany and two in Turkey and $15 million in ransom. The Lufthansa plane made an enormous tour of the Middle East for several days until it finally arrived in Mogadishu, Somalia, the pilot having been savagely shot in the throat by one of the hijackers.

The one direct result of the episode in Munich in 1972 had been the creation of the GSG9 counterterrorist team. This team, with the help of SAS advice and stun grenades, managed to storm the plane and kill three of the hijackers without any loss of life. This event signaled the West German move from a response of "flexibility" to one of "no compromise." It had been a long, hard lesson for the West Germans to learn. Even in August 1978 the West German government wavered when two East Germans hijacked a Polish plane to Berlin. In an effort to avoid jurisdiction in the politically sensitive case, and thereby to duck responsibility for punishing the hijackers, the West German government appealed to the United States to invoke its postwar rights to oversee air corridors to West Berlin. But many more escaping refugees continued to hijack in the 1980s, and West Germany convicted and imprisoned them, as well as greatly strengthening its airport security.

HOLLAND

Holland was introduced to air piracy during an unsuccessful attempt to hijack a KLM plane in 1965, but the first intense period of hijacking between 1968 and 1973 left the Dutch relatively unscathed. After 1973, however, KLM planes were hijacked; Palestinians and Japanese Red Army cadres launched operations in The Netherlands, and hijackers thousands of miles away presented nonnegotiable demands.[36] At first, the Dutch opted for a policy of "conciliation and accommodation" consistent with their fairly permissive social ethos. But events after 1974 radically changed the Dutch position. On September 24, 1974, three members of the Japanese Red Army seized the French Embassy in The Hague. With the memory of the Lod Airport massacre still vivid, the Dutch government persuaded the French to release Japanese prisoners in exchange for the French ambassador and other hostages. A French jet with a Dutch crew then flew the four Japanese terrorists to Damascus.

On November 22, 1974, a British plane was hijacked by the Palestinians, who demanded that the Dutch release two Fedayeen who had been arrested in March and sentenced to five-year terms for hijacking. The Dutch capitulated. On November 25, three days later, a KLM B747 was hijacked with 247 hostages aboard. It embarked on an odyssey that took it to Damascus, Nicosia, Tripoli, Malta, and finally Dubai. Passengers were released in groups for three days, and the Dutch government was forced to make a solemn promise that no arms or immigrants would pass through its territory en route to Israel. If anything was a compromise of Dutch sovereignty, it was this decision. But the Dutch insisted that their policy was flexible and that concession was granted "only when the event was beyond control or when loss of life seemed certain."[37] In October two members of the Fedayeen, using arms that had been smuggled in, seized a chapel in the penitentiary near The Hague. They captured a visiting choir, released seven hostages, but demanded a plane to fly them out of Holland. Finally, after 105 hours, Dutch marines and police stormed the chapel and freed the remaining hostages after overpowering the Palestinians. But later they were exchanged for the earlier-mentioned hostages in the British jet seized on November 22. The Dutch government was taking a battering.

On December 2, 1975, seven South Molluccan terrorists seized a local train at Beilen in the northern Netherlands. They shot and killed the engineer and one passenger before settling in for a siege. The Dutch government decided on no concessions and no leaving the country. One more hostage was killed. On December 4 the situation was complicated by the seizure of the Indonesian consulate in Amsterdam by seven other South Molluccans. After 12 days of bleak winter conditions the terrorists on the train surrendered, and after 16 days those in the consulate gave up. Fairly heavy prison sentences were given all of them, and "the general feeling in The Netherlands and elsewhere was that the Dutch strategy of extended negotiations while refusing to compromise had been highly effective."[38]

In September 1976 a KLM DC9 flying between Nice and Amsterdam was hijacked by three Arabs. They surrendered finally to Libyan authorities and the Dutch government, and especially its prime negotiator, psychiatrist Dick Mulder, "felt that negotiations—especially on non-substantive matters—would gradually transform the terrorist situation into one where surrender would become inevitable and the hostages' safety certain."[39] The Dutch felt the "no-compromise" posture of silence employed by the Irish and British police was not so effective. Eighteen months later, on May 23, 1977, 6 heavily armed South Molluccans seized an elementary school four miles southwest of Assen taking 105 students and 6 teachers hostage. Simultaneously, 7 other South Molluccans stopped a train near Ohnen and held 50 hostages. The prime minister denounced "a horrible act of terror," and the minister of justice refused to release 24 imprisoned South Molluccans and fly them to an unspecified country in a B747. The siege dragged on and on, until the children contracted a mysterious illness and were finally released. But finally, the government ran out of patience after three weeks of negotiation and standoff. On June 11 Dutch marine commandos backed by five Lockheed F104 Starfighters attacked the school and train simultaneously. The final toll was 8 dead (2 hostages and 6 South Molluccans) and 12 wounded (9 hostages, 1 terrorist, and 2 marine commandos).[40] Although the government and the negotiators disagreed over the final outcome, the Dutch had come full circle, from "concession" to the Japanese Red Army to repression with no concessions (albeit after three weeks). By 1977 the Dutch government had learned the same lessons as the West Germans and henceforth joined them in the category of "no compromise" with terrorist hijacking.

JAPAN

Between 1970 and 1977 the Japanese Red Army (JRA) was involved in eight of the nine attacks that challenged the Japanese government. This terrorist group had been dangerous and difficult for all governments because of its ruthlessness, internal discipline, and skillful use of international bases and links with other terrorist groups. Paul Wilkinson has been one of the few commentators to mention the JRA, and he stated that "even the dangerous qualities just described do not adequately explain the JRA's success rate. They reaped maximum advantage from the ineptness and weakness of governments' responses to their attacks."[41] The Japanese government in this period was a study in weakness and capitulation. It clearly preferred to pay millions of dollars in ransom than to take a tough line against international terrorism.

The Japanese were faced early on with the hijacking dilemma for on March 3, 1970, the group known as the Samurai Nine struck. As described in Chapter 2, nine members of the JRA seized a Japanese Air Lines B727 and flew it first to Fukuoka, Japan; then to Seoul, South Korea; and finally, to Pyongyang in North Korea. It was the first skyjack to be televised in progress, and millions of Japanese stayed at home to watch the saga. Deputy Minister of Transport Yamamura negotiated directly with the terrorists in both Fukuoka and Seoul. The Japanese government was so unprepared for this supposedly Western malady that it had not even signed the 1963 Tokyo convention on hijacking. The South Koreans wanted to take a tough line to discourage an increasing habit of hijacking from South to North Korea. But the Japanese government was committed to saving all lives aboard even if it meant Yamamura standing in for the hostages himself and traveling to North Korea. One of the main lessons from this hijack observed and learned by the PFLP was the indecisiveness of governments in the face of a determined hijack. As Phillips pointed out, "a political group had detained an airliner full of passengers for four days at an airport while it negotiated with *governments.*"[42] Later in the year the PFLP found its own airport at Dawson's Field, renamed it Revolution Airstrip, and negotiated over three airplanes hijacked and sitting on the tarmac.

On May 31, 1972, three Japanese Red Army terrorists killed 26 people and wounded 76 in an attack at Lod Airport in Tel Aviv. The incident shocked the world as no previous hijacking had done. It also horrified the Japanese government, which offered profound apologies and compensation. On July 20, 1973, a group of three Arabs and one JRA member hijacked a Japan Airlines B747 between Amsterdam and Tokyo. The aircraft flew around the Middle East for four days until it arrived at Benghazi, where passengers were released and the plane was blown up. Once again, the Japanese government was anaemic and quiescent over the attack on its airline. Inevitably, this led to fresh attacks, and on January 31, 1974, two Palestinians and two JRA members attacked a Shell Oil Company fuel installation in Singapore. They seized a boat and five hostages, which they held for a week until five more JRA terrorists took over the

Japanese embassy in Kuwait. Finally, all nine terrorists were picked up by a Japanese Air Lines plane and flown to South Yemen. The Japanese government was making it very easy for the terrorists to thrive as they capitulated to all their demands.

Success breeds success, and on September 13, 1974, three JRA terrorists attacked the French Embassy in The Hague, taking 12 hostages. In the end the French and Dutch governments had to deal with the episode. It is known that the Dutch consulted periodically with Japanese embassy officials.[43] But this seems to have been the latter's only input into a situation in which, once again, the soft line of nonresistance prevailed. On August 4, 1975, the U.S. Consulate and the Swedish Embassy in The Hague were secured by Japanese Red Army terrorists demanding the release of seven imprisoned terrorists. The Japanese gave in again, and although two refused to go, five were flown to Libya. On May 1, 1976, a Japan Air Lines DC8 was hijacked without intervention by the Japanese government, and finally, on September 28, 1877, the Red Army hijacked a Japan Air Lines flight in Bombay. The terrorists demanded the release of six Red Army prisoners and a $6 million ransom. The Japanese government capitulated and paid the entire ransom while facilitating the terrorist's escape to Baghdad to join Wadi Haddad and Carlos. In 1978 at the Western Economic Summit meeting the Japanese agreed with the declaration on dealing toughly with hijacking but did nothing concrete to accomplish its aims.

It was likely because the Japanese Red Army ceased operations as a separate unit that no hijacks were aimed at Japan after 1979. Also, that country was geographically removed from the center of hijacking activity in Western Europe. But Japan is as far off the scale in the direction of "concession and accommodtion" as Israel is in the opposite direction of "retaliation." Either the Japanese learned nothing or else they deeply believe in buying their way out of hostage situations. Certainly, the security at Narita Airport in Tokyo is among the most efficient in the world. But the airport is an armed fortress, which might not be the way the West wants to deal with airport security.

AUSTRIA

Austria was a soft target for terrorists in the 1970s. It was a country with many guest Arab laborers. Also, Chancellor Bruno Kriesky was a Jew and would not risk striking back at Palestinians. In early 1970 a bomb exploded in an Austrian airliner, but the plane held together. In September 1973 two Arabs extorted a promise from the Austrian government, through a terrorist heist, to close down Schonau Transit Camp for Russian Jews en route to Israel.[44] The Austrians considered the safety of the hostages to be their priority and were jubilant over their handling of the incident until a chorus of criticism came not only from Israel but also from the United States and other Western governments. Austrian weakness no doubt played a part in the calculations of Carlos, when on December 21, 1975, he walked into the OPEC headquarters in Vienna and captured all 12 OPEC oil ministers. The next day the compliant Austrian authorities had an Austrian Airways DC9 with a crew of three ready for a flight to Algiers. They even shook hands with the terrorists as they left. Carlos wanted a manifesto broadcast in French on Austrian radio and television every two hours, and again the Austrians complied. En route to Algiers, Carlos reportedly told the Austrian pilot that "violence is the only language the Western democracies can understand."[45] But the size of the ransom was the true indicator of the extent of the Austrian defeat. The government reportedly transferred more than $5 million from a Swiss bank to Aden. Along with Saudi and Iranian payments, it was undoubtedly a world record ransom payment. It certainly served to encourage terrorists to demand more and to attack Western governments further. During that period, and subsequently, the Austrian government has occupied the far left of the response spectrum under the heading of "concession and accommodation."

According to John Bowyer-Bell, the spectrum of governmental response to international terrorism during the period from 1973 to 1977 appeared as follows:

Concession and Accommodation	Flexibility	No Compromise	Retaliation
Cyprus	Sweden	France	Israel
Spain	West Germany	Britain	
Austria	United States	Holland	
Japan			

During the next ten years, the cast of actors changed, and several governments moved across the spectrum of response. The governments that are examined are India, Kuwait, Egypt, Italy, Greece, France, Britain, and the United States.

INDIA

Between 1981 and 1988 India experienced eight terrorist-related incidents to civil aircraft. In every case the cause was the Sikh problem in the Punjab. On September 29, 1981, an Indian Airlines B737 was hijacked by seven Sikh terrorists on a flight between New Delhi and Amritsar. Using their ceremonial daggers the hijackers overpowered the crew and demanded to be flown to Lahore, Pakistan. There, they demanded the release of Sikh terrorists in prison, a press conference, an autonomous Sikh state, and $500,000.[46] In the end the Pakistanis sent army personnel disguised as airport employees aboard the plane and ended the hijack. This was the same year in which an increasingly nationalist Punjab state had made 45 demands of the central Indian government. One of these demands was that members of the Sikh religion be allowed to wear their ceremonial Kirpan, or dagger, on both domestic and international flights.[47] They were now banned on all flights.

On August 4, 1982, a lone Sikh terrorist hijacked an Indian Airlines B737 again between New Delhi and Amritsar. Permission to land at Lahore was denied so the plane landed at Amritsar where the hijacker was overpowered. Just 16 days later an identical hijack occurred, but the hijacker was shot and killed. From 1982 onwards, serious violence erupted in the Punjab, which then developed into a siege of the Sikh Golden Temple at Amritsar by the Indian government. The siege lasted from June 2 to 5, 1984, and ended with thousands dead, including the charismatic Sikh leader Bhindranwale. On July 5, 1984, eight Sikhs hijacked an Indian Airlines A300 airbus flying between Srinagar and New Delhi. Armed with pistols, knives, axes, and a fake bomb, they demanded the release of all Sikhs captured in the temple fighting in June. They also demanded $25 million for the damage done to the temple and the return of stolen treasures.[48] The demands were not met and the hijackers had to surrender to Pakistani authorities in Lahore. On October 31, 1984, "the most powerful woman on earth," Indian Prime Minister Indira Ghandi, was assassinated by two of her Sikh bodyguards and near civil war erupted briefly in India.[49]

When the Golden Temple was stormed in June, 25,000 Sikhs marched in the streets of Vancouver, Canada. Among them, no doubt, marched members of the Babbar Khalsa. This organization, led by Talwinder Singh Parmar and estimated to have 400 Canadian followers, strongly supported an independent state in the Punjab. The Babbar Khalsa "has often offered support to hijackers of Indian Airlines jets on trial in Pakistan as symbols of defiance."[50] Beginning in early 1985 there were warnings that it would be unsafe to fly overseas in Air India (formerly Indian Airlines) planes. But Canadian authorities were dubious and security was lax.

Suddenly, on June 23, 1985, a double sabotage took place, planned, enabled, and executed on Canadian soil. Within an hour of each other, Air India 182 flying between Toronto and London and CP Air 003 between Vancouver and Tokyo experienced explosions. The first destroyed the plane in the air high above the Irish Sea, killing 329 people, and the second killed two baggage handlers and wounded four others at Narita Airport in Tokyo as the baggage from the CP Air flight was being off-loaded. Sikh extremists are under deep—but as yet unproved—suspicion for having placed the bombs aboard both planes. Subsequently, in 1986 two Sikhs were convicted in Canada of trying to place bombs aboard planes leaving New York for India. They were given life sentences.

The real impact of these events is best mirrored in their effect on Indian airport security and government policy toward hijacking. The Sikh problem alone has led the Indian government to a policy of strong "no compromise." When an Indian airplane is hijacked, the policy is no negotiation over hostages and no concessions. At all cost, hijacks must be contained within the state of India. Hostages taken on aircraft are deemed to be expendable. India's five main international airports, at Calcutta, Bombay, New Delhi, Madras, and Kerala, resemble armed camps. Passengers have to show an airline ticket before entering the airport terminal and then go through four separate check points. Luggage is

X-rayed for explosives before passengers reach the holding area, and both domestic and international luggage is automatically X-rayed during the check-in procedure. Indeed, airplane and airport security is so tight as to be almost absurd. On many flights, cutlery is counted before and after eating meals, and photography over airports is strictly forbidden. The nation's three antihijacking teams, which were trained by the East Germans, are ready to operate at any time.

Initially, the Sikhs objected to going through metal detectors in their turbans. But when they gave trouble, they were hauled away and searched because of the climate of suspicion against them. Even small batteries are not allowed inside the body of the plane, because they could be easily used to ignite a bomb. Thus, within a five-year period, the Sikh problem has effectively revolutionized Indian airplane and airport security. The Indian government stands firmly in the ranks of states with a "no compromise" response to terrorist hijacking. Even so, the government admits that its system is not fail-proof and has anticipated hijackings with a broad range of responses, including posthijack stress therapy. It is interesting to note that there have been no major hijacks since 1985, though between October 15 and 20, 1988, there were two suspicious crashes of Air India planes. One, an A300 airbus, crashed with a loss of 209 lives. The other, a Fokker, crashed in Assam killing 165. Whether the cause was sabotage, mechanical failure, or pilot error has not yet been established. Of the 329 passengers killed in Air India 182 in 1985, 290 were Canadian citizens; thus it was no surprise when Canada's foreign minister, Joe Clark, signed an extradition treaty with India in 1986. The two countries also agreed to bilateral intelligence service cooperation over terrorism.

KUWAIT

In the 1980s Kuwait emerged dramatically as a victim on the international hijacking scene. There were a number of reasons for this. First, one-third of the population was Shiite Moslem, although the nation has a Sunni Moslem ruler. Second, Kuwait, an oil-rich state, took a decisive stand with Iraq in the Iraq-Iran War. This alone was enough to earn the angry displeasure of Iran. Third, Kuwait had developed an excellent airline service, which plied the Middle Eastern and West Asian routes. Finally, the oil industry attracted impoverished workers to Kuwait, many of them disinherited Shiites from disintegrating Lebanon. Together, these factors set the scene for a remarkable series of attacks on the national airline, Kuwait Airways.

On July 8, 1977, six men hijacked a Kuwait Airways B707 flying between Beirut and Kuwait. It was diverted to Damascus, Syria, where the hijackers surrendered to the Syrian authorities. On July 24, 1980, a more serious hijack took place. A Kuwait Airways B737 was hijacked between Beruit and Kuwait by at least five hijackers armed with pistols, hand grenades, and dynamite. Ordering the plane to Kuwait, the hijackers demanded payment of a debt owed by a Kuwaiti businessman of between 200,000 and 1 million Kuwaiti dinars. The plane flew to Manama, Bahrain, next and then returned to Kuwait. An electrical outage at Kuwait airport forced the plane to Abadan in Iran. Next, it tried to land in Teheran where the runway was blocked, forcing the plane to return to Kuwait. Finally, the pilot and copilot leaped out of the cockpit window and escaped, and the hijackers were persuaded to surrender.[51] Apparently, the weapons used had been smuggled in after the hijackers had passed through the screening process.

The third Kuwait hijack took place, again on a Kuwait Airways flight in Beirut headed for Kuwait, on February 24, 1982. Firing submachine guns in the air, the hijackers rode up to the aircraft in a car and boarded. They demanded the release of their Shiite Moslem spiritual leader, who had disappeared on a trip to Libya in August 1978. They wished to fly to Iran, but that country made it known that the aircraft would not be permitted to land. During nine hours of negotiations, they fired bursts at the control tower and finally surrendered when assured of a U.N. inquiry into their leader's disappearance. But these attacks on Kuwaiti planes were only a prelude to what was still to come.

In 1983 Islamic Jihad was created in collusion between Iran and the Shiites in Southern Lebanon. The first target of this Shiite International was to be Kuwait. On December 12, 1983, a truck laden with high explosive crashed through the gates of the U.S. Embassy in Kuwait and blew up ten feet from the building. There were seven other simultaneous explosions throughout the city, including one at the French Embassy. A massive plot to assassinate government leaders and perhaps even to attempt a coup was uncovered by American and Kuwaiti intelligence sources.[52] A total of 18 conspirators, all Iraqi-born Shiites and Lebanese belonging to the group known as Al Dawa (The Call), was discovered. It was a highly professional team, and the explosion at the U.S. Embassy killed 5 and wounded 87 people. Seventeen of the 18—the other died in the embassy explosion—went to prison, where some of them remain under sentence of death.

These were the circumstances when, on December 4, 1984, a fourth and far more serious hijack was launched against Kuwait by the Shiite International. It was a brutal affair that lasted six days and resulted in the murder of two U.S. overseas aid workers and the wounding of two Kuwaitis. Others were beaten and tortured. The terrorists struck exactly one year after their outrage in Kuwait and now demanded the release of the 17 prisoners. Four men hijacked a Kuwait Airways A310 flying between Kuwait, Dubai, and Karachi. The plane was hijacked to Teheran where, during the six days, 153 passengers and crew were released. What became quickly apparent was that Iran was aiding and abetting the hijack. More arms appeared on the plane, and the Iranian authorities enabled the screams and terror of the 166 passengers to be broadcast for all the world to hear. A Kuwaiti negotiating team was sent to Teheran but was not allowed to meet with the Kuwaiti copilot. (The pilot was British.) As G. H. Jansen of the *Los Angeles Times* wrote: "The usually supple and accommodating Kuwaitis . . . now untypically showed great determination in refusing to release (the 17 prisoners)."[53] This strong exhibition of national will was supported by all Kuwaitis, save the Shias. Even when the Iranians finally moved in and ended the hijack, the Kuwaiti leaders thanked the Iranian authorities, nursed their doubts about Iranian collusion, but still refused to allow any of the 17 prisoners to be freed. President Reagan sent a message to Kuwait's emir, Sheik Jaber al-Ahmed al-Sabah, praising his "firm stand" in rejecting the demands of the terrorists.[54] Kuwaiti airplane and airport security tightened considerably after this episode, but it faced the same constraints as that in India: not every one of the 200,000 Shia living in the region could be treated as a suspect.

Islamic Jihad had not finished with Kuwait. When TWA 847 was hijacked in Beirut on June 14, 1985, one of the principal demands made of the Americans was that they should lean on the Kuwaitis to release those 17 prisoners. Neither government was willing to give in on that score, thus making another hijack almost inevitable. That incident came in April 1988 and lasted for 16 days.

On April 5, 1988, a Kuwait Airways B747 flying between Bangkok and Kuwait was hijacked by terrorists from Hezbolah (The Party of God) over the Strait of Hormuz and diverted to Mashad in Iran. During a two-week period, the plane flew to Larnaca in Cyprus and finally to Algiers in a 3,200-mile journey. The 112 passengers aboard included 3 distant members of the Kuwaiti royal family. Several more hijackers joined the plane in Iran, along with more weapons, and it is strongly suspected that Imad Mughniyah, the mastermind of the 1984 and 1985 TWA hijacks, joined the nine hostage takers. The Syrians would not allow the terrorists to land in Damascus, and Larnaca was used because the jet was running out of fuel. The most interesting aspect of this hijacking, however, was the standoff between the terrorists seeking the release of the 17 prisoners in Kuwait and the Kuwaiti government. Iran was clearly behind the terrorists; the United States was equally clearly behind the Kuwaiti government. In fact the Kuwaiti government is hated by Iran for the additional reason that it brought U.S. naval power into the Persian Gulf to protect Kuwait's oil shipments. During the long siege, the United States publicly and privately urged the Kuwaitis not to yield to the hijackers. Kuwaits' policy of "no compromise" was severely tried during the crisis. The hijackers shot two Kuwaiti soldiers at Larnaca; they threatened to blow up the plane; they got one of the royal personages to call on the Kuwait government to release the 17 prisoners. But none of the threats, torture, or hype worked.

When the Algerians entered the picture in a mediatory capacity, "they blamed Kuwait's intransigent refusal to discuss the 17 jailed terrorists for the lack of progress in the talks."[55] The Kuwaiti minister of state for foreign affairs insisted the radicals would not be released.[56] "Kuwait has a firm policy of not yielding to terrorism." He also stated: "We are a nation of laws, and we will remain a nation of laws."[57] On April 13 Kuwait's defense minister affirmed his country's "unwavering and principled stance of rejecting blackmail."[58] On April 14, the chief editor of the *Al-Anbaa* newspaper in Kuwait stated, "Even if they kill all the hostages there on the plane, we'll never, ever release the killers who are here in Kuwait.''[59] There were demonstrations of support in Kuwait at the funerals of the two slain Kuwaiti soldiers.

Finally, the hijackers were forced to leave Algeria empty handed, and the remaining 36 hostages were freed unharmed and given a rapturous welcome on their return to Kuwait. Under severe pressure from experienced hijackers, who had killed and were backed by Iran, the government of Kuwait retained intact its firm policy of ''no compromise'' on hijacking.

It is also likely Imad Mughiyah now knows that further hijacks to release his cousin will be of no effect. This is the second case of a non-Western government taking a firm and principled national stand against international hijacking.

EGYPT-ITALY-GREECE

Italy, Greece, and Egypt are included together in this section because they represent the soft underbelly of European hijack terrorism. Although only a few major hijacks have directly involved these states, Rome and Athens are two of the busiest centers of hijacking in the whole of Europe, and their government policies are clearly apparent. As stated earlier, the Italians have a special sympathy for the Palestinians, which has made them soft on Palestinian hijacks. Italy is also particularly vulnerable geographically to strikes from the Arab world.

Greek policies toward hijacking are similar to Italian policies though the strong anti-Americanism of the Papandreou government tended to favor the terrorist cause more than is the case of Italy. Athens is also a natural hub of travel not only for Europe but for the world, and combined with this geographical factor is the sad truth that the Greeks seem incapable of mounting effective airport security. At the same time they do seem able to absorb the enormous tourist revenues that accrue from the constant use of Athens and its airport by travelers worldwide.

In the case of Egypt there is a natural sympathy for the Palestinian cause, though this has been muted by Egypt's 25-year campaign of making common cause with Western Europe and the United States. Egypt has been in a divided frame of mind and has paid the price in hijacking. Three incidents in 1978 and 1985 have clearly illustrated the dilemmas faced by Egypt's policy-makers. On February 18, 1978, two gunmen from the Abu Nidal faction murdered Egyptian editor Yusuf Sebal in Larnaca, Cyprus. The terrorists then siezed a Cypriot airliner, and in the ensuing standoff with the Cypriot authorities a costly misunderstanding arose in which Egyptian commandos, trying to achieve an Entebbe-style rescue, ended up in a gunfight with the Cypriot national guard in which 15 commandos died. The terrorists were captured, sentenced to death, and then set free by the Cypriot government.

On October 7, 1985, the Italian cruise ship *Achille Lauro* was hijacked by a PLO faction. The whole scheme went wrong when they were prematurely discovered; so instead of the attack on Israel, which had been planned, a cruise ship hijack ensued. In the course of it an American citizen, Leon Klinghoffer, was brutally murdered. The pirates finally surrendered to the Egyptian authorities, since the ship was visiting Alexandria at the time of the seajack. Abul Abbas, the PLO planner of the whole operation, joined the four captives in Cairo, but Egyptian President Mubarak lied about the presence of the five terrorists in Egypt, insisting they had already left. U.S. intelligence knew they were still there, however, and even managed to intercept the Egyptair B737 carrying them to Tunis, south of Crete in the Mediterranean. The Egyptian plane was forced down at Sigonella base in Sicily on October 11. Mubarak was embarassed by the whole episode, and in trying to save face at home, he "demanded an apology from President Reagan for all Egyptians."[60] There were demonstrations by students and a U.S. flag burning in Cairo, but Mubarak's face-saving attempt was clearly a failure internationally.

These events probably explain why, a month later, President Mubarak tried to take a tough line again. On November 23, the Abu Nidal faction hijacked an Egyptair B737 on a flight between Athens and Cairo. A midair gunfight ensued with the plane being forced to land at Luqa, Malta. The terrorists began to murder Jewish and U.S. citizens systematically. After a ten-hour hiatus the plane was stormed by Egypt's elite "Thunderbolt" force, but again, as at Larnaca, the operation went wrong. In one of the bloodiest hijack episodes yet, nearly 60 people were killed in order to save 40 others. The Maltese would not allow any American special forces to join in but gave the fatal go-ahead signal to the Egyptians. Like his predecessor Anwar Sadat, President Mubarak had failed to carry out successfully a hard-line response to terrorist hijacking.

The Italian government revealed its attitude to hijacking early, when in 1972 U.S. Marine Raffaele Minichiello, of Italian parentage, hijacked a U.S. plane from San Francisco to Rome. It was a clear violation of army, civilian, and international norms, a dangerous and ill-advised hijack. Yet in Italy the hijacker was received like a national hero. The Italian government refused extradition of a U.S. citizen and then gave Minichiello only a six-month prison term. In February 1973 the Italian government released two members of Black September just six months after arresting them with a bomb that they intended to place on an El Al B707 at Rome Airport.[61] By 1978, The Red Brigades in Italy had been dealt a lethal blow by the Carabinieri under General Dalla Chiesa, but still the lesson had not been learned.

There were four hijacks of Alitalia planes in 1979, 1980, and 1982. All of them were Middle-East related, and in three of the four cases the Italian governmental reaction was weak and ineffective.

On October 11, 1985, the five terrorists involved in the *Achille Lauro* seajacking were forced down at Sigonella base in Sicily. The government of Italy under Prime Minister Bettino Craxi refused to allow the United States to arrest the hijackers. They then allowed the mastermind of the operation, Abul Abbas, to escape to Belgrade where he spoke freely to Western reporters. This action was taken without consultation with the defense minister in a coalition government, and as a result the Craxi government fell. As Gayle Rivers wrote: "Washington might have foreseen that the Italians would not have the courage to go along with the big play."[62] The intimidation of the Italian government by Libya and the Palestinian factions was now all but complete. Italy now belonged to the permissive extreme of governments in the category of "concession and accommodation." With Rome airport being one of the busiest and most-attacked airports in Western Europe, the scene was now set for a supreme demonstration of terrorist disdain and contempt. On December 27, 1985, Abu Nidal terrorists attacked Rome and Vienna airports, killing 19 and wounding more than 100 people. In terrorist eyes, the Italian government was simply irrelevant and was to be exploited whenever an occasion arose.

On May 11, 1986, Brigadier General Ambrogio Viviani, former chief of Italian military counterespionage, disclosed that Italy and Libya had worked out a deal whereby Moammar Qaddafi would not conduct terrorist operations against Italians if they would turn a blind eye to activities of his men and the PLO faction under his control. Viviani revealed that Italy not only provided Qaddafi with help against his enemies but also showed the Libyans how to set up a secret service. Ironically, the man who made the deal was none other than the former Italian prime minister who was later murdered by the Red Brigades, Aldo Moro.[63] It became very clear that any Western European attempt to tighten up airplane and airport security on a coordinated basis would run immediately into a two-faced attitude from the government of Italy.

On July 22, 1970, the Greek government firmly established its own unique approach to hijacking. On that date an Olympic Airways plane was hijacked and the lives of Greek passengers exchanged for imprisoned terrorists in Greece. The government, the Red Cross, and even Aristotle Onassis were all involved in a situation in which the Greek government was blackmailed on its own soil. There was considerable international protest over this cave-in, but the Greek government was adamant that a deal was a deal. This episode was a prelude to the multiple hijacking at Dawson's Field later that year.

It was clear that lacking a major international airline, Greece would become a victim of terrorist convenience as an attack point in the center of international air travel. On August 5, 1973, 5 passengers were killed and 55 wounded in a Palestinian machine gun and grenade attack on a TWA plane landing in Athens on a flight from Tel Aviv. TWA was soon to have other problems in Athens, for on September 7, 1974, another TWA plane was blown up in midair out of Athens, from Israel, with a loss of all 88 passengers.

But it was in the 1980s that the security of Athens airport came under close scrutiny as a result of several hijacks and because of an American-Greek political standoff. In 1984 the "suitcase bomber" referred to earlier was traced by a foreign intelligence agency to his apartment in Athens, where one of the lethal suitcases was discovered.[64] Although tipped off about the suitcase, Greek intelligence failed to discover the bomb sealed inside it and so bungled the investigation. As a result the CIA was accused of taking unilateral action in Greece. In the ensuing furor, the State Department designated the Greek performance in this matter as "directly traceable to Papandreou's harshly anti-American political style."[65]

In the TWA 847 hijack of June 1985, a Lebanese Shiite, Ali Atwa, failed to board the crowded flight in Athens. The Greek government seized him but quickly exchanged him, ostensibly for the life of a Greek popstar aboard the plane in Algiers. The result was that through the offices of the Greek government Ali Atwa rejoined TWA 847, a craven capitulation to international terrorism. As Nikos V. Skoulas, secretary-general of the Greek National Tourist Organization, said, "We understand that some countries refuse to negotiate with terrorists, but to save lives we do negotiate."[66]

On November 23, 1985, the Abu Nidal faction hijacked the plane out of Athens en route to Cairo, a hijack that ended in tragic circumstances at Luqa Airport in Malta. On April 2, 1986, a bomb exploded aboard TWA 840, blowing a hole in its side as it approached Athens. On April 7, 1986, *Newsweek* complained that "the European approach has been to avoid retaliation by accommodating the Libyans and not trying to provoke terrorists."[67] It pointed out that Greece had simply expelled a terrorist caught red-handed in a Mercedes packed with explosives. Also in 1986, it was Greek opposition to sanctions that broke up the potential for a whole unified European front against Syria in the wake of the Hindawi arrest in London in April of that year. In 1986, as in 1988, the United States was ready to brand Athens airport as a Dangerous Foreign Airport and forbid American planes to land there. Behind-the-scenes arrangements were hastily made through the good offices of an IATA official, who happened to be in Athens, to upgrade the security at the airport. Despite all this, the Greek government is unrepentant, and in the words of Gayle Rivers: "Terrorist activity from this Mediterranean launching pad is rampant, and Athens is viewed as perhaps one of the most dangerous aerial crossroads in the world."[68] The Greek government, along with the Italian government, belongs to the "concession and accommodation" side of the spectrum of government responses.

FRANCE

As Edward Moxon-Browne wrote, "In the 1970s France was relatively free from the kind of terrorism that predominates elsewhere."[69] Nevertheless, the first French encounter with terrorism in 1974 very quickly established the nation's future response to terrorist blackmail. At The Hague on September 13, 1974, the French ambassador and other members of his embassy were taken hostage by the Japanese Red Army. The Dutch were ready to storm the building with their special troops, who were actually already in the building and poised to strike, when the French insisted on a soft-line approach. As Paul Wilkinson wrote, "Due to French insistence a policy of capitulation to terrorist demands was adopted.''[70] Once such a pattern is established, it is difficult to reverse because the terrorists have already made a judgment about the government's will to resist. Gayle Rivers wrote, ''The French government has an appalling record of compromising in the fight against terrorists. The Arab groups consider France a soft touch.''[71] In the months before the Entebbe hijack the French police arrested German Baader-Meinhof Gang member Wilfred Bose. His deportation was eagerly awaited by the Federal German Border Guard. But the French instead drove Bose to the German border unannounced and let him go. Bose was next heard from in the hijacking of the Air France A300 at Entebbe. Although the hijacked plane was French and more than 100 passengers were Jewish, the government of France seems to have done very little to resolve the crisis. In the end it was the Israelis who acted.

Presumably, the French believed that the problem of terrorism would simply go away if they waited it out. In 1975 alone there had been three dangerous attacks on El Al planes and passengers at Orly airport mounted by Carlos and the PFLP, but the French government did little to upgrade airport security in the wake of these attacks.

In September 1976 the Croatian hijack from New York to Paris presented the French government with the opportunity to embrace a hijack policy of "no compromise." Minister of the Interior Michel Poniatowski and President Giscard d'Estaing both stated that negotiations were out of the question and would be a concession to blackmail.[72] At DeGaulle Airport the French did not even want to allow the Croatians to confirm that various leaflets had been dropped. This was the condition of release of the passengers. After all, no French nationals were involved, and there was nothing to lose by being tough. Unfortunately, the Croatian hijack did not mark a change in French behavior toward hijacking, for on January 3, 1977, the French let Abu Daoud, the planner of the Munich Massacre, go after correctly identifying him. There was a week-long, worldwide storm of protest that included the recall of the Israeli ambassador to France. But international castigation of the "the Butcher of Munich" had little or no impact on the government, and as the 1970s came to a close the French government was firmly established in the category of "flexibility," if not "concession and accommodation."

In 1981 the terrorist scene changed dramatically in France with the emergence of at least 12 terrorist groups in that country.[73] In the same year Euroterrorism began to be felt in France, Germany, and Belgium. Put simply, in the words of Moxon-Browne, "The choice of Paris as the scene for violent incidents is attributable to the policy of welcoming political exiles to France and that welcome being abused by the individuals or groups concerned."[74] In the early 1980s, France almost guaranteed a plague of terrorist attention by three pieces of legislation. The first abolished capital punishment, the second confirmed France as *Terre d'asile* or sanctuary for political refugees, and the third consisted of a French refusal to extradite politically motivated suspects to other European jurisdictions.[75] Then, on top of all that, the French government tempted the fates by pursuing a high-profile foreign policy in the Middle East. France became involved in Lebanon in the peacekeeping force there, infuriated Iran by siding with Iraq in the long war between the two states, and directly confronted Libya over Chad.

In 1983-1984 there were three hijacks of Air France planes, all of which involved Middle Eastern factions. On August 27, 1983, an Air France jet between Vienna and Paris was hijacked and flown to Teheran. The terrorists demanded the release of Lebanese terrorists in French prisons but finally surrendered. On March 7, 1984, another Air France B737 was hijacked between Frankfurt and Paris, but the hijackers were overpowered in Geneva. Finally, on July 31, 1984, another Air France B737 on the same run was hijacked to Teheran. This incident lasted for two days and again involved the demand for release of prisoners. The hijackers surrendered after blowing up the plane's cockpit. Late in 1985 U.S. intelligence sources received information that Imad Mughniyah was planning to go to France. The United States tipped off its French counterpart, but the French spotted Mughniyah and then let him go. As Gayle Rivers wrote, ''The Americans were dismayed by this clear attempt by the French to appease the terrorists in the hope that they might get their hostages in Lebanon released.''[76] The French also remained opposed to extraditing terrorist fugitives to the United States on the grounds that Americans had refused to extradite to Britain wanted IRA members caught in the United States.[77]

When Socialist President Mitterrand came to power in France, he immediately granted amnesty to 31 convicted terrorists, including Jean Marc Rouillan and Natalie Menigon, the coleaders of Action Directe. He also eliminated the State Security Court, which had jurisdiction over terrorist offenses. These were great mistakes, and France would pay for them. In addition, successive French governments, whether socialist or conservative, had believed it was possible and fruitful to negotiate with international terrorists in the hopes of leaving France untouched. This, too, was a big mistake. On January 25, 1985, General René Audran, an important member of the Ministry of Defense, was shot outside his home by members of Action Directe. On December 7, 1985, there was bombing and random terror at French department stores in Paris. In February 1986 the Champs Elysées was bombed by pro-Khomeini forces, and outrages continued into February and March. This last rash of Lebanese-related terrorism developed because Georges Ibrahim Abdullah turned himself in to the French Police in 1984 in fear of Israeli reprisal. It was subsequently discovered that he was responsible for the death of the deputy U.S. military attaché in Paris and the second secretary of the Israeli Embassy, both of which had taken place in 1982. The French were going to try to exchange him for their hostages in Lebanon, when the Americans instituted civil proceedings against Abdullah for the death of their deputy military attaché. The result was a series of terrorist attacks in Paris, even worse than those in the final stages of the Algerian War in 1961-1962. When the government realized that 85 percent of the French people were against the freeing of Abdullah, a life sentence was passed on him by a French court, and the government was forced to take stern measures against terrorism. The attacks, which outraged Parisians, seemed to illustrate the futility of trying to play off Middle Eastern factions against each other as the French have done repeatedly. In the case of Abu Nidal, France agreed to parole two convicted Palestinians provided that Abu Nidal's group would commit no terrorist acts on French soil. The result was that Abu Nidal proceeded to commit a bloody procession of terrorist acts in the rest of the world, many of them carried out from the sanctuary of France. The 1986 bombings brought to an end the French conviction that terrorism was none of France's business as long as it killed people other than French citizens and was carried on outside France; they had even hinted that terrorism within France was acceptable as long as French citizens were not killed.[78]

By October 1986 French premier Jacques Chirac, speaking to the U.N. General Assembly, "denounced the leprosy of terrorism that has become a systematic weapon of a war that knows no borders or seldom has a face."[79] He spoke after a brutal wave of terrorist bombings in Paris had left 9 dead and 163 wounded since September 8 of that year. Both the Center-Right Chirac government and its successor, the Socialist Rocard government, continued the general thrust of a strong counterterrorism policy established in 1987, and French police scored a number of successes against terrorism in 1988.[80]

Paris airports, however, remain a target too attractive for terrorists to resist as is evident from this list of attacks on various airports.

Rome	10 attacks
Paris	10 attacks
London	8 attacks
New Delhi	7 attacks
Athens	7 attacks
Frankfurt	6 attacks
Tel Aviv	6 attacks
Tokyo	5 attacks
Karachi	5 attacks
Vienna	5 attacks

Beirut, Teheran, and Manila have all experienced too many hijacks to mention, especially since those countries have been subject to heavy instability.

Thus French policy over terrorism, including terrorism in the skies, has come full circle. The lesson was not learned in the 1970s, but France became inundated in the mid-1980s and finally changed its policy from one of "concession and accommodation" to one of "no compromise" by the end of the decade. It was a case of coming full circle as a result of bitter experience.

GREAT BRITAIN

The British have experienced a great deal of terrorist violence in the past 20 years. The overwhelming majority of attacks have been linked to the Provisional

Irish Republican Army and the troubles in Northern Ireland. A considerable amount of Middle Eastern activity has also taken place in the United Kingdom, but very little of it has been connected to airplanes and airports. Between September 1970 and December 1988 there were only five significant hijacks of British planes, a comparatively good record. Writing in the early 1980s, the American authority on terrorism, Neil Livingstone, stated, "The U.K. may well have the tightest airport security in the world as a result of the spillover of violence from the conflict in Northern Ireland."[81]

Early on, the British took a less than firm and uncompromising stand over hijack blackmail. In September 1970, during the multiple hijack at Dawson's Field, they were in the thick of the action. Because the El Al plane had landed in London, the British took custody of hijacker Leila Khaled. To spring her from prison, the PFLP hijacked a British VC10 bound for London from Bahrain. Among its passengers were 21 unaccompanied children returning to school in England.[82] The British were forced to release Khaled. As one of the five governments involved in the ensuing negotiations, the British took the middle line between Israeli refusal to negotiate and the Swiss and German desire to give in quickly and independently. In agreeing to free Khaled and six other terrorists, the British insisted that this would be achieved only if the five governments negotiated as a united front.[83]

In January of 1974 army assistance was called on to deal with a serious threat posed by Palestinian terrorists who were believed to be planning a SAM-7 missile attack on a plane at Heathrow Airport.[84] Fortunately, this attack did not take place, "but this and the successive army-police joint exercises at Heathrow in June, July and September 1974, certainly provided valuable practice for countering the more serious terrorist attacks with really effective forces."[85]

On March 3, 1974, a British VC10 was hijacked en route from Bombay to London and blown up in Amsterdam by Abu Nidal's group, the NAYLP. There wasn't much the British could do about airport security in Bombay. On November 22 another British Airways airliner was hijacked from Dubai to Tunis by the same Abu Nidal group. In exchange for the release of passengers, two terrorists imprisoned in Holland for a previous hijacking of a British plane and the prisoners from Rabat were freed.[86] In January 1975 the British learned the consequences of their failure to institute universal search procedures for domestic as well an international flights. This oversight left the door open for a potential hijacker to seize an aircraft on an internal flight and divert it overseas. In January 1975 a BAC 1-11 was hijacked on a flight from Manchester to London and diverted abroad, to the embarrassment of the British government.[87] The Americans had already experienced this kind of hijack with Rafaele Minichiello and several other hijackers. To the humiliation of a domestic hijack gone international is added the potential danger of a crash should the fuel consignment prove inadequate for an international flight. On August 20, 1978, Palestinians mounted an armed attack on an El Al bus departing from a London hotel, killing a flight attendant. On March 22, 1984, a hijacker commandeered a British Airways B747 between Hong Kong and Peking. The hijacker got to his demanded destination of Taiwan but was arrested and imprisoned on arrival. Again, there was little British authorities could do about the situation.

Because a virtual state of war has existed over Northern Ireland, with the IRA launching numerous attacks on mainland Britain and its major cities, that country has had to stay alert to terrorism in a way perhaps only the Israelis really understand. British policies, which involve wide-ranging connections to the Arab world, combined with a residue of British-Israeli antagonism from the Palestine Mandate, may be an additional explanation for the relative freedom from hijacking. Perhaps most important, however, is the emphasis the British have long placed on intelligence gathering, and it is likely that good airport security in its broadest sense has saved Britain from much hijack embarrassment. One other factor that looms large in the calculation of potential hijacks of British planes is the menacing presence of the SAS. This elite parachute and special operations group has terrified the IRA; it contributed to the victory of the West Germans at Mogadishu in 1977, and it very decisively ended the Iranian Embassy siege in London in 1980. The likelihood of sure and sudden death for hijackers from the SAS is an effective deterrent. The mere mention of SAS involvement over the radio brought the Balcombe Street siege in London to an abrupt halt after six days of standoff in December 1975.

It is true that British airport security had had its weak moments, and hijack policy has at times been inconsistent. One such episode occurred after the Entebbe raid in 1976, in the discussion of the role of the British and French governments at that time. "The idea of the British Labour government," wrote Paul Wilkinson, "lending any assistance to such an operation is truly laughable. It transpires that the British Foreign Office, not satisfied with merely failing to follow the American lead in congratulating Israel on her action, actually sent a message of condolence to Amin."[88] On April 17, 1986, another slipup occurred when El Al security found a plastic bomb in the luggage of a pregnant Irish chambermaid most assuredly going to her death along with 400 other passengers on board an El Al B747. The bomb had been missed by British airport security. Such a mistake seems much more significant in light of the terrible explosion aboard Pan Am 103 in December 1988. The plane disintegrated above the Scottish town of Lockerbie, killing 269 people including 11 inhabitants of the town. The flight had originated in Frankfurt, where it appears the bomb was put on the plane, but a crisis erupted in the British Parliament nevertheless, with sustained calls for the resignation of the British minister in charge of airport security, Paul Channon.

The record of British security is uneven but markedly improved, however, in the past decade. Initially "flexible" in their negotiations with terrorists, the British later espoused a policy of "no compromise" and negotiations without capitulation. Under Margaret Thatcher, Britain has been tough and hard line over terrorism for almost ten years. The IRA very nearly blew up both Thatcher and her entire cabinet in a Brighton Hotel at the Conservative party convention in October 1984. Her answer was to make common cause with President Reagan in his bombing of Libya in 1986; to entrench sweeping antiterrorism powers in parliamentary legislation in 1988; and to state unambiguously on April 6, 1988, in the wake of the Lockerbie tragedy, "We do not give in to (terrorist) blackmail, it only leads to further incidents."[89]

THE UNITED STATES

In the mid-1980s the American preoccupation with Star Wars gradually gave way to a much greater concern over the reality of terrorist wars waged mercilessly against American civil aviation worldwide. In the short period between 1985 and 1989, the following incidents directly engaged the United States:

June 14, 1985	TWA 847 hijack
October 7, 1985	Seajack of *Achille Lauro*
October 19, 1985	U.S. diversion of Egyptair 737
December 27, 1985	Attacks on Rome and Vienna airports
March 25, 1986	United States sinks two Libyan vessels in the Gulf of Sidra
April 2, 1986	Bomb explosion on TWA 840
April 5, 1986	Bombing of West Berlin disco
April 14, 1986	U.S. attack on Libya
May 19, 1986	Attack on heads of state at Tokyo summit
September 5, 1986	Pan Am 73 in Karachi
July 3, 1988	USS *Vincennes* shoots down Iranian Airbus in Persian Gulf
December 21, 1988	Pan Am 103 explodes over Lockerbie

These attacks and counterattacks fully engaged the United States in the terrorist wars after a period of hiatus in the early 1980s. This battle against civil aviation terrorism, however, was taking place offshore. Attacks on U.S. personnel and embassies in the Mediterranean were bound to have a greater impact on European governments than on Washington. In October 1985 Secretary of State George Shultz made a speech in which he stated that the United States should stop equivocating and resolve to use military force against terrorist groups, even if such measures led to the death of innocent people and American servicemen.[90] "We may never have the kind of evidence that can stand up in an American court of law," said Shultz, "but we cannot allow ourselves to become the Hamlet of nations, worrying endlessly over whether and how to respond."[91] Secretary of Defense Caspar Weinberger was skeptical "about responding with force to terrorism of uncertain origin and against enemies who may not be identifiable, let alone accessible."[92] Shultz and a small group of advisers cited Israel's approach in taking the war to the terrorists themselves with preemptive strikes across borders and on other continents. In the end, the argument was resolved by the stream of events that engulfed the United States after June 1985. The attack on TWA 847 has been dealt with elsewhere in this book, and the traumatic effect that it had on U.S. thinking was evident. The December attacks on Rome and Vienna airports were aimed as much at the United States as Western Europe and set the scene for an extraordinary year in civil aviation terrorism. It was a year in which George Shultz's retaliatory philosophy was implemented as policy. But the pivotal event of 1985 was the seajacking of the *Achille Lauro* on October 7, 1985. The United States was drawn into this affair because of the brutal murder of Leon Klinghoffer, a vacationing American citizen of Jewish ancestry. Three times the United States had promised revenge: when the U.S. Embassy in Beirut was bombed in 1983; when 230 Marines were massacred in a Beirut bombing the same year, and when a young U.S. Navy diver, Robert Stethem, was tortured and then shot aboard TWA 847. Three times nothing had happened, and unless President Reagan wished to look weak and vacillating, action was called for. Thus on October 10 an Egyptair B737 with the *Achille Lauro* hijackers aboard was diverted to Sigonella base in Sicily without a shot being fired. At least four terrorists would now go on trial for their action even if the mastermind of the seajack had escaped.

Beneath the surface a counterterrorism policy was slowly taking shape. U.S. officials said that policy gradually focused on Libya, because Qaddafi was more open than other leaders in avowing his support of terrorism and because Libya's infrastructure of terrorism—training camps, military installations, and communications centers—appeared easier to hit without doing damage to civilians. The confrontation with Libya over the Line of Death drawn across the Gulf of Sidra by Qaddafi ended the post-Vietnam inhibition against military action as the United States sank two Libyan gunboats on March 25 in the Mediterranean. There followed three more events in April 1986 that quickly cemented the growing U.S. retaliatory policy. A bomb exploded abroad TWA 840 on April 2; there was a bombing in a West Berlin disco in which an American serviceman died on April 5; and finally, on April 14, the United States launched an attack on Libya that came close to killing Qaddafi. The administration had tried economic sanctions and appeals to allies to isolate Libya diplomatically, and neither had had much effect. Now it was time to begin to retaliate against terrorist attacks. In the view of George Shultz: "If you let people get away with murder, you'll get murder."[93] The urge to hit back at international terrorism was driven by the new assertiveness of Reagan's foreign policy. A series of successes from Grenada to the Philippines had shown that the United States could pull off military and diplomatic coups without destablizing the system. Putting new muscle into American policy and avenging the death of its citizens served notice that the terrorists had better think twice before acting in the future.

In May 1986 the annual summit meeting of the major industrial countries took place in Tokyo, where an unusually direct communiqué was issued condemning state-sponsored terrorism. American Secretary of State Shultz's long and lonely struggle to develop a concensus in the United States as well as among U.S. allies on the need to strike back at terrorists was affirmed when Japanese terrorists attempted to fire homemade bazookas at the Akasaka Palace where the leaders were meeting. President Reagan found firm support for vigorous action against state-sponsored terrorism from Prime Ministers Margaret Thatcher and Brian Mulroney of Canada.

On September 5, 1986, the attack against Pan Am 73 took place at Karachi airport. The earlier attack on TWA 847 and the later attack on Pan Am 103 that destroyed the plane over Scotland combined with this one to show that the United States still had a long way to go in the area of deterrence and prevention. These three episodes illustrated dramatically that retaliatory hits against terrorists are no substitute for an effective policy of airplane and airport security at home and abroad. This has now become an internationally cooperative venture in which countries have to work closely together to defeat terrorist attacks. So it can be seen that the United States moved from a posture of ''flexibility'' in the mid-1970s to one of ''non compromise'' in the mid-1980s. But by the end of the 1980s the ''no compromise'' policy was overlapping into a ''retaliation'' posture like that long followed by the Israelis. Such a posture was causing concern to American allies in Western Europe who were bearing the brunt of terrorist attacks while no really visible concomitant improvement in U.S. aviation security seemed to be taking place.

THE WESTERN ALLIANCE

Since 1985-1986 terrorist actions have concentrated on American targets. The United States, however, has been too far from the Middle East and too difficult to enter for terrorists to yet threaten homeland America. Therefore the majority of terrorist attacks are on American targets located in the Mediterranean and Western Europe, and the new U.S. determination to fight terrorism in retaliatory fashion is taking place largely on Western European territory. There is now a growing assertiveness of the Western Europeans on foreign policy issues expressed through the framework of European Political Co-operation (EPC). The EPC has tried to constrain the American use of military force against terrorists: What many Europeans fear is a deadly cycle of vengeance—terrorism begetting U.S. strikes, which then prompt more terrorism in return. There is a school of thought on both sides of the Atlantic that is convinced that antiterrorism policy must be accompanied by concerted diplomatic efforts to bring about some resolution of Arab-Israeli conflicts—the Palestinian question, Islamic fundamentalist violence, and other root causes of tension in the Middle East. As Christopher Hill pointed out: ''The enlargement of the EC to include

Greece, and later Spain and Portugal, has hardly strengthened the voices of those inclined to support American counter-attacks on terrorism."[94] Perhaps Western Europe is at a different stage of development than the United States in coping with irregular warfare. European governments now display a diplomatic reflex when faced with problems that once might have called forth a military response. There is also, as Hill pointed out, "a certain ennui, a distaste for the prospect of military operations, overt and covert, which is not currently seen in the United States."[95]

The Americans, for their part, are sick of being attacked abroad and are becoming uneasy about the thin line between negotiation and appeasement. The Europeans, on the other hand, are reluctant to allow terrorism to damage their relations with Arab states, including Libya, because of vital trade relations. They are also resisting a model of clear state sponsorship for terrorism. This clear-cut East-West division was compounded by increasing anti-Reaganism in Europe and impatience with European "disloyalty" in the United States during the late 1980s.

The American attack on Libya in April 1986 brought these smoldering differences to a head. Prime Minister Craxi of Italy declared that "the problems of the Mediterranean certainly cannot be settled by a military blitz."[96] Chancellor Kohl of West Germany added, "my advice would always be to avoid such acts of military reprisal until you know what you are starting and how you are going to get out of it at the end."[97] The Spanish, Italian, and Greek governments were especially concerned about the price to be paid for the raid. Italy, where 40,000 demonstrators protested the bombings in various cities, was particularly vulnerable since it conducts $7 billion of Western Europe's $17 billion in trade with Libya.

In November 1986 the British decided to break off diplomatic relations with Syria over the Hindawi incident in which the Syrian Embassy in London was clearly found to be involved in the attempt to bomb the El Al plane flying out of Heathrow. Hindawi himself was sentenced to 45 years in prison, the stiffest jail sentence ever handed down by a British court. As one senior British Official put it: "By her tough and unflinching stance, the Prime Minister has confirmed her position as one of the world's leading antiterrorists, perhaps the most resolute of all."[98] At the end of January 1987 Canadian External Affairs Minister Joe Clark and British Foreign Secretary Sir Geoffrey Howe agreed that Western countries needed to move beyond merely reacting to terrorist attacks to developing a long-term strategy to prevent terrorism.[99] Canada and Britain have long been two of the staunchest Western countries calling for concerted action against terrorism, although the former has faced few situations of hostage taking against its own citizens. It was in December 1988 when Pan Am 103 disintegrated over Lockerbie that the U.S., British, and West German governments began to understand that a concerted policy to tighten airport and aircraft security was urgently needed.

CONCLUSION

This chapter set out to explore the good, the bad, and the ugly in terms of government postures toward hijacking of international civil aviation. A consistent picture emerges from this study of the attitudes of 13 governments of mostly Western origin. In the 20-year period studied, from 1968 to 1988, several governments have changed position in their national policies. Some, who initially vacillated over their policy, soon sorted out their basic response to terrorism under the heat of terrorist attack. There appears at the simplest level to be a clear-cut distinction between soft-line and hard-line responses to terrorism that were defined earlier in the chapter. The list of governments to be found in both categories follows:

Soft-line approach: Japan, Austria, Italy, Greece, Spain, Cyprus, Egypt, Belgium, Malta, Thailand, and Pakistan

Hard-line approach: Israel, United States, Britain,* India, West Germany,* Kuwait,* Holland,* France,* Jordan,* and South Korea

The countries marked with an asterisk (*) changed from a soft-line to a hard-line policy during the period under study. Using Bowyer-Bell's categorization of government policies, it is possible to create a spectrum of government response starting on the extreme end of hard-line response and ending at the extreme end of soft-line response. This categorization of governments studied appears as follows:

Retaliation	No Compromise	Flexibility	Concession and Accommodation
Israel	Britain	Sweden	Cyprus
United States*	India		Austria
	West Germany	Canada	Spain
	Holland	Belgium	Italy
	Kuwait	Switzerland	Greece
	Jordan	Japan	ᵒ
	South Korea	Pakistan	Malta
	France*	Egypt*	Thailand

The asterisk (*) indicates that in 1989 certain states appeared to be moving from one category to another, usually in a hard-line direction.

It soon became clear that governmental response to attacks on international civil aviation can be approached from a number of perspectives. At least four are considered here: prevention, the immediate reaction, the reaction to the terrorist host-state, and the long-term response.

Prevention

The prevention of terrorism against civil aviation comes principally through deterrence and penalties. Deterrence includes the use of counterterrorist groups ready at any moment to move against hijacked planes. Such forces exist in India, West Germany, Holland, Canada, the United Kingdom, Israel, the United States, and South Korea. Deterrence is also implemented when captured terrorists are imprisoned and not released under any circumstances and is furthered when security at major international airports is not only declared to be good by selective media exposure but also is seen to be good in action during a crisis. Airports in Israel, West Germany, Holland, and Singapore and Narita Airport in Japan, as well as London's Heathrow, all fit in this category. The severest penalty aimed at terrorist-harboring or terrorist-sponsoring countries seems to be the threat of an airline boycott. Even the threat of such a strike by the IFALPA has been very successful at upgrading security in airports like Rome and Athens. But the pocketbook is still the place where countries feel the impact of penalties and sanctions the most. In the summer of 1986 a drastic drop in American tourism to Western Europe badly damaged revenues and caused considerable government action on behalf of airplane and airport security. On the matter of prevention of attacks on civil aviation, joint action by governments is the only realistic and effective option for the future. Paul Wilkinson has called for more intensive international cooperation than currently exists, though he, like General Richard Clutterbuck, stressed that we are talking about the reduction,not the elimination, of terrorism.

The Immediate Reaction

When confronted by terrorist demands after hijacks, the immediate reactions of governments have usually fallen into three categories of response: The first, the "flexible" response, include immediate negotiations. The second, "safe release," concerns itself chiefly with the safety of the hostages and sees the "Bangkok solution," or release of hostage plus safe passage for terrorists, to be the optimum one. The third is "strict noconcessions," in which the chief concern is the discouragement of future acts of terrorism by not allowing this one to bear any fruit.[100] These scenarios of immediate reaction correspond to the Bowyer-Bell categories of governmental response.

Reaction to the Terrorist Host State

Western European states are not likely to punish states that sponsor terrorism because the onus of guilt cannot always be attached. After the United States mounted its attack on Libya in 1986, there was strong evidence that Syria was involved. Having attacked Libya, would the United States then mount a similar attack on Iran, Syria, or North Korea? The attack on Libya satisfied psychological needs for revenge among Americans, but it also threatened to bring reprisals to the more vulnerable Western European states. A reaction of this type also supplies much desired publicity for terrorism, without doing much harm to the sponsoring state. Knowing where to stop when targeting countries that aid terrorists is also a problem. In a speech before the American Bar Association in 1986, President Reagan mentioned Libya, Cuba, North Korea, Syria, and Iran as the principal terror-sponsoring states. But Brian Jenkins of the Rand Corporation has prepared a list of 20 such states and maintains that it could easily be doubled.

The Long-Term Response

The long-term response of governments to terrorism evolves "as a result of a mix of factors, habit, history, personalities of the moment, traditional prejudice, intuition and usually an eye on the public's desires," wrote Bowyer-Bell.[101] It is probably safe to add that the idiosyncratic has and will continue to affect national policies on civil aviation. Again quoting Bowyer-Bell, "No Western democracy can really be expected in the future to adopt a coherent national policy toward a terrorist threat, however defined. When President Nixon announced that the U.S. could not give in to terrorist blackmail, he expressed a posture and an aspiration, not a policy."[102] What is really needed to beat the terrorists is a flexible and carefully coordinated program of national and international measures, but such a panacea is still a long way off. A proper common policy on counterterrorism for Western Europe alone would require judicial integration of a kind that is still years away. Different philosophies, different extradition laws, and different attitudes toward political refugees still deeply divide European states, meaning a common policy on terrorist prevention will be a long time in the making.

In the meantime, practical steps can and should be taken by governments to mitigate the impact of terrorist attacks on international civil aviation. Gayle Rivers suggested that an ounce of prevention is worth a pound of cure and that most of today's terrorism has been born out of past political experience. He added that terrorists always attempt to escalate their outrages, and therefore firm action, not appeasement, is the only effective response. Instead of reacting to terrorist acts, the emphasis of states must change so as to anticipate, preempt, and preclude them. This is the function of good intelligence.

International civil aviation spans all countries and all jurisdictions of the world by definition. Therefore the only way to combat hijacking effectively is to coordinate national policies on a regional and international basis. It is clear that different states bring differing philosophies to bear on hijacking, but they all involve a mixture of military, political, economic, legal, and psychological means to a greater or lesser degree. Therefore the way to combat a hijacking successfully lies in coordination of existing institutions.

These institutions would include Interpol, which is the main framework for police cooperation among Western states. It was limited to criminal matters until 1984, however, and it is too large to be really effective. The ICAO has made some slow progress toward common procedures in civil aviation and the seven Economic Summit nations have become increasingly political, turning their attention specifically in 1986 toward state-sponsored terrorism. But they are not committed to practical changes of policy. The Council of Europe has been important in the juridical field. It produced the European Convention on the Suppression of Terrorism in 1977, which fostered a climate in which European Community action could take place at the political level. In 1976, after heavy IRA attacks in London and the seizure of the German embassy in Stockholm, the members of the European Community set up, on a British initiative, what has become known as the TREVI system of working groups. It consists of representatives of ministers of the interior, police forces, and security services and is answerable to those ministers in member states who are responsible for counterterrorism. The TREVI has been sufficiently successful politically to generate outside demands by states to join its ranks. The IATA, representing the world's airlines, has developed an increasingly important role in the field of airport security and it continues, like IFALPA, to work in concentrated fashion on closing the gaps in international civil aviation that allow terrorists to operate. Finally, NATO is not an inappropriate place for the formulation of a coordinated Western response to the problems of terrorism. The diplomatic role of NATO in Western policy discussion has always been strong, and as real detente moves ahead in East-West relations, NATO might well find itself in a coordinating role that reflects the more North-South orientation of international terrorism.

In the final analysis, the hub of international airports and national airlines is at the center of the hijacking problem, and it is here the action must take place. Each time terrorist outrages against international civil aviation escalate, the system of security is forced to improve. In the long run, the system of security is likely to outlive, if not outperform, the terrorist problem itself. The explosion aboard Pan Am 103, which killed 269 people in December 1988, is one of those deeply felt tragedies that seems to give impetus to national governments to put real teeth into international provisions for aviation security. When international cooperation against terrorism is put in place, some of the more hesitant nations will take their lead from the stronger ones. Pan Am 103 has certainly catapulted the United States into the center of security reform. The growing number of hijacks in the Soviet Union and Eastern Europe and the impact of Glasnost may well give both superpowers common cause to make civil aviation safe. In the meantime, the assault on Western Europe civil aviation has placed those countries in the forefront of the battle with the hijack terrorists.

Chapter 7

Outlook: Aerial Piracy and Airport Security

LOOKING AHEAD

A clear-headed understanding of the past is absolutely essential to creating effective policies for the future, which is why this book has detailed 30 years of hijacking. Trends and patterns can be seen and insights gained by examining the many faces of security in civil aviation, but now it is necessary to look ahead. Terrorists are opportunists whose effectiveness is based on continually seizing the moment. Governments, therefore, have to be far-sighted, patient planners. This process of planning and continually upgrading security in response to terrorist acts may in the end outlast if not overcome the terrorist threat. It may even push governments into relinquishing and pooling their sovereignty for the greater good of all states.

Indeed, at this juncture in history, international civil aviation is under severe pressure to close the loopholes in its security processes and form a common front against the terrorists. Such a response is possible only if security is treated as a complete system with diverse components. As the terrorists strike at weak components, governments must be strengthened to meet the challenge. For the sake of simplicity, these components are divided into nine parts that logically follow one another in importance and international scope.

First, the whole process begins with the gathering of timely intelligence, which in turn must be communicated quickly and effectively to the appropriate airports. Second, airport security is still, after all these years, at the heart of the struggle against international terrorism. Third, the psychology of the terrorist-hijacker at a given time is of great importance to the forces of security; the type of hijacker in action has varied over the years and knowing one's enemy is important in the terrorist war. Fourth, a significant component in the system is the passengers. The whole point of the civil aviation industry is to serve the traveling public, business people, tourists, diplomats, and families whose combined travel amounts to billions of dollars for which the airlines vie. The passenger as obvious victim has seemed unimportant until recently, but this is beginning to change. Fifth, if airport security is circumvented, a hijacking takes place, and a unique set of human, technological, psychological, and international problems is created in a very fragile environment. In many respects, the airplane is one of the weakest links in the security system, because so little training and preparation has taken place to make it safe.

Sixth, as a result of hijacks, national policies are forced to evolve and states have to respond on behalf of their nationals and their airlines and often have to cooperate with other governments in terminating the hijack. Seventh, the world nevertheless falls naturally into regions, and regional policies and agreements are frequently the most effective way to deal with a persistent terrorist threat. Eighth, beyond regional solutions, international measures need to be taken because terrorism operates throughout the global village, effortlessly crossing national borders and challenging states to cooperate and integrate. Ninth, the final step in the process of security against air terrorism must be the political solutions. In the case of many terrorist groups, political solutions could prove to be the needed ounce of prevention, but national pride complicates such remedies, and governments are often slow to come to such conclusions.

INTELLIGENCE

Paul Wilkinson pointed out that the Lockerbie incident has revealed grievous security weakness in the three countries involved. Britain and the United States have no coherent policy on public information in response to specific threats to aircraft.[1] Only a small number of U.S. embassy staff were able to benefit from the warning of a threat to Pan Am flights leaving Frankfurt. The British Department of Transport did not see fit to alert Heathrow's security staff. The fact that warnings had been issued, possibly by the terrorists themselves, and those warnings had not been communicated to airport authorities is a serious failure in intelligence. The resultant controversy has focused on what constitutes a serious threat and to what extent such a threat should be communicated to the traveling public. Obviously, some balance needs to be reached in resolving this controversy, since there are legal cases pending over the Lockerbie incident Instead of reacting to acts of terrorism, the emphasis of states must change to anticipate, preempt, and preclude them. Effective police and intelligence cooperation within international alliances and communities is the only way to anticipate terrorist behavior.

Writing in the October 1989 edition of *Security Management,* in the article "Air Terrorism: Flight or Fright," Colonel William T. Corbett, an experienced counterterrorist, dealt with the issue of whether or not to notify the public of threats to airlines. The Israeli position is never to make such threats public in order to entrap the terrorist as he embarks on the airline. For a small airline, this policy is feasible. Commensurate with recent Israeli influence on American security policy, on April 3 and 27, 1989, the U.S. Department of Transport confirmed that the United States would not publish threat information. Colonel Corbett is strongly of the opinion that keeping threat information secret in the effort to catch terrorists, as opposed to announcing such information in trying to prevent attacks, must be seriously questioned.

As is well known, dealing with terrorism involves two main considerations— antiterrorist security and counterterrorist operations. The purpose of antiterrorist security is to prevent attacks, and the very best way to prevent an attack is to inform the planners that you know of their plans. Counterterrorist operations are the separate task of neutralizing the terrorists. To mix these two functions is a design for disaster, since it risks using innocent people as bait. To be successful, such a plan would require a 100 percent success rate against attacks, which is a manifest impossibility.

Another issue is just how secret the threat information is kept. Threat advisories, for instance, are routinely disseminated to U.S. and foreign embassies, aviation agencies, airlines, airports, official and contract airport security organizations, and the relevant U.S. military command headquarters. So if tens of thousands of people know about a threat and can tell their own families, why shouldn't the few travelers on the affected route also be warned? Colonel Corbett is convinced that experience shows that publicizing threat information causes prospective attackers to abandon their plans. He insisted that the policy of not releasing threat information creates bitterness and distrust between the traveling public and the government. He also pointed out that not only does public announcement of terrorist plans cause most actions to be cancelled but also that the use of secret threat intelligence has never demonstrated its success with apprehended terrorists.

The policy of secrecy leads to still worse effects when leaks occur, particularly as the media gets wind of an operation. The middle ground would be for the government to issue general threat information but hold on to sensitive intelligence details. Once the issue becomes desensationalized, insiders would have less motivation to leak the intelligence to the media, which would then be more responsive to government requests for restraint.

Therefore the traveling public has a right to know if it is being exposed to life-threatening situations. The government has a right to protect sensitive intelligence, and nothing is to be gained by confrontation between the parties concerned. Colonel Corbett believes that a compromise on the matter of sharing threat information is both necessary and sensible.

Since 1977, the TREVI group has provided a means of communication within the European Economic Community in which "government ministers, high-ranking policy officers and senior officials discuss current issues in terrorism and share intelligence information between states."[2] It was only in September 1986, at the height of the French bomb crisis, that the European Economic Community (EEC) ministers of the interior agreed to set up a "hot-line" of intelligence information on the movement of known terrorists. It was the old story of reacting to terrorist outrages rather than anticipating their crimes and gaining an advantage over them. Both within Western Europe and the Atlantic Alliance an institutional system of intelligence sharing is long overdue. As

Rodney Wallis of the IATA pointed out, "if government acceptance of responsibility is a major plank in civil aviation's defence platform, then effective communication must be another."[3] The development of the delivery of effective and timely intelligence information to airports requires communication and cooperation among all parties in aviation—governments, airports, and airlines. The IATA's Security Advisory Committee was replaced in June 1988 with a smaller Security Task Force to check on conditions in airports worldwide. Today communication flows along several channels, including IATA security and the International Criminal Police Organization (INTERPOL). Information about the movements of suspect personnel and hijack threats are channeled by airlines through their communications networks to the IATA's director of security. The director maintains close liaison with INTERPOL.[4] Speaking at The Hague in January 1987, Schiphol Airport manager Jan Wegstapel said, "IATA's Security Advisory Committee and the recently-established Aviation Security Panel (AVSEC), a body made up of experts from 15 countries and AACC, IATA, IFALPA, and INTERPOL, are currently busy developing new techniques and procedures to prevent terrorist actions."[5] In addition to this proliferation of international security committees are the intelligence agencies of individual Western countries. Probably, the most frequent problems concern systems overload and lack of correct evaluation of threats that should be passed on to airports where terrorists are likely to attack.

AIRPORT SECURITY

In a 1988 study by the Jaffee Centre for Strategic Studies (JCSS) Project on Low Intensity Warfare, Ariel Merari identified 229 actual or attempted attacks on international civil aviation between 1983 and 1987. He found that bombings constituted nearly 80 percent of the attacks on airports and airline offices but only 26 percent of the attacks on airlines.[6] Apart from hijacks, armed assaults were the other main form of attack on airports. He also found that most of the effort invested in securing the safety of civil aviation has focused on airlines. Airports and airline offices have therefore remained as vulnerable to attack as they were 20 years ago. "This disparity," Merari wrote, "explains the fact that hijackings have declined in the course of the recent two decades, while attacks on airports and airline offices have increased."[7]

In the wake of the Lockerbie disaster, the FAA issued much stricter baggage inspection requirements including the screening of all checked baggage and matching of all luggage to the passengers. These rules, however, applied only to flights from Europe and the Middle East. Additional regulations included checked baggage being accepted only from ticketed passengers and only at ticket counters inside the airport terminal. All checked baggage must be X-rayed or hand searched. U.S. airlines are responsible for maintaining positive control of checked baggage at all times after it is checked. The FAA criteria will be used to identify certain passengers for additional screening, which is to include a personal search of an individual and his luggage. Freight is to be accepted only from established customers, unless it can be held by the airport for 24 hours before boarding. All U.S. aircraft must be under the observation of one or more guards at all times and must be security sealed when parked overnight. All cleaners, baggage and cargo handlers, caterers, mechanics, and others on board U.S. aricraft must be screened and must work under observation. Finally, for originating flights, aircraft searches must include the cabin, cockpit, and cargo areas before cargo and passenger boarding to ensure against concealed weapons or explosives.[8] U.S. carriers are concerned that the new strict rules will cause them to suffer an unfair business penalty when compared to their European competition. But the FAA has also insisted on monitoring the security arrangements of foreign carriers flying into the United States. This arrangement could raise the standard of security throughout the Western world.

But the FAA has its critics. Among them are private security firms, who are warning clients not to fly U.S. airlines abroad because terrorists have demonstrated an ability to penetrate American security. They also believe it is a mistake to upgrade security only in Europe and the Middle East, because there has already been evidence of Abu Nidal operating in Latin America. Vance International has warned against using Athens airport at all. Said Charles Vance, "There are 50 ways to beat the system no matter what you do."[9] One of those ways is the Libyan development of disguising plastic explosives, forming them into the shape of a blowdryer, a calculator, or other devices typically found in luggage.

The most serious critic of all is Issac Yeffet, El Al's director of security from 1978 to 1984. He said flatly: "There is no airline security in the United States. What little is being done to protect passengers is not done well."[10] He thinks security is being pursued in the wrong way and therefore that money is being spent without a good security return. Again in his words, "Security pays for itself in decreased insurance fees and increased ridership, but airline executives have made security a low priority. There is no reason to believe this will change until there is a major disaster at an American airport."[11] Yeffet has a number of specific criticisms of U.S. airport security to which the FAA has no real answer.

To sum up, Yeffet stated: "From poorly phrased or non-existent preboard questioning, ineffective use of X-ray machines and metal detectors to curbside check-in, there is nothing that Americans do well when it comes to airport security."[12] Such criticism from an Israeli might well be resented in a country where conditions are very different. At no time, however, has the United States been subjected to the campaign of political terrorism against civil aviation that either Israel or Western Europe has experienced. Guarding American planes in Western Europe against terrorist attack is nothing like the upheaval that will be caused when a concerted attack on the domestic traffic of North America occurs. That attack will surely come, and when it does, the whole security system at America's 531 major airports will have to undergo radical change.

In the meantime, we are lucky to have thoughtful and farseeing international civil servants like Rodney Wallis of the IATA. Not only has he spoken out on these matters, but he has introduced new thinking into the security of airports worldwide. At The Hague conference of January 1987, Wallis specified what he considered to be the areas of airport security in need of upgrading: First is the ramp area, including the ramp itself and the area surrounding it. Both saboteurs and hijackers have increasingly used ramp personnel to place bombs on board planes and to introduce weapons that the hijackers retrieved after coming clean through security. The fight to prevent illegal transportation of illicit narcotics by air also profits from security weaknesses in the ramp area. As Wallis pointed out, there are in excess of 40,000 people rampside in some major airports, and airports and airlines must cooperate in ensuring that the screening of these people and the security procedures rampside are well organized and foolproof.

The second area of weakness is baggage security, particularly the threat of sabotage from a checked bag that is boarded without its owner. Baggage-passenger reconciliation became well known in 1989 in the wake of the Lockerbie disaster, but Wallis was advocating it as early as 1986. Passenger-baggage reconciliation is not only a security must on international flights, but it is also a cost-effective way to ensure that passengers and their baggage remain a single entity.

The third weakness is in the area of cargo security, where more stringent time-lag periods and X-ray activity are needed to combat sabotage. The tragedies of Air India 182 and Pan Am 103 dramatically emphasized this point by 1989.

The fourth area of weakness is in passenger screening, where millions of dollars are spent in no obviously beneficial way. The process of screening has not approached maximum cost-effectiveness, since, according to Wallis, "There is no established international standard against which the competence of passenger screeners can be tested and I know of few countries where any attempt has been made to lay down national criteria."[13] In North America, passenger screening is generally conducted by the staff of private companies. In the United Kingdom, security personnel are engaged by the airport authority. Some other European countries use civilian passenger screeners answering to the police. Germany, Holland, Scandinavia, and Belgium have security costs borne directly by the state. The Japanese use a private organization with what airlines consider to be a very professional force.

The fifth area of weakness lies in the human factor. As Wallis pointed out, "it is pointless having high-tech equipment if we use low-tech people."[14] Current weaknesses in selection, training, and supervision must be dealt with. Profile-identification and behavior patterns of terrorists as well as expertise in explosive detection must be taught to personnel. With state sponsorship of terrorism increasing, security officials must not overlook diplomatic personnel, which have long been ignored. The policing of public airport areas also requires security people who can quickly sense unusual individual behavior within a noisy crowd. The commercial arguments alone probably outweigh the case for sterilization of airport concourses. Besides, meeters and greeters spend a lot of money at concessionaires and ease the still widespread pain and fear of separation and flying. Until future airport designs incorporate security more thoroughly, police will have to be doubly effective in monitoring public concourses.

The sixth area of weakness is with high technology itself. At first the X-ray system seemed to be a panacea; the equipment was relatively simple to use and kept passengers moving. With the advent of plastic guns and plastic explosives, however, a quantum leap forward is now needed in the realm of weapon and explosive detection. Thermal neutron activation may help to sniff out potentially destructive bombs and weapons, but the human mastery of this new process, not to mention the period needed for further technical development, puts a heavy stress on human security abilities. It can be seen, therefore, that airport security is indeed at the very heart of civil aviation safety and that this is the point at which systems succeed or fail.

PASSENGERS

As Rodney Wallis has said, "It needs to be remembered that aviation is all about service to the travelling public."[15] Geoffrey H. Lipman added, "Men and women have the right to travel without fear."[16] Lipman is the director-general of the IFAPA, the airline passenger association, and after the eighteen months of carnage that preceded January 1987, he not surprisingly had things to say on behalf of passenger safety. As he pointed out, "Passengers may not understand the political or diplomatic machinations, nor the problems of creation of adequate defences, nor the legalities involved . . . but passengers are exposed to the daily media outpouring and they are most certainly aware of the dangers."[17]

In 1985 and 1986 passengers did make their views known. Voting with their feet, Americans stayed home from Europe in droves. The economic impact was immediate and dramatic, according to Geoffrey Hill. "The United States administration estimated that in 1985, one billion dollars in tourist revenue was lost as a result of terroristic acts staged in Europe."[18] The massive fall off of traffic continued in 1986, and there was evidence from polls that passengers developed a new fear of flying. This new fear did not prevent them from traveling generally, but it induced them to avoid certain carriers and certain destinations. It made them more politically sensitive to shifting climates around the world, and it produced passengers more critical of security detection processes, security staff attitudes, and border control procedures at certain airports. The feeling of unease has been heightened by the public debate in the United States and Europe about air safety, particularly after the destruction of Pan Am 103. As Lipman pointed out, "Passengers are increasingly grouping their concerns in these areas, together with security, as the downside of air travel."[19]

Direct charges for security (U.S. airlines introduced a $5 surcharge in 1986) have annoyed passengers who see no visible improvement in their own security. Not only is there no accountability for the extra charge, but there is also no evidence of improved security and very little likelihood of the charge being rescinded when times get better and terrorism comes under control. Geoffrey Lipman said, "Most of the letters we receive on this subject draw attention to the lack of proper physical inspection at certain airports—particularly domestic airports—and to disinterested or inattentive detection machine staff. Another complaint involves the exceptions to control at some airports for diplomats, airport staff or crew.''[20]

Air travelers themselves could contribute to enhancing security by keeping alert, refusing to receive goods from other people, and informing the authorities of anomalies they see. Security awareness could be promoted all over the world among air travelers, and an established set of security guidelines could be inculcated into the mind of the traveling public. After all, you soon learn not to feed the bears in national parks, so why not learn to recognize and speak up over sloppy airport security.

In 1989 a study entitled ''A Survey of Travelling Americans'' was conducted by Louis Harris and Associates for *Travel and Leisure* magazine. Airplane bombings, airport violence, cruise ship terrorism, were all a source of quiet anxiety among Americans. The study, ''for perhaps the first time, shows the long-term impact of terrorism on foreign travel: about 1-in-10 foreign travellers have, at some time, cancelled their plans due to terrorism fears. This translates into about 1.8 million people. Concern over security shows up across the board.''[21] According to the Harris study, ''Airport security is the number one criterion in selecting a foreign destination—a high concern of 79 percent—ranking above all the traditional considerations one might think people weigh in deciding where to go overseas.''[22]

A much smaller number of passengers need help with a much more critical problem—what to do when their airplane is hijacked. The passenger in a hijack may have to sit through hours or even days of psychological uncertainty, facing the possibility of death. Even a modicum of instruction and training could dramatically assist passengers with emotional survival.

PSYCHOLOGY OF THE HIJACKER

Rodney Wallis pointed out:

Although the number of hijackings has generally decreased over the last 15 years, individual incidents have become more violent. Hijackers seem less willing to negotiate terms for the safe release of passengers, crew and aircraft. Today's terrorists appear to be out to kill and maim simply to bring worldwide attention to their political or religious beliefs and to pressure governments into submission.[23]

Combatting such political and psychological fanaticism is no easy task for security, and the evolution of terrorist cells to embrace sabotage has caused a sea of change in the nature of terrorism. Not only are the religious fundamentalists ready on occasion for martyrdom, but they have also learned a whole new range of special methods and means of penetrating security. One is the recruitment of naive couriers who are unwittingly sent to die with the other passengers. Special explosive and sophisticated concealment methods are among the arsenal of

contemporary terrorists, as are detonators activated at certain heights by
barometric pressure.[24]

HIJACK IN THE AIR

Drawing on the JCSS study by Ariel Merari, it can be seen that the main
countries targeted by terrorist attacks on civil aviation between 1983 and 1987
are as follows:[25]

France	36	Iraq	6
United States	35	Kuwait	6
Japan	17	Soviet Union	6
Iran	16	Peru	5
United Kingdom	15	South Africa	4
Israel	14	Italy	4
West Germany	11	Libya	3
Jordan	10	Syria	3
Saudi Arabia	10		

Whereas terrorist attacks on civil aviation are indiscriminate, hijackers
nevertheless almost always chose their target as a means of harming a particular
state or states.[26] But the location of incidents by region of occurrence is
interesting. It tells us not only where the heaviest concentration of terrorist
activity is, but where the next scenes of violence are developing. Regional
occurrence of civil aviation attacks between 1983 and 1987 are as follows:[27]

	Incidents	Percentage
Western Europe	86	36.0
Middle East	49	10.5
South America	20	8.4
Sub-Saharan Africa	19	7.9
Far East	18	7.5
South Asia	16	6.7
North Africa	7	2.9
Central America	7	2.9
Caribbean	6	2.5
East Europe	4	1.7
North America	3	1.3
Southeast Asia	3	1.3
Oceana	1	0.4

If we now know the most likely civil aviation routes on which hijacks are likely to occur, pilots, flight attendants, and passengers can begin to equip themselves for the possibility of a hijack and how it should be handled. Although pilots would be the last people to start crying for help, they nevertheless are individually extremely concerned about the possibility of a hijack. It has now happened more than 900 times in 20 years, and each hijack is a flirtation with death. From the perspective of the flight attendants, the training for anticipating a hijack is inadequate. Flight attendants have made this clear in public statements and at conferences on airplane and airport security. What is more, they are unhappy with the almost complete absence of joint training with pilots. While the pilot is being a silent hero at the controls of a hijacked plane, the flight attendants absorb the greatest part of the stress and the responsibility for the lives and sometimes the deaths of passengers. Time and again in hijacks, the passengers owe their release to the courage and bravery of flight attendants. This group of people feels that training for the ordeal is inadequate and that more is definitely needed.

Passengers, too, need better briefing about the emotional consequences of a hijacking. Practically no advances have been made in caring for the long-term effects of a hostage-taking situation on its victims. Thousands of people have now survived lengthy hijacks and have tried to readjust to life, without psychological counseling. Some of them suffer recurrent flashbacks of the horror for years. Yet little work has been done in the field of posthostage distress. Although the airlines have come under fire in a series of court cases launched by passengers, the government, which holds many of the ultimate solutions for air terrorism, should probably be held liable for bearing the cost of such psychological treatment. But this matter, like treatment for the victims of rape and assault, is still in its infancy.

GOVERNMENT POLICIES

The behavior of governments is at least as important in effecting civil aviation security as is the condition of airport security. Rodney Wallis said, "All too often governments have made decisions in isolation which have actually led to a decrease rather than an increase in the effectiveness of security measures."[28] Governments are capricious and inconsistent in their approach to aviation security. A government that has experienced a terrorist attack will quickly invoke increased security measures, but this often has no effect whatsoever on a neighboring country that has been spared terrorist activities. Governmental ambivalence toward aviation security leads one to conclude that the effects of terrorism extend to the very heart of political systems. By the same token, the political climate prevailing in an individual state will often be critical in determining its response to terrorist action. A current example is France's ambivalent attitude toward Syria.

Schiphol Airport manager Jan Willem Wegstapel believes that an effective approach to international terrorism rests on three pillars. "The first is that of prevention. This is the field in which airports and airlines can do a great deal themselves and where they bear important responsibility."[29] The second pillar is legislation, which is primarily a state affair, and the third is response, combatting terrorism through arrests, prosecution, and extradition of perpetrators of terrorist acts.[30] This is also the primary responsibility of states. As Rodney Wallis pointed out, "Hijacking of a political nature could be ended today if all governments adhered to the terms and conditions of the three relevant security conventions."[31] He went on to state that "honest application by all states would eliminate the safe havens currently open to the terrorists. Without these refuges we believe much of their enthusiasm would disappear."[32] Twenty-five of the 155 member states of the ICAO have not yet ratified these three conventions. Of these renegade states, Jan Wegstapel believes that "the collusion of offending governments and the passivity of others are the crucial assumption on which international terrorism operates. International terrorism would simply not be possible if all states denied sanctuary to terrorists and stopped promoting their activities."[33] Wegstapel is also critical of his own Dutch government because it plans to pass on both the responsibility and the cost of security measures at Dutch airports to the airports themselves. Differing policies by governments toward their airport authorities especially in the field of security only serve to weaken counterterrorism.

Athens airport became the scene of an intergovernmental dispute after the TWA 847 hijack in 1985. Thousands of Americans assumed security to be so lax that they cancelled summer trips to Greece to avoid passing through the Athens corridor. Greek aviation officials insisted their airport got a bad rap from President Reagan in a crisis period. Others, including journalists, disputed such an interpretation and cited security personnel laughing, smoking, and ignoring security screens.[34] Both Greek pride and the country's economy have suffered badly for apparently allowing the Shiites to smuggle hand grenades and a gun aboard TWA 847. The Greek prime minister tried to dismiss the effect of the U.S. State Department travel advisory by implying that only about 8 percent of the visitors were American. The average American visitor, however, stays longer and spends three times more than other foreign visitors.

It was suggested that both the State Department advisory and the president's attack on Greek airport security had more to do with politics than with security. As Coleman Lollar put it, "Few in Greece doubt that Washington's real intent is to put pressure on what it views as a renegade government within NATO. That infuriates the Socialists, frustrates the largely pro-American Greek travel industry and even amuses some of Papandreou's rightist opponents."[35] Within days of the TWA hijacking an IATA team came to Athens to study the airport's security procedures. Changes began immediately with teams of five security agents assigned to each inspection station. Operators monitoring X-ray machines were changed every 30 minutes. Armed guards were placed at all entrances to the departure lounge. A new training program for security guards was initiated. Construction began on an airport perimeter security fence. In short, despite all the national posturing, the incident did lead to improved security, largely through the intervention of the IATA.

The reactions of governments to political terrorists is as political as the terrorists themselves. The recent onslaught of terrorism in France has had a salutary effect upon that country. It prompted many changes in French legislation in its policies toward terrorism. France instituted higher penalties for terrorist offenses and incentives that encouraged accused terrorists to act as informants. The government tightened security measures and became more willing than ever before to improve its extradition procedures. In 1986 Prime Minister Jacques Chirac formed the National Security Council to coordinate counterterrorist activities between government departments.[36]

In the United Kingdom, as Robin Hill pointed out, "The overlap of competence in airport security has caused concern within the House of Commons Select Committee on Transport, which recently reported that 'where there is power (the Department of Transport) there is no responsibility and where there is responsibility (the airports) there is very little power.'"[37]

But it is the unilateral activities of the United States that in many respects now lead the counterattack against terrorism. The United States has been discontented with foreign airport security and angry at the attacks launched on its airlines abroad. Having tried unsuccessfully in the late 1970s to encourage international enforcement machinery, the United States has enacted its own Foreign Airport Security Act, under which a strict inspection program is operating. Said Hill, "If Federal Aviation Administration inspectors find inadequacies to exist in any airport's security, warnings may be issued to the authorities concerned, with the expectation of improvements being made."[38] Inspectors have identified areas for improvement in foreign countries that have usually been rectified following "strong, though discreet, FAA and embassy representations."[39]

REGIONAL MEASURES

A number of bilateral agreements have been reached between states wishing to stop the flow of hijackers. They include the Afghanistan-U.S.S.R. Agreement on the Hijacking of Aircraft (1971); the Cuba-U.S. Memorandum of Understanding on the Hijacking of Aircraft and Vessels (1973); the Canada-Cuba Agreement on Hijacking (1973); the Cuba-Mexico Agreement on the Illicit Seizure of Aircraft and Seacraft (1973); The Iran-U.S.S.R. Agreement on the Hijacking of Aircraft (1974); the Columbia-Cuba Agreement on the Unlawful Seizure of Aircraft (1974); the Finland-U.S.S.R. Agreement on the Hijacking of Aircraft (1974); and the Bulgarian-Yugoslavian Agreement on Hijacking (1977). Bilateral agreements between Arab states, while politically risky, would be one possible means of reducing the hijacking in that region. The Cubans and Americans finally wearied of the complications ensuing from acting as a haven or a point of origin for terrorists. But even in the 1980s, planes are still hijacked regularly to Cuba.

Apart from bilateral agreements, the possibility of regional treaties to deal with hijacking exists. The EEC has moved to develop a common position on the problem, but progress is painfully slow because of different legal traditions and political outlooks. In Europe the cooperation of INTERPOL and TREVI must be seen as a breakthrough in dealing with terrorism. Regional measures against terrorism must include NATO, the alliance of North Atlantic nations, and the overlapping Economic Summit Seven. The Bonn Declaration on Hijacking (1978) was simply a declaration by each of the seven Economic Summit states to take sanctions against states harboring terrorists. Nevertheless, according to Dan Fiorita, the Canadian representative on the ICAO council, "it is a very valuable assertion of the political will of states."[40] The Venice Declaration (1987) expanded the Bonn Declaration to include offenses under the Montreal Convention.[41]

The NATO Council has always been a forum for the discussion of Western policy in East-West confrontations. Furthermore, the council has always discussed both political and military issues, so there would be nothing radical about NATO discussing or even attempting to resolve cross-Atlantic differences on counterterrorist strategy. On the whole, regional arrangments have been convenient and helpful but by no means crucial to countering the hijack threat.

INTERNATIONAL MEASURES

Real, effective countering of terrorism against international civil aviation rests on a three-cornered tripod consisting of airport security, national policies, and international measures. Coordination of these three levels internationally would effectively shut down the terrorist threat to international aviation, but such coordination is no easy matter to achieve. It is puzzling to note that long after terrorist groups have developed sophisticated regional and international networks of logistical support and refuge, Western states have, for one reason or another, failed to coordinate their action in one common front against the terrorist threat. For a long time it was possible to explain away the situation by saying that the international mechanisms to suppress terrorism were not in place. But now such mechanisms exist, and it is clear that what is lacking is the will to take advantage of them.

For some people, this is a political problem that goes back to governments; for others, it is a matter of legal conventions and penalties needing to be put in place. Likely, both will have to be part of any international solution to terrorism. In the meantime, the structure of international organization in place against terrorism resembles an overloaded ark. It includes the United Nations, which works through the Security Council, the General Assembly, and the ICAO, headquartered in Montreal; the IFALPA, representing airline pilots; the AACC, which represents more than 400 airports worldwide; and the International

Federation of Airline Pilots Association (IFAPA), located in Geneva. It also includes the European Civil Aviation Conference (ECAC), based in Paris; INTERPOL, which coordinates police intelligence; and TREVI, which, though European, is gaining worldwide jurisdiction and influence. How can so many organizations fail to develop effective international policies? Yet how could they all manage to cooperate?

According to Claude Bergeron, "The United Nations' attempt to find a solution to the skyjacking problem was conducted largely at the initiative of the Secretary-General as a result of overtures made to him by INTERPOL, IFALPA and IATA."[42] Both the Security Council and the General Assembly have passed resolutions on the subject of terrorism, but they defer to the ICAO, which specializes in the problem. The ICAO has been studying crimes aboard aircraft since 1950 and was responsible for the Tokyo, Hague, and Montreal conventions. Yet, as Bergeron indicated, "The problem with the above three conventions' approach is the inability of nations to find a method of taking appropriate action against states who violate the convention."[43] Even before the diplomatic conference had convened at The Hague in December 1970 to adopt the antihijacking treaty, the legal committee of the ICAO had been at work to create the Montreal Sabotage Convention, which paralleled The Hague convention, but pertained to sabotage of aircraft. The use of sanctions or the creation of an international criminal court have not received enough support to be implemented and certain nations persist in harboring terrorists. The editor of *Aviation Week* and *Space Technology* wrote on January 9, 1989, "While bolstering international resources is within ICAO's purview, this is not the agency to carry the load of investigative, enforcement and judicial proceedings. A new organization is needed; perhaps a variation on the UN Peacekeeping Force, but focused on terrorism."[44]

The IATA is a private association of the major airline companies of the world. Although most interested in air routes, rates and fares, and traffic rights, it has been increasingly drawn into counterterrorism. Members of the IATA have not mounted any sustained pressure against airlines of states that welcome, harbor, or encourage hijackers; yet its Security Advisory Committee and, more recently, its Security Task Force have become increasingly important in counterterrorism. So often it is the personnel of an organization who have a vision that can give real impetus to change. Rodney Wallis, whose ideas are dealt with below, is such a person in the IATA.

The IFALPA has been the most vocal organization over hijacking and, in many ways, the most effective. It has been inclined to take concrete measures against states that assist hijackers either before or after the act.[45] The association actually called a worldwide strike that had the potential to cripple air travel. Again, vigorous leadership was provided by Tom Ashwood, and a quiet but deeply determined Canadian working out of Montreal for Air Canada security, Fred Deveaux. The latter has been outspoken in calling for better airport security in Canada and more training for flight attendants and pilots.

Nevertheless, in recent years it is two men on opposite sides of the Atlantic who have appeared to be the driving force behind a fiercer and more effective war against aviation terrorism: One is Rodney Wallis of the IATA; the other is Paul Wilkinson of Aberdeen University in Scotland.

Rodney Wallis's motto is: "We must be on our toes at all times to stay ahead of the terrorist. Preempting him or her is our best chance of saving lives."[46] Wallis was undoubtedly behind the IATA's Eight Points, which define basic security standards for international airports. The revised points now additionally focus on antisabotage measures. In the wake of the Pan Am 103 destruction over Lockerbie, Wallis has been deeply involved in an attempt to give urgent reality to internationalizing the response to sabotage of aircraft. This is a five-point response program that involves the establishment of an international advisory group to support governments during a hijacking, the establishment of an international team of experts to investigate acts of unlawful interference after the event; the establishment of an international force working in conjunction with the international advisory group mentioned above, the establishment of an international court to try captured hijackers or other criminals; and finally, the establishment of an international detention center where terrorists could complete their sentences.[47] An explanation of these points suggests that "the intent of these proposals is to strengthen the resolve of states who find themselves under intolerable pressure when an act of unlawful inteference takes place involving their territories."[48] This involves the refueling of aircraft to get rid of a hijacking and the denial of landing rights by closing a runway. One day a major disaster will result from these practices. The object of this plan would be to spread the burden evenly across an international platform and thereby strengthen national resolve to resist terrorism in the air.

On the other side of the Atlantic Ocean, Paul Wilkinson is chairman of the Research Foundation for the Study of Terrorism and security advisor to the International Foundation of Airline Passengers Association, based in Geneva. In an article for *The Times* of London, he outlined some of the international measures that would reduce hijack terrorism: "We need a global aviation security strategy and an international security fund, ideally administered by the International Civil Aviation Organization, to introduce updated technology and training even for the airports of the poorest countries. Otherwise, terrorists will exploit these weak links."[49] Security can be improved without sacrificing passenger convenience by using new technologies for detecting explosives, he believes, adding, "We should use existing vapour-sniffing machines to augment our inadequate X-rays and develop detection methods using neutron bombardment, dielectric measurement and thermal imagery."[50] Security can further be improved, Wilkinson maintained, through the international use of a high-technology identity document. A computerized air travel permit the size of a credit card could carry a finger print code that could be checked against the bearer, thus preventing the use of stolen or forged permits. A check would take no longer than four seconds per passenger.[51] More than 90 percent of aviation terrorism involves the use of false passports, and this system would deal with all but the terrorist-sponsoring states, which would not participate. There is also a need for expert spot checks on airport security worldwide, coupled with the threat of aviation sanctions against those who persistently fail to meet required standards. Although the ICAO ought to be doing these things, it is the AACC and IATA that in fact seem to be taking the initiative.

Since 1976, the IATA security survey team have been created to visit airports, and government response to this program has been excellent. At the invitation of national governments the teams have visited more than 20 countries each year. Furthermore, these visits and surveys have been accomplished at no expense to the governments in question. In September 1986 Israel made a proposal to the ICAO that

the Chicago Convention, as ICAO's constituent document, be amended so as to establish a Commission of Unlawful Interference, to supersede the Committee, which currently exercises competence in that field. Responsible directly to the ICAO Council and appointed by it, the Commission would comprise 15 members suitably qualified in aviation security and with appropriate practical experience.[52]

In his study, *International Terrorism and Civil Aviation, 1983-87,* Ariel Merari said that "the conclusion is unavoidable that international agreements have by and large failed to achieve their purpose."[53] Robin E. Hill Stated: "There must develop as part of a general anti-terrorism scheme a distinct and coherent response to airborne crime in governments, in alliances, in ICAO and within the industry itself, with increasing collaborative efforts between these tiers of authority."[54] Hill is probably closest to the mark, and horrendous aircraft explosions may in the end drive governments to practical measures and sterner actions against terrorism.

POLITICAL SOLUTIONS

Finally, and I feel like a voice crying in the wilderness in this respect, the whole question of controlling terrorism must be approached from the angle of settling political problems. It must be stressed that many terrorist attacks on international civil aviation stem from frustration at unresolved nationality problems. In the field of hijacking this problem becomes evident when the record of hijacks is examined. The Armenians, Sikhs, Lebanese, Palestinians, Shiites of the Persian Gulf states, Filipinos, Tamils, and IRA are all groups that skillful political negotiation could lead to compromise solutions, greatly benefiting the safety of civil aviation. This is not to suggest capitulation to terrorism or even concession and accommodation. But the avenue of political negotiation could and should be explored. Only one person in the field of aviation security has gone on record on this subject, Rodney Wallis. At the Hague conference in 1987, he said,

Terrorism against civil aviation will continue. The conflicts in the Middle East show no sign of abatement—governments appear not to have the political will to solve this problem. Certainly the solution is outside the scope of airlines, thus the fertile incubators of radical young people will continue to be fuelled by distrust and hatred.[55]

There is considerable evidence to suggest that a number of the terrorist groups mentioned above have deliberately chosen hijacking to bring to the attention of an uncaring world that they feel desperate and either want help or desire the international community to bring pressure to bear on their supposed or real oppressors. There is no doubt that if Israel were willing to take the political risk of acknowledging and enabling the principle of self-determination for the Palestinians, as the British did for the Israelis in 1917, the bottom might completely fall out of international terrorism. The rejectionist groups like the PFLP and Abu Nidal might attempt to run their own courses of bitterness, but an independent Palestinian entity would soon bring an end to their hijacking activities. Perhaps, as suggested recently, Ahmed Jabril of the PFLP-GC carried out the bombing of Pan Am 103 for hire to satisfy Iran's desire for revenge for the destruction of an Iranian airliner by the USS *Vincennes* earlier in 1988. The whole "war" between Iran and the United States is negotiable, and there is a failure in the West to understand the disastrous human rights and economic conditions that led to the Shah's downfall and the tyranny that later led to the fundamentalist, religious regime. The problems in Sri Lanka and the Punjab are susceptible to negotiated settlement. The Armenian attacks on Turkish diplomats and Western airlines could be curtailed by economic restitution and an official apology by a Turkish successor government.[56] A lot of hijacking took place in and among Iraq, Iran, Kuwait, and other Gulf states as a result of the Iran-Iraq War; since the ceasefire, the hijacking has largely subsided.

In the period between 1983 and 1987, the Soviet Bloc countries were plagued by hijackings almost as much as Western countries. According to FAA statistics, in the period from 1977 to 1986 there were 38 hijackings in East European countries, compared with 34 in West European countries.[57] Just as the Middle Eastern protagonists are trying to bring pressure to bear on Western European countries for a solution to their political problems, so the Soviet Union is now encountering similar political pressure through hijackings over its problems with ethnic minorities.

International terrorism against civil aviation is far more linked to political aspirations than people suspect, and the present dearth of diplomatic initiatives in international relations is a reflection of the poverty of human potential in the times in which we live.

If help is not forthcoming from the diplomatic community, perhaps it is fitting to end with some advice from the practical mind of the counterterrorist. After all, he is the person who has been closest to the terrorist and knows the enemy well both in theory and practice. In his useful little book *The War Against Terrorists and How to Win It,* Gayle Rivers did not advocate a Rambo-like provocation of Armaggedon in the skies. Instead, he ended by giving some practical advice. He spent some pages showing how national policies of "appeasement" simply make the terrorists go for more rather than slaking their apparent thirst for violence. He put his finger on a serious problem when he asserted, "There are, in fact, influential people in the U.S., British and European governments and the media who advocate appeasement, though they cannot demonstrate a single instance in which it has worked against terrorists."[58] Really firm policies toward terrorism with an absolute minimum of concessions are the only way to deal with fanatics, and this need not damage the internal fabric of democracy.

The second issue with which Rivers dealt at some length is the question of retaliation. "Retaliation," he said,

in simpler language, means tit for tat, an eye for an eye. Tit for tat may momentarily quench the thirst for vengeance. It may make a politician feel that he is doing something. It may make the public feel that the politicians are doing something. But tit for tat sends no message to the enemy. It is merely an invitation for him to think up some bigger or better response. If tit for tat balloons, it can become a costly and useless conventional war as it did when Israel invaded Lebanon.[59]

The final issue with which Rivers dealt is "prevention." He insisted that

deporting a known terrorist does not mean a country is successfully exporting his trouble-making capacity. It is setting him free and washing its hands of the problem. A policy of prevention requires that living, active terrorists be detained, not released; if deported, they should be sent only to a country that wants to try them for crimes committed there and not to countries that offer terrorists safe havens and rest periods until their next offense. Most of today's terrorism has been out of past political expediency.[60]

That expediency produces betrayal and distrust, even among supposed allies. Rivers's final admonition could be a fitting message for Western governments. "Until we send—and terrorists everywhere get—the message that they are not safe anywhere in Western democracies, we will continue losing the terrorist war."[61]

Notes

CHAPTER 1

1. It is not easy to describe accurately the main subject matter of this book. In international law it is called "unlawful seizure of aircraft." That has now been modified to "unlawful interference." *Hijacking*—meaning the seizing of an airliner—was first used by *The Times* (London) on February 19, 1958. *Skyjack* was first used by *The Times* On August 10, 1961. David Hubbard suggested that a *hijacker* is a qualified pilot competent to take over the controls, and a *skyjacker* is a passive rider dependent on the flight crew. Some sources use the term *air* or *aerial piracy.* Most of these distinctions are tenuous and often difficult to discern. Therefore they are used interchangeably in this book. I prefer the word *hijack* since everyone seems to know what it means. *Hijack* and *Hijacking* became current American slang during Prohibition and meant "to steal in transit," especially "to rob a bootlegger of his liquor." See D. Phillips, *Skyjack: The Story of Air Piracy* (London: Harrap, 1973), p. 259.

2. Phillips, *Skyjack,* p. 45.

3. Ibid.

4. Cofrisi was the first of a long line of mentally disturbed hijackers, especially in the United States.

5. Phillips, *Skyjack,* p. 47.

6. Perhaps the hijacks were symbolic of the enduring poor Cuban-U.S. relationship.

7. Phillips, *Skyjack,* p. 261.

8. J. Arey, *The Sky Pirates* (New York: Scribners, 1972), p. 59.

9. Ibid., pp. 57-58.

10. D. G. Hubbard, *Winning Back the Sky: A Tactical Analysis of Terrorism* (New York: Saybrook, 1986), p. 31.

11. Arey, *Sky Pirates,* p. 51.

12. Phillips, *Skyjack,* p. 40.

13. Hubbard, *Winning Back the Sky,* p. 32.

14. R. Clutterbuck, *Living with Terrorism* (London: Faber and Faber, 1975), p. 95

15. Hubbard, *Winning Back the Sky,* pp. 32-33.

16. Phillips, *Skyjack,* p. 69.

17. I heard Tshombe's last speech in London just days before his kidnap. I was also in Algiers near the time of Tshombe's death. There was a lot of newspaper publicity worldwide about the Tshombe case.

18. Arey, *Sky Pirates*, p. 67.

19. Department of Transportation, Federal Aviation Administration, Office of Civil Aviation Security. *U.S. and Foreign Registered Aircraft Hijackings, 1931-1986* (Washington, D.C.: Federal Aviation Administration, 1986), 132 pp.

CHAPTER 2

1. R. Clutterbuck, *Living with Terrorism* (London: Faber and Faber, 1975), p. 97.

2. D. Phillips, *Skyjack: The Story of Air Piracy* (London: Harrap, 1973, p. 71.

3. J. Arey, *The Sky Pirates* (New York: Scribners, 1972, p. 69.

4. *Phillips, Skyjack,* pp. 72-73.

5. P. Clyne, *An Anatomy of Skyjacking* (London: Abelard-Schuman, 1973), p. 188.

6. Phillips, *Skyjack,* p. 76.

7. Ibid.

8. Ibid., p. 78.

9. Ibid., p. 79.

10. Ibid.

11. Ibid., p. 80.

12. Ibid.

13. Ibid.

14. Ibid., p. 184.

15. Ibid.

16. Ibid., p. 185. See also Department of Transportation, Federal Aviation Administration, Office of Civil Aviation Security, *U.S. and Foreign Registered Aircraft Hijackings, 1931-1986* (Washington, DC: Federal Aviation Administration, 1986), p. 32.

17. A film was made of D. B. Cooper's exploit with an FBI officer hunting him down. Some of the money was found in a creek bed, but it is most likely that he died in his jump attempt.

18. Phillips, *Skyjack,* p. 187.

19. Arey, *Sky Pirates,* p. 188.

20. Ibid., p. 97.

21. Ibid.

22. Ibid., p. 182.

23. Ibid., p. 76.

24. Ibid., p. 127.

25. Ibid., p. 163.

26. Ibid., p. 175.

27. Ibid., pp. 148-49.

28. Phillips, *Skyjack,* p. 83.

29. D. G. Hubbard, *The Skyjacker: His Flights of Fantasy* (New York: Macmillan, 1971), p. 70.

30. Phillips, *Skyjack,* p. 212.

31. Arey, *Sky Pirates,* p. 215.

32. Ibid.

33. Ibid., p. 246.

34. Phillips, *Skyjack,* p. 218.

35. Ibid., p. 236.

36. Ibid.

37. Ibid., p. 267.

38. Ibid., p. 241.

39. Ibid., p. 244.

40. Ibid., p. 245.

41. Ibid., p. 246.

42. Ibid., p. 251.

43. Ibid., p. 91

44. Ibid., p. 97.

45. Ibid., p. 100.

46. Ibid.

47. Ibid., p. 266.

48. Ibid.

49. Ibid., p. 100.

50. Ibid., p. 131.

51. Ibid., p. 116.

52. Ibid., p. 129.

53. Ibid., p. 138.

54. Arey, *Sky Pirates,* p. 94.

55. C. Dobson and R. Payne, *The Never-Ending War: Terrorism in the 80's* (New York: Facts on File, 1987), p. 235.

56. Phillips, *Skyjack,* p. 153.

57. Ibid., p. 154.

58. Ibid., pp. 154-55.

59. Ibid., p. 161.

60. Clutterbuck, *Living with Terrorism,* p. 114.

61. Ibid.

62. Phillips, *Skyjack,* p. 171.

63. Ibid.

64. Clutterbuck, Living with Terrorism, p. 103.

65. Ibid.,p. 119.

66. Ibid., p. 103.

67. Ibid., pp. 103-4.

68. C. Dobson and R. Payne, *Counterattack: The West's Battle Against the Terrorists,* (New York: Facts on File, 1982), p. 8.

69. Dobson and Payne, *Never-Ending War,* p. 24.

70. "Shiite International" means a coalition of Shiite groups operating in different countries whose relationship is deliberately blurred.

71. Dobson and Payne, *Never-Ending War,* p. 24.

72. Ibid., p. 25.

73. Stethem was an underwater diver for the U.S. Navy, but the German word *closest* meant marine, and the marines had lobbed a shell into one of the terrorist's village killing his wife and child. He was beside himself with rage.

74. Dobson and Payne, *Never-Ending War,* p. 51.

75. Ibid., p. 229.

76. Ibid., p. 236.

77. The author was in the airport near the time of the explosion.

78. One step backward in order to jump two steps forward.

79. There is a fascinating description of this flight in A. Cave-Brown, *The Bodyguard of Lies* (London: Bantam, 1976). See operations "Flash" and "Valkyrie," pp. 241-42.

80. See above, Chapter 1, note 1.

81. I owe much of the legal material here to an excellent term paper called "Air Terror—A Look at Skyjacking," by Lisa Pindera (Winnipeg: University of Manitoba, Counter Terror Study Center, March 1983).

82. D. G. Hubbard, *Winning Back the Sky: A Tactical Analysis of Terrorism* (New York: Saybrook, 1986).

83. Dobson and Payne, *Counterattack,* p. viii.

CHAPTER 3

1. J. M. Post. "What Makes Terrorists Tick," *Washington Post,* reprinted in *Winnipeg Free Press,* Sept. 3, 1988, p. 52.

2. Ibid.

3. Ibid.

4. Ibid.

5. Ibid.

6. Ibid.

7. Interview with L. Breen, Winnipeg, Manitoba, June 28, 1989.

8. Ibid.

9. D. G. Hubbard, *Winning Back the Sky: A Tactical Analysis of Terrorism* (New York: Saybrook, 1986).

10. N. D. Joyner, *Aerial Hijacking as an International Crime* (New York: Oceana, 1974), p. 207.

11. P. Clyne, *An Anatomy of Skyjacking* (London: Abelard-Schuman, 1973), p. 121.

12. Department of Transportation, Federal Aviation Administration, Office of Civil Aviation Security, *U.S. and Foreign Registered Aircraft Hijackings, 1931-1986* (Washington, DC: Federal Aviation Administration, 1986).

13. F. J. Hacker, *Crusaders, Criminals, and Crazies: Terror and Terrorism in Our Time* (New York: Bantam, 1976), p. 9.

14. Clyne, *Anatomy of Skyjacking,* p. 121.

15. D. Phillips, *Skyjack: The Story of Air Piracy* (London: Harrap, 1973), pp. 86-100.

16. Ibid., p. 228.

17. Clyne, *Anatomy of Skyjacking,* p. 121.

18. Ibid., pp. 122-23.

19. Hacker, *Crusaders, Criminals, and Crazies,* pp. 8-9.

20. Clyne, *Anatomy of Skyjacking,* p. 125.

21. Hacker, *Crusaders, Criminals, and Crazies,* pp. 104-5.

22. Clyne, *Anatomy of Skyjacking,* p. 22.

23. E. Rich, *Flying Scared* (New York: Stein and Day, 1972), p. 146.

24. Ibid., p. 22.

25. Hacker, *Crusaders, Criminals, and Crazies,* p. 105.

26. Rich, *Flying Scared,* p. 58.

27. Hacker, *Crusaders, Criminals, and Crazies,* p. 104.

28. Ibid.

29. Ibid., p. 111.

30. Ibid., p. 112.

31. Ibid., p. 9.

32. Ibid., p. 10.

33. E. Morris and A. Hoe, *Terrorism: Threat and Response* (London, Macmillan, 1987), p. 54.

34. Hacker, *Crusaders, Criminals, and Crazies,* p. 9.

35. Clyne, *Anatomy of Skyjacking,* pp. 125-26.

36. Y. Melman, *The Master Terrorist: The True Story Behind Abu Nidal* (New York: Adama, 1986), p. 159.

37. "World Terrorism," *Calgary Herald* (Calgary, Canada), June 5, 1972.

38. Melman, *The Master Terrorist,* p. 117.

39. Ibid., p. 79.

40. Ibid., p. 218.

41. Ibid., p. 145.

42. Ibid., p. 160.

43. Morris and Hoe, *Terrorism,* p. 59.

44. Melman, *The Master Terrorist,* p. 160.

45. Ibid., p. 146.

46. Ibid.

47. J. Adams, "Terrifying Partnerships: Abu Nidal Joins Moammar Gadaffi," Sept. 24, 1986, p. 9.

48. B. M. Jenkins, ed., *Terrorism and Beyond: An International Conference on Terrorism and Low-Level Conflict* (Santa Monica, CA: Rand, 1982), pp. 52-70.

49. Melman, *The Master Terrorist,* p. 169.

50. Ibid., p. 192.

51. Morris and Hoe, *Terrorism,* pp. 55-56.

52. R. Wright, "Deadly Terrorist Takes Own Lead," *Los Angeles Times,* reprinted in *Winnipeg Free Press,* Feb. 7, 1988.

53. Ibid.

54. Ibid.

55. C. Dobson and R. Payne, *The Never-Ending War: Terrorism in the 80's* (New York: Facts on File, 1987), pp. 42-43.

56. T. M. Ashwood, *Terror in the Skies* (New York: Stein and Day, 1987), p. 55.

57. Ibid.

58. R. Clutterbuck, *Living with Terrorism* (London: Faber and Faber, 1975), p. 144.

59. A. Cave-Brown, *The Bodyguard of Lies* (Toronto: Bantam, 1976).

60. Clutterbuck, *Living with Terrorism,* p. 86.

61. Dobson and Payne, *Never-Ending War,* p. 235.

62. Ibid.

63. Ibid., p. 237.

64. Ibid., p. 239.

65. After a 23-hour flight to Seoul I passed that same garbage receptical exiting the airport just a few hours before it exploded.

66. Interview with an informed and involved Pakistani diplomat.

CHAPTER 4

1. A. Enns, "Counter-Terrorist Activities within the Civil Aviation Industry," Paper (Winnipeg: University of Manitoba, Counter Terror Study Center, March 1988).

2. W. Biddle, "Keep It Simple and Reliable," *Discover*, June 1986, pp. 22-31, 24.

3. A. Merari, "International Terrorism and Civil Aviation," In INTER, *International*

Terrorism in 1987, JCSS Project on Low Intensity Warfare (Jerusalem, 1987), pp. 71-84, 77.

4. Memorandum on ICAO, 13th ed. (Montreal: Public Information Office, 1987), p. 38.

5. "Is the U.S. Sabotaging Its International Airlines?" *Business Week,* Jan. 26, 1981, pp. 74-80.

6. *Newsweek,* July 1, 1985, p. 26.

7. Merari, "International Terrorism," p. 80.

8. Interview with P. Hanappel, Associate Dean, McGill Law School, Montreal, Feb. 1989.

9. G. Rivers, *The War Against the Terrorists* (New York: Charter Books, 1987), p. 58.

10. Ibid.

11. Ibid., p. 67.

12. Ibid.

13. N. C. Livingstone, *The War Against Terrorism* (Toronto: Lexington Books, 1982), p. 82.

14. Enns, "Counter-Terrorist Activities, p. 7.

15. C. Dobson and R. Payne, *Counterattack: The West's Battle Against the Terrorists* (New York: Facts on File, 1982), p. 82.

16. Ibid.

17. See appendix 4.

18. Enns, "Counter-Terrorist Activities," p. 8.

19. Ibid.

20. R. G. Bell, "The U.S. Response to Terrorism Against International Civil Aviation," *Orbis* (Foreign Policy Research Institute), 19 (Winter 1976): 191-205, 193.

21. R. Clutterbuck, *Living with Terrorism* (London: Faber and Faber, 1975), p. 116.

22. Ibid., p. 103.

23. Livingstone, *War Against Terrorism,* p. 92.

24. Ibid., p. 87.

25. Bell, "The U.S. Response," p. 199.

26. Ibid., p. 200.

27. M. Martinez, "Eradicating Aerial Hijacking," *Air Line Pilot,* Oct. 1974, p. 7.

28. Ibid., pp. 6-9, 41, 8.

29. Ibid., p. 43.

30. Ibid., p. 9.

31. Ibid., p. 41.

32. Bell, "The U.S. Response," p. 202.

33. J. J. O'Donnell, "Statement before the Governmental Affairs Committee, United States Senate," Washington, DC, Jan. 30, 1979, p. 4.

34. Ibid.

35. Ibid., p. 3.

36. Ibid., p. 6.

37. Ibid., p. 5.

38. Ibid., p. 4.

39. Ibid., p. 5.

40. Ibid., p. 7.

41. See appendices for hijack statistics worldwide.

42. "Viewpoint," *Air Line Pilot* (Washington, DC), Mar. 1983.

43. *Aviation Week and Space Technology* Apr. 28, 1986, p. 29.

44. This period is the most dangerous to the traveler as he confronts the terrorist.

45. Ibid.

46. *Newsweek,* July 1, 1985, p. 37.

47. Ashwood, *Terror in Skies,* p. 90.

48. *Newsweek,* July 1, 1985, p. 27.

49. T. M. Ashwood, *Terror in Skies* (New York: Stein and Day, 1987), p. 89.

50. Ibid.

51. Ibid., p. 87.

52. Ibid., p. 86.

53. *Newsweek,* July 1, 1985, p. 36.

54. Ibid.

55. Ashwood, *Terror in Skies,* pp. 107-8.

56. S. Ashley, "Can Technology Stop Terror in the Air?" *Popular Science,* Nov. 1985, pp. 69-71, 99, 100.

57. P. Wilkinson, "Vital Steps to Air Safety," *The Times* (London), Jan. 7, 1989.

58. Ibid.

59. Ibid.

60. Ibid.

61. Ashley, "Can Technology Stop Terror in the Air?" p. 70.

62. Ibid.

63. Ibid., p. 71.

64. Ibid., p. 69.

65. Ibid.

66. Biddle, "Keep It Simple," p. 26.

67. Ibid.

68. Ashley, "Can Technology Stop Terror in the Air?" p. 100.

69. Ibid.

70. Wilkinson, *Terrorism and the Liberal State* (London: Macmillan, 1977), pp. 206-24.

71. I. Yeffet, "the Next Bomb," *Life,* Mar. 1989, pp. 130-38.

72. Ibid., p. 132.

73. Ibid.

74. Biddle, "Keep It Simple," p. 69.

75. Yeffet, "The Next Bomb," p. 132.

76. Ibid.

77. Ibid., p. 133.

78. Ibid.

79. Ibid., p. 137.

80. Ibid.

81. "Security in the Skies," *Macleans,* Jan. 11, 1988, p. 30.

82. Interview with S. Gieg, Graduate Student, University of Manitoba, July 1988.

83. Yeffet, "The Next Bomb," p. 134.

84. Rivers, *War Against Terrorists,* p. 49.

85. Yeffett, "The Next Bomb," p. 133.

86. Ibid., pp. 133-34.

87. Ibid., p. 134.

88. The airport security seemed to be excellent, and I was impressed; however, I remember seeing the white garbage container as I left the airport. The next day I had to speak on airport security at the Military Staff College.

89. Yeffet, "The Next Bomb," p. 132.

90. "Security in the Skies," p. 31.

91. Ibid., p. 32.

92. Yeffett, "The Next Bomb," p. 138.

93. Ibid.

94. Winnipeg Free Press, Special section on Winnipeg International Airport, May 20, 1988, pp. 27-32, 27.

95. Ibid.

96. W. Shea, "Airports: The Way Ahead," *American Airport Management* 2, no. 1 (Nov. 1985): 6-10, 8.

97. Merari, "International Terrorism," p. 72.

98. Ibid., p. 73.

99. Rivers, *War Against Terrorists,* p. 54.

100. Paul Koring, "Airline Baggage Slips Through Canada's Anti-Terrorist Net," *The Globe and Mail,* May 25, 1986, p. A4.

101. Ibid.

102. Peter Moon, "No Screening Required to Get Airport Security Pass," *The Globe and Mail,* May 3, 1986, pp. A1-A2.

103. Ibid.

104. Victor Malarek, "Airport Staff Fingerprinting Opposed by Union," *The Globe and Mail,* Sept. 30, 1986, p. 1.

105. Ibid.

106. K. Bremer, "Airports Await New Access Control Rule," *Airport Services*, Dec. 1988, pp. 21-25.

107. Ibid.

108. Ibid.

109. Ibid.

110. *Aviation Week and Space Technology*, Jan. 16, 1989, p. 64.

111. Interview with Robert Selig, Director, Grand Forks Regional Airport, ND, Part 1: Oct. 1988; Part 2: June 1989.

112. "The U.S. Government Antiterrorism Program" (Washington, DC: Special Coordination Committee, National Security Council, June 1979), p. 11.

113. Ibid.

114. Ibid.

115. Ibid.

116. "Viewpoint," Oct. 1974, p. 41.

117. Interview with Selig, Oct. 1, 1988.

118. "U.S. Government Antiterrorist Program," p. 13.

119. Commonwealth Air Transport Council, "Organization of Canadian Aviation Security," 13th meeting, Ottawa, 1987, pp. 1-5, 1-2.

120. Ibid., p. 3.

121. Honorable W. M. Kelly, "The Report of the Senate Special Committee on Terrorism and the Public Safety," (Ottawa: Minister of Supply and Services, 1987, p. 34.

122. Ibid., p. 65.

123. "Viewpoint," Apr. 1986, p. 15.

124. Ibid., p. 16.

125. Ibid.

126. R. Wallis, "Staying Ahead of the Terrorist," International Air Transport Association. (Montreal, 1988).

127. *Aviation Week and Space Technology,* May 26, 1986, p. 31.

128. Ibid.

129. Ibid., June 29, 1987, p. 36.

130. Ibid.

131. Ibid.

132. Ibid.

133. Ibid., Jan. 9, 1989, p. 29.

134. Ibid., p. 62.

135. Ibid., p. 31.

136. J. H. Cushman, "Airport Security," *New York Times,* News Service, May 13, 1989.

137. Ibid.

138. Ibid.

139. Ibid.

140. J. Wegstapel, quoted in *Aviation Security: How to Safeguard International Air Transport,* Conference at the Peace Palace (The Hague, Jan. 1987), p. 97.

141. Ibid., p. 99.

142. Ibid., p. 100.

143. Ibid., p. 102.

144. Interviews with R. Selig.

145. Ibid.

146. A. T. Wells, *Airport Planning and Management* (Blue Ridge Summit, PA: Tab, 1986), p. 35.

147. Ibid., p. 36.

148. Ibid., pp. 36-37.

149. Ibid., p. 37.

150. "Rating the 10 Busiest Airports," *Condé Nast's Traveller,* Jan. 1, 1989, pp. 107-14, 112-13.

151. C. Dobson and R. Payne, *The Never-Ending War: Terrorism in the 80's* (New York: Facts on File, 1987), pp. 308-43.

152. Cushman, "Airport Security."

153. Ibid.

154. Ibid.

155. Ibid.

156. Ibid.

157. Ibid.

CHAPTER 5

1. E. Rich, *Flying Scared* (New York: Stein and Day), p. 11.

2. Ibid., p. 41.

3. D. Hubbard, *Winning Back the Sky: A Tactical Analysis of Terrorism* (New York: Saybrook, 1986), pp. 59-60.

4. J. Schreiber, *The Ultimate Weapon: Terrorists and World Order* (New York: William Morrow, 1978).

5. Hubbard, *Winning Back the Sky,* pp. 66, 58-59.

6. Ibid., pp. 17-18.

7. This diagram is taken from Schreiber, *Ultimate Weapon,* p. 18, but I have added to it.

8. Schreiber, *Ultimate Weapon,* p. 19.

9. Hubbard, *Winning Back the Sky,* pp. 45-46.

10. Rich, *Flying Scared,* pp. 58-59.

11. Hubbard, *Winning Back the Sky,* p. 46.

12. Ibid., p. 47.

13. Schreiber, *Ultimate Weapon,* p. 42.

14. E. Morris and A. Hoe, *Terrorism: Threats and Response* (London: Macmillan, 1987), p. 47.

15. Ibid.

16. Ibid., p. 48.

17. Schreiber, *Ultimate Weapon,* p. 50.

18. The author helped make a video for just such a purpose in April 1990 in Montreal, Canada for Air Canada flight attendants.

19. Hubbard, *Winning Back the Sky,* p. 47.

20. Ibid., p. 52.

21. Flight attendants need to see videos and films of hijack situations and also to train together with pilots.

22. Hubbard, *Winning Back the Sky,* p. 55.

23. Morris and Hoe, *Terrorism,* p. 48.

24. Quoted from L. Khaled and G. Hajjar, *My People Shall Live: Autobiography of a Revolutionary* (London, Hodder & Stoughton, 1973), pp. 131-43, 179-91.

25. Ibid., p. 131.

26. Ibid.

27. Ibid., p. 135.

28. Ibid., p. 142.

29. Ibid., p. 146.

30. Hubbard, *Winning Back the Sky,* p. 51.

31. Ibid.

32. Ibid., pp. 48-50.

33. R. Perrett, "Skyjacking: The Infant Crime of the Modern Era Grows Up," Paper (Winnipeg: University of Manitoba, CTSC, Mar. 1988, p. 24.

34. Hubbard, *Winning Back the Sky,* p.54.

35. Rich, *Flying Scared,* p. 147.

36. Minichiello suddenly took his gun apart and started to clean it piece by piece. The crew watched him do it. The hijack might have been terminated then and there.

37. Interview with B. Dunn, Flight Attendant and Officer, Canadian Air Line Flight Attendants Association, Vancouver, June 23, 1989.

38. T. M. Ashwood, *Terror in the Sky* (New York: Stein and Day, 1987), p. 46.

39. Ibid., p. 47.

40. Ibid.

41. Ibid., p. 53.

42. Ibid., p. 55.

43. Interview with B. Dunn.

44. Ibid.

45. Ibid.

46. Ibid., p. 26.

47. Arey, *The Sky Pirates* (New York: Scribners, 1972), p. 136.

48. Interview With B. Dunn.

49. "Terrorism," R. Bonisteel's program "Man Alive," CBC Television, Canada, Oct. 1986. The man was interviewed at some length about his reactions and emotions throughout this harrowing experience.

50. It has not been established whether the terrorist's grenades or the Egyptian commandos's weapons set alight the interior of the plane. Many trapped passengers simply suffocated.

51. I am suggesting here that passengers on planes should begin to consider how they might react to a hijacking. Reading a book about it is a start.

52. This list has been developed by O. P. St. John and L. Breen as a result of lectures, experience, and other lists developed. It also acknowledges F. Bolz and E. Hershey's *Hostage Cop* (New York: Rawson Wade, 1980), pp. 313-16.

53. It is difficult to obtain information on the details of hijacks, but so much controversy surrounded these two situations that a lot of information has emerged as to what happened. Both hijacks are therefore useful to this study.

54. One of the people who participated in the killing of Robert Stethem was put on trial by U.S. authorities in 1988-1989, and it meant to a lot of Americans that at least partial justice was done.

55. Hubbard, *Winning Back the Sky,* p. 77.

56. Ibid., p. 79.

57. Ibid.

58. This action is nearly always taken to seize and maintain the initiative in a hijack.

59. *Time*, Sept. 15, 1986, p. 31.

60. Perrett, "Skyjacking," p. 33.

61. *Time*, Sept. 15, 1986, p. 31.

62. Perrett, "Skyjacking," p. 33.

63. *Newsweek,* July 1, 1985.

64. Ibid., Sept. 15, 1986, p. 22.

65. Ibid.

66. The U.S. Embassy was suddenly and unaccountably burned to the ground in 1982 by rioting Pakistanis. Also, in 1980, what was for some years the longest hijack on record took place in a successful attempt by opponents of the regime to force Zia-ul-Haq to free political prisoners. The mastermind of this hijack was said to be Benazir Bhutto's brother.

67. *Newsweek,* Sept. 15, 1986, p. 22.

68. *Time*, Sept. 15, 1986, p. 29.

69. Interview with B. Dunn.

70. Ibid.

71. Ibid.

72. Interview with L. Breen, Winnipeg, Manitoba, June 28, 1989.

73. Ibid.

74. Ibid.

75. Interview with B. Dunn.

76. Ibid.

CHAPTER 6

1. P. Wilkinson, "Trends in International Terrorism and the American Response," in *Terrorism and International Order,* ed. L. Freedman et al. (London: Routledge & Kegan Paul, 1986), p. 49.

2. R. Hill, quoted in *Aviation Security: How to Safeguard International Air Transport,* Conference at the Peace Palace (The Hague, Jan. 1987), p. 8.

3. G. Lipman, quoted in *Aviation Security: How to Safeguard International Air Transport,* Conference at the Peace Palace (The Hague, Jan. 1987), p. 109.

4. N. Smit-Kroes, quoted in *Aviation Security: How to Safeguard International Air Transport,* Conference at the Peace Palace (The Hague, Jan. 1987), p. 3.

5. J. Wegstapel, quoted in *Aviation Security: How to Safeguard International Air Transport,* Conference at the Peace Palace (The Hague, Jan. 1987), p. 104.

6. Ibid., p. 102.

7. Ibid.

8. O. Von der Gablentz, quoted in *Aviation Security: How to Safeguard International Air Transport,* Conference at the Peace Palace (The Hague, Jan. 1987), p. 116.

9. C. Hill, "The Political Dilemmas for Western Governments," in *Terrorism and International Order,* ed. L. Freedman et al. (London: Routledge & Kegan Paul, 1986), p. 77.

10. Ibid., p. 80.

11. Ibid., p. 81.

12. A. Enns, "Counter-Terrorist Activities within the Civil Aviation Industry, "Paper (Winnipeg: University of Manitoba, CTSC Collection, Mar. 1988), p. 12.

13. Hill "Political Dilemmas," p. 82.

14. P. Wilkinson, "International Dimensions," in *The New Terrorism,* ed. W. Gutteridge (London: Mansell, 1986), p. 12.

15. Ibid., p. 15.

16. Ibid.

17. Ibid., p. 16.

18. J. Bowyer-Bell, *A Time of Terror: How Democratic Societies Respond to Revolutionary Violence* New York: Basic Books, 1978), p. 172.

19. Ibid., p. 173.

20. The account of this hijack opens *A Time of Terror,* by Bowyer-Bell.

21. Bowyer-Bell, *A Time of Terror,* p. 173.

22. Ibid., p. 201.

23. D. Phillips, *Skyjack: The Story of Air Piracy* (London: Harrap, 1973), pp. 166, 173.

24. Ibid., pp. 154-55.

25. Ibid., p. 166.

26. C. Dobson and R. Payne, *The Never-Ending War: Terrorism in the 80s* (New York: Facts on File, 1987), p. 314.

27. Wilkinson, "International Dimensions," p. 12.

28. Phillips, *Skyjack,* p. 140.

29. Ibid., p. 153.

30. Ibid.

31. Ibid., p. 172.

32. Ibid.

33. Bowyer-Bell, *A Time of Terror,* p. 86.

34. Ibid.

35. G. Rivers, *The War Against the Terrorists* (New York: Charter Books, 1987), p. 58.

36. Bowyer-Bell, *A Time of Terror,* p. 174.

37. Ibid., p. 175.

38. Ibid., p. 176.

39. Ibid.

40. Ibid., p. 177.

41. Wilkinson, "International Dimensions," p. 13.

42. Phillips, *Skyjack,* p. 129.

43. Wilkinson, "International Dimensions," p. 14.

44. Bowyer-Bell, *A Time of Terror,* p. 194.

45. Ibid., p. 196.

46. Department of Transportation, Federal Aviation Administration, Office of Civil Aviation Security, *U.S. and Foreign Registered Hijackings, 1931-1986* (Washington, DC: Federal Aviation Administration, 1986), p. 94.

47. S. Jiwa, *The Death of Air Indian Flight 182* (London: Star Book, 1986), p. 186.

48. Department of Transportation, *U.S. and Foreign Registered Hijackings,* p. 121.

49. Jiwa, *Death,* p. 192.

50. Ibid., p. 193.

51. Department of Transportation, *U.S. and Foreign Registered Hijackings,* p. 81.

52. Dobson and Payne, *Never-Ending War,* pp. 33-47.

53. G. H. Jansen, "Hijacking Tars Iran," *Los Angeles Times,* reproduced in *Winnipeg Free Press,* Dec. 5, 1984.

54. *Winnipeg Free Press,* Tuesday, Dec. 11, 1984, p. 18.

55. *Time,* Apr. 25, 1988, p. 21.

56. Ibid.

57. *Winnipeg Free Press,* Apr. 15, 1988, p. 1.

58. *The Globe and Mail,* Apr. 14, 1988, p. 1.

59. *Winnipeg Free Press,* Apr. 15, 1988, p. 4.

60. *Time,* Oct. 18, 1985, p. 16.

61. Phillips, *Skyjack,* p. 265.

62. Rivers, *War Against Terrorists,* p. 123.

63. Dobson and Payne, *Never-Ending War,* p. 342.

64. Ibid., p. 137n.

65. Dobson and Payne, *Never-Ending War,* p. 52.

66. C. Lollar, "Drawing the Line in Athens," *Frequent Flyer,* Sept. 1985, pp. 71-78, 75.

67. *Newsweek,* Apr. 7, 1986, p. 33.

68. Rivers, *War Against Terrorists,* p. 231.

69. E. Moxon-Browne, "Terrorism in France," in *The New Terrorism,* ed. W. Gutteridge (London: Mansell, 1986), pp. 111-34, 111.

70. Ibid., p. 114.

71. Rivers, *War Against Terrorists,* p. 235.

72. Bowyer-Bell, *A Time of Terror,* pp. 173-74.

73. Moxon-Browne, "Terrorism in France," pp. 111-34.

74. Ibid., p. 126.

75. Ibid., p. 134.

76. Rivers, *War Against Terrorists,* p. 167.

77. Ibid., p. 168.

78. "France and Terrorism," *Los Angeles Times,* reproduced in *Winnipeg Free Press,* Sept. 20, 1986.

79. *Time,* Oct. 6, 1986, p. 46.

80. U.S. Department of State, "Patterns of Global Terrorism: 1988," Report (Washington, DC, 1989), pp. 25-26.

81. N. C. Livingstone, *The War Against Terrorism* (Toronto: Lexington Books, 1982), p. 88.

82. R. Clutterbuck, *Living with Terrorism* (London: Faber and Faber, 1975), p. 101.

83. Ibid.

84. P. Wilkinson, *Terrorism and the Liberal State* (London: Macmillan, 1977), p. 148.

85. Ibid.

86. Dobson and Payne, *Never-Ending War,* p. 243.

87. Ibid., p. 214.

88. CTV "National News" (Canada), Apr. 6, 1988.

89. *Newsweek,* Nov. 5, 1984, p. 44.

90. Ibid.

91. Ibid.

92. *Time,* Apr. 21, 1986, p. 24.

93. Hill, "Political Dilemmas," p. 83.

94. Ibid., p. 92.

95. *Time,* Apr. 21, 1986, p. 26.

96. Ibid., p. 28.

97. *Time,* Nov. 3, 1986, p. 35.

98. *Winnipeg Free Press,* Jan. 30, 1987, p. 42.

99. Wilkinson, "Trends," p. 104.

100. Bowyer-Bell, *A Time of Terror,* p. 197.

101. Ibid., p. 270.

102. Ibid.

CHAPTER 7

1. P. Wilkinson, "Vital Steps to Air Safety," *The Times* (London), Jan. 7, 1989.

2. R. Hill, quoted in *Aviation Security: How to Safeguard International Air Transport,* Conference at the Peace Palace (The Hague, Jan. 1987), p. 17.

3. R. Wallis, quoted in *Aviation Security: How to Safeguard International Air Transport,* Conference at the Peace Palace (The Hague, Jan. 1987), p. 79.

4. International Air Transport Association, "Backgrounder," (Montreal: Information Department, 1988), p. 2.

5. J. Wegstapel, quoted in *Aviation Security: How to Safeguard International Air Transport,* Conference at the Peace Palace (The Hague, Jan. 1987), p. 103.

6. A. Merari, "International Terrorism and Civil Aviation," In *INTER, International Terrorism in 1987,* JCSS Project on Low Intensity Warfare (Jerusalem, 1987), p. 73.

7. Ibid., p. 81.

8. *Aviation Week and Space Technology,* Jan. 9. 1989, p. 31.

9. Ibid., p. 60.

10. I. Yeffet, "The Next Bomb," *Life,* Mar. 1989, p. 132.

11. Ibid.

12. Ibid., p. 137.

13. Wallis, quoted in *Aviation Security,* p. 86.

14. Ibid., p. 87.

15. Ibid., p. 89.

16. Ibid., pp. 111-12.

17. Ibid., p. 107.

18. Hill, quoted in *Aviation Security,* p. 20.

19. G. Lipman, quoted in *Aviation Security: How to Safeguard International Air Transport,* Conference at the Peace Palace (The Hague, Jan. 1987), p. 107.

20. Ibid., p. 110.

21. L. Harris and Associates, "The Travel and Leisure Study: A Survey of Travelling Americans, *Travel and Leisure,* May 1988, pp. 10-11.

22. Ibid.

23. "Backgrounder," p. 1.

24. *Newsweek,* Sept. 15, 1986, p. 27.

25. Merari, "International Terrorism," p. 75.

26. Ibid., p. 74.

27. Ibid., p. 76.

28. "Backgrounder," p. 4.

29. Wegstapel, quoted in *Aviation Secutity,* p. 101.

30. Ibid.

31. Wallis, quoted in *Aviation Security,* p. 78.

32. Ibid., p. 79.

33. Wegstapel, quoted in *Aviation Security,* p. 102.

34. C. Lollar, "Drawing the Line in Athens," *Frequent Flyer,* Sept., 1985, p. 71.

35. Ibid., p. 74.

36. Hill, quoted in *Aviation Security,* p. 17.

37. Ibid., p. 18.

38. Ibid.

39. Ibid.

40. D. Fiorita, "Aviation Security: International Responses, Paper (Montreal: International Civil Aviation Organization May 10, 1988), p. 15.

41. Ibid.

42. C. Bergeron, "Hijacking," Paper (Ottawa: Carleton University, Apr. 10, 1982), p. 13.

43. Ibid.

44. *Aviation Week and Space Technology,* Jan. 9, 1989, p. 9.

45. Bergeron, "Hijacking," p. 14.

46. R. Wallis, quoted in International Air Transport Association "Staying Ahead of the Terrorist" (Montreal, 1988), p. 3.

47. Memorandum on ICAO, 13th ed. (Montreal: Public Information Office, 1987), pp. 1-2.

48. Ibid., p. 2.

49. Wilkinson, "Vital Steps."

50. Ibid.

51. Ibid.

52. Hill, quoted in *Aviation Security,* p. 16.

53. Merari, "International Terrorism," p. 83.

54. Hill, quoted in *Aviation Security,* p. 8.

55. Wallis, quoted in *Aviation Security,* p. 94.

56. See my article "Why Armenian Terror in Canada?" *The Globe and Mail,* Apr. 1, 1985, p. 7.

57. Merari, "International Terrorism," p. 83.

58. G. Rivers, *The War Against the Terrorists* (New York: Charter Books, 1987), p. 163.

59. Ibid., pp. 187-88.

60. Ibid., p. 207.

61. Ibid., p. 208.

Aircraft Hijackings and Other Criminal Acts Against Civil Aviation Statistical and Narrative Reports

U.S. Department
of Transportation

Federal Aviation
Administration

Updated to January 1, 1986

Notice:

This edition is the final publication covering all known hijackings and explosions aboard aircraft since 1931.

Future publications will include only data covering the latest 10 year period.

Section	Title
A	U.S. Registered Aircraft Hijacking Statistics
B	Chronology of Hijackings of U.S. Registered Aircraft and Legal Status of Hijackers
C	Legal Status of Hijackers-Summarization
D	U.S. and Foreign Registered Aircraft Hijackings
E	U.S. and Foreign Registered Aircraft Hijackings-Summarization
F	Explosions Aboard Aircraft
G	Worldwide Significant Criminal Acts Involving Civil Aviation—1985

May, 1986
Washington, D.C. 20591

This publication was prepared by the Federal Aviation Administration, Office of Civil Aviation Security

208

US Department
of Transportation
**Federal Aviation
Administration**

Hijacking Attempts on U.S. General Aviation Aircraft

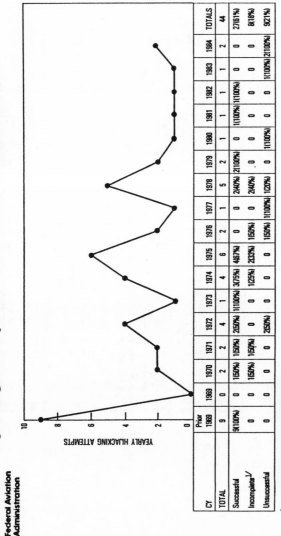

YEARLY HIJACKING ATTEMPTS

CY	Prior 1969	1969	1970	1971	1972	1973	1974	1975	1976	1977	1978	1979	1980	1981	1982	1983	1984	TOTALS
TOTAL	9	0	2	2	4	1	4	6	2	1	5	2	1	1	1	1	2	44
Successful	9(100%)	0	1(50%)	1(50%)	2(50%)	1(100%)	3(75%)	4(67%)	0	0	2(40%)	2(100%)	0	1(100%)	1(100%)	0	0	27(61%)
Incomplete[1]	0	0	1(50%)	1(50%)	0	0	1(25%)	2(33%)	1(50%)	0	2(40%)	0	0	0	0	0	0	8(18%)
Unsuccessful	0	0	0	0	2(50%)	0	0	0	1(50%)	1(100%)	1(20%)	0	1(100%)	0	0	1(100%)	2(100%)	9(21%)

[1] Hijacking in which hijacker is apprehended/killed during hijacking or as a result of "hot pursuit."

General Aviation Aircraft Hijacking Attempts Since Jan. 1, 1984

Date 1984	Aircraft	Number Aboard	Hijacker's Boarding Point	Hijacker's Destination/ Objective
1/11	Piper-35	2	Polson, MT	Escape Attempt
2/18	Piper-Navajo	10	Evanston, WY	Escape Attempt

As of: 1/1/85

Hijacking Attempts on U.S. Scheduled Air Carrier Aircraft[1]

US Department of Transportation
Federal Aviation Administration

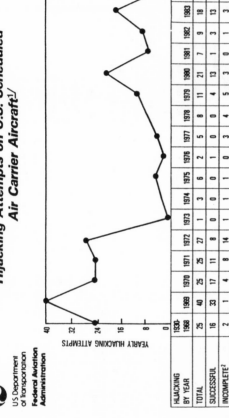

HIJACKING BY YEAR	1930-1968	1969	1970	1971	1972	1973	1974	1975	1976	1977	1978	1979	1980	1981	1982	1983	1984	TOTALS
TOTAL	25	40	25	25	27	1	3	6	2	5	8	11	21	7	9	18	5	238
SUCCESSFUL	16	33	17	11	8	0	0	0	1	0	0	4	13	1	3	13	4	124
INCOMPLETE[2]	2	1	4	8	14	1	1	1	0	3	4	5	3	0	1	3	1	52
UNSUCCESSFUL	7	6	4	6	5	0	2	5	1	2	4	2	5	6	5	2	0	62

[1] Effective September 1981--Includes all certificate holders as defined in Code of Federal Regulations Title 14 Part 108.
[2] Hijacking in which hijacker is apprehended/killed during hijacking or a result of "hot pursuit".

U.S. Aircarrier Hijacking Attempts Since Jan.1, 1984

Date 1984	Airline-Flt/ Aircraft	Number Aboard	Hijacker's Boarding Point	Hijacker's Destination/ Objective
2/11	AA-658/B-727	152	Port Au Prince, Haiti	New York, N.Y. (JFK)
3/27	PI-451-B-737	59	Charleston, S.C.	Cuba
3/28	DL-357-B727	26	New Orleans, LA.	Cuba
11/29	EA-1962-HP-13	13	Augusta, GA.	Atlanta, GA.
12/31	AA-626-DC-10	198	St. Croix, Virgin Islands	Cuba

As of: 1/1/85

210

US Department
of Transportation
Federal Aviation
Administration

Hijacking Attempts on U.S. And Foreign Aircraft*

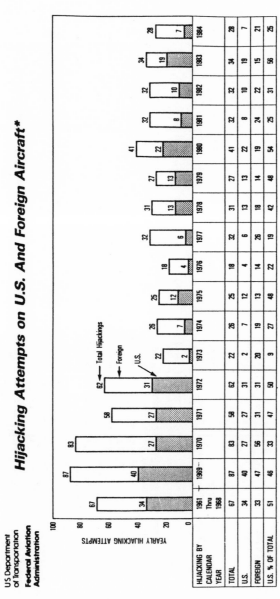

HIJACKING BY CALENDAR YEAR	1961 Thru 1968	1969	1970	1971	1972	1973	1974	1975	1976	1977	1978	1979	1980	1981	1982	1983	1984
TOTAL	67	87	83	58	62	22	26	25	18	32	31	27	41	32	32	34	28
U.S.	34	40	27	27	31	2	7	12	4	6	13	13	22	8	10	19	7
FOREIGN	33	47	56	31	31	20	19	13	14	26	18	14	19	24	22	15	21
U.S. % OF TOTAL	51	46	33	47	50	9	27	48	22	19	42	48	54	25	31	56	25

*Includes General Aviation Aircraft

As of: 1/1/85

211

DEPARTMENT OF TRANSPORTATION
FEDERAL AVIATION ADMINISTRATION - OFFICE OF CIVIL AVIATION SECURITY
U.S. AND FOREIGN REGISTERED AIRCRAFT HIJACKINGS - SUMMARIZATION
UPDATED: JANUARY 1, 1986

CY	1931-69	1970	1971	1972	1973	1974	1975	1976	1977	1978	1979	1980	1981	1982	1983	1984	1985	TOTAL
U.S. Successful	58[9]* (55)**	18[1] (14)	12[1] (10)	10[2] (6)	1[1] (0)	3[3] (1)	4[4] (0)	1[0] (0)	0 (0)	2[2] (0)	6[2] (2)	13[0] (13)	2[1] (1)	4[1] (3)	13[0] (11)	4[0] (3)	2[1] (0)	153[28] (119)
Incomplete***	3[0] (3)	5[1] (1)	9[1] (1)	14[0] (1)	1[0] (0)	2[1] (0)	3[2] (1)	1[1] (0)	3[0] (0)	6[2] (2)	5[0] (3)	3[0] (0)	0 (0)	1[0] (0)	3[0] (1)	1[0] (0)	1[0] (1)	61[8] (13)
Unsuccessful	13[0] (7)	4[0] (0)	6[0] (3)	7[2] (1)	0[0] (0)	2[0] (0)	5[0] (0)	2[1] (0)	3[1] (0)	5[1] (1)	2[0] (1)	6[1] (4)	6[0] (2)	5[0] (1)	3[1] (1)	2[2] (0)	2[0] (0)	73[9] (21)
SUB-TOTAL	74[9] (65)	27[2] (15)	27[2] (14)	31[4] (7)	2[1] (0)	7[4] (1)	12[6] (1)	4[2] (0)	6[1] (0)	13[5] (3)	13[2] (6)	22[1] (17)	8[1] (3)	10[1] (4)	19[1] (13)	7[2] (3)	5[1] (1)	287[45] (153)
FOREIGN Successful	100[7] (40)	37[5] (17)	10[1] (3)	13[1] (3)	10[0] (2)	5[1] (1)	3[0] (0)	6[0] (0)	16[0] (0)	8[1] (1)	8[2] (0)	9[1] (2)	13[2] (3)	12[0] (1)	6[0] (0)	17[1] (1)	19[9] (0)	292[31] (74)
Unsuccessful	27[1] (9)	19[2] (4)	21[0] (6)	18[0] (1)	10[0] (1)	14[1] (1)	10[1] (1)	8[1] (0)	10[1] (0)	10[0] (0)	6[0] (0)	10[1] (0)	11[0] (0)	10[1] (0)	9[0] (1)	4[0] (0)	12[0] (0)	209[9] (27)
SUB-TOTAL	127[8] (49)	56[7] (21)	31[1] (9)	31[1] (4)	20[0] (4)	19[2] (2)	13[1] (1)	14[1] (0)	26[1] (0)	18[1] (1)	14[2] (0)	19[2] (4)	24[1] (3)	22[1] (1)	15[0] (1)	21[1] (1)	31[9] (0)	501[40] (101)
WORLDWIDE Successful	158[16] (95)	55[6] (31)	22[2] (13)	23[3] (9)	11[1] (2)	8[4] (2)	7[4] (0)	7[0] (0)	16[0] (0)	10[3] (1)	14[4] (2)	22[0] (15)	15[3] (4)	16[1] (4)	19[0] (95)	21[1] (4)	21[1] (0)	445[59] (193)
Incomplete (U.S.)	3[0] (3)	5[1] (1)	9[1] (1)	14[0] (0)	1[0] (0)	2[1] (0)	3[2] (1)	1[1] (0)	3[0] (0)	6[2] (2)	5[0] (3)	3[0] (0)	0 (0)	1[0] (0)	3[0] (1)	1[0] (0)	1[0] (1)	61[8] (13)
Unsuccessful	40[1] (16)	23[2] (4)	27[0] (9)	25[2] (2)	10[0] (2)	16[1] (1)	15[1] (1)	10[2] (0)	13[2] (0)	15[1] (1)	8[0] (1)	16[2] (6)	17[0] (2)	15[1] (1)	12[1] (2)	6[2] (0)	14[0] (0)	282[18] (48)
TOTAL	201[17] (114)	83[9] (36)	58[3] (23)	62[5] (11)	22[1] (4)	26[6] (3)	25[7] (2)	18[3] (0)	32[2] (0)	31[6] (4)	27[4] (6)	41[3] (21)	32[3] (6)	32[2] (5)	34[1] (14)	28[3] (4)	36[10] (1)	788[85] (254)

* G/A - FIGURES IN BRACKETS REPRESENT THE NUMBER OF GENERAL AVIATION FLIGHTS. THESE FIGURES ARE INCLUDED IN THE TOTAL FIGURE.

** FIGURES IN PARENTHESIS REPRESENT ATTEMPTED HIJACKINGS TO CUBA.

*** AN INCOMPLETE HIJACKING IS ONE IN WHICH THE HIJACKER IS APPREHENDED/KILLED DURING HIJACKING OR AS A RESULT OF "HOT PURSUIT".

EXPLOSIONS ABOARD AIRCRAFT
ANNEX A
NUMBER INCIDENTS AND PERSONS KILLED BY YEAR

Year	No. of Incidents	No. Killed	Year	No. of Incidents	No. Killed	Year	No. of Incidents	No. Killed
1949	2	36	1965	1	52	1975	4	1
1950	1	0	1966	1	28	1976	5	168
1952	1	0	1967	4	66	1977	1	0
1955	2	60	1968	1	0	1978	3	5
1956	1	0	1969	4	33	1979	2	0
1957	2	1	1970	9	84	1980	1	0
1959	1	1	1971	3	25	1981	3	2
1960	2	47	1972	7	114	1982	2	1
1962	1	45	1973	5	92	1983	2	112
1964	1	15	1974	5	161	1984	3	0
						1985	7	390
						TOTAL	87	1539

213

Terrorism from Below and Above

TERROR FROM BELOW		
Crazy	*Criminal*	*Crusading*
Self-centered and sacrificial	Selfish and self-protective	Unselfish and sacrificial
Thought processes: highly personal, often nonrational or irrational	Thought processes: task-oriented, rational, conventional in terms of prevailing values	Thought processes: task-oriented, functionally rational * but unconventional in terms of prevailing values
Sometimes delusional	Realistic	Realistic, often in service of unrealistic ends
Abstract goals	Concrete goals	Concrete and abstract goals
Anticipated gain: psychological and idiosyncratic	Anticipated gain: personal and material	Anticipated gain: collective, symbolic, publicity, or material
Often "incomprehensible"	Commonly "understandable"	"Understandable" to sympathizers, "senseless" to antagonists
Cry for help, self-dramatization (psychodrama), therapeutic attempt, attempt at self-cure	Materially, not psychologically, oriented	Attention-getting, ostentatious, dramatic, spectacular, publicity-conscious
Amateurish M.O.**	Professional, mostly repetitive M.O.	Theatrical M.O. follows trends and fashions
High risk taking	High risk avoidance	Indifferent to high risk
Predominantly inward-directed aggression, intrapunitive, suicidal	Predominantly outward-directed aggression, extrapunitive, homicidal	Intrapunitive and extrapunitive, suicidal and homicidal
Loners or small groups, not organized	Loners or organized in a businesslike (e.g., syndicates, corporations) or familylike (e.g., clan, brotherhood) manner, often subject to terror from above (Mafia)	Small or large groups, organized in armylike manner (e.g., leagues, fronts, units), with hierarchical command structure, often submissive to terror from above
Unstable, immature, often distractible and inept individuals with weak ego and overt behavior disturbances	Detached, often dehumanized individuals, often unstable and inept but also often with seemingly intact ego and without overt behavior disturbances	Fanatical individuals, often with seemingly intact ego, without overt behavior disturbances

MOTIVATION

CAST

TERROR FROM BELOW (*continued*)

Crazy	Criminal	Crusading	
Conspicuous through bizarre conduct or attire	Mostly inconspicuous	Inconspicuous	
Often overt sexual disturbance	No overt sexual disturbance	No overt sexual disturbance, little or no overt sexual interest	
Unpredictable, vascillating, hesitating	Predictable, mostly determined, ruthless	Predictably unpredictable, determined, ruthless	
Indifferent to immediate success	Exclusively interested in concrete immediate success	Predominantly interested in immediate and long-range publicity and success	CAST
Frequently imitative	Frequently imitative	Frequently innovative and violence-escalating	
Eager for alliances with audience, often on any terms	Disinterested in alliances but interested in specific deals	Interested in deals and alliances on their own terms	
Cannot be deterred by ordinary means, can be persuaded but not bought	Can be deterred by ordinary means, can be bought but not persuaded	Cannot be deterred by ordinary means, incorruptible	
Selection: random or according to delusional system (with attraction to the powerful and prominent)	Selection: purely instrumental (the rich and prominent for trade and blackmail value)	Selection: for symbolic and/or publicity value, often from emotional, highly charged enemy target group as instruments for barter but may become targets for brainwashing and eventual allies	VICTIMS
Highly endangered for short periods of time	Danger varying according to response; the more professional the criminal, the less endangered the victim	After initial phase, danger almost entirely dependent upon responses	
Selection: random or vaguely defined target group, visualized as possible allies and helpers	Selection: usually small groups, such as the victim's family	Selection: largest group possible (the nation, the world)	OBJECTS (AUDIENCE)
Recipients of moral appeals	Recipients of business propositions	Recipients of specific blackmail threats and vague moral appeals	
High ambivalence	Indignation not tempered by ambivalence	High ambivalence	REACTION OF OBJECTS
Merciless removal ("Kill him; he's crazy anyway") or pity (poor-devil phenomenon)	Buying offers and/or severe punishment	Extreme measures (e.g., repressive counteraction, death penalty) advocated by antagonists; understanding advocated by sympathizers	

TERROR FROM BELOW (continued)

Crazy	Criminal	Crusading	
Emphasis on protection rather than punishment	Emphasis on punishment and deterrence	Emphasis on punishment for protection and deterrence by antagonists; emphasis on little or no individual punishment by sympathizers	REACTION OF OBJECTS
Quick retaliation or advocacy of flexible negotiations	Advocacy of immediate nogotiations, often with the use of guile and trickery	Various coping styles; show of strength (e.g., no negotiation, no concession), but negotiations obligatory if victims are sufficiently valuable	

TERROR FROM ABOVE

Crazy	Criminal	Crusading	
Same as terrorism	Same as terrorism	Same as terrorism	MOTIVATION
Erratic, bizarre conduct with emphasis on self-aggrandizement	Professional conduct of administrators and executors in tight business organizations demanding discipline and submission, strict division of labor	Professional conduct of generals and soldiers in military organizations demanding discipline and submission with specific rules for propaganda and image making	CAST
Untrained, often unskilled	Often well trained and highly skilled	Often well trained and highly skilled	
Often manipulated	Often manipulators	Often manipulated manipulators	
Same as terrorism	Same as terrorism	Same as terrorism	VICTIMS OBJECTS (AUDIENCE)
Selection: random, vague, and inconsistent, no discernible pattern	Selection: captive limited target groups	Selection: captive total population, everyone a potential victim	
Wait-and-see attitude	Quick, limited response, often through manoeuvers, tricks, and without moral scruples	Ambivalent reaction according to political conviction and/or gravity of threat	REACTION OF OBJECTS
Attempted exploitation of terrorist's self-destructive tendencies (give enough rope to hang)	Attempted deals and short-range accommodations, limited submission, or escape attempts, frequently, long-range accommodation and submission	Short-range escape attempts or "inner" escape by demonstrative apathy; different coping devices depending on degree and duration of "total institution"; frequently long-range accommodation, submission, and conversion (joining)	
Ridicule and faked submission	Indignation and disgust	Indignation and disgust, sometimes changing to resignation or enthusiasm	

---

*According to Karl Mannheim, a distinction is to be made between functional rationality, referring to the appropriate relationship between ends and means, and substantive rationality, referring to the "appropriateness" of ends.

**M.O.: modus operandi, method of procedure.

Sabotage of Aircraft, 1949–1988

05/07/49	Philippine Air; Doet/Manila; bomb; criminal; 13 dead
09/09/49	Quebec Air (CP) Quebec City/Bay Comeau; bomb explosion; 23 dead
04/11/55	Air India Hong Kong/Djakarta; bomb in wheel well; 16 dead.
11/01/55	United Airlines U.S.Denver/Portland; bomb in baggage; 44 dead
07/25/57	Western Airlines L.Vegas/L.A. bomb in lavatory; 1 dead
01/06/60	National Airlines NY/Miami; bomb explosion; 34 dead
04/28/60	Linea Aero Venezuela Caracas/P.Ayacucho; bomb; 13 dead
05/22/62	Continental Air Chicago/Kansas City; bomb in lavatory; 45 dead
12/08/64	Bolivian Airlines Tipuani/La Paz; dynamite; 15 dead
07/08/65	CP Air (Canada) Vanc/Whitehorse; bomb in fuselage; 52 dead
11/22/66	Aden Airways near Aden; bomb in baggage-hold; 28 dead
10/12/67	B.E.A. Comet. Rhodes; bomb in tourist cabin; 66 dead
12/26/68	Athens; ElAl 707 attacked with grenades; 1 dead
02/02/69	Zurich ElAl 707 attack with grenades and guns; 2 dead
08/05/69	Philippine Air. 2am boanger; gelignite in lavatory; 1 dead
12/22/69	Air Vietnam NrNha Trang; bomb in lavatory; 32 dead
02/21/70	Swiss Air; Over Würenlingen; bomb explosion; 47 dead
02/02/70	Austrian Airliner; Vienna; bomb explodes; plane lands safely
04/21/70	Philippine Air. Nr Manila; explosion in lavatory; 36 dead
06/02/70	Philippine Air. Roxas; bomb under seat explodes; 1 dead
09/07/70	PanAm 747. on ground, Cairo; plane demolished on ground
09/12/70	TWA707, on ground, Dawson's Field; destroyed, Jordan
09/12/70	Swissair DC-8, on ground, Dawson's Field; destroyed, Jordan
09/12/70	British OAC VC10; destroyed, Dawson's field, Jordan
08/24/71	Royal Jordanian Air 707; explosion in lavatory; on ground in Madrid
11/20/71	China Airlines; S.China Sea; bomb explosion; 25 dead
01/26/72	Yugoslav, DC9; explodes over Czechoslovakia; 27 dead
05/25/72	Lan-Chile 727, nr Cuba; bomb explodes; plane lands safely
06/15/72	Cathay Pacific Air, over S.Vietnam; bomb under seat; 81 dead
08/16/72	ElAl 707, over Rome; bomb in cassette player; lands safely
09/16/72	Air Manila, near Roxas; explosion cargo compartment; lands safely
12/08/72	Ethiopian Airlines, near Addis Ababa; grenade; 6 dead
03/19/73	Air Vietnam DC-4, S. Vietnam; explosion in cargo; 59 dead
04/24/73	Aeroflot TV104, near Leningrad; bomb; 2 dead
07/20/73	Japanese Air Lines 747; destroyed; 1 dead; explosive
08/05/73	Athens; TWA plan from TelAviv; grenade attack; 5 dead; 55 wounded
11/17/73	Rome; PanAm; thermite bomb kills 32; 40 injured
12/17/73	Pan Am 707; Rome, on ground; incendiary grenades; 30 dead
02/20/74	Air Vietnam, DC-4; S. Vietnam; explosives detonated; 3 dead
03/22/74	Air Inter (France), Corsica; bomb explodes; no deaths
07/23/74	Belfast-London Aer Lingus; bomb fires but not exploded; 92 survive
08/26/74	TWA 707; Rome; explosive device fires but no explosion
09/08/74	TWA 707; Ionian Sea; explosion in cargo-hold; 88 dead
09/15/74	Air Vietnam; S.Vietnam; hand grenades; 70 dead
01/75	Attempt to shoot down ElAl 707 with missile; fails

06/03/75	Philippines BAC-111 near Manila; bomb in lavatory; 1 dead; 45 injured
07/05/75	Pakistan Airlines 707; Rawlpindi; bomb under seat; 4-foot hole
12/19/75	Paris Boudia group attack passengers; 20 wounded
12/29/75	LaGuardia; bomb explodes in luggage; 62 dead 1 injured
01/01/76	Middle East Airlines, S.Arabia/Kuwait; explosion; 82 dead: n.s.
05/21/76	Philippine Airlines; Zamboauga; grenades; 13 dead; 14 injured
07/02/76	Eastern Airlines; Electra; on ground; bomb destroys aircraft
09/07/76	Air France 707; Corsica; explosion aboard plane on ground
10/06/76	Cubana; DC8; Barbados; explosion; 73 dead: n.s.
10/77	Singapore Airlines; explosion aboard and crash; 100 dead: n.s.
08/18/78	Philippine Airlines; explosion in lavatory; 1 dead; 3 injured
09/07/78	Air Ceylon; on ground, Colombo; aircraft destroyed by bomb
03/25/79	TWA jet, Kennedy Airport; bomb explosion; 4 injured
04/03/79	Frankfurt cargo terminal: suitcase; ElAl explodes; 10 injured
04/26/79	Indian Airlines 737, over Madras; explosion; 8 injured
11/15/79	American Airlines; bomb; smoke; landed safely
/80	Pan Am; San Francisco/Tokyo; bomb of Ibrahim discovered
09/09/80	United Airlines; explosion in hold, Sacramento; 2 injured
10/13/81	Air Malta 737; on ground, Cairo; bomb in luggage; 2 dead; 8 injured
12/12/81	Aeronica Nicaragua 727; on ground, Mexico City; explosion; 5 injured
07/12/82	People's Republic of China; in-flight bomb explosion; lands safely
08/11/82	PanAm 747; 140 miles from Honolulu(Tokyo); bomb explodes; 1 dead; 15 injured; May 15 org.
08/19/83	Syrian Airlines 727; Rome; incendiary device burns aircraft
09/23/83	Gulf Air (Bahrain), 30 miles from Abu Dhabi; bomb explodes; 112 dead: n.s.
01/18/84	Air France 747, 70 miles from Karachi; explosion; 2-metre hole; landed
03/10/84	Union Des Transport (France), Chad; explosion on ground; 24 injured
07/31/84	Air France 737; on ground, Teheran; hijackers destroy aircraft
01/23/85	Bolivian Lloyd Aero 727; in flight; bomb in lavatory; 1 dead
03/09/85	Royal Jordanian Air L-1011; on ground, Dubai; bomb explodes
06/88/85	Royal Jordanian Air 727; Beirut, on ground; hijackers blew up plane
06/23/85	Air India 182 (747); sabotaged 90 miles off Ireland; 329 dead
06/23/85	CP Air (Canada; bomb explodes at Narita; 2 dead
06/85	Frankfurt airport; bomb explodes; 3 dead, plus wounded
10/30/85	American Airlines 727; on ground, Dallas; explosiou after landing
11/23/85	Egyptair 727; Valletta, Malta; explosion; 60 dead; 35 injured
04/02/86	TWA 840 into Athens experiences bomb explosion; 4 dead
04/17/86	London, Heathrow; ElAl discover bomb (Hindawi-Murphy)
05/08/86	Colombo Air Lanka; bomb explodes in tail; 20 dead; 41 wounded
05/30/86	Air India; JFK; security finds bomb. Sikhs
09/05/86	Pakistan, Karachi Pan Am 073; Abu Nidal grenade attack; 20 dead
11/25/86	Iraq-Air 737; hijackers & security in firefight; crashes; 65 dead; 42 wounded
11/29/87	Baghdad-Abu Dhabi-Korea; Korean Air 858; sabotaged; 115 dead
12/10/87	US Pacific Southwest Air (L.A to S.F.); sabotage by gunfire; 43 dead
07/03/88	Iran, Persian Gulf; USS Vincennes shoots down Iranian A-300; 290 dead
08/17/88	Peshawar, Pakistan; President Zia & Am.Amb.die in sabotaged C-130; 29 dead
10/15-20/88	India; two separate crashes; sabotage suspected; 374 dead
12/22/88	Lockerbie, Scotland; PanAm 103; bomb-sabotaged; 270 dead

1949-1988: 2939 people died by sabotage or explosions
1949-1988: 356 people were wounded
      (This does not include a 1977 Air India suspected sabotage in which 216 died.)
Since 1968 there have been 80 clear-cut attempts to destroy planes.

My People Shall Live:
Autobiography of a Revolutionary
by Leila Khaled
as told to George Hajjar

Introduction to
Canadian Edition

My People Shall Live was written in the fall of 1971. It was intended as a political statement of the Arab revolutionary position on the Palestine question. Leila Khaled was selected as the subject of the book. The transformation of her life from refugee to revolutionary typifies and symbolizes the reemergence of the Palestinian people on the political scene.

My People was supposed to have been published in the U.S. and in Canada, which is held as a minor part of the U.S. "domestic market", by Bantam Books of New York. It was suppressed under Zionist pressure, though Bantam had already marketed My People internationally, including such countries as Britian and the Commonwealth, excluding Canada but including South Africa, Rhodesia, and Australia, West Germany, France, Hong Kong, Lebanon, Egypt, Japan and Turkey.

The book did meet opposition overseas. In London, England the Pilots' Association sought an injunction banning serialization of My People in the Sunday Telegraph because it promoted 'terrorism' and 'skyjackings'. The High Court of England dismissed the charge and pontificated "the book is a handbook on communism and revolution". Then the Zionists turned their attention to distribution where they also failed, with the exception of W.H. Smith and Sons who refused to stock My People but expressed readiness to accept orders for it.

But the shocking story of suppression takes place in New York where Bantam had advanced the date of publication from March '74 to February and then cancelled after it had typeset the book and printed the cover. (The author has both the cover and the galley proofs in his possession.) I was told in writing by Marc Jaffe, senior editor of Bantam, that it was "not the appropriate moment

To Bertrand, Bonnie and Sophie and the children of the earth.

"It is not enough to hate and believe in the past to make a revolution. Hatred and belief in the past are sufficient prods for the rebellion phase. We must love and be future-oriented if we wish to carry out the revolution."
Ghassan Kanafani, Editor *Al Hadaf*,
the organ of the Popular Front for the
Liberation of Palestine.

Kanafani was assassinated by Israeli agents July 8. 1972. The Revolution Lives!

George Hajjar has written a book on Kanafani entitled *Kanafani, Symbol of Palestine.*

legality in his own terms and decides to apply his ethical and legal doctrines against me because he has the power as well as the means of communications to justify his inhumanity, I am under no moral obligation to listen, let alone obey his dictates. Indeed, I am under a moral obligation to resist and to fight to death the enemy's moral corruption. My deed cannot be evaluated without examining the underlying causes. The revolutionary deed I carried out on August 29, 1969 was an assertion of my spurned humanity, a declaration of the humanity of Palestinians. It was an act of protest against the West for its pro-Zionist (therefore anti-Palestinian) posture. The list of the sins of the West is overwhelming.

*

* * *

Germany, according to Zionism, has "atoned" for the incineration of six million Jews by the payment of nine billion marks in "reparations" to the state of Israel, the "haven" of a united Zionist Jewry. It has since 1965 almost wholly identified with Israel, especially before and during the June War, when the former Nazi chancellor offered to give the Israelis "gas masks" to protect them from "Arab bacteriological warfare". Israel for her part has entertained Joseph Strauss and sold Uzzi rifles to Germany.

France has not only supplied Israel with Mystères, Super Mystères and Mirages, but has allowed the Israelis to "steal" French gunboats from Cherbourg, contrary to De Gaulle's wishes. De Gaulle merely "relieved" the general who turned over the boats to Israel. Guy Mollet, the French Socialist prime minister, conspired with Ben Gurion and Anthony Eden and invaded Egypt in 1956. France provided Israel with the scientific know-how and material to manufacture the atomic bomb at Dimova and labelled the plutonium-producing plant a "textile factory".

Switzerland, the neutral country, has not only detained Arab revolutionaries and released the murderers of Palestinians, but has also closed its eyes to Zionist kidnappers who killed scientists working for my people. Switzerland has let go practically unpunished Zionists who stole its own state secrets and advanced Mystère blueprints.

England has been guilty of every imaginable crime against my people. Its historic crime is the assassination of my personality, the rape of my land, the obliteration of my history.

America has perpetuated Britain's crimes. It has supplied Israel with Hawk missiles, Skyhawk and Phantom fighter-bombers. America is the defender, apologist and financier of Israel in every world forum, at every bankers' conference. America is Israel; Israel is America and Europe combined in Palestine.

I do not wish further to burden my reader by our indictment of the West for the crimes it has committed against me and my people, because that alone requires a volume in itself. I merely wish to make some references to the policies of the chief imperialist, America, in order to explain the timing of my revolutionary deed and to illustrate further the bitterness and animosity we harbour towards US imperialism.

*

* * *

On August 29, 1969, Richard Milhous Nixon, the President of the United States, was scheduled to address the 72nd annual meeting of the Zionist Organisation of America. The Popular Front knew what Nixon was going to say because he had said it all before and said it very vociferously when he visited "victorious" Israel in August of 1967 in the aftermath of the June War. He told the Israelis that they would be "foolish to give up any of the territory occupied in the June War without receiving the "guarantees of a just peace" that the Israeli leaders were demanding. Furthermore, Nixon made a joint appearance with Hubert Humphrey before the Jewish B'nai B'rith on September 8, 1968 in Washington. (Mr. Humphrey seized this opportunity to make his first formal speech of the election campaign, and he too demonstrated his political loyalty and friendship to "besieged Zion".) Here is an excerpt from Mr. Nixon's speech before B'nai B'rith, the "humanitarian-inclined" Zionist organisation:

America knows that, and America is determined that Israel is here in the family of nations to stay. America supports Israel because we believe in the self-determination of nations. America supports Israel because we oppose aggression in every form. America supports Israel because its example offers a long range hope to the Middle East.

Vice-President Humphrey, along with Senators Robert F. Kennedy and Eugene McCarthy, had promised to continue military aid to Israel, including jets, until peace was established in the Middle East. Nixon, however, was much more emphatic. In Houston, Texas, on September 6, 1968 he had declared:

I have the general principle that to maintain the uneasy peace in the Middle East, it is vital that Israel maintain a superiority as against its neighbours, and if it takes Phantom jets, then they shall have Phantom jets.

Israel must possess sufficient military power to deter an attack. As long as the threat of an Arab attack remains direct and imminent, "sufficient power" means the balance must be tipped in Israel's favour. For that reason – to provide Israel a valid self-defence – I support a policy that would give Israel a technological military margin to more than offset her neighbour's numerical superiority. If maintaining that margin should require that the United States supply Israel with Phantom F4 jets, we should supply those jets.

Nixon also stated that "the danger of war increases in direct proportion to the confidence of certain Arab leaders that they could win the war". What generates that confidence and impels the Arabs to think of war is, of course, the Soviet Union, a state that has "stepped up their anti-semitic propaganda, concocting a 'Zionist plot' in Prague to win support in the Middle East".

It is my view that for Israel to take formal and final possession of the occupied territories would be a grave mistake [but] it is not realistic to expect Israel to surrender vital bargaining counters in the absence of a genuine peace and effective guarantees. Israel's enemies can afford to fight and lose and come back to fight again; Israel cannot afford to lose once.

Although we had expected Mr. Nixon to appear in person at the Zionist meeting in Los Angeles on August 29, 1969, as TWA flight 840 took off from Rome, he did not. Instead, he sent a letter to the president, Mr. Jacques Torczyner, who read it to his fellow Zionists on behalf of Mr. Nixon. The letter stated that America was committed to "friendly relations with Israel" and cited the organisation "for strengthening Israel's social and economic foundations and the cultural ties between its people and their friends in America". Nixon regarded "these efforts" as being "in the highest American tradition", and assured the Zionists that his government sought "a Middle East arms balance" that favoured Israel's "continued military superiority". As the Zionists were gathering in Los Angeles with California Governor Ronald Reagan and Golda Meir, I was having a pleasant chat with the Singer Sewing Machine Company's Middle East agent on my way to Rome to divert TWA flight 840 to Damascus.

*

* *

*

I had trained for every conceivable contingency; I had mastered most operational details of the great Boeing 707. There was something, however, I did not train for: the human situation. How to deal with idle or curious conversationalists. How not to arouse their suspicions or be rude to a seat-mate. I had to improvise and felt very uncomfortable. I imagined that all the Westerners aboard knew about my mission.

My seat-mate from Beirut to Rome was a clean-cut sociable American on his way to New York. I knew that Americans, like most other tourists, like to make casual conversation about everything under the sun. I didn't realise that they posed personal questions so directly and so nonchalantly. Mr. Holden must have been bored, and he wanted to talk. "Where are you going?" he asked to open the conversation. "I am going to Rome," I said. "Why are you going to Rome?" he continued.

I paused momentarily to fabricate an answer, and said with simulated shyness, "I am going to meet my fiancé who is coming from London to meet me in Rome in a few days." I suddenly realised I had made a slip. What if he too were going to Rome, and asked me to dinner or something while I was waiting for my "fiancé". I swiftly corrected my mistake by adding, "It is quite possible that he might surprise me and be waiting for me at the airport."

Then I asked him, "Where are you going?"

"To New York," he said, much to my relief.

He was determined not to let the conversation lapse. "How on earth would an Arab girl be going to Rome to meet her fiancé alone and get married?" he asked. I answered in a superficially self-assured tone, "I've known him since we were children,"

and we've been engaged for several years; besides, we are modern, not traditional Arabs." "That's good," he said, and started telling me how he and his wife had eloped because her parents had disapproved of him. As I assured him that I was not eloping, the stewardess cheerfully announced that there was a newly-married couple on the plane and they had a huge cake they would like us to share. "Who would like to have some cake?" she said. Everybody, including Mr. Holden and I, chanted in a chorus of "I would." In the midst of this jolly atmosphere, Mr. Holden asked, as if to dampen my enthusiasm for marriage,. "How come you're getting married when your fiancé is still a student and without a career?" I smiled. "We're not filthy-rich oil kings, but we're rich enough to afford it while we're young." "Then," he said, "may I suggest that you spend your honeymoon on a yacht by yourselves, on a Mediterranean cruise." I interrupted, protesting "I'd rather be among people." He slyly asked, "Are you going to marry the people?" "No," I said, "but I love being with people."

As I cleared customs and claimed my luggage, I had to face a porter who insisted on helping me, and then asked "When can I see you – tonight?" I was angered by his forwardness, and firmly said, "I am engaged; I am sorry," resorting to the traditional stewardess's reply. I had to face the same problem with another man on the bus into Rome. By now I was running out of patience, especially as my suitor squeezed close to me and practically tried to hold me in his arms without having spoken to me. I said furiously, "Take your hand off me. You're about to drive me out of the bus with your pushiness." He did, and he didn't dare make any other overtures all the way.

I spent two days at the hotel fending off invitations for personally guided tours of Rome. During these two days, I walked the streets of Rome alone. It is strange, but I had no desire to purchase anything, see Rome's ancient glory, or even go to a film. I only walked and walked, contemplating my mission and reciting its details to myself.

Early on the morning of August 29, I checked out of the hotel and caught a bus to Fiumicino Airport on the outskirts of Rome. Happily, the only snag was a half-hour flight delay. My associate, whom I recognised only from a photograph, appeared on schedule and we exchanged pre-arranged signals. His name was Salim Issawi; he was a Palestinian from Haifa who had been raised in Syria. Salim sat quietly nearby and we tried to ignore each other.

All was going smoothly when suddenly the human element threatened our careful planning. A few seats away there was a little girl with a button on her dress cheerfully proclaiming "Make Friends". That message brought me up short, forced me to remind myself, as I watched her playing with her little sister, that this child had committed no crime against me or my people. It would be cruel to imperil her life by hijacking a plane, the symbolic meaning of which she had no conception – a plane that could explode during our attempted seizure or be blown up by Israeli anti-aircraft fire when we entered the "Israeli airspace".

While these qualms pricked my conscience, the whole history of Palestine and her children came before my eyes. I saw everything from the first day of my exile. I saw my people homeless, hungry, barefoot. The twice "refugee" children of Bagan camp near Amman seemed to stand, a humiliated multitude, in front of me saying, "We too are children and we are a part of the human race." The scene strengthened me enormously. I said to myself, "What crime did I and my people perpetrate against anyone to deserve the fate we have suffered?" The answer was "None". The operation must be carried out. There can be no doubt or retreat. My children have spoken.

On the bus across the field to the Boeing 707, another unscheduled problem developed. A handsome man in his early thirties came up to me and said "Hello" in a most jovial, enthusiastic manner. "Hello," I replied nonchalantly, as I calmly tried to read *My Friend Che* by Ricardo Rojo. He seemed very eager to talk and asked me who I was and where I was going. I couldn't very well repeat the marriage tale and couldn't invent anything quickly enough. I said, "Guess."

He tried, "Greek, Spanish, Italian?" I asked him where he was from. "I am from Chicago," he answered, and continued his questioning. "You wouldn't be South American, would you?" Now that I knew where he was from, I figured it was safe to say that I was a South American. I thought it might end his questioning, at least. "From Brazil?" he asked, looking admiringly at me, and ogling my whole body. "You're getting closer," I said.

"Bolivia?" "Yes," I replied, "but how did you know?" "It's your book that gave you away," he declared. I asked him what he thought of Che. "Good man," he said. "Where are you going?" I countered, trying to change to a less controversial topic. "To Athens, to see my mother. I haven't seen her in fifteen years. I bet she's there already, waiting for me at the airport." I was astounded, and almost told him, "You bloody fool, you'd better get off this plane, because it isn't going to Athens." I tried to ignore him and closed my ears to keep his voice from penetrating my inner conscience. I plunged into a nervous reading of *My Friend Che*.

This encounter made me stop and think, because I understood the longing for one's own country. However, I rationalised his plight by making a distinction between his "exile", which was voluntary, and mine, which was forced. But these human encounters made me decide to be extra careful not to jeopardise the lives of the passengers unnecessarily. Their welfare, however, did not and could not cripple my operation. The deed had to be carried out. There was no turning back.

The plane was airborne for only twenty minutes before the hostesses were graciously trying to serve their five first-class passengers. Neither Salim nor I was anxious to eat. The stewardesses were very solicitous. They offered us drinks and peanuts. Anything we wanted. I settled for a coffee, Salim for a beer. But they made us nervous, as they kept returning and asking us if we wanted anything else. I pretended that I had a stomach ache and asked for a blanket. I innocently placed it over my lap, so I could take my pistol right in the top of my trousers without being noticed. Salim asked for an aspirin tablet. I was afraid the stewardess might suspect something had she realised that two passengers opposite each other in the first row were sick. In any case, I dreaded the prospect of having a companion with a headache, so was relieved when he merely pocketed the aspirin. Seconds after the only other male passenger in the first class section returned from the small lounge, I gestured to Salim to proceed to the cockpit. Just at that moment, another hostess carrying the crew's lunch trays was opening the door of the cockpit. Salim seized the opportunity and leapt in ahead of her. She screamed, "Oh no!" and her trays flew in the air, causing much noise but no injury. I was behind Salim and ordered the stewardess to get out of the way. She did, quivering and watching us over her shoulder. Salim was so huge that he blocked my view, and I couldn't see the reaction of the crew. I could, however, hear him say that the plane had been taken over by the Che Guevara Commando Unit of the PFLP, and announce that the new captain was Shadiah Abu Ghazalah.

In the middle of his speech, my pistol slipped down the leg of my trousers and, as I bent down to pick it up, I saw the bewildered looks on the crew's faces. I suppose all they could see was part of my wide-brimmed chic hat. I felt ridiculous for a moment, laughed at my ineptness, put the pistol away, and entered the cockpit solemnly brandishing my hand grenade and declaring I was the new captain. The crew were completely shocked to see me there, but they showed no fear. To demonstrate my credibility, I immediately offered my predecessor, Captain Carter, the safety pin from the grenade as a souvenir. He respectfully declined it. I dropped it at his feet and made my speech. "If you obey my orders, all will be well; if not, you will be responsible for the safety of passengers and aircraft."

"Go to Lydda," I instructed. "To Lod?" he queried, using the Israeli name. "You understand English, don't you?" I said curtly. "You just listen to my orders and don't ask silly questions." Since I knew the plane carried fuel for almost three hours and 45 minutes, I decided to reaffirm my authority by testing the flight engineer. I turned towards him and asked, "How much fuel do you have, flight engineer?" "For two hours," he promptly replied, without even looking at the fuel gauge. "Liar," I shouted, and told him that I knew just as much as he did about the Boeing, and that if he ever lied to me again I'd break his neck. The pilot tried to calm me down. He thought I was angry, but I was actually overjoyed. He warned the crew not to be obstinate in dealing with their new captain.

Realising that he was prepared to co-operate, I asked Captain Carter to radio Rome so that I could explain my action to the Italian people. He explained that we were too far away. I insisted that he try. He did. We had no luck. I asked a steward to bring our hand luggage forward, and then ordered him and the other first-class passengers to move to the tourist section. Next I demanded that the intercom system be turned on. All orders were complied with, and I read the following message to the passengers:

Ladies and gentlemen, your attention please. Kindly fasten your seat belts. This is your new captain speaking. The Che Guevara Commando Unit of the Popular Front for the Liberation of Palestine which has taken over command of this

TWA flight demands that all passengers on board adhere to the following instructions.

Remain seated and keep calm.

For your own safety, place your hands behind your head.

Make no move which would endanger the lives of other passengers on this plane.

We will consider all your demands within the safe limits of our plan. Among you is a passenger responsible for the death and misery of a number of Palestinian men, women and children, on behalf of whom we are carrying out this operation to bring this assassin before a revolutionary Palestinian court. The rest of you will be honourable guests of the heroic Palestinian people in a hospitable, friendly country. Every one of you, regardless of religion or nationality, is guaranteed freedom to go wherever he pleases as soon as the plane is safely landed.

Our destination is a friendly country, and friendly people will receive you.

As I completed reading the message, I observed that the plane had swerved off the course I charted for it. I ordered the captain not to play games if he wanted to reach our destination safely and put him on course again. Then Salim reminded me that fifteen minutes had elapsed since the passengers were asked to hold their hands behind their heads. I quickly advised them to relax and to drink champagne if they so desired, and offered an apology for inconveniencing them.

Shortly afterwards, a stewardess came in and explained that most of the passengers didn't understand English, didn't know what we had said, and would like us to repeat the message. She even offered to translate it into French for them. I repeated the message and assured them that everything was normal, that there was only one person on the plane we were after. Later,

this was interpreted by the press as indicating that we were after the Israeli ambassador to the US, General Izhak Rabin of June War fame. We were not, and if we had been, I would not have boarded flight 840 at Rome, since I saw all the passengers and knew that Rabin was not among them. Saleh Al Moualim, an Israeli Arab on board, must have thought that he was the person we meant, because he became very jittery and frightened. The selective terror tactic worked; the passengers' fear diminished and everyone co-operated with us. In explaining the message to the passengers, I told them that we detested the American government's Middle East actions, and held no grudge against any individual person. They were frightened, however, when I announced that we intended to blow up the plane upon arrival in a friendly country. I announced this only an hour before reaching Damascus.

Meanwhile, I resumed radio contact with the ground, sending messages of solidarity to the Greek revolutionaries and to the people of South Europe. I demanded that the Greek colonels release our imprisoned revolutionaries, and said that the CIA plotters would be toppled by the Greek people. All went according to plan, until we got the Egyptian observation tower on our wave-length. I identified myself to the controller in Arabic and asked him to convey to the Egyptian people the greetings of the Palestinian revolution. I advised him that I was going to Lydda, and his voice crackled: "Allah, to Lydda, what will you do there?" "Visit the fatherland," I said. "Are you sure of that?" "I certainly am," I replied enthusiastically. He tried to tell me that it was too dangerous. I switched him off, then relented momentarily as he screamed, "Oh Front, Oh Popular, Oh Arab Palestine!" but the rest of the appeal was too incoherent and inaudible.

Within minutes, I could see the coast of my Palestine in the haze. As we approached the land of my birth, it seemed that my

Planes blown up by Palestinian revolutionaries

Publisher's Note: We regret that the quality of this photograph was inadequate for reproduction purposes. In our judgment, however, the illustration is not essential for an understanding of the surrounding text or the article as a whole.

love and I were racing towards each other for an eternal embrace. I rushed towards my beloved and saw Palestine for the first time since my forced exile in 1948. I was lost in a moment of passion and meditation. Then I remembered the mission and ordered the pilot to descend, and I addressed a message in Arabic to my fellow exiles in occupied Palestine, telling them we shall return and we shall recover the land. I advised them to remain steadfast and promised to smash the Zionist fortress of conceit. I told Lydda tower in Arabic that we were going to land. He didn't understand, the pilot said, and told us we should ask for clearance and wait. I said, "This is my country. I do not need permission from the Zionist vultures to land."

I spoke to the tower in English, saying: "Here we come again. Shadiah Abu Ghaselah has come back to life. There are millions of Shadiahs who will be returning again and again to reclaim the land." The Israeli tower must have been terrified for a while because I said that we intended to blow up the plane right in the airport. In seconds three Israeli Mirages appeared on the horizon and tried to prevent us from landing. I turned the intercom on so that the passengers could hear the exchange.

I declared anew that the pilot and the Israelis were responsible for the safety of the passengers and the plane, and that we intended to do no harm to anyone if our orders were obeyed. The co-pilot asked if he could speak to the Israelis and I let him. He said, "Popular Front, Free Arab Palestine, Armed people have threatened to explode the plane with hand grenades if your Mirages don't clear out." Until this moment the Israeli tower was still addressing us as TWA 840. My patience ran out and I told him to shut up and turned him off, saying that there will be no further communications until he addressed us as Popular Front, Free Arab Palestine.

In seconds he did so as we swung around my beloved Haifa. The pilot asked, "What shall I do now?" I said, "Let's take a

229

seven-minute tour of the fatherland." My father's image appeared before my eyes, and I could hear his voice saying "When will we return home?" My whole world came together. I was silent. I looked out at the greenery and mountains of Palestine. I could see Tel Aviv below. I wept out of affection and longing, and said softly, "Father, we shall return. We shall redeem your honour and restore your dignity. We shall become the sovereign of the land some day." Suddenly, I remembered that the mission preceded personal emotions. I instructed the pilot, "Go to Lebanon, where my people live as refugees." The Israeli planes continued to pursue us. At the Lebanese border, they zoomed away. I called Cyprus and sent greetings to its heroic anti-imperialist fighters, and sent messages to my people in South Lebanon. The pilot interrupted. "We must ask for clearance from Beirut." "We don't need to ask for clearance," I said. "This is an Arab country." We circled Beirut briefly before I ordered the pilot to go on to Damascus. He objected, "The airport there couldn't accommodate the Boeing 707." "Look, do you think we're so backward that we couldn't handle your damned plane?" I said strongly. He didn't respond. I took the microphone and addressed the passengers for the last time: "Evacuate immediately on landing; have a happy holiday in Syria. I trust we shall have a smooth landing."

The fuel gauge was reading empty; the pilot sought clearance and I ordered him to land immediately on the runway farthest from the air terminal. "Let's have a smooth landing," I said, "because if I fall, the hand grenade could explode and that would be a terrible anticlimax to a happy journey." He landed smoothly and in less than three minutes the plane was empty. Salim and I tried to tell the passengers to slow down and to take their personal belongings with them. Most ran out barefooted. Even the crew left their jackets behind. As Captain Carter stepped out, I saluted and thanked him for his co-operation. He

looked at me in astonishment. The co-pilot said, "You're most welcome."

I checked the plane. All the passengers had left. Salim wired the cockpit and lit the fuse. I slid out on one of the torn emergency chutes and fell to the ground on my rear. Salim followed and landed on my shoulders. The plane did not explode as scheduled. Salim's personal courage made him climb back in and set everything in motion once more. When Syrian soldiers arrived on the scene, I distracted them by saying, "The Israeli officers ran in that direction. Go and get them." Salim was still in the plane. I feared for his safety, but admired his heroism and selfless devotion. I tried to leap in and couldn't. Suddenly he appeared and waved reassuringly. The Boeing still did not explode. He fired a few shots into the wing of the plane, but there was no fuel left, so it wouldn't readily ignite. When sparks finally fluttered, we took cover twenty yards away. Half a mile away, the passengers in the terminal watched the bonfire and the explosion of the Boeing. The Syrian soldiers returned, astounded. They were even more surprised when Salim and I surrendered to them and turned over our weapons. The *Al-Hadaf* photographer, who was parachuted by the Front to film our landing and the explosion, was so excited that he forgot to remove the lens cap from his camera.

Our Syrian hosts took us to the air terminal, where I delivered a brief speech to the passengers:

Ladies and gentlemen, thank you for your kind attention and co-operation during the flight. I am captain Shadiah Abu Ghazalah. That's not my name; my name is Khaleda. Shadiah is an immortal woman who wrote: "Heroes are often forgotten, but their legends and memories are the property and heritage of the people." That is something historians and analysts cannot understand. Shadiah will not be forgotten by the

Popular Front and by the generation of revolutionaries she helped mould in the path of revolution. I would like you to know that Shadiah was a Palestinian Arab woman from Nablus; that she was a schoolteacher and a member of the Popular Front underground; that she died in an explosion at her own home at the age of twenty-one on November 21, 1968, while manufacturing hand grenades for the Front. She was the first woman martyr of our revolution. I assumed her name on flight 840 to tell the world about the crimes the Israelis inflict upon our people and to demonstrate to you that they make no distinctions between men, women and children.

But for their own propaganda objectives they repeatedly state in your press how we attack their "innocent" women and children and how cruel we are. I want you to know that we love children, too, and we certainly do not aim our guns at them. We diverted flight 840 because TWA is one of the largest American airlines that services the Israeli air routes and, more importantly, because it is an American plane. The American government is Israel's staunchest supporter. It supplies Israel with weapons for our destruction. It gives the Zionists tax-free American dollars. It supports Israel at world conferences. It helps them in every possible way. We are against America because she is an imperialist country.

And our unit is called the Che Guevara Commando Unit because we abhor America's assassination of Che and because we are a part of the Third World and the world revolution. Che was an apostle of that revolution. We took the plane to Haifa because Comrade Salim and I come from Haifa. Both of us were evicted in 1948. We took you to Tel Aviv as an act of defiance and challenge to the Israelis and to demonstrate their impotence when the Arabs embark on offensive rather than defensive strategy. We brought you to Damascus because Syria is the pulsating heart of the Arab homeland and because

the Syrians are a good and generous people. We hope you will enjoy your stay in Damascus. We hope you will go home and tell your friends not to go to Israel—to the Middle East war zone. Please tell your neighbours that we are a people like you who wish to live in peace and security in our country, governing ourselves. Please tell the Americans that if they hate war and the exploitation of others, they should stop their government from making war on us and helping the Israelis to deprive us of our land. Tell your people that coming to Israel helps her to deny our rights. Revolution and peace. Greetings to all lovers of the oppressed!

It was nearly seven p.m., August 29, 1969. As I concluded my speech, I saw my Greek friend sobbing, and an American woman trying to assuage him. I do not think he recognised me as his bus companion. Salim and I mixed with the passengers and distributed sweets to the children. Two old ladies were consoling each other; one was saying she was "wet" and the other was telling her to thank God for having arrived in Damascus alive. The Syrian authorities cleared the passengers through customs and took them to hotels in Damascus. They released all of them with the exception of six Israelis. One American woman was taken to hospital with a broken ankle. On September 3, four Israelis were released; later the other two were exchanged for two Syrian air force pilots in Israeli custody and a handful of imprisoned fighters. Salim and I were taken to police headquarters.

Although we had arrived at the airport to the cheers of the Syrian crowds, the Syrian officials were not that friendly. An arrogant colonel started his investigation by demanding, "What do you think you are?" "Soldiers, like you," I said. "No," he angrily replied, "you are a terrorist organisation." "Hey," I said, "am I in Israel or the Syrian Arab Republic, the advocate of revolutionary warfare?" The colonel didn't like my tone of voice. "This action is not *fedayeen*-like. It is terrorism," he said. "Look," I explained, "I am a soldier who carried out her assignment. If you wish to debate the validity and legitimacy of our revolutionary strategy, we'll be happy to do it with you, but not in a police station." "Where did you train?" "I will answer no further questions, since I already gave you my name and told you what party I belong to."

The colonel ordered us to be held in dingy little rooms and gave us two blankets each. At about eleven-thirty p.m., we were taken from our cells to the second floor for further interrogation. I gave my name as Khaleda and they obviously knew it was false. The officer in charge was rather suave and clever. He ordered his assistants to bring us dinner and proceeded to tell us how he strongly identified with the Palestine revolution. I interrupted, "That is not the colonel's view." "What colonel?" he said. "You should know," I answered.

The assistants brought food, and I declined it, declaring, "I won't eat until I am released." "Where will you go if released?" he asked. "To my country, Palestine," I said. The officer enquired about many things, and my answer was an emphatic "No comment" to every question. Late that night, I asked to go to the bathroom, and I was accompanied by a male policeman who was under orders to search me before I went in. I dared him to touch me, and threatened to attack him and scream rape if he did. He ignored the orders and took me back to my windowless cell. I asked the male guard to buy me a packet of cigarettes; he refused, doling out one cigarette at a time for the remainder of the night. Since I was unable to sleep, see anyone or talk, I kept the guard marching me back and forth to the bathroom all night. I do not know who was more exhausted by morning. I continued that strategy for the next four nights.

On the morning of August 31, breakfast was brought in and

I declined to eat again, announcing that I was on a hunger strike. By then I hadn't had a good meal in three days and I was smoking very heavily. I was also getting bored being in isolation but knowing full well that my comrades were joyously celebrating my deed. Around noon, I twisted the edge of the rusty iron partition between me and Salim and we started whispering to each other face to face. I told him about the "wet lady" at the airport, and we laughed boisterously about it. The guard heard the noise and ran towards the cell thinking I must have gone mad. He asked me to share the joke with him. I refused to say anything. But when he realised that I was still sane, he looked around my cell, and found the hole. He accused me of being a terrorist, and threatened dire consequences if I widened the hole. I dared him, "Go and tell your superiors."

That afternoon, another colonel came to visit us, but he was in civilian clothes. He was smoother than his predecessors. He introduced himself as a Palestinian pilot with the Syrian air force from Al-Nassera. "My name is Azzani," he said, "and I have just returned from the front bringing you the revolutionary greetings of the fighters." I said, "If you recognise us as revolutionaries, why are you holding us in prison?" "Why are you on a hunger strike?" he asked, without answering my question. I said, "Because I am being treated like a criminal, and I protest very strongly against these insulting interrogations of intelligence officers like yourself." He asked if I needed anything or any money. I replied proudly, "I have money and the only thing I want is departure from this Baath prison." He left without comment.

On September 1, I felt very weak and tired. Stomach ache, headache, general fatigue seemed to have overtaken me. I began to feel dizzy, but I still refused to eat. That evening I fainted on my way to the bathroom, and it took them a few minutes to revive me. The Syrians were very disturbed and called in a shall convert our existence into bombs to redeem the land, the coast, the mountain. We shall fight and fight . . .

"Oh! I seem to be forgetting myself. I am writing as if I were a poet. Poetry is also part of our armoury, but deeds are a sharper aspect of our weaponry.

"Oh God! When will the deprivation end? When will I return to my home—to embrace life in its fullest? There in Haifa I shall live, for I feel choked here.

"I feel oversatiated for having beaten the CIA. And why not? Hadn't Salim Issawi and I hit at the heart of America and its power? Let America give Israel all the weapons she requests. I am sure my people shall live. I am in the observation tower and nothing frightens me. My people are being steeled by struggle against the imperialist and Zionist enemies.

"I remember the moment I entered the pilot's cabin and how he shivered before me. How the words of surrender flowed from his lips: 'O.K., all right. I'll do whatever you want. Now tell me what to do.'

"He was stunned by my deed. I am certain he cursed Israel and America a thousand times in the silence of his heart.

"What an exciting occasion to force every air tower, including that of Israel to broadcast our slogans: 'Popular Front, Free Arab Palestine.'

"The pilot was the first to shout our slogan. He said it with a quivering voice. He is a middle class American who was taught to love himself more than anything else. I have no doubts that selfishness is an American virtue that manifests itself when Americans are not acting collectively under a victorious leadership. I remember how they fled from the Japanese and how they retreated like sheep in the Far East. I don't think the pilot cared to sacrifice himself for America.

"What a splendid moment in my life when I flew over the homeland in an enemy plane. Oh, my God! What a beautiful

doctor who tried to persuade me to eat some yoghourt or drink something other than coffee. I insisted "No" and passed out again. All I remember after that was a nurse bathing my face, and Salim carrying me to a hospital ambulance. I was not fully conscious until the morning of September 2, when, with a sense of inner peace and self-fulfilment, I sat down in the hospital and wrote a few notes, taking my inspiration from Che's immortal dictum: "We must grow tough, but without ever losing our tenderness."

*

* *

"What a beautiful passage, but more beautiful is the tradition of revolutionary tenderness. I am not sure that I have practised that art effectively. Others will have to pass judgment on my deed. I am certain, though, that the capitalist press regarded my deed as an 'outrage' and urged their governments to prosecute those criminals ruthlessly or to extradite them to other countries where they could be prosecuted.

"I am somewhere in Damascus. I was placed here after I carried out my mission. After I performed my revolutionary duty against the enemy.

"It was a momentous second in my life when I put my fingers on the trigger and ordered the enemy to obey my command. All my life I dreamt of carrying arms to aim at the enemy—that vengeful enemy who raped our land and has expropriated our homes without compensation.

"Oh Palestine! I am ready to die and I shall live by dying for thee!

"Oh my homeland! My love, my only love! I shall revolt against thine enemies, all enemies. I shall make bombs from the atoms of my body and weave a new Palestine from the fabric of my soul. With all my power and the power of my sisters, we land. I felt like landing and dying at the hands of my enemy. To land, to melt into the eternity of the land and to form part of the soil of Palestine ... But our revolutionary nobility impelled me to sacrifice my personal wishes for a union with the land in order to save the children who committed no sin against me or my people. The passengers are not guilty of any crime. As for our part, aren't we the friends of all peoples?

"Now I remember the moment I communicated with Cairo and conveyed our revolutionary greetings to the Egyptian Arab people. The Cairo tower wanted to know where we were heading. I told him Lydda. 'Lord, no!' he said. 'Yes, Lydda,' I said. 'God!—and what are you going to do there?' 'We are going for a visit,' I said.

"Moments after I was in touch with the Lydda tower, which insisted on calling me TWA 840. I told him sternly to shut up and refused to answer him until he addressed me: Popular Front, Free Arab Palestine—exacting such concessions from a Zionist stooge was indeed an achievement.

"The Israelis thought that Salim and I were going to explode the plane and its passengers. What fools! They must think we're a bunch of suicidal gangsters like their leaders.

"In Damascus we indeed exploded the cockpit of the imperialist plane as an expression of our strategy, which aims at hitting the imperialist interests wherever they may be. The Popular Front will destroy the treasonous enemy—the enemy of humanity, right and justice. Blessed be the arms that carry out deeds and the revolutionary brains that conceive of deeds and plan them. We shall be victorious.

"Sleep has fled from my eyes. I hear the cries of prisoners being tortured in Syrian dungeons. I cannot condone torture, no matter what the crime was. I hate to hear of a man crying in pain. I hate the infliction of pain on any person, because I know what it is to feel pain—pain and anguish for the loss of the homeland, for the loss of a whole people, the pain of my entire nation. Pain truly affects my soul; so does the persecution of my people. It is from pain that I derive the power to resist and to defend the persecuted.

"My people, my land, my Palestine! For thee I shall resist, for your honour I shall accept pain."

Palestine, my love!
for you I shall fight
fight
and open the road
the road of return
victorious return
to all parents
to all lovers.

Today I am a volcano
a revolutionary volcano
the Front—Volcano
the Front—revolution.
Yes—the revolt of return
My Front is free
My Front to Palestine
paving the way to all,
to all my Arab people
with guns, cannons my Front acts
and with brains.

Yes, with brains we act, act, act! I reflected briefly, and wrote a note to my mother, to my mother and to all mothers.

"To you, my dearest, I write these lines. Where are you? I see you only in my imagination ... you are waiting for my return ... be patient, Mother ... I shall return ... I see you, beloved, in the hands of thine enemies . . . I am choking . . . on the verge of death, every time I imagine you . . . .

"Oh Lord, safeguard her and safeguard my people as you protected me. Safeguard them from the persecution of the enemy. Blind the enemy whenever he tries to violate my domicile . . . for my Palestine is not only my mother . . . she is my sister, friend and companion.

"Oh, how I long for Palestine, for my beloved, for my brothers and sisters in this little Syrian cage where I feel physically bound and spiritually boundless and universal, for I have overcome the particular and reached for the true good—the good of the oppressed.

"The feeling of being uprooted accompanies me everywhere, the feeling of being stateless, without a homeland, is a feeling that can only be obliterated by the return! Oh, Lord, what a dreadful human dilemma to be separated forcefully from one's own country!

"Yes, I feel unanchored . . . for my land is raped . . . it is under the hoofs of the Zionists . . . a people that have evicted my mother and other mothers and raped my true Mother Palestine.

"I swear by my revolution, by my humanity, that we shall return the Palestinians to their homes and we shall recover our lost humanity!"

Yes, we have lost everything:
we have lost life and its meaning;
we have lost the humanity of man;
we are a people that lost its land;
and he who loses his land
loses his life—for land is
the source of life.

My beloved, I shall return on the
wings of eagles to you;
I shall return repeatedly to
spread terror in the heart of the enemy.
I shall flag the enemy;
I shall pulverise him.
And why not? How can I forget
the rage of the tempest that struck
my dear father . . . a thousand greetings I send
to your soul, my father, and
the souls of Palestinian fathers in the beyond.
Tortured, you left Palestine and
uprooted you lived;
desire replaced health,
sadness joy, hatred love,
humiliation pride.

Father, rest assured I shall avenge your honour and
redeem your dignity . . .
the honour and dignity of all martyrs!
By cannons, bullets, bayonets!
from the heavens we shall descend,
from the sea we shall come,
from Mount Carmel we shall leap to the
heart of Haifa.
My Front shall do this to
tend the wounded, succour the needy
and inspire the children of despair.

Mother, I can no longer keep my secret:
I am a lover of Palestine, and I have
no other love . . .
Therefore remain firm and constant . . .
unafraid my people face tyranny and oppression.

Leila and fellow hijackers after their release

Publisher's Note: We regret that the quality of this photograph was inadequate for reproduction purposes. In our judgment, however, the illustration is not essential for an understanding of the surrounding text or the article as a whole.

Be with me, my beloved, remember our martyrs,
remember the stolen lands.
Take all difficulties with steadfast revolutionary
violence!
For the path is long and steep
and the recovery of the homeland needs absolute
firmness.
Henceforth we shall not bend our heads.
The enemy may be strong . . . but we are much stronger.
Our cause is right and just
and we have begun to believe in ourselves.
We no longer know fear.
Wait for me. Wait for victory.
We shall return!"

*

*

*

On September 3, I was shocked to hear that the Syrians had released four Israelis, while Salim and I were still detained. I lashed out at the Syrians, threatening retaliation. The nurses tried to calm me, explaining that the hospital was not a prison and urging me to eat if I wanted to be released quickly. I promised to behave if they brought me newspapers and let me listen to the radio. They agreed and I felt compensated for my fatigue when I heard a broadcast in which the story of the hijacking was told according to the pilot. Moments later, the Commander-in-Chief of the Syrian armed forces, General Mustafa Tlass, entered my room—my most distinguished visitor. The General said he disapproved strongly of my deed and insinuated that I was a UAR agent who had brought the plane to Syria to embarrass the Syrians and give President Nasser a propaganda boost.

I assured him that the Front was totally autonomous and took orders from no one. I raised the issue of the released Israelis and he explained that I was "the guest, not the prisoner of Syria".

236

"I would rather not be anybody's guest, because I must return to my base to carry on with my work," I said, and asked him to see if he could arrange a meeting for me with President Attassi. The President was in Egypt for a meeting of the front-line states, he explained, and he didn't know when he was coming back.

The General left, and Salim and I were moved to an apartment with four other people. We began to realise that the more indignant we behaved, the more lenient and accommodating the Syrians became. We demanded to know why we were being kept there and how long it was going to continue. There was no reply. Around ten that evening, we were visited by Colonel Ali Zaza (he is presently the Minister of the Interior under President Hafez Al-Assad), and got an inkling of what was in store for us. Zaza came with two other men who identified themselves as Saiqa commanders. (Saiqa is the Syrian-supported section of the resistance.) They were eager to talk. For the next four hours we debated the whole history of the resistance, the role of Fateh, the Palestine National Congress and its value, the nature of socialism. It became increasingly obvious that Saiqa was a branch of the Syrian Baath, and had no independent personality of its own. Although we agreed on some points, we felt that, on the whole, the Baath of Attassi, Jedid and Makkous (the current ruling triumvirate of Syria) believed in left-wing Baathism, not scientific socialism and dialectical materialism.

By September 4, we must have become very fashionable and respectable. Four ladies of upper-class appearance and attitudes came to visit us and presented me with a bouquet of flowers. Three introduced themselves as representatives of the Syrian, Palestinian and Lebanese Union of Women, and one as a member of Fateh. I looked at them with contempt and asked if their bouquet was a fitting tribute to a living revolutionary who had accomplished her mission. They were taken aback. One had the

audacity to criticise the Front for the operation, calling it an attempt on our part to eclipse the burning of the Al-Aksa mosque, an action which was gaining sympathy for the Arabs and unifying the Moslem world behind one policy. (At one hurriedly called summit conference of Arab states, Israel was held responsible for the burning of the mosque and accused of desecrating a Moslem Shrine and attempting to Judaise it.)

I explained that the Al-Aksa incident had occurred more than a week before our attack, and had no relation to our action. Furthermore, I insisted, we did not strive for a unity based on religious bigotry, but we were fighting for the unity of the anti-imperialist forces. My congenial guests were not impressed. They were upset that an "upstart" like myself could dare cast aspersions on their idols. They walked out in a huff never to return to amuse me with their feminine slave passions and fashions.

The evening of September 4 was a sad one for me. I learned of the death of a great revolutionary leader, Ho Chi Minh. Ho's death struck me like lightning. I felt part of me had died. It was the same feeling as when I heard about the assassination of Che. I knew Ho's principles would live, and that he was an old man who had lived a full life and helped liberate a substantial part of his homeland. Yet I was sad and contemplated for an entire sleepless night the greatness of Ho and what we Palestinians could learn from him and his example. The next morning, I sat down and wrote a poem.

* * *

* * *

During a five-week period, from September 5 until October 11, Salim and I were held in three different "guest houses" in Syria. The Syrians, I am certain, were not afraid of Salim or me. They feared the Front and its heroic exploits. They must have remembered vividly how Dr. Habash, whom they imprisoned in fire. I grabbed eight-year-old Hani, and ran up and down the stairs shouting "Fire, Fire". Hani was bleeding from the chest and his feet looked squashed. A neighbour invited us to take refuge in her apartment and called the fire brigade. I was anxious, but Hani was absolutely calm and silent. He forced a smile and said to me, "Leila, revolutionaries of the Front ought not to be fearful. You ought to be ashamed to be frightened." I was a little shocked by the reminder from this child revolutionary, and I pounced on him and carried him outside to take him to the hospital. I stopped a cabby, who refused to transport us, and I spat in his face. Suddenly Abu Dardock, a member of the Front, appeared on the scene and away we went to the American University hospital's emergency ward. As I rushed in with Hani in my arms, blood covering both of us, I cried, "Find me a doctor please". Within minutes a doctor was there but before he even looked at the child, he callously enquired if I had the money to pay for the treatment. I shrieked at him, "Are you a doctor or a carpet salesman?" He firmly explained that AUB was a "hospital not a charity centre". "Since you are in business, take me for ransom, but please look after the child," I begged. At that moment Dr. Haddad and his wife stormed in looking for their child. His mother was almost hysterical. The American doctor recognised Dr. Haddad, a fellow MD. He was taken aback and apologised profusely. His apologies fell on deaf ears. I voiced my threats loudly, "Yankee doctor, the revolution will make AUB's hospital a hospital for the poor and your kind of doctor will have to be disbarred or sent back to America." He flashed a barefaced grin and said "I'm sorry".

*

The attack on Dr. Haddad's apartment strengthened our resolve to fight the enemy with all the power at our command. We were much more determined to die for the cause than ever

before. The sight of the apartment in flames was constantly on my mind as I flew to Frankfurt in August. In Frankfurt, I stayed at a moderately-priced hotel whose owner turned out to be Jewish. He greeted me in Arabic and I hesitated momentarily before replying, then casually reciprocated his greeting, pretending that I was a non-Arab. He persisted in talking Arabic to me and boastfully announced: "I am a Jew you know." I promptly replied, "I am an Arab and I am not against the Jews; I am against the Zionists and the people who occupied Arab territory." He countered agreeably, "I am a Zionist for religious reasons, but I am not interested in politics." Our confrontation ended, I went upstairs to my room and stayed put until the following morning. Finally I became restless and hungry and decided to go out to eat and take a long walk. My Jewish friend was at the desk. He greeted me volubly and asked if I would like to go to Amsterdam on a trip he was organising for his guests. I smiled, declined the invitation and rushed out to fetch some food. On the way I purchased several English newspapers; all were filled with news from Jordan and some had editorial comments on the impact of the Rogers proposals on the Arab world, Israel, and great power relations. Practically every paper I read speculated on forthcoming hijackings. I felt uneasy at first, but then relieved when I read that the hijackings were supposed to be taking place in Zurich and elsewhere, not in Amsterdam.

I was obsessed with the idea of my mission. I rehearsed it on the hour every hour of my waking days. I roamed the city of Frankfurt for a few days, bored with the waiting; then I went to Stuttgart briefly and on to Amsterdam. Our rendezvous with history was approaching: all plans had to be translated into action; history was ours to write; Patrick Arguello was to write it in blood, I was not so honoured.

*

*

*

I met Patrick Arguello for the first time in September, 1970, in front of the air terminal at Stuttgart. We briefed each other on our mutual assignment and reviewed the plan thoroughly. The following day we flew together to Frankfurt. At Frankfurt airport, Mr. Diaz (Patrick) was inspected as I watched the passengers of a TWA Tel Aviv-bound flight being thoroughly searched. I felt very happy that we were causing the enemy so much trouble. "What fools, that's the plane we're going to hijack on its way back from Tel Aviv," I thought to myself. Patrick was cleared through customs without suspicion.

The next stop was Amsterdam. On September 6 Patrick and I met in front of the El-Al counter at ten a.m. We waited for half an hour for the El-Al Office to open. It never opened that day. We checked the flight schedule; the bulletin board still showed El-Al flight 219 as departing for New York at eleven twenty a.m. We asked the KLM ground hostess for assistance. She took our tickets and called El-Al office. There was no answer.

The KLM hostess seemed a little surprised. She asked, "Why take El-Al flight, there are others, which are better and more comfortable." We assured her that "we'd rather travel El-Al." As we waited Pan Am flight 840 arrived and I happily remembered TWA flight 840 of August 29, 1969. I was not aware at that moment that two of our comrades, having been barred in an earlier attempt by the Israelis, were on their own to seize Pan Am flight 840 a half-hour after take-off. They took the 747 to Cairo where they blew it up as a declaration of Palestinian independence. Neither Patrick nor any of the other five male hijackers knew that three planes were our target that day. Only the three female Palestinian captains and a handful of other leaders knew of the entire plan. We lingered in the waiting room until about twelve-o-five. There was still no sign of the El-Al counter-staff.

Suddenly an armed police officer in Israeli uniform emerged.

"Why are you late?" he demanded. I accommodatingly explained, "We arrived at ten o'clock, officer," and suggested that he ask the KLM hostess, who vouched for us. "Your passport please," he said. Both Patrick and I showed him our passports without comment. The officer carefully examined each page. He looked at my photograph and then back at me several times. He paced back and forth as he addressed us. He asked me to empty my handbag and identify every item in it which I did. I looked completely normal. Patrick was wearing a business suit and I was dressed in a mini-skirt and jacket. I did not pretend to be other than calm Maria Sanchez from Honduras. Routine questions went on for several minutes. Suddenly I heard loud voices. I saw three Arabs walking in my direction. My heart sank. I knew and recognised one of them. What if he greeted me? We would be exposed immediately. Fortunately the Israeli officer had his back to them. Since we were already holding hands for his benefit, I quickly threw my arms around Patrick. He seemed a little surprised, but what man will rebuff a woman under such conditions? The embrace lasted until my Arab friend passed by unnoticed by the El-Al officer or anyone else. The officer seemed untroubled by us. Politely he invited us to go with him to the basement to check our baggage. "Officer, our luggage is open, you could inspect it anytime you like," I said. "Regulations state, Madam," he explained, "that owners must be present." We happily agreed. The officer was no amateur. He systematically went through every item not once, but twice. He asked informal but pertinent questions as he inspected our possessions.

Then he pointedly turned to me and asked: "Has anyone given you any gifts?" "No," I replied emphatically. "Do you have anything sharp or dangerous?" "Such as?" I said. "Such as a pistol, a knife or anything sharp?" "No Sir. What would a girl like me ever do with a pistol or knife, officer?"

He smiled apologetically and said, "You can go back to the transit hall." Then it suddenly dawned on him to ask me in English if I spoke Spanish. "Si, senor," I blurted out boldly. "Have a good journey," he said. Patrick was a little surprised. "Why would you say to him you spoke Spanish when you don't?" "Look Patrick," I said, "if he knew how to speak Spanish he would have addressed us in Spanish from the beginning. Calm down, we're clear."

As we re-entered the hall, I saw some thirty or forty youngsters waiting to board EL-Al flight 219. I was shocked and secretly lamented that once again I had to face the agonising problem of what to do to avoid hurting children. I love children and I know they are free from guilt. Although I remembered the children of Palestine napalmed by the Israelis and Dr. Haddad's child running out of his flaming room, I nevertheless vowed to do my utmost not to jeopardise the lives of the passengers needlessly. I sat semi-paralysed for a few seconds wrestling with the moral issues of our action. Meanwhile Patrick was walking around the hall trying to spot our two comrades. As I looked at the children a beautiful little girl walked towards me, her eyes directed longingly towards the sandwich in my hand. Her mother pulled her away as I almost said to her, *"Taali ela houna."* (Come here and take it.) No sooner did I hold my tongue, than her mother called *"Taali ela houna ya binti,"* (Come here my child). I was startled. Patrick had just joined me. I tried to dispel any sign of anxiety by whispering furtively to him "Guess what?" "Yes," said Patrick, thinking I had spotted our comrades. "The lady with the children opposite us is an Israeli; imagine if she were assigned to hijack this plane and she wanted to take it in one direction and we in the other. Who is likely to win the contest?" I asked. Patrick laughed and assured me "We shall win."

We waited. Minutes seemed like hours. No Israeli plane was in sight. Only the damned KLM planes were there and we had no use for them. The jumbo jet had taken off at eleven-thirty. It was now a little after twelve. The Israeli officer reappeared and we went through the same routine inspection. We were ordered to another side of the room. I tried not to show my frustration. The third inspection started and we were told to move back to our original places. By the end of this inspection, it was one-thirty. The hijack proclamations were supposed to have been simultaneously announced at twelve-twenty. I figured that either the hijackings were announced and the blasted Israelis had heard about them and decided to transfer us to KLM, or they had captured our two other comrades and were desperately looking for us. I had two hand grenades; Patrick had one hand grenade and a pistol. I said to Patrick who was aware only of our own hijack plans, "Commandos do not surrender, we have to play Samson if they discover us." Patrick resolutely agreed. We were asked to walk downstairs. The same officer was standing at the gate checking every passport and passenger. I said "Officer, we are late." "That's all right, madam, we're doing it for your own security," he declared. We marched to the plane surrounded by all kinds of armed guards. I was delighted that the resistance was causing so many difficulties and making the Zionists paranoid and jittery. I felt that Patrick and I had already conquered the enemy and accomplished half of our mission by making a fool of him and proving that his precautionary measures were not foolproof. I realised that the enemy's fortress was not impregnable as I ascended the plane with twelve guards of honour bearing sub-machine guns guaranteeing my "security". When I stepped into the El-Al plane, I felt for the first time since April 13, 1948, that I was at home again in Haifa. I was indeed in a lion's den. Never before had I felt so elated and proud of being a member of the Popular Front than at that moment.

• •

•

240

Patrick and I searched for two empty seats. We were moved around twice until we were finally seated together in the second row of the tourist class. We heaved a sigh of relief as a hostess asked if we were comfortable. I was exhilarated and looked forward to the second half of our mission. Patrick seemed a little frightened as EL-AL finally took off around one-thirty. Patrick knew me only as Shadiah. I thought if I revealed my identity his morale would be greatly boosted. I did. Patrick was heartened. He gave me a victory salute. The lady next to me fell asleep immediately. All the passengers seemed tired. At one-fifty-five, we noticed that someone was watching us from the back of the plane. I told Patrick to stay still. I turned around and looked directly at the man for a minute. He was in civilian clothes. When he saw that I was watching him he shyly looked the other way. At that moment Patrick prepared his hand grenade and pistol, and I pulled the safety pins off my two hand grenades and rushed forward through the first class section and towards the cockpit. We shouted "Don't move," as some of the passengers tried to take cover. Three stewards were in front of us wielding hand guns. In a couple of seconds I could count six guns. But we had anticipated a battle. A hostess fell to the ground crying to me in Arabic. I threatened to blow up the plane if anyone fired at us. I displayed my two grenades and dropped the safety pins on the floor hoping to convince everyone we intended business and to avert a bloody battle. Patrick held the armed stewards and the passengers at bay. "Go ahead, I'll protect your back," he instructed me. I forced the hostess to stand up and walk ahead of me. The moment she opened the door, she staggered forward in a state of panic. I couldn't see the captain or crew. Shots were fired. There was another door before we could reach the pilot's cabin. Both of us banged on the door. No one opened the door. Suddenly someone was looking at us through a spyhole. I brandished my hand grenades and ordered him to open the door or else. I heard more shots and the plane went into a spin.

Several people attacked me at the same moment. I thought the plane was disintegrating. The firing continued and suddenly I found myself besieged by a pack of wolves, EL-AL staff as well as passengers. Someone screamed "Don't shoot at her! She has two hand grenades." No one fired at me. But some people were kicking me, others hitting. A few just stepped all over me. Two were holding my hands and trying to take away the grenades. One finally succeeded in prying one grenade from me without exploding himself and the plane. I held tightly to the other until I was knocked unconscious for a second and was overpowered.

At first I didn't know what was happening to Patrick. Within a few minutes I was dragged to the first-class compartment where Patrick was lying, bleeding profusely and breathing heavily. I could see he was still alive. The Zionists were acting like mad dogs. They trampled over every part of our bodies. By that time Patrick was too weak to resist. I was fighting like a caged lion. I fought until I was completely exhausted. Then a vicious thug pounced on me, pulled my hair mercilessly, called me a wicked bitch, a malicious Arab and all sorts of obscene names. I spat contemptuously in his face. I bit his hands. He and the others around me beat me incessantly for several minutes.

The plane was travelling smoothly; the remaining passengers were staying in their seats. Suddenly an Israeli guard emerged from the cockpit area. Patrick was lying on his side. The man turned him over on his stomach and started tying him up with wires and a necktie. Someone asked "How are they?" A voice replied "We don't know. He is ... we're not sure. She's three-quarters dead." The man stepped on Patrick's hips and Patrick looked at me in agony, his hands tied behind his back. Then the Zionist guard fired four shots into Patrick's back. Someone screamed from the back of the plane "Please stop the bloodshed."

"Please, Please, Please!" The four shots that were fired into Patrick's back were fired from a distance of less than one foot. Patrick looked at me, gave me a deathly smile, and bid me an eternal goodbye.

Then came my turn. I was tied up in the same fashion: hands behind my back, my feet and legs immobilised with wires. I expected to join the ranks of our martyrs as Patrick had just done. But the Zionists did not execute me. I was certain they were not moved by any humanitarian concern or by the pleading voice from the back of the cabin. They needed me for display purposes in their human zoo in Israel. I presumed they wanted a witness to testify to their "bravery" – a prisoner to torture and to extract confessions from. As they finished tying me up, the pilot announced, "We are going to Tel Aviv." Yet within minutes, I felt the plane descend and then touch down. As it hit the runway I fell off my seat and my "bodyguard" fell on top of me. He pulled me back up shouting obscenities and kicking me ruthlessly. The passengers disembarked. I could hear the sound of an ambulance outside. Two uniformed officers walked in. I didn't know where we were. Another officer walked in to the first-class compartment where I was being held. He demanded that I be turned over. An Israeli officer declared, "She is our prisoner. Get out of here. This is Israeli property." The first two men stood their ground. Then the Israeli pilot, yes the pilot, in the presence of two British officers, came out of his cockpit, lifted me off my seat and gave me a couple of vicious kicks in the bottom. The British officers screamed, "Shame," and pushed him aside. More British officers stepped into the fray, identifying themselves as members of Scotland Yard. The captain told them, "To hell with you and your government. She is my prisoner. Get out of this plane." The British officers tried to seize me. Three Israelis pulled me in one direction by my trussed up legs; the British pulled my hands in the other in a

tug-of-war which the British won. A great husky English officer carried me over his shoulders and threw me down to the waiting arms of two other officers below. I was in British hands. I knew it would be safer for me than in Tel Aviv.

* * *

The British placed Patrick and me in some kind of police ambulance. I was hoping against hope that Patrick would live. In a few minutes, a nurse told an officer beside her something, but I didn't hear it. Then she took the oxygen mask off Patrick's mouth. I knew he was dead. I pleaded with the British to untie me. They did after they persuaded me to remain calm. I stood beside Patrick's body: I held his hands; I surveyed his wounds; I touched his smashed head; I kissed his lips in a spirit of camaraderie and love, I wept unashamedly. I spoke to him, "Patrick, now you have joined Che in revolutionary love. You are an inspiration for the weak and oppressed. The Palestinians shall build you monuments in their hearts and in their liberated homeland. I long for the hour of liberation under leaders of our stature and selfless dedication." In less than twenty minutes, the ambulance arrived at Hillingdon hospital. Patrick Arguello, age twenty-seven, father of three children, a Nicaraguan citizen of the world, born in San Francisco, USA, was pronounced dead. What had prompted someone half-way across the world from Palestine to undertake this dangerous mission? Patrick was a revolutionary Communist. His gallant action was a gesture of international solidarity. A flame of life was extinguished; it lit the world for a moment; it blazed a trail on the road back to Palestine. Arguello lives, so do my people, so does the revolution!

At Hillingdon hospital, I was given a general check-up and X-rayed. I was surrounded by a crush of people who seemed to have very little to do with my medical examination. The doctor pronounced me "fit to go", though neither he nor anyone as I could, to ease my boredom. But one guard provoked me, "Why did you do it? It's a monstrous act," she said. I left without being able to explain to her why. However, she was kind to me and assisted me when the police moved me to Ealing. She put a blanket over my face and wished me well.

❋

❋ ❋ ❋

I was moved to Ealing police station on September 7. Here I was placed in a cell by myself. Two women officers guarded me. At first both seemed to resent me. We exchanged few words. I refused to eat. I only smoked and drank black coffee. I asked to see newspapers. They said I could read a women's magazine if I wanted I said, "No thanks." On September, 8, I met Chief Superintendent Frew, and Inspectors Bruce and Laidlaw. I said to them, "I will talk if I am recognised as a commando." They agreed on the condition that I would tell the truth.

Frew: "What's your name?"
Khaled: "Leila Khaled."
Frew: "That's a lie."
Khaled: "Then, what is my name?"
Frew: "Khaled is an assumed name."
Khaled: "My assumed name is Shadiah Abu Ghazalah, she was one of our great fighters . . ."

Frew interrupted me, "Oh, please, please don't harangue us. Answer questions specifically." He showed me a pistol and asked me to identify it. I said it was one of several Israeli pistols brandished in my face. He showed me a pistol which I later found out had been Patrick's, but since I hadn't seen it before, I said I didn't know to whom it belonged. He didn't believe me. He then demanded, "How did you obtain those strange bodies?" referring to the hand grenades. I answered him tersely: "They were given to me by the PF." "Who issued this passport to you?" "The PF," I said. "Where were you going to take the plane?"

else around me could have imagined how beat I was and how everything in me ached. I was asked by someone who didn't look like a nurse who I was. I said, "I am a commando from the Popular Front for the Liberation of Palestine." "This is not a name," a voice shouted. "That's my name. I do not wish to talk further." As people wandered around trying to extract confessions from me or statements, the familiar face of a journalist appeared in the crowd, but I couldn't place him. He must have recognised my voice immediately. He said, "That's Leila." A police officer said, "What Leila?" "That's Leila Khaled, the girl who hijacked the TWA last year," the journalist replied. "Are you sure?" "Yes I am." The officer asked if Leila was my name. I smiled but refused to comment. I was taken to West Drayton police station where I spent the night. Here the police tried to interrogate me. I absolutely refused to utter a single word beyond "I am a commando from the Popular Front," unless they agreed to recognise me as a commando and treat me as a war prisoner. At West Drayton, the only unpleasant incident was when an immigration officer came in with a sheaf of papers, read me all sorts of legal instructions, and informed me that I was refused legal entry to Britain. I said, "Wonderful. Release me now." He said "No," and wanted me to sign his ridiculous papers and acted as if I were some kind of a British outlaw. I ordered him out.

The first two nights were a nightmare. I worried about what was taking place in Jordan and what had happened to the other planned hijackings. I felt terrible because I had failed to seize and retain El-Al flight 219 and I felt shattered over the death of comrade Arguello. These two thoughts were constantly on my mind. I couldn't sleep for an hour without waking up, finding myself engaged in another make-believe battle. I was lonely and exhausted. I said very little to the women who constantly accompanied me. The only relationship I had with them was "What time is it?" A question posed as frequently paused briefly, then said: "It is quite possible that there were others on the plane whom I didn't know. Why, did you find someone else?" I inquired innocently. "Miss Khaled," Frew said, "I have grey hair." I promptly interrupted, "That's not from me. That's because you have a nagging wife." Frew smiled to himself, "I think you are a very intelligent woman." "I reject your compliments," I shot back as the verbal battle continued. I tried unsuccessfully to appear indignant and told the trio that as an Arab-Palestinian woman I refused to accept compliments from Fascist pigs who held me as prisoner.

Frew shuffled through his collection of documents and retorted, "Why would an Arab-Palestinian woman try to blow up a plane on which there were Palestinian Arabs?" I was not antagonised. "Oh," I said, "you have already decided that I am guilty of a crime that wasn't even committed before giving me the benefit of a British trial in court." "All the witnesses said you tried to blow up the plane." "Mr. Frew," I said, "they are a bunch of Zionist liars. Besides, why don't you hold a public inquiry and let every one of the witnesses be cross-examined?" He cleverly interjected: "Do you think you're a coward Miss Khaled?" "Look," I replied, "I had orders to seize the plane, not to blow it up. I am no Kamikaze pilot. I care about people. If I wanted to blow up the plane no one could have prevented me."

"Where did you board the plane? In Tel Aviv?" Frew inquired. "I boarded it at Schiphol airport in Amsterdam." "How many other hijackings did you plan?" "None." "Two others have taken place," he informed me. Surprised and pleased, I tried not to show any reaction to his statement. Then Frew said to me, "The Israelis have asked for your extradition. Would you like to be extradited to Israel?" I didn't know the meaning of the word extradition and asked him to explain the implications. He did, and added, "If you're extradited the Israelis are likely

"Somewhere." "Where?" "Somewhere," I insisted. "Who is Abd Arheem Jaber?" Now I brightened up and decided to deliver my first brief speech and refuse to talk further if I were stopped. The officers sensed my determination and remained silent.

"Jaber is a Palestinian hero in Zionist dungeons. He is one of our underground commando leaders who struck terror in the heart of the enemy, and throughout his cities. Before he was captured by the enemy on September 21, 1968, he fought courageously until his ammunition ran out. He held the enemy until most of his comrades managed to disappear in the face of American-made Sikorsky helicopters. He lived among the peasants of Palestine and he organised and trained them and spread revolutionary ideas. His most daring act was his challenge to General Sharif Nassir, uncle of King Hussein. Sharif Nassir was addressing a Jordanian platoon before the reactionary regime dispatched them to Yemen to help with the counter-revolutionary attempt to restore the deposed Imamate there. Jaber stood up to Sharif Nassir and said, 'Instead of sending us to Yemen to fight UAR troops and Yemeni radicals, why not send us to Tel Aviv to fight the real enemy of Palestine?' Sharif Nassir, who is quick with the gun, found Jaber a bit quicker. Jaber was dishonourably discharged, but upheld his dignity. I could tell you a lot more about the operations he masterminded in the occupied territories, but I want you to understand one thing: Jaber was held incommunicado for four months and the enemy couldn't break his will in spite of the torture—physical and psychological—inflicted on him. I assure you I am of the same stuff. I trust you understand now why my unit was called the Abd Arahman Jaber Commando Unit."

The British officers listened stony-faced. When I had finished Frew resumed his questioning. "In this note written by you, Miss Khaled," Frew said, "it says Shadiah and her colleagues. Who are your colleagues?" "What colleagues?" I asked. I to torture you." "Well Mr. Frew, then you know about Israel's torture chambers, brainwashing sessions, and physical shaming. That's good. I am glad you know. I think others should too. Anyhow, if I am extradited I will only be number twenty thousand and one. Just a statistic. I assure you, I won't break down under Zionist torture." "I insist you're a very intelligent girl," Frew declared. "I insist I do not accept your compliments. Give me a cigarette and a drink of water please," I said humorously. In this relaxed atmosphere, I told the officers that I had committed no crime against the British and I could see no reason why I was being kept in a British jail. They said they didn't know either. I asked if any Israelis were also held in jail. "None" they said. I exploded: "Why not? Don't you know they executed my comrade in cold blood." "Your colleague was killed in battle. The coroner's verdict says his death was 'lawful homicide'," Frew pointed out. "Shame on the British courts," I cried out. "How could they make such a decision on the basis of biased evidence and without even interrogating me? It is the Star Chamber all over again. This time it is directed from Tel Aviv and Washington." The atmosphere became tense as I gazed furiously at each officer. I muttered, "That's British justice," as they filed out. I was taken back to my cell. I had an intense headache that evening. The guards watched me closely as I marched back and forth restlessly.

On September 9, Mr. Frew visited me once again. He asked where I would like to go if extradited. I said to my homeland, Palestine. I demanded that I be released immediately and threatened dire consequences if the British continued my detention. That very day a BOAC VC-10 was hijacked. I knew my release was imminent. Mr. Frew returned to tell me that evening that I must have known what was going on. I said, "The Front knows what it is doing. I need not wait for a recommendation of clemency from a British jury."

On September 10, the ghost of Patrick haunted me. I couldn't stay my tears. I couldn't eat because Patrick had died hungry; I remembered that every day and tried to stop eating to pacify myself. The matron tried to calm me; she was a kindly woman and gave me helpful advice, but feelings of sadness and anguish aren't something that can be erased by a few motherly words. I was cheered up a little however, when I learned that the PF was demanding my return in exchange for BOAC passengers. Mr. Frew came in to enquire about Patrick's passport and asked: "Who was your partner, Leila?" He had closed the door behind him. I said, "My name is not Leila, but Miss Leila Khaled, a commando from the Popular Front. Is that clear Mr. Frew?" He was surprised that I was being so formal. I chuckled and tantalised him further: "According to your own rules, you have no right to be here in the absence of another female companion. By the way, when will I have the pleasure of facing British justice?" Frew was confused. He mumbled a few incoherent words and withdrew to reopen the door. He was somewhat apologetic as he asked if there was something he could do for me. "Yes," I said, "I would like to knit sweaters for our commandos. Would you be kind enough to provide me with some wool and needles?" He promised to try but didn't think the rules would allow it. I requested a pencil and a piece of paper. He gave me a two-inch pencil. Though I felt drowsy and had a toothache I penned my first note to Patrick.

Today is day four since we embarked on our immortal journey. Your spirit fills me with hope that the cause we embraced is just and honourable. You have given your life for a people you didn't know, for a people continents apart from your homeland, for a people who haven't seen your photograph. Though I know you not, I know you more than any other man I encountered in my life or any other hero I read or dreamt about. I always longed to know people who love others more than themselves; I always admired men who sacrificed their lives for the cause of liberty; I always adored people who walked naked before the sun not fearing its scorching rays and said no to the enemies of light, life and progress. In dying for Palestine you have become the symbol that lightens our oppression; you have also become the joyous burden that propels us onward to end that oppression. In joining our struggle for dignity and peoplehood, you have given us a lesson in international solidarity and brotherhood and cemented the bond of affection between the people of Latin America and the people of Palestine. You wrote history by shedding your blood for others; you united continents by your all-encompassing spirit; you ascended to the realm of Olympian gods by your life-inspiring commitment. You are at once a Lafayette, a Byron, a Norman Bethune, a Che Guevara—a Patrick Arguello, a martyr for Palestinian freedom. You are not dead. You live. You will live forever! You are the patron saint of Palestine. In revolution,

Leila.

September 11 was a day for banter. It started with a visit from the envoy of Honduras, a corpulent, moustached feudal lord. Mr. Frew introduced him as his excellency, the Consul of Honduras. He asked, "How did you obtain this Honduran passport?" I answered contemptuously: "Did the Popular Front disguise you and send you here as a fictitious banana republic ambassador?" His excellency was infuriated. He departed like a vanquished Napoleon. What a sad state of affairs for officialdom, for a Latin consul to be ridiculed and insulted by a Palestinian or a nobody hijacker. How humiliating! Mr. Frew was appalled, but not surprised by my reaction. I blamed him for failing to fulfil his promise of knitting material.

He apologised and explained, "You are not allowed to have sharp instruments in your possession." He wanted to know if the Front would explode the plane with the passengers as was reported by the "objective" British press that day. "Yes," I said unhesitatingly. "What?" he asked, "have you no humanity?" "Humanity my foot!" I shouted. "You should be ashamed to utter such a word in the West. If you have any integrity you'd remove that word from your dictionaries and declare it a non-English word." I started making a speech on Zionism and imperialism and how the British vampired the Arab world, but Mr. Frew deflated me this time. He interrupted, "Miss Leila Khaled, perhaps our government is imperialist. Please stop your speech-making." I felt undercut and later asked my "bodyguards" why Mr. Frew didn't defend the government. They explained that there were many members of the Labour Party at Ealing who were not necessarily sympathetic to the Conservative government.

On September 12, I tried to take a different tack after hearing that the imperialist planes had been blown up. Since all kinds of strikes were going on in Britain, I thought my "bodyguards" should go on strike in sympathy with their fellow workers. I suggested since they were "my prisoners" they should stage a revolt and join their fellow workers on strike. As I was urging them to rebel Mr. Frew walked in. He took a deep breath and said, "What are you up to now?" "Mr. Frew," I said, "these prisoners deserve to be free." "What prisoners?" he enquired. "Those poor masses working night and day here." "O.K. You win this time," he said paternally. As Mr. Frew sat checking his files I decided to badger him. "I know the Home Office is violating British justice, habeas corpus and other concepts of justice, but does the Ealing Hilton have to violate the laws of hygiene too Mr. Frew?" He scratched his head and enquired further. I informed him that I hadn't had a bath in six days.

He quickly arranged for me to be marched to the fifth floor accompanied by four police matrons who insisted on having me undress in their presence as each guarded a corner of the narrow shower room.

September 13 was a bad day for me. I felt ill most of the day and couldn't sleep that night. The doctor was called in. He pleaded with me to eat more than just a cheese sandwich and coffee and gave me two sleeping tablets. They had a terrible effect on me. That night was a nightmare for everybody except me. They thought I was about to die, but I surprised them and woke up feeling as if my head weighed a ton. When I opened my eyes at five-thirty a.m. everyone was practically in tears. That charming little matron was truly relieved and delighted to see me revive. It was apparent that she had had a sleepless night as had most people around me.

The next two weeks I settled into an established routine. There were no further interrogations. I was allowed to use the matron's rooms and to roam within a ten-yard radius without being followed. Political issues in Jordan, especially after the seventeenth, preoccupied me and became the focal point of my discussions with Frew and others. I was given a bundle of letters that had arrived at Ealing: some denounced me; others supported the cause; one contained a marriage proposal. I was not permitted to answer any of them, but I was permitted to write to my parents and some close friends. I volunteered to translate the contents but Mr. Frew told me that Her Majesty's Government had its own interpreters.

*

*

*

It didn't surprise me that a full-scale massacre was under way in Jordan. Isolated in a British cage, however, I did not appreciate the magnitude and extent of Hussein's terror. It seemed, judging from reports in the British press, that the incident was a con-

tinuation of the policy of harassment, intimidation, and terror instituted in November of 1968 and continued sporadically since then. Although it was obvious that the latest combat engulfed the whole country, it was not so obvious as the final liquidation attempt on the part of the monarchy.

*

*

Many have alleged, without justification, that the PFLP precipitated the massacres by the Jordanian regime of September 1970 with the multiple "hijackings" we undertook. Such a simple explanation of the well-conceived plot on the part of the Jordanian authorities to eliminate the Palestinian revolution cannot be accepted. The massacre of September and the subsequent mopping-up operations that took place while the Arab states fulminated should convince everyone that, indeed, the Arab kings and colonels regarded the Palestinian resistance as a dangerous movement that could threaten their very regimes and engulf the whole region in an international civil war of the working class versus the forces of oppression. One thing was made clear during those momentous months: Hussein was prepared to invite Israel to take over "his kingdom", rather than allow the resistance to topple him, and America almost intervened to "rescue" its citizens and maintain Hussein in power. The components in this drama were a power-hungry Hashemite ruling clique, prepared to commit any treachery to keep the reins of power in its hand; general Arab silence, which can only be interpreted as acquiescence to the massacre; and the American-Zionist conspiracy hatched between Golda Meir and Nixon in Washington.

*

*

*

On September 17, the British guards, whether on their own initiative or under instructions from their superiors, urged me to ask for political asylum. To me it was a repugnant form of abdication. I rejected the idea immediately. In fact, I demanded that I be released so that I could go and join my comrades in Jordan. The British bided their time and negotiated as partners of the so-called "Berne Five", under pressure from the Americans and the Israelis. I am certain the Germans, the Swiss and the British would have exchanged hostages for our prisoners had it not been for Zionist and American insistence on a unified front - an action, which, in effect, showed how little the Europeans cared for their own citizens compared with those of Zionist Israel and the American behemoth. I know that their justification for such callous deeds was that they were upholding international law and morality and defending "innocent passengers", but let's not deceive ourselves; the interests of Dick Nixon and Golda Meir were placed ahead of those of Britain, Germany, and "neutral" Switzerland.

The turmoil in Jordan disturbed me deeply. I tried to maintain my composure and act naturally, but it was a difficult job. Mr. Frew was a daily visitor. He wondered why Moslems fought each other instead of the enemy. I lectured him on the nature of class society and explained that the good little British-manufactured King of Jordan was part of the enemy camp. Frew listened intently but like most of his Western compatriots, he was unable to grasp the idea of social class and its historic implications. He only accused me of being bitter. I said I was more then bitter, I was full of class hatred and aspired for nothing less than the complete obliteration of the Jordanian monarchy and retinue. Frew's prescription for the remedy of my class consciousness was a week's stay in "democratic" Britain after my release. I said, "I'll be happy to stay in Britain until Christmas if I were released immediately so as to enjoy the fruits of British democracy." Frew detected my sarcastic tone. "Now," he said, "I wish you would go back to Jordan before I

lose my wife." "Tell your wife not to worry, Mr. Frew. I have no intention of marrying a fatherly British cop. If I do marry, it will be an Arab revolutionary or a simple peasant, not a British lord, not a Greek shipping magnate, not an American industrial baron. Is that clear Mr. Frew?"

I followed the Jordanian civil war in the British press. When I began reading reports about the "Syrian intervention", I deduced from fragmented editorial comments that an Israeli-US invasion was being contemplated. When, however, it was reported that the "Syrian column" had been defeated by "brave" Jordanians and forced to withdraw, I realised that the regime was not on the verge of dethronement. But when I saw Hussein and Arafat shake hands in the presence of kings and presidents I knew the revolution was betrayed. At that moment, I am sure I could have unhesitatingly gunned down every participant in that conference. I could no longer withhold my fury, I could see the writing on the wall: the resistance was dead as a historic force. I truly cried for the blood of martyrs in Jordan, the blood bartered away at the Cairo Hilton, the Kubbe Palace and the Arab League Headquarters. I could not forgive the Arab League for the blood of Patrick, whose body still lay in a British morgue while counter-revolutionary "peace" was signed. I knew the fighters would repudiate the leadership and in time form their own revolutionary vanguard party. I knew it had to be done; I knew the Front was going to do it. In the ensuing months, however, Arafat and Co. still refused to understand that the Palestinian Arab revolution was in fundamental contradiction to the Arab decadent social orders. Hussein crushed the resistance physically in Jordan and drove the guerrillas out in July 1971, and the "resistance leaders", with the exception of the Popular Front and a few independents, accepted Saudi-Egyptian mediation and were still prepared to negotiate with Jordan and embrace Hussein and Hassan.

Early on September 28, it was reported that President Nasser was dying. The news didn't strike me as real nor did I fathom the implication of his impending death. I was still too frenzied over the Arafat-Hussein accord to think clearly. Late in the day, however, it was reported that President Nasser had died. I was stunned, emotionally paralysed. The feelings I had when Che and Ho died returned. This time perhaps more poignantly, for I was, as every Arab was at one time or other, an admirer of Nasser. He was one of the greatest Arab leaders of the modern era. As a giant among dwarfs, he symbolised everything noble, great and weak among the Arabs. He was from us and one of us; he was a leader of men. I felt a part of me died with him. I was happy I had lived in the age of Nasser. I will only be happier to live in a liberated Palestine.

Mr. Frew and those around me saw how sad I was. They couldn't understand why I should be so distressed over the death of someone I had denounced the day before. They couldn't understand that Nasser was the first champion of anti-imperialism in my world.

On September 29, Frew intimated that I might soon be released. I checked the newspapers closely for clues as to when the last six hostages were going to be surrendered to the International Red Cross Committee. They finally were on the thirtieth of September, 1970. The moment the hostages reached Cyprus, I was instructed to prepare for departure. There was no indication of my destination. I bade my British friends farewell, kisses and all, and promised to send more customers to the Ealing Hilton where clients have bodyguards and accommodation is free.

At six-thirty, Mr. Frew came and asked me to which country I would like to go. I said confidently, "The decision has already been taken by my commanders. By the way, where am I being taken?" Frew didn't answer and no one answered the question in the next few hours. I was told that since I was a soldier,

I was expected to abide by the rules as I was being moved out of Britain. I agreed and followed orders to the letter. The matrons told me that people were lining up in the streets to see me, but they were going to be sadly disappointed as I would be taken out lying, covered up in a van. I was surprised to be accompanied by a whole convoy of police cars and motorcycles. I was allowed one quick look at the crowd assembled around Ealing police station before being taken to a military airport. As I boarded the helicopter I flashed a victory sign to the photographers. I said goodbye to Mr. Frew and promised to visit the "Ealing" again. "No," he cried out, "come to Britain, not to the 'Ealing'." We travelled by helicopter for about an hour and then landed at another nameless airport. I noted to the captain that helicopters are more difficult to hijack than regular planes. He didn't appreciate my sense of humour. Then we boarded a Comet for an unannounced destination. I still couldn't find out where I was going. Then I heard a member of the crew saying "there is another woman to come". I knew instantly it had to be Amina Dhahbour who was being held by the Swiss in Zurich. Suddenly we descended in Munich. The airport was a garrison. From my window I counted the armoured cars. I was ordered to take the last seat on the plane. Three brothers, from the Action Organisation, Mufid Abdul Rahman, Hanabi and Nashaat, were brought aboard. I knew none of them and we were not allowed to shake hands. Next stop was Zurich where my inspiration, Amina and comrades Ibrahim Tewfiq and Mohammad Abu Al-Haija came aboard. I wanted at least to hug Amina, but it was not permitted. We just greeted each other from afar. Each of the passengers had his own bodyguard. None was handcuffed. The night of September 30 was a long one. The journey to Cairo was the longest I ever endured. I slept periodically. We had to remain seated at all times.

We arrived in Cairo, October 1, 1970, at eight a.m. The city was in mourning for the death of President Nasser. The British, German and Swiss consuls met us at the airport. Each one of us was dutifully taken in hand by "his" consul and turned over to the Egyptian authorities. Protocol reigned. I was astonished to find out that Patrick's body wasn't with us, but there were no British around to denounce or Arab leaders to threaten. We were taken to an Egyptian "guesthouse" and held there for eleven days. We were told that we were being held there for "security reasons".

On October 12, we were flown to Damascus and each commando rejoined his or her unit. Before returning to Beirut, however, I visited my friend Colonel Ali Zaza, the man who had accused me of working for Egyptian intelligence in the TWA affair.

"Colonel," I said, as I barged into his office, "I trust you are convinced now that the Popular Front and I are nobody's tools." "I am," he said. "Wouldn't you like to keep me in your guesthouse again?" "No, Leila, this time you can be my guest for lunch." "No thank you, colonel," I said. "I have to report back to my unit in Beirut within two hours. See you on the battlefield in Palestine!"

I went to Beirut in mid-October and held a press conference at *Al-Hadaf*'s office pointing out that Patrick was murdered by the Israelis and that the British excused the crime that took place in their airspace. To this date, the British have refused to put their "evidence" before a competent authority for inspection and the autopsy report remains confidential.

*

*

*

For the next few weeks, I spent most of my time giving press interviews and preparing to marry a fellow fighter, Bassim, an Iraqi Arab revolutionary. We got married on November 26, 1970, spent a week together and then returned to our separate tasks.

The Secure Terminal

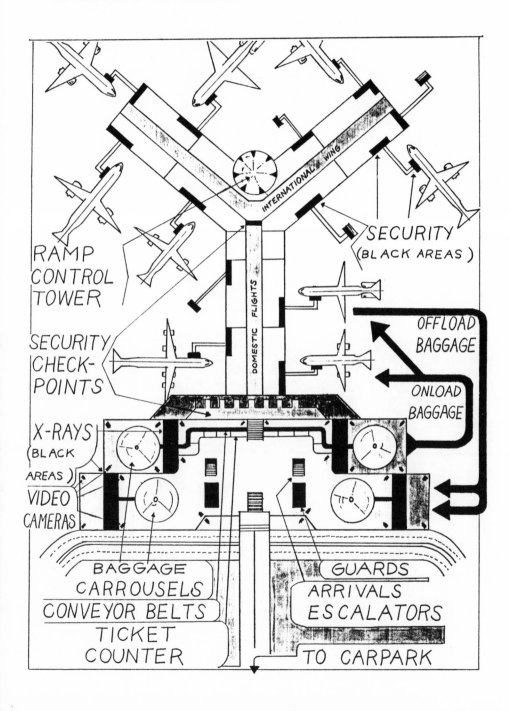

The Secure Airport

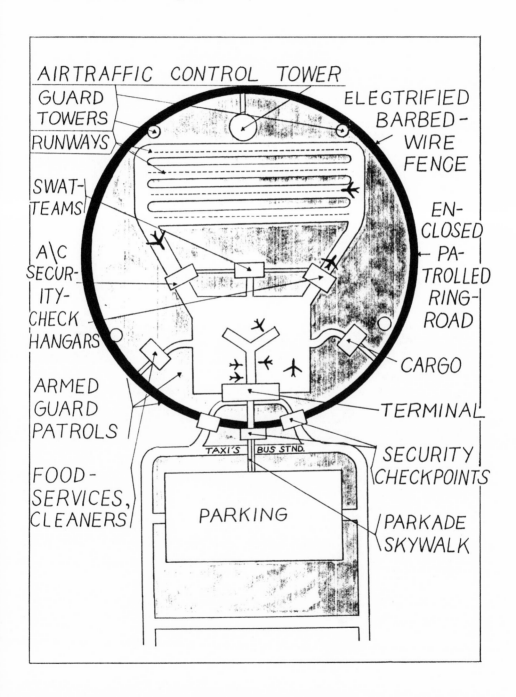

AIRTRAFFIC CONTROL TOWER
GUARD TOWERS
RUNWAYS
SWAT-TEAMS
A\C SECUR-ITY-CHECK HANGARS
ARMED GUARD PATROLS
FOOD-SERVICES, CLEANERS

ELECTRIFIED BARBED-WIRE FENCE
EN-CLOSED PA-TROLLED RING-ROAD
CARGO
TERMINAL
SECURITY CHECKPOINTS
PARKADE SKYWALK

TAXI'S   BUS STND.
PARKING

A Short List of Important Hijacks, 1968–1989

02/02/68	Hijack of Delta DC8 by L. Rhodes Jr.; first since 1961
07/22/68	Israel ElAl 707; Rome-Tel Aviv, by PFLP; to Algiers; 2 mos. negotiations
07/12/68	USA, O.D. Richards hijacks Delta Convair; Baltimore-Houston; fails
11/04/68	USA, R. Johnson hijacks National Airlines 727; Houston-Miami-Cuba; $
12/28/68	Israeli retaliation strike destroys 13 M.E.airlines planes; Beirut
01/08/69	USA, C.Belon hijacks TWA 707, Paris-Rome-Beirut; 1st Am hijack abroad
03/15/69	USA, J. DeVivo hijacks Eastern DC9, Newark-Boston "Fly East"
06/04/69	USA, A. Barkley hijacks TWA 727, Wash-Phoenix; fails
08/02/69	USA, R.Rivera Rios hijacks lst USA jumbojet PanAm 747, NY-P.Rico-Cuba
08/29/69	Israel adopts principle of not giving in to hijackers' demands
08/29/69	USA, Leila Khaled hijacks TWA 840, L.A-Tel Aviv-Rome-Damascus
11/01/69	USA, R. Minichiello, US Marine, hijacks TWA 85 S.Francisco-Rome; 6900 miles
02/21/70	SwissAir Coronado jet bomb explosion destroys plane; 47 dead (13 Israelis)
03/31/70	Japan; JRA 1st hijack of JAL jet to Korea; Takashi Okamoto; Samurai 9
08/22/70	Greece. Olympic Airways 727; Beirut-Athens; hijacked for POW exchange
19/06/70	Jordan. Dawson's Field; multiple hijack; TWA 707; Frankfurt-NY Swissair DC8; Zurich-NY ElAl B707; NY-Amsterdam; Khaled PanAm jet to Cairo blown up (last hijack of Israeli plane)
09/08/70	PFLP; British VC-10; London-Bahrain-Bombay; to free L. Khaled
04/17/71	USA, R.F. McCoy hijacks TWA 727, Denver-S.Francisco, with $ but caught
05/28/71	USA, J.E. Bennett hijacks Eastern, NY-Miami-Nassau, for $; fails
07/24/71	Jordan. Attack by Fatah on Alia plane; Cairo
07/28/71 + 09/01/71–Israel. Suitcase bombs given to Dutch and Peruvian girls. PFLP-GC. Fail
11/12/71	Canada. Paul Cini hijacks Air Canada Edmonton-Toronto for $; fails
11/24/71	USA, D.B. Cooper hijacks 727 out of Seattle. $200,000; never seen again
02/22/72	W. Germany Lufthansa, New Delhi-Athens-S.Yemen; PFLP; $5m. ransom
05/08/72	Belgium. Sabena hijacked to Lod, Israel. BSO; fails
05/31/72	Israel. JRA-PFLP attack at Lod; Kozo Okamoto; 26 dead, 76 wounded
09/05/72	W. Germany. Munich Olympics; 11 Israeli athletes killed; BSO
09/12/72	Israel. P.M. Golda Meir declares war on Arab terrorists
10/29/72	W. Germany. Lufthansa, Beirut-Munich-Damascus; BSO swap for POWS
11/10/72	USA; 3 blacks hijack Southern Airways; 29 hrs; Cuba; Oak Ridge threat
02/21/73	Israel shoots down Libyan plane over Sinai suspecting attack on Israel
07/20/73	Japan. PFLP-JRA hijack JAL 747, Amsterdam-Tokyo; blow it up; 1 dead
08/05/73	USA. TWA flight Tel Aviv-Athens attack by NAYLP; kills 5; wounds 55
09/05/73	Italy. Rome. BSO attack Israeli plane with Strela SAM-7; missile; arrested

12/17/73   USA. Rome; PanAm plane set on fire by thermite bomb; 32 dead; NAYLP
03/03/74   UK. Amsterdam VC-10; Bombay-London; hijacked by NAYLP
09/07/74   USA. TWA Athens-NY; blown up over Ionian Sea; 88 dead
11/22/74   UK. Br.Airways; Dubai-Tunis; NAYLP; POW exchange
11/25/74   Holland. KLM 747 jet hijacked to Dubai via Damascus
11/25/74   Canada. CPAir 737; Wpg-Edmonton; hijack foiled by captain
01/13/75   France. Paris; Carlos-PFLP; rocket attack on El Al plane; fails
01/19/75   France. Paris; Carlos gun fight in lounge of airport
12/19/75   France. Paris; Boudia commando attack on passengers; 20 wounded
12/21/75   Austria. Vienna; Carlos captures OPEC oil ministers flies to Algiers
05/01/76   Japan. JRA hijack JAL DC-8; finally surrender
05/21/76   Philippines. Phil Air; 6 Moslems demand $375,000 ransom; 10 dead
07/04/76   Philippines. Phil Air; BAC III to Manila; $300,000 ransom; 6 days
06/27/76   France/Israel. Fch Air bus A-300; Tel Aviv-Athens-Entebbe-Israeli rescue
09/41/76   Holland. KLM DC-9; Nice-Amsterdam; hijacked by 3 Arabs
10/09/76   USA. TWA 355; Croatian hijack, Chicago-Montreal-Gander-Paris
10/28/76   Czech. Cz Airlines Il-18, Prague-Munich; 8-yr sentence
11/04/76   Poland. Lot.TU-134; hijack to Vienna; 11-year sentence
03/17/77   Japan. Tokyo hijack 727 JAL; hijacker dies of cyanide pill
07/08/77   Kuwait. Airways 707, Beirut-Kuwait-Damascus; surrender
09/28/77   Japan. JAL DC-8, Bombay-Tokyo-Dacca; 5 hijackers demand $6million and
            POWS; JRA
09/30/77   France. Air Inter, Paris-Lyon; grenade explodes; 1 dead
10/13/77   W.Germany. Lufthansa 737, Palma-Frankfurt-Mogadishu; GSG9 attack; 3 dead
12/04/77   Malaysia. 737 Penang-K.Lumpur; shoot-out; crash; 80 dead
02/18/78   Cyprus. Cypriot liner hijacked; Abu Nidal; Egyptian commandos dead
08/25/78   USA. TWA 707, NY-Geneva; 17-year prison sentence for hijacker
01/16/79   Lebanon. Beirut M.E. Airlines 707; Amman; demands of political nature
09/07/79   Italy. Alitalia DC-8; hijack over spiritual leader in Libya
01/14/80   Italy. Alitalia demand for Tunisian POWS
01/18/80   Lebanon. M.E. Airlines, Beirut-Larnaca; spiritual leader in Libya
07/22/80   U.S.A. Delta Miami-San Juan-Cuba; black Muslims; 40 yrs
07/24/80   Kuwait Air 737, Beirut-Kuwait; demand of $1million; surrender
03/02/81   Pakistan. Al Zulfiquah hijacks PIA 12 days; 54 POWS freed
09/29/81   Indian. Indian Airlines 737; Sikh hijack N. Delhi-Amritsar
02/24/82   Kuwait Air 707, Beirut-Kuwait; Moslem leader Libya; UN inquiry
05/21/82   Philippines BAC1-11; hijacker with grenade overcome
06/30/82   Italy. Alitalia 747, New Delhi-Bangkok; 20 years prison
07/25/82   China Il-18. 5 hijackers Xian-Shanghai; shoot-out
08/04/82   India. Indian Airlines 737, N.Delhi-Amritsar; Sikhs
08/20/82   India. Indian Airlines 737; Sikh killed ending hijack
09/25/82   Italy. Alitalia 727, Algiers-Rome; surrender of hijacker
05/05/83   China. 6 hijackers Trident 2-E, Shenyang-Shanghai; jailed
07/06/83   Iran Air 747, Shiraz-Teheran-Paris; surrender of hijackers
08/27/83   France. Air France 727, Vienna-Damascus-Teheran; surrender
03/07/84   France. Air France 737, Frankfurt-Paris-Geneva; Arabs arrested
03/22/84   U.K. Br.Air 747, Hong Kong-Peking-Taiwan; prison
05/07/84   India Air A-300; hijacked by Sikhs; $25million ransom, but surrender
07/05/84   India. 8 hijackers hijack Air India; demand $25million ransom; surrender
07/31/84   France. Air France 737, Frankfurt-Paris-Teheran; plane blown up
08/24/84   India. 7 hijack Indian Air 737; Sikhs with daggers; surrender
12/04/84   Kuwait. Kuwait Air A-310, Dubai-Karachi-Teheran; 6 dead

02/07/85	Cyprus. Cyprus Air 707, Beirut-Larnaca; 4 Shiites; surrender
02/27/85	W. Germany. Lufthansa 727, Frankfurt-Damascus; surrender
02/??/85	W. Germany. Lufthansa 737, Hamburg-London; mentally ill hijacker
05/18/85	S. Korea. Korean Air 727, Seoul-Cheju; hijacker overpowered
06/11/85	Jordan. Alia 727, Beirut-Amman; 5 Arabs hijack at Larnaca
06/14/85	U.S.A. TWA 847, Athens/Rome-Beirut-Algiers; 1 dead; 15 days
06/23/85	Canada. CP Air 007, Vancouver-Tokyo; bomb explodes; 2 dead
10/11/85	U.S.A. Intercept Egyptair, Sicily, with Achille Lauro hijackers
11/23/85	Malta. Luqa Egyptair 737, Athens-Cairo; 22 hours; 60 dead
12/27/85	Italy/Austria. Abu Nidal attack on Rome and Vienna airports
04/02/86	U.S.A TWA 727, Athens-Rome; bomb explodes; 4 dead
04/17/86	U.K. El Al, Heathrow. Hindawi-Murphy; bomb discovered
08/05/86	Shri Lanka. Colombo. Air Lanka bomb explodes; 20 dead; 41 wounded
05/30/86	India. Air India 747; Sikh attempt to sabotage; Washington DC
09/05/86	Pakistan. Pan Am 073; Abu Nidal hijack; 17 hrs; 20 dead
09/14/86	S. Korea. Kimpo airport bomb explosion; dead and wounded
11/25/86	Iraq.-Air 162. Firefight with terrorists; 65 dead; 42 wounded; crashes
11/29/87	S. Korea. Korean Air 858; sabotaged by N. Koreans; 115 dead
12/10/87	USA Pacific South West Airlines, LA-S.Francisco; sabotage; 43 dead
04/05/88	Kuwait Air 422. Hijacked by Hezbollah to Algiers; 16 days
07/03/88	Iran. USS Vincennes shoots down Iran airbus; 290 dead
08/17/88	Pakistan. C-130 Transport of President Zia; sabotaged; 29 dead
09/29/88	Brazil. Rio hijacker shot after hijack attempt
15/10&20/88	India. Two Air India crashes; suspected sabotage; 374 dead
12/01/88	USSR. 5 Soviets hijack to Israel; handed back to Russians
12/21/88	USA. Pan Am 103 sabotaged over Lockerbie; 269 dead

States Whose Planes Were Hijacked/Attacked, 1968–1988

U.S.A. 1968 (3 times), 1969 (6 times), 1970 (2 times), 1971 (3 times), 1972, 1973 (2 times), 1974, 1976, 1978, 1980, 1985 (2 times), 1986, 1987, 1988

Israel. 1968 (2 times), 1970, 1971 (2 times), 1972 (2 times), 1973 (2 times), 1976, 1986, 1988

Swiss. 1970 (2 times)

Japan. 1970, 1973, 1976, 1977 (2 times)

Greece. 1970, 1974

U.K. 1970, 1974 (2 times), 1984, 1986

Jordan. 1971, 1985

Canada. 1971, 1974, 1985 (2 times)

West Germany. 1972 (3 times), 1977, 1985 (2 times)

Belgium. 1972

Holland. 1974, 1976

France. 1975 (3 times), 1976, 1977, 1983, 1984 (2 times)

Austria. 1975, 1985

Philippines. 1976 (2 times), 1982

Czech. 1976

Poland. 1976

Kuwait. 1977, 1980, 1982, 1984, 1988

Malaysia. 1977

Cyprus. 1978, 1985

Egypt. 1978, 1985 (3 times)

Lebanon. 1979, 1980

Italy. 1979, 1980, 1982 (2 times), 1985

Pakistan. 1981, 1986, 1988

India. 1981, 1982 (2 times), 1984 (3 times), 1985 (2 times), 1988

China. 1982, 1983

Iran. 1983, 1988

S. Korea. 1985, 1986, 1987

Malta. 1985, 1986

Sri Lanka. 1986

Iraq. 1986

Brazil. 1988

USSR. 1988

States Experiencing Hijacks, 1968–1988

Poland	Hong Kong
DDR	France
Czechoslovakia	Switzerland
Roumania	Italy
USSR	Austria
Bulgaria	Malta
Yugoslavia	Greece
Hungary	Turkey
Costa Rica	Spain
Haiti	Algeria
Cuba	Iraq
Chile	Syria
Honduras	Israel
Panama	Libya
Mexico	Yemen
El Salvador	Kuwait
Nicaragua	Iran
Argentina	Lebanon
Kenya	Jordan
Uganda	Bahrein
S. Korea	Qatar
China	Tunisia
S. Vietnam	Djibouti
Singapore	Dubai
India	S. Arabia
Pakistan	
Thailand	
Taiwan	

Hijacks in the Communist Orbit, 1968–1988

	Escapes
Poland	26
Cuba	74
Czechoslovakia	12
USSR	13
Bulgaria	4
Roumania	3
DDR	1
Hungary	1

Freedom escapes from Communist World, 1968-88: Total: 134.
Escapes to Cuba: 74.   Source: FAA Study

Bibliography

DOCUMENTS AND REPORTS

"Air Piracy and Airport Security: A Symposium," Jan. 17-18, 1986, St. John's College, University of Manitoba, under the auspices of the Counter-Terror Study Centre, Winnipeg, 1986.

Commonwealth Air Transport Council. "Organization of Canadian Aviation Security." 13th Meeting, Ottawa, 1987, pp. 1-5.

Department of Transportation, Federal Aviation Administration, Office of Civil Aviation Security. *U.S. and Foreign Registered Aircraft Hijackings, 1931-1986.* Washington, DC: Federal Aviation Administration, 134 pp.

Federal Aviation Administration. "Explosions Aboard Aircraft." Washington, DC: Department of Transportation, Office of Civil Aviation Security, updated Jan. 1, 1986.

International Air Transport Association. "Backgrounder." Montreal: Information Department, 1988. p. 2.

_____. "Staying Ahead of the Terrorist," Montreal, 1988.

Kelly, Honorable William M. "The Report of the Senate Special Committee on Terrorism and the Public Safety." Ottawa: Minister of Supply and Services, 1987.

Memorandum on International Civil Aviation Organization. 13th ed. Montreal: Public Information Office, 1987.

O'Donnell, J. J. "Statement before the Governmental Affairs Committee, United States Senate." Washington, DC, Jan. 30, 1979.

Transport Canada. "Security Guidelines for Aircrew." Ottawa: Civil Aviation Security Branch, Dec. 1984.

"The U.S. Government Antiterrorism Program." Washington, DC: Special Coordination Committee, National Security Council, June 1979.

U.S. Department of State. "Patterns of Global Terrorism: 1988." Washington, DC, Mar. 1989.

U.S. Department of Transportation "Criminal Acts Against Civil Aviation 1986." Washington, DC: Federal Aviation Administration, Office of Civil Aviation Security, 1986.

U.S. Department of Transportation. "Semiannual Report to Congress on the Effectiveness of the Civil Aviation Security Program, July 1, 1987-Dec. 31, 1987." Washington, DC, June 1988.

U.S. House of Representatives. *Antiterrorism Measures: The Adequacy of Foreign Airport Security.* Washington, DC: U.S. Government Printing Office, 1986.

BOOKS

Arey, James. *The Sky Pirates.* New York: Scribners, 1972.

Ashwood, Capt. Thomas M. *Terror in the Skies.* New York: Stein and Day, 1987.

Atala, Charles. *Le Hijacking Aerien.* Ottawa: Lemeux, 1973.

Aviation Security: How to Safeguard International Air Transport. Conference at the Peace Palace. The Hague, Jan. 1987.

Baumann, Bommi. *How It All Began.* Vancouver: Pulp Press, 1975.

Bolz, Frank, and Edward Hershey. *Hostage Cop.* New York: Rawson Wade, 1980.

Bowyer-Bell, J. *A Time of Terror: How Democratic Societies Respond to Revolutionary Violence.* New York: Basic Books, 1978.

Brenchley, F. *Living with Terrorism: The Problem of Air Piracy.* London: Institute for the Study of Conflict, 1986.

Cave-Brown, Anthony. *The Bodyguard of Lies.* Toronto: Bantam, 1976.

Cline, Ray S., and Yonah Alexander. *Terrorism as State-Sponsored Covert Warfare.* Fairfax, VA: Hero Books, 1986.

Clutterbuck, Richard. *Living with Terrorism.* London: Faber and Faber, 1975.

Clyne, Peter. *An Anatomy of Skyjacking.* London: Abelard-Schuman, 1973.

Crelinson, Ron, ed. *The Impact of Terrorism and Skyjacking on the Operations of the Criminal Justice System.* Montreal: International Centre for Comparative Criminology, 1976.

Dobson, Christopher, and Ronald Payne. *Counterattack: The West's Battle Against the Terrorists.* New York: Facts on File, 1982.

_____. *The Never-Ending War: Terrorism in the 80's.* New York: Facts on File, 1987.

Freedman, Lawrence, R. J. Vincent, P. Wilkinson, P. Windsor, C. Hill, and A. Roberts. *Terrorism and International Order.* London: Routledge & Kegan Paul, 1986.

Gutteridge, William, ed. *The New Terrorism.* London: Mansell Publishing, 1986.

Hacker, Frederick J. "Contagion and Attraction of Terror and Terrorism." In *Behavioral and Quantitative Perspectives on Terrorism,* ed. Y. G. Alexander and J. M. Gleason. New York: Pergamon, 1981.

_____. *Crusaders, Criminals, and Crazies: Terror and Terrorism in Our Time.* New York: Bantam, 1976.

Haeck, Louis. "Le Droit International et le Terrorisme aerien." In *Annals of Air and Space Law.* Vol. 13. Montreal: McGill University, 1988.

Hewit, Christopher. *The Effectiveness of Anti-Terrorist Policies.* Lanham, MD: University Press of America, 1984.

Hill, Christopher. "The Political Dilemmas for Western Governments." In *Terrorism and International Order,* ed. L. Freedman et al. London: Routledge & Kegan Paul, 1986, pp. 77-100.

Hubbard, David, M.D. *The Skyjacker: His Flights of Fantasy.* New York: Macmillan, 1971.

_____. *Winning Back the Sky: A Tactical Analysis of Terrorism:* New York: Saybrook, 1986.

Jenkins, Brian M., ed. *Terrorism and Beyond: An International Conference on Terrorism and Low-Level Conflict.* Santa Monica, CA: Rand, 1982.

Jiwa, Salim. *The Death of Air India Flight 182.* London: Star Books, 1986.

Joyner, Nancy D. *Aerial Hijacking as an International Crime.* New York: Oceana, 1974.

Kellett, Anthony. *International Terrorism: A Retrospective and Prospective Examination.* Operational Research and Analysis Establishment Report no. R78. Ottawa: Department of National Defence, May 1981.

Khaled, Leila, and George Hajjar. *My People Shall Live: Autobiography of a Revolunary.* London: Hodder & Stoughton, 1973.

Koch, Peter, and Hermann Kai. *Assault at Mogadishu.* London: Corgi Books, 1979.

Livingstone, Neil C. *The War Against Terrorism.* Toronto: Lexington Books, 1982.

McKnight, George. *The Terrorist Mind: Why They Hijack, Kidnap, Bomb, and Kill.* London: M. Joseph, 1975.

McWhinney, Edward. *Aerial Piracy and International Law.* New York: Oceana, 1973.

_____. *The Illegal Diversion of Aircraft and International Law.* Leyden: A. W. Sizthoff, 1975.

Melman, Yossi. *The Master Terrorist: The True Story Behind Abu Nidal.* New York: Adama Books, 1986.

Merari, Ariel. "International Terrorism and Civil Aviation." In *INTER, International Terrorism in 1987.* Jaffee Center for Strategic Studies Project on Low Intensity Warfare. Jerusalem, 1987, pp. 71-84.

_____, ed. *On Terrorism and Combatting Terrorism.* Frederick, MD: University Publications of America, 1985.

Morris, Eric, and Alan Hoe. *Terrorism: Threat and Response.* London: Macmillan, 1987.

Moxon-Browne, Edward. "Terrorism in France." In *The New Terrorism,* ed. William Gutteridge. London: Mansell, 1986, pp. 11-134.

Mulgrew, Ian. *Unholy Terror: The Sikhs and International Terrorism.* Toronto: Key Porter Books, 1988.

Phillips, David. *Skyjack: The Story of Air Piracy.* London: Harrap, 1973.

Rich, Elizabeth. *Flying High.* New York: Stein and Day, 1972.

_____. *Flying Scared.* New York: Stein and Day, 1972.

Rivers, Gayle. *The War Against the Terrorists.* New York: Charter Books, 1987.

Schreiber, Jan. *The Ultimate Weapon: Terrorists and World Order.* New York: William Morrow, 1978.

Scotti, Anthony J. *Executive Safety and International Terrorism.* Englewood Cliffs, NJ: Prentice-Hall, 1986.

Stevenson, William. *90 Minutes at Entebbe.* New York: Bantam Books, 1976.

Thompson, Leroy. *The Rescuers: The World's Top Anti-Terrorist Units.* Boulder, CO: Paladin Press, 1986.

Turi, Robert. *Descriptive Study of Aircraft Hijacking.* Huntsville, TX: Sam Houston University, 1972.

Wells, A. T. *Airport Planning and Management.* Blue Ridge Summit, PA: Tab, 1986.

Whelton, C. *Skyjack.* New York: Tower Publications, 1970.

Wilkinson, Paul. "International Dimensions." In *The New Terrorism,* ed. William Gutteridge. London: Mansell, 1986, pp. 29-56.

_____. *Terrorism and the Liberal State.* London: Macmillan, 1977.

_____. "Terrorism versus Liberal Democracy: The Problems of Response." In *The New Terrorism,* by William Gutteridge, ed. London: Mansell, 1986, pp. 3-28.

PERIODICALS

Ashley, S. "Can Technology Stop Terror in the Air?" *Popular Science,* Nov. 1985, pp. 69-71, 99, 100.

Aviation Week and Space Technology, Apr. 28, 1986, p. 29; May 26, 1986, p. 31; June 29, 1987, p. 36; Jan. 9, 1989, pp. 9, 29, 31, 62. Jan. 16, 1989, p. 64.

Bell, R. G. "The U.S. Response to Terrorism Against International Civil Aviation." *Orbis,* (Foreign Policy Research Institute), 19 (Winter 1976): 191-205.

Biddle, W. "Keep It Simple and Reliable." *Discover,* June 1986, pp. 22-31.

Bremer, Karl. *Airport Services,* Dec. 1988, pp. 21-25.

Brown, Peter J., "Viewpoint: Should Americans Sit Still for Hijackers?" *Security Management,* 30, no. 4 (1986): 47-49.

Cetron, Marvin J. "The Growing Threat of Terrorism." *The Futurist,* July–Aug. 1989 pp. 20-24.

Chancey, R. "Deterrence, Certainty, Severity, and Skyjacking." *Criminology* 12 (1975): 447-73.

Dailey, J. T. and E. W. Pickerel. "Some Psychological Contributions to Defenses against Hijackers." *American Psychologist* 30 (Feb. 1975): 161-65.

Evans, A. E. "Aircraft Hijacking: Its Cause and Cure." *American Journal of International Law* 63 (1969): 695-710.

Harris, L., and Associates. "The Travel and Leisure Study: A Survey of Travelling Americans," *Travel and Leisure,* May 1988, pp. 10-11.

Holden, Robert T. "The Contagiousness of Aircraft Hijacking," *American Journal of Sociology* 91, no. 4 (Jan. 1986): 874-904.

"Is the U.S. Sabotaging Its International Airlines?" *Business Week* Jan. 26, 1981, p. 74-80.

Leach, Norman S. "Terrorism in Your Own Back Yard." *Security Management,* May 1989, pp. 57-60.

Lollar, C. "Drawing the Line in Athens." *Frequent Flyer,* Sept. 1985, pp. 71-78.

Martell, D. F. "FBI's Expanding Role in International Terrorist Investigations." *Law Enforcement Bulletin* 56 (Oct. 1987): 28-32.

Martinez, Marty. "Eradicating Aerial Hijacking." *Air Line Pilot,* Oct. 1974, pp. 6-9, 41.

Miller, R. "Acts of International Terrorism: Government Responses and Policies." *Comparative Political Studies* 19 (Oct. 1986): 385-414.

Minor, W. W. "Skyjacking Crime Control Models." *Journal of Criminal Law and Criminology* 66 (1975): pp. 94-105.

Mintz, M. A. "Note on the Hijacker: His Criminal Evolution from Hijinks to Revolution." *Sociological Inquiry* 43 (1973): 89-93.

Moss, Robert. "International Terrorism and Western Societies." *International Journal* 28, no. 3, Summer 1973, 418-30.

Newsweek, Nov. 5, 1984, p. 44; July 1, 1985, pp. 27, 36, 37; Apr. 7, 1986, p. 33; Sept. 15, 1986, pp. 22, 27.

Newhouse, John. "Annals of Intelligence: Changing Targets." *New Yorker,* July 10, 1989, pp. 71-82.

_____. "The Diplomatic Round: A Freemasonry of Terrorism." *New Yorker,* July 8, 1985, pp. 46-63.

Norton, G. "Tourism and International Terrorism." *World Today* 43 (Feb. 1987): 30-33.

Oakley, Robert. "International Terrorism." *Foreign Affairs* 65, no. 3 (1987): 611-29.

Port Authority of New York and New Jersey. "The Future of Terrorism in the United States." *Office for Special Planning,* Jan. 10, 1986, p. 5.

_____. "Terrorism and Aircraft." *Office for Special Planning,* Jan. 31, 1986, p. 3.

_____. "Terrorism and Tourist Travel." *Office for Special Planning,* Mar. 26, 1986.

Post, J. M. "What Makes Terrorists Tick? *Washington Post;* reprinted in *Winnipeg Free Press,* Sept. 3, 1988.

"Rating the 10 Busiest Airports." *Condé Nast's Traveller,* Jan. 1, 1989, pp. 107-14.

"Security in the Skies." *Macleans,* Jan. 11, 1988, pp. 30, 31.

St. John, Peter. "Analysis and Response of a Decade of Terrorism." *International Perspectives,* Sept./Oct. 1981, pp. 1-5.

Shani, Col. Joshua. "Airborne Raids: A Potent Weapon in Countering Transnational Terrorism." *Air University Review,* 1985, pp. 41-55.

Shea, William (Bill). "Airports: The Way Ahead." *American Airport Management* 2, no. 1 (Nov. 1985): 6-10.

Simon, R. I., and R. A. Blum. "After the Terrorist Incident: Psychotherapeutic Treatment of Former Hostages." *American Journal of Psychotherapy* 41 (Apr. 1987): 194-200.

Sochor, Eugene. "Civil and Military Aviation: Who Rules Over the Rulemakers?" *Comparative Strategy* 7, no. 3 (1988): 311-29.

Stevens, Capt. D. C. "International Terrorism: The Canadian Perspective," *Canadian Defence Quarterly* 16, no. 1 (Summer 1986): 39-41.

Strentz, Tom. "A Hostage Psychological Survival Guide." *Law Enforcement Bulletin* (FBI) 56 (Nov. 1987): 1-8.

Time, Oct. 28. 1985, p. 16; Apr. 21, 1986, pp. 24, 26, 28; Sept. 15, 1986, pp. 29, 31; Oct. 6, 1986, p. 46; Nov. 3, 1986, p. 35; Apr. 25, 1988, p. 21.

"Viewpoint." *Air Line Pilot* (Washington, DC), Oct. 1974, p. 41; Mar. 1983; Apr. 1986, pp. 15-16.

Wilkinson, P. "State-Sponsored Terrorism: The Problems of Response." *World Today* 40 (July 1984): 292-98.

Yeffet, Isaac. "The Next Bomb." *Life,* Mar. 1989, pp. 130-38.

NEWSPAPER ARTICLES

Adams, J. "Terrifying Partnership: Abu Nidal Joins Moammar Gadaffi." *Winnipeg Free Press, Sept. 24, 1986.*

Cushman, J. H. "Airport Security." New York Times, News Service, May 13, 1989.

Jansen, G. H. *Los Angeles Times;* reproduced in *Winnipeg Free Press,* Dec. 5, 1984. *The Globe and Mail,* Apr. 14, 1988, p. 1.

Hamizrachi, Yoram. "Lax Security Makes Terror too Easy." *Winnipeg Free Press,* Jan. 31, 1986, p. 7.

Koring, Paul. *The Globe and Mail,* May 25, 1986.

Malarek, Victor. *The Globe and Mail,* Sept. 30, 1986.

Meisler, S. *Los Angeles Times;* reproduced in *Winnipeg Free Press,* Sept. 20, 1986.

Moon, Peter. *The Globe and Mail,* May 3, 1986.

St. John, Peter. "Steps for Terror-Proofing Canada's Airports." *The Globe and Mail,* Mar. 28, 1986. p. 7.

_____. "Why Armenian Terror in Canada?" *The Globe and Mail,* Apr. 1, 1985, p. 7.

Wilkinson, Paul. "Vital Steps to Air Safety." *The Times* (London), Jan. 7, 1989.

Winnipeg Free Press, Dec. 11, 1984, p. 18; Jan. 30, 1987, p. 42; Apr. 15, 1988, pp. 1, 4.

_____. Special section on Winnipeg International Airport, May 20, 1988, pp. 27-32.

"World Terrorism." *Calgary Herald* (Calgary, Canada), June 5, 1972.

Wright, Robin. *Los Angeles Times;* reprinted in *Winnipeg Free Press,* Feb. 7, 1988.

TELEVISION

CTV "National News" (Canada), Apr. 6, 1988.

"Terrorism." Roy Bonisteel's program "Man Alive." CBC Television Canada, Sept. 29 and Oct. 6, 1986.

PAPERS

Almond, Harry H., Jr. "Countering International Terrorism: The Challenge for Legal Control." Washington, DC: Georgetown University, 1985.

Bergeron, Claude. "Hijacking." Ottawa: Carleton University, Apr. 10, 1982.

Enns, Andrew. "Counter-Terrorist Activities within the Civil Aviation Industry." Winnipeg: University of Manitoba, CTSC, Mar. 1988.

Ferguson, Maj. R. K. "Terrorism in the Skies." Winnipeg: University of Manitoba, CTSC, Mar. 1986.

Fiorita, Dan. "Aviation Security: International Responses." Montreal: May 10, 1988.

Fontaine, Daniel. "Airport Security: A Problem of Priorities." Winnipeg: University of Manitoba, CTSC, Mar. 1988.

Henry, Hugh. "An Analysis of What the Contemporary Western Response to International Terrorism Should Be." Winnipeg: University of Manitoba, CTSC, Aug. 1987.

Morden, J. R. (Director, CSIS–Canada). "Notes for Remarks on the Terrorist Threat to Canada." Presented to CASIS meetings, Quebec City, Canada, May 31, 1989.

Perrett, Maj. R. "Skyjacking: The Infant Crime of the Modern Era Grows Up." Winnipeg: University of Manitoba, CTSC, Mar. 1988.

Pindera, Lisa. "Air Terror: A Look at Skyjacking." Winnipeg: University of Manitoba, CTSC, Mar. 1983.

St. John, Peter. "Terrorist Threats to Canada." Presented at the Canadian Association of Security and Intelligence Studies meeting of the Learned Societies at Windsor, Ontario, June 11, 1988. (See CTSC Collection.)

INTERVIEWS

Ben Shack, Rehavia. Chief of Security, Canada, for El Al Airlines, Montreal, Feb. 8, 1989.

Breen, Lawrence. Winnipeg, Manitoba, June 28, 1989.

Bruneteau, John. Senior Flight Attendant, Air Canada, Winnipeg, Nov. 1988.

Deveaux, Capt. Fred J. Chairman, Security Committee, Canadian Air Line Pilots Association, Montreal, Feb. 9, 1989.

Dunn, Barbara. Flight Attendant and Officer, CALFAA, Vancouver, June 23, 1989.

Gieg, Scott. Graduate Student, University of Manitoba, July 1988.

Gregory, Jim. Office of Security, Federal Aviation Administration, Washington, DC, Aug. 4, 1988.

Hanappel, Peter. Associate Dean, McGill Law School, Montreal, Feb. 1989.

Mazor, John. Chief of Publicity, American Air Line Pilots Association, Washington, DC, Aug. 4, 1988.

Motiuk, Larry, and Allan Poynter. Montreal, Feb. 10, 1989.

Selig, Robert. Director, Grand Forks Regional Airport, ND. Part 1: Oct. 1988; Part 2: June 1989.

Shea, William. Professor and Chairman, Department of Aviation, Center for Aerospace Sciences, University of North Dakota, Grand Forks, ND, Feb. 1989.

Wallis, Rodney. Chief of Security, International Air Transport Association, Montreal, Feb. 8, 1989.

Index

AACC. *See* Airport Associations Coordinating Council

Abdullah, Georges Ibrahim, 161

Achille Lauro, 166

Action Directe, 161

Action Group for the Liberation of Palestine, 22

Adams, James, 59

"Aden coup," 145

Air Canada, 121, 134

Aircraft security: components, 173-74; flight attendants, 116, 120-23; passengers, 123-26; pilots, 118-20

Air France, 26, 29, 31

Air piracy, 21, 23-29, 41, 173-90

Airport Associations Coordinating Council (AACC), 101, 107, 176, 188

Airport Operators Council International (AOCI), 95

Airport security, 18, 29, 67-107, 173-90; detection devices, 10, 28, 73, 80-84, 185-88; electronic surveillance, 59, 80, 99; intelligence, 173-76; manager, 100-102; "new skin" theory of airport security, 50, 77-80; passenger security, 27-29, 102-7; security personnel, 84-91, 183-85; western response, 28-31

Air Transport Association, 99

Al Dawa (Call of Islam), 61, 154. *See also* Shiite Moslems

Algiers, 10, 34, 127, 143; hijacker's sanctuary, 20-21; mediation, 156. *See also* Greece, exchange of popstar in Algiers

ALPA. *See* American Airline Pilots Association

Amal (Hope), 45, 61, 127. *See also* Berri, Nabih

American Airline Pilots Association (ALPA), 75-76, 95

American Airlines, 11, 18

American airports: Atlanta-Hartsfield, 104; Chicago O'Hare, 96, 104; Dallas-Fort Worth, 104; Denver-Stapleton, 86, 104; Dulles, 14, 104; Grand Forks, 202, 215; John F. Kennedy, 12, 76, 104; La Guardia, 104; Los Angeles International, 104, 143; Miami International, 95; Reno, 87; San Francisco International, 87

American Association of Airport Executives, 98

American-Cuban Hijack Agreement, 11, 14, 29, 184

AOCI. *See* Airport Operators Council International

Arabs: conflict with Israel, 21, 28, 62; cooperation with Japanese Red Army, 26; prisoner exchange, 25; terrorism, 25, 138

Arab Skyjack War, 21-31, 143

Arafat, Yasser, 59

Arey, James, 7, 9, 16, 43, 124

Arguello, Patrick, 24, 143

Armenians, 47; Secret Army for the Liberation of Armenia (ASALA), 65, 189

ASALA. *See* Secret Army for the Liberation of Armenia

Ashley, Steven, 81